STRATEGIC ANALYSIS FOR HOSPITAL MANAGEMENT

Roger Kropf, Ph.D.
University of Massachusetts
at Amherst

James A. Greenberg, Ph.D.
Brooklyn College

AN ASPEN PUBLICATION®
Aspen Systems Corporation
Rockville, Maryland
Royal Tunbridge Wells
1984

Library of Congress Cataloging in Publication Data

Kropf, Roger.
Strategic analysis for hospital management.

Includes bibliographies and index.
1. Hospitals—Administration—Data processing. 2. Hospitals—Planning. 3. Information storage and retrieval systems—Hospitals. 4. Management information systems. I. Greenberg, James A. II. Title.
RA971.6.K76 1984 362.1′1′068 84-2885
ISBN: 0-89443-855-7

Publisher: John Marozsan
Associate Publisher: Jack W. Knowles, Jr.
Editor-in-Chief: Michael Brown
Executive Managing Editor: Margot G. Raphael
Managing Editor: M. Eileen Higgins
Editorial Services: Martha Sasser
Printing and Manufacturing: Debbie Collins

Library of Congress Catalog Card Number: 84-2885
ISBN: 0-89443-855-7

Printed in the United States of America

1 2 3 4 5

To Marcia and Andrew,
Dena and Katie

Table of Contents

Preface

This book is devoted to the subject of how management information systems can be used to improve hospital strategic planning. We have used the term *strategic analysis* in the title to stress the difference between this book and others that focus on the organization and politics of hospital planning. Our concern is how information can be acquired and analyzed to improve decisions on hospital strategy.

Relevant and accurate information is needed by every hospital that hopes to prosper in an increasingly regulated and competitive environment. Information is needed to understand and react to changes in reimbursement methods, to control expenditures, and to develop and implement strategies for changing the mix of services being provided.

Hospitals are responding to this pressure for improved information by acquiring access to new computer technology. Before committing scarce resources, hospital managers should specify the questions to be asked, the decisions to be made, and what information could result in better decisions. This is a difficult task in strategic planning. An initial list of questions and decisions may lead to others that have never been dealt with before, and the information acquired will rarely dictate the decision to be made. We hope that this book will assist managers who are faced with the problem of specifying information needs before committing the hospital to purchase or lease computer hardware and software or before signing a shared services agreement.

Rather than just thinking about how information and analyses could theoretically improve strategic planning, we have spent considerable time looking at hospital plans and talking with hospital managers, consultants, and other professionals who work in strategic planning and the development of management information systems (MIS). The reader will find throughout this book numerous cases and examples of how relevant and accurate information can make a difference in strategic planning.

Hospital managers will find this book most useful in the early stages of specifying their need for computer services. This is the stage at which the hospital's data processing staff, consultants, and salesmen ask what the MIS should produce to support strategic planning.

An examination of the capabilities of hardware and software now on the market is also essential. We have not attempted to provide such a survey or to evaluate specific products. In the period of time necessary to produce this volume, such technical information would have become outdated. However, Chapter 11 describes a few of the products on the market as the book went to press. This provides us with the opportunity to discuss how changes in computer technology have affected—and will continue to affect—hospital strategic planning.

We hope that this book will be read by both hospital management and data processing professionals. We thus felt an obligation to define and explain basic terms in both strategic planning and MIS rather than refer readers to other works. Those readers who possess considerable knowledge and skills in either MIS or strategic planning will find it helpful to move quickly through this basic material in their areas of expertise. It is our hope, however, that by reading this work specialists in both areas will become more aware of how they can work productively together.

We also could not present in this single volume a discussion of each advanced topic in MIS and strategic planning that could be found in a separate volume on each subject. We have had to be selective, examining in considerable detail only those topics (e.g., market analysis) that in our judgment would be a high priority in any hospital's strategic planning process.

Hospitals across the country operate in regulatory and competitive environments that differ considerably. We have sought to achieve a balance between cases and other materials that reflect conditions in areas with and without considerable regulation and competition.

Hospitals also have access to data of varying quality and comprehensiveness. Access to computer hardware and software and expertise in their uses also vary considerably. We have therefore included material relevant to a range of hospitals.

A hospital's information system can make a major contribution to the quality of strategic planning if enough time is taken to consider what information is really needed. Since each hospital's decision makers have their own values, preferences, and management styles, we do not expect complete agreement. We hope, however, that this book will assist hospital managers in determining what information is really needed to make strategic decisions about the future.

Acknowledgments

There are a number of people whose help has made this book possible. First and foremost, we would like to thank Seth Goldsmith, Professor of Health Administration at the University of Massachusetts. The anxieties of becoming authors were considerably reduced by his words of wisdom and sense of humor. He also put us in touch with numerous other people in the hospital field who provided us with information and advice that made this a substantially better book.

Mark Toso, Vice-President of Amherst Associates, also deserves special thanks for his continual willingness to share ideas and information, and especially for his assistance in preparing Chapter 10 of this book.

Philip Reeves of George Washington University and Harry Gifford of the University of Massachusetts deserve our thanks for their careful reading of the manuscript and their valuable suggestions.

Mark Gottlieb and Barry Eisenberg deserve our thanks for allowing us to use the plan prepared for "Memorial Hospital" while they were employed by Block, McGibony, + Associates.

Lucinda Lagasse of the University of Massachusetts Medical Center provided invaluable assistance in the preparation of the case study that appears in Chapter 10. Alex Szafran of BayState Medical Center in Springfield, Massachusetts, also provided us with valuable suggestions. While the case study does not concern their hospitals, the information they provided was invaluable in preparing an analysis of the data we acquired.

Elliot Stone of the Massachusetts Health Data Consortium provided examples of the work of his organization. He also gave us valuable advice on the content of Chapter 5.

A number of hospitals provided valuable assistance and data. They include Mount Sinai Hospital in Hartford, Connecticut; Kenmore Mercy Hospital in Kenmore, New York; Mercy Hospital in Wilkes-Barre, Pennsylvania; and The Health Central System, a multihospital system based in Minneapolis, Minnesota.

A number of organizations that provide information products and services to hospitals contributed materials for the book and deserve our thanks. They include Amherst Associates, Inc.; Mediflex Systems Corporation; Shared Medical Systems, Inc.; Arthur Andersen & Co.; Ernst & Whinney; Electronic Data Systems Corp.; Hospital Administrative Services of the American Hospital Association; the Commission on Professional and Hospital Activities; the Financial Analysis Service of the Healthcare Financial Management Association; Iowa Servi-Share; the Missouri Health Data Corporation; and Management and Planning Services, Hospital Association of New York State.

Introduction

This book is designed to assist hospital managers in evaluating whether their current or planned information systems could improve their decisions in strategic planning. It focuses on the first steps of any such evaluation: the specification of the questions that need to be asked, the decisions that need to be made, the information that is required, and the analytical techniques that are available to produce this information. The questions that need to be asked and the decisions that need to be made are determined by the external environment in which the hospital must operate, by internal conditions, and by the characteristics of the planning process the hospital has chosen to follow.

The major objective of Part I of the book is to lay the groundwork for a discussion of what information is needed for hospital strategic planning and what analytical techniques might produce it.

Chapter 1 describes the current external environment faced by hospitals, some of the internal changes that are occurring in hospital organization and management, and why information systems that support strategic planning are needed. The importance of developing an information system that supports strategic planning is explained.

Chapter 2 presents our definition of the strategic planning process. The tasks involved in strategic planning are defined. Some of the questions and decisions that arise in carrying out each of these tasks are also presented. Both the context (internal and external environment) and the process of strategic planning are therefore examined before the questions and decisions involved in strategic planning are specified. Information must then be created from data to respond to those questions and to support decision making.

The objective of Chapter 2 is not to present rigid specifications for a hospital planning process, but to provide an example, based on a study of hospital plans and the literature on hospital planning, of how the process of specifying questions and decisions might proceed. Hospital managers are left to decide which of the questions and decisions are pertinent to their situation, and what others must be added.

In Part II, the sources of data and information for hospital strategic planning are examined. Faced with the need to make a decision, managers are likely to ask what information is available that describes current conditions or suggests the impact of future actions by the hospital and others. Before examining what information could be useful for specific questions and decisions, potential sources of information are described. We cannot, of course, provide a complete description for every hospital of the sources of internal and external information for strategic planning. We do, however, suggest what information is likely to be easier to acquire, and what alternatives various hospitals have chosen to meet their need for internal and external data.

Chapter 3 examines the information systems that operate in the hospital. The evolution of computerized hospital information systems is discussed, and the types of hospital information systems that now exist and their relevance for strategic planning are examined.

Chapter 4 examines government data sources, with an emphasis on the national data systems that can provide some data to all hospitals. The importance of state data systems, which vary widely in content, is also discussed.

Chapter 5 discusses shared information systems, which allow a hospital access to the data of other hospitals. The focus here is not just on what data such systems can provide, but also on the difficulty of establishing such systems, since sharing data involves risks as well as rewards.

Part III describes the types of information and analytical techniques that are useful for strategic planning. Three important topics in strategic planning are discussed: the analysis of service areas and markets (Chapter 6), medical staff analysis (Chapter 8), and financial planning (Chapter 10). In each of these chapters, techniques are presented for analyzing data to yield information that is useful for planning. Also, information that would be useful in answering some of the questions and making some of the decisions presented in Chapter 2 is described.

The purpose of these three chapters is not to present an exhaustive catalog of techniques for data analysis. It is rather to show how hospital managers have used data to create useful information for decision making. In a few cases, we have also applied techniques from other industries that we believe are useful for hospital decision making.

Chapters 6, 8, and 10 have as unifying elements two questions: What information do we need to answer the questions and to make the decisions in strategic planning? What analytical techniques are available to turn data into relevant information?

In Chapters 7 and 9, case studies on the development and use of information in hospital strategic planning are presented. Our objective here is to share some of the work actually being done by hospitals and to demonstrate the applicability of techniques we have discovered during the preparation of this book. We hope that hospitals faced with similar decisions and questions will save valuable time and resources by reading these cases and borrowing what appears to be appropriate for their purposes.

Numerous organizations are now offering to hospitals information services that range from printed reports to the computer hardware and software necessary for generating management reports internally. In Chapter 11, we examine a few of these services. We do not provide a survey of such services nor evaluate their quality. As we have noted, any such survey would be quickly outdated. Our major concern is with the information needs of the strategic planning process and the analytical techniques that could be used, not with the technical characteristics of the combinations of computer hardware and software being developed to meet those needs.

The objective of Chapter 11 is to help hospital managers avoid two pitfalls. The first is to assume that these information services have nothing to offer—that they cannot improve strategic planning. The likely result of accepting this assumption is higher expenditures on expensive professional staff and making do with less information than could actually be made available. The second pitfall is to assume that much of the strategic planning process can be carried out by computers. The result of accepting this assumption is that managers, trustees, and other decision makers are likely to be disappointed and frustrated with the answers provided (or with the lack of them).

In Chapter 11, we therefore focus on the general capabilities of the information services being offered and how they can contribute to the strategic planning process. We also examine the extent to which the products and services being offered can be combined to produce a "decision support system." Particular attention is paid to the usefulness of various information services in carrying out the tasks described in Chapters 6, 8, and 10, since the reader will by then be familiar with the information that is needed.

A major assumption of this work is that the steps involved in determining (1) the questions to be asked, (2) the decisions to be made, (3) the information that is useful, and (4) the analytical techniques that are available are critically important in the selection or development of a management information system for strategic planning. In this context, we have not focused on the politics of hospital strategic planning, or on how to organize a planning process. A number of other books deal with these issues in great detail. The process of leading trustees, management, medical staff, and hospital employees through a decision-making process that often threatens their perceived self-interest is complex and difficult. Planning remains in this sense a political process. Providing decision makers with useful information—and deciding where and how to get this information—are also important management tasks. We hope that this volume will provide some assistance in these areas.

In describing the information that may be most relevant for a variety of decisions, we have made our judgments based on examinations of hospital plans, a reading of the literature on hospital planning and management, and conversations with hospital management and consultants. We hope our work will assist in the evaluation of what information is really important to a hospital's strategic planning process and what analytical techniques are needed. The result, we trust, will be the development of more efficient and effective hospital management information systems.

Part I

The Strategic Planning Process

Chapter 1

The Context of Strategic Planning

EXTERNAL AND INTERNAL ENVIRONMENTS

The external environments faced by hospitals and internal changes in hospital organization and management are increasing the pressure to engage in strategic planning. This is resulting in a greater demand for useful information. This, together with the growing availability of analytical techniques and computer hardware and software, will lead to the continued development of information systems and services. An understanding of both the hospital's external environment and the internal changes that are occurring in hospitals is therefore essential for understanding why information systems and services will become more and more important to hospitals in the future, and why it will become increasingly important for hospital managers to define their need for information and analytical techniques.

The environment in which hospitals now operate is not one in which increasing demand, a growing market share, and increases in revenue can be taken for granted. Nor can hospitals assume that their current organizational structures and mix of services are appropriate. The demand for all of a hospital's services may not continue to grow in the future. This is primarily due to shifts in demand resulting from the aging of the population, a reduced birth rate, the geographic redistribution of the population, and the development of new ways of organizing health care (e.g., HMOs and outpatient surgery). Health promotion and prevention services are increasingly viewed as less costly and more effective alternatives to the acute care that has traditionally been the primary source of hospital revenue.

The federal government and some state governments have indicated a willingness to view the Medicare and Medicaid programs not as ''entitlement'' programs, in which expenditures are set by the level of demand, but as programs in which spending is determined through the political process. A few state governments, as well as some employers and insurance companies, have begun to contract with groups of providers. Such preferred provider organizations (PPOs) give the contracting providers exclusive or preferential access to a market that was once open to everyone.

The implementation of a prospective reimbursement system for Medicare as a result of the Social Security Amendments of 1983 offers hospitals some new opportunities, but also creates some new risks. Hospitals can keep the difference between a prospectively determined hospital-specific cost-per-case and their actual cost. If their actual cost exceeds the stipulated amount, they will not be given additional reimbursement. A separate prospective price will be set for patients in each diagnosis related group (DRG). Hospitals can theoretically now either make or lose money depending on the resources they spend on specific types of patients and how many they can treat.

One major response to these potential changes in demand and revenue is a reconsideration of the hospital's structure and legal status. Third party reimbursement policies and government tax laws have led some hospitals to consider separate corporations as a means of protecting certain assets and sources of revenue in order to provide funds for the development of services considered essential for the hospital's growth and survival. In addition to divesting themselves of some activities, hospitals have also considered using their unique strengths to engage in new activities (e.g., for-profit management consulting). Shared services corporations and multihospital systems have also become increasingly attractive as a way of gaining flexibility in allocating resources, improving productivity and lowering costs, and gaining access to more specialized staff expertise.

Threats to traditional sources of hospital revenue and new forms of hospital organization have led some observers to conclude that hospitals will increasingly compete with one another. Competition introduces the further threat that utilization, market share, and revenues will decrease.

These new opportunities and threats have resulted in increased interest by the hospital industry in strategic planning. Such planning involves the asking of a series of questions that are essential to the development of strategy:

- What business should we be in?
- What is our desired future state?
- Whom do we serve? What are our markets?
- Who are our competitors? What are their intentions?
- What are our strengths, weaknesses, opportunities, threats?

INFORMATION SYSTEMS FOR STRATEGIC PLANNING

Answering the above questions and making decisions about hospital strategy require information. There are a number of different types of decisions made in hospitals, and information systems have been developed to assist managers in making them. To understand the capabilities of these information systems, the differences in the kinds of decisions made by managers must be understood.

Robert Anthony has categorized management decisions in a useful way. He classifies management decisions as (1) operational, (2) managerial, and (3) strategic.[1] Operational decisions concern the use of resources to perform specific tasks. Managerial decisions concern the allocation of resources to meet defined goals. Strategic decisions concern the selection of goals and the determination of what should be produced in order to pursue those goals.

These categories can be used to define how the evolving capabilities of data processing have been used in hospitals (a subject that is examined in more detail in Chapter 3). Computer-based hospital information systems are now frequently used to make operational decisions. The tasks involved include maintaining supply inventories, allocating charges to specific patients, and patient billing. Hospital information systems also frequently generate the information needed at the managerial level to monitor and control expenditures, productivity, revenues, and cash management.

Information systems for strategic decision making are relatively recent. Many focus on financial decisions concerning the growth or termination of services. The decision maker is asked to provide the underlying assumptions, the objectives sought, and the conditions that would make the results unacceptable. A number of scenarios can therefore be generated and analyzed. Because of the current interest in hospital reorganization and competition, decision-making models and related computer software for examining the effect of such scenarios have also begun to emerge (a few of those models are described in Chapters 10 and 11).

STRATEGIC PLANNING AND MANAGEMENT INFORMATION SYSTEMS

As we have seen, the current environment in which hospitals must operate presents both opportunities and threats to their growth and survival. This is likely to increase the importance of strategic planning. The development of an effective management information system is likely to improve the ability of hospitals to answer the questions and make the decisions involved in the strategic planning process.

Information systems that merely provide support for operational and managerial decisions are insufficient. Hospitals will need to develop information systems that provide the information needed specifically for strategic planning, including the analytical techniques needed to produce that information. At the same time, the pressures to reduce the costs of health care will lead to more careful scrutiny by both managers and regulators of whether the costs of the new information systems and services are justified.

This book will be successful if it stimulates some careful thinking about what information and analytical techniques are needed for strategic planning. The development or selection of an appropriate information system (or individual services) for strategic planning will then be much easier. In this way, hospital managers may avoid the depressing situation described by "Finagle's Laws on Information:

1. The information you have is not what you want.
2. The information you want is not what you need.
3. The information you need is not what you can obtain."[2]

REFERENCES

1. R.N. Anthony, *Planning and Control Systems: A Framework for Analysis* (Cambridge, Mass.: Harvard University, Graduate School of Business Administration, 1965).

2. J.H. Murnaghan, "Health Services Information Systems In The United States Today," *New England Journal of Medicine* 290 (1974):603–610.

Chapter 2

Strategic Planning as a Decision-Making Process

INTRODUCTION

Strategic planning is the process of making and implementing decisions concerning the use of resources to achieve an organization's goals and to fulfill its mission. Strategic planning is concerned with the alternative uses of resources rather than the immediate control of how targeted resources are spent (which distinguishes it from program planning). It is concerned with the definition of the structure of the organization and its major services, products, and markets. Above all, it is concerned with how the decisions made today will impact on the future of the organization.

The terms *strategic planning* and *long-range planning* are sometimes used interchangeably. Since strategic planning takes a long-range view (five or more years into the future), the interchangeability is understandable. We will use the term *strategic planning* in this book because we feel that the process of defining alternative uses of resources and subsequent actions is so important. Long-range planning suggests only the time frame for planning.

Strategic planning also encompasses more than planning the construction or modernization of the hospital's physical plant. While new construction is an often used strategy, it is just one type. A strategic planning process should also explore other strategies that concern changes in markets and services.

Exhibit 2–1 shows the major steps in the strategic planning process. The major questions that need to be asked in order to make decisions at each step in the process are shown. "Decisions" specify actions that are to be taken, while "questions" define the types of information (quantitative and qualitative) that would assist in making the decisions. (In Part III, we define in greater detail the information and analytical techniques needed for carrying out some of these steps.)

We have not restricted the Exhibit 2–1 questions to those that require quantitative information, even though the remainder of this book focuses on data

Exhibit 2–1 Major Steps in the Strategic Planning Process

Major Questions	Major Steps
Who are we?	Initial mission statement
	Internal Analysis / External Analysis
Where are we now?	Assessment of present position
Where are we going if we follow our present course?	Development and evaluation of alternative scenarios
Where do we want to go?	Revision of mission statement and development of goals
How can we get there?	Development and evaluation of alternative strategies
	Determination of strategies and objectives
What if the situation changes?	Development of contingency plans
What actions must we take?	Development and implementation of program plans
Who will be responsible and what will they do?	Development and implementation of operational plans
How will we know if we are succeeding?	Development of evaluation, monitoring, and control systems
Do we need to change course?	Revision and implementation of contingency plans

sources, information needs and analytical techniques. This reflects our belief that managers use both quantitative and qualitative information, values, judgment, and even intuition in strategic planning. While quantitative information is extremely important for strategic planning, it must be supplemented with other types of information. Several recent books are available to help the reader understand how strategic decisions are made and the range of information that is needed.[1–3]

While the development of an effective MIS requires that steps, questions, and decisions be defined, we do not mean to imply that strategic planning is a rigid process in which steps are always carried out in sequence. Moves by competitors, the need to seize one-time opportunities, and other events may result in some of the steps in Exhibit 2–1 being skipped. Steps already completed may have to be repeated as new information arrives. Analyses already completed may have to be discarded or reworked because new information (or the results of the analyses themselves) suggests the need for a different approach.

Flexibility is critically important, and the existence of data bases in computers and the software to analyze them can greatly increase the ability of the hospital manager to be flexible. New scenarios can be developed and their impact explored with the computer rapidly performing the necessary data retrieval and analysis.

The number of steps, questions, and decisions presented in the remainder of this chapter may suggest that we envision hospital strategic planning as always requiring voluminous reports. However, the size of the memos, reports, and other documents needed to support strategic planning (or a strategic plan, if one is prepared) will depend on the time and resources that managers are able and willing to devote and on the magnitude of the consequences of the changes being contemplated.

Each piece of information usually makes some contribution to the manager's understanding of what decision would have the greatest impact in achieving the hospital's mission and goals. Each manager has to make a decision as to whether more or less, or different, information would be more valuable. There will also be circumstances in which waiting for the arrival of further information would result in the loss of a one-time opportunity or in serious damage to the hospital's financial condition or ability to provide services. Decisions must then be made quickly, with fingers crossed.

This should not be interpreted as advocating frantic, last-minute planning when work could have been done earlier. Nor are we suggesting that an ongoing strategic planning process is not necessary. Many of the long-range decisions a hospital needs to make—especially those concerning its mission and the services it will provide—are neither made nor undone in a week. Often, a formal or informal process of consulting important groups and individuals is implemented. Thus, when the time is available, the acquisition and analysis of data to create useful information should be a high priority for hospital managers.

THE STRATEGIC PLANNING PROCESS

Development of an Initial Mission Statement

Mission statements are often criticized either for being vague or for reinforcing outmoded definitions of what a hospital should be doing. A vague mission statement that implies that the hospital can provide any service to anyone in its community or region provides no basis for making strategic decisions. On the other hand, a detailed mission statement that is written before an examination of the hospital's internal and external environment can discourage the hospital from questioning its current allocation of resources.

The development of a somewhat detailed initial (under no circumstances, final) mission statement is an important first step. No hospital enters the strategic planning process without some sense among its leadership, staff, and community of its traditional role. Agreement on what that mission has been—not necessarily what it always should be—provides the context for examining the internal and external conditions under which the hospital must operate. Those involved in the planning process can then begin asking not only what the hospital should be doing, but, in the light of the traditional beliefs concerning the hospital's mission, what shifts it will need to make in order to implement changes.

We agree with Pascale and Athos that too little attention has been paid in American organizations to "superordinate goals."[4] These are the shared values that the organization places above all others. For voluntary community hospitals, the superordinate goals are frequently the highest quality care for patients, the welfare of citizens of a particular community, and the rendering of service consistent with religious or philosophical values. For investor-owned hospitals, superordinate goals can be the rate of return to investors, quality care for patients, and growth in assets.

A mission statement should set down these superordinate goals, viewing them not as vague, meaningless statements but—as recent studies of successful Japanese and American businesses suggest—as essential elements in achieving the unity of purpose that motivates employees, provides a direction to growth, and ultimately attracts support from the community.[5] In addition, the hospital needs to define functions, levels of care, services, populations, and service areas in order to provide a focus for the analysis of its internal and external environments.[6]

At this point, the hospital should also be defining its basic attitude toward important groups. Is it interested in a competitive relationship with other hospitals, or is it interested in joint planning and cooperative approaches to resolving the problems of mutual survival? If the hospitals in its community are now competitive, the hospital should be defining an acceptable response to that situation in light of its values, beliefs, and superordinate goals.

The development of an initial mission statement requires answers to the following questions:

1. What are our basic beliefs? Our "superordinate" goals?
2. What does the hospital see as its major functions?
3. What levels of care and services do we wish to provide?
4. What population groups and geographic areas does the hospital wish to serve?
5. What type of relationship do we want to have with external groups, including our competitors and third party payers? Cooperative, competitive, or antagonistic?

Internal Analysis

Two major subjects of an internal analysis are (1) how resources are currently being used and (2) what the capabilities of the hospital are. The services provided to specific markets (i.e., groups of patients and physicians) using one or more technologies need to be described. The description of the technologies is especially important, since similar services (e.g., diagnostic radiology) can be provided using alternative technologies, but with significant implications for the hospital's competitive position. The need and demand of existing markets for services and technologies not currently being provided must also be assessed as part of the internal analysis.

Pascale and Athos present a useful set of concepts for evaluating the capability of an organization. The performance of an organization can be influenced by its structure, systems, staff, skills, strategy, style, and superordinate goals.[7] *Structure* refers to the type of organization, for example, whether a hospital is part of a multihospital system or is one unit of a larger, diversified corporation. *Systems* refers to how information is managed and processes controlled, for example, through a formal system of routine reports or through informal meetings. *Staff* refers to the important human resources of the organization and their characteristics, for example, the age of the physicians and their orientation to technology. *Skills* refers to the distinctive abilities of the organization that set it apart, for example, tertiary services. *Strategy* refers to the decisions that have been made concerning the allocation of resources and the direction in which the organization is going, for example, to diversify and become a leader in community services to the elderly. *Style* refers to the patterns of behavior of senior management, for example, is it oriented to facts or does it prefer intuition in making decisions. (*Superordinate goals* were defined earlier.) Finally, to this list should be added an understanding of the condition of the hospital's assets, including its physical plant, equipment, and financial resources.

An internal analysis requires answers to the following questions:

1. What services do we provide?
2. What consumer and physician groups do we serve?
3. What technologies do we utilize? Is there a need and/or demand for other services and technologies in the consumer and physician groups we now serve?
4. Who constitutes the hospital's medical staff?
5. What is the current level of skills among the hospital's management and professional and non-professional staff?
6. What is the hospital's organizational structure, and what systems are used to manage it?
7. What is the "style" of hospital management?
8. What is the condition of the hospital's existing financial and capital assets?
9. How have the factors listed above changed in the last five to ten years?

External Analysis

The hospital needs to identify its areas of potential growth in terms of patients and physicians (market groups), services, and technologies. The hospital can then ask what other providers are likely to want to meet the same needs and demands and what government agencies and third party payers it must deal with.

The current policies and future intentions of government and third party payers represent both constraints and opportunities for the hospital. The hospital must gain some understanding of the likely reaction of these external groups to its current activities and possible initiatives. It must assess the extent to which it can call on the support of influential groups and the likelihood of their effective intervention on its behalf.

The hospital must also develop what Porter has called a "competitor response profile" in order to understand the potential seriousness of a competitor's offensive and defensive moves.[8] This is important even if the hospital has decided as part of its mission statement to seek cooperation rather than competition. The profile asks what the competitor's future goals are, what its current strategy is, what assumptions it holds about itself and the hospital industry, and what its capabilities are. The hospital may find itself competing even if it does not want to. By making moves that deeply threaten another hospital, it may find itself in a more hostile and aggressive competitive atmosphere than it had intended.

An external analysis requires answers to the following questions:

1. How does the hospital define its total market, including the population it is not currently serving?
2. What government agencies and third party payers have some authority over the population the hospital wishes to serve, and over the hospital and other providers of service in these markets? What opportunities and constraints does this place on the hospital?
3. What other providers wish to serve the same needs and demands?
4. What future goals and current strategies do they have?
5. What assumptions do they hold about themselves and the hospital industry? What are their current capabilities?
6. What population needs are not currently being met?
7. What physician needs are not being met?
8. What groups in our service area are likely to support the hospital financially and in political controversies? What resources do they possess and are they likely to use them?

Assessment of Present Position

The purpose of the internal and external analyses of the hospital's environment is to arrive at a realistic assessment of the hospital's current position. After assembling the necessary information, we can ask what the hospital's strengths, weaknesses, opportunities, and threats are. The urgency with which the hospital must act depends on the rate at which the hospital's situation has been deteriorating (or improving) and on the immediate threats to the hospital's survival that exist.

The assessment of the hospital's present position requires answers to the following questions:

1. Based on the internal and external analyses, what are the hospital's current strengths, weaknesses, opportunities, and threats?
2. What has been the rate of change in the hospital's improving or deteriorating situation?
3. Are there immediate threats to survival that should receive priority attention?

Development and Evaluation of Alternative Scenarios

In the absence of immediate threats to survival, the hospital's attention should be on the future rather than just current conditions. Forecasting future events is, to say the least, difficult. We must deal with imperfect information and unforeseen changes in economic conditions, government policies, and staffing within our own and competing hospitals.

Forecasting the hospital's future environment therefore requires thinking through alternative scenarios concerning future events, asking what the probabilities of their occurrence are, and what the potential impact on the hospital would be. While decision makers in the hospital cannot spend long periods of time thinking through every possible event, the analysis of the hospital's present situation will suggest what possible events are likely to have the most serious implications for the hospital. The financial consequences of these events are likely to be of great concern. A range of computer-based financial models now on the market can assist in determining the potential impact of these events (some of the capabilities of these models are examined in Chapters 10 and 11).

The development and evaluation of alternative scenarios require answers to the following questions. What would be the probability of occurrence and the impact on the hospital's services and financial condition of:

1. no major change in the hospital's services, markets, staffing, and other internal factors discussed above, while the external environment remains on its present course
2. effective controls on utilization and payment by third party payers
3. adverse economic conditions that result in a change in consumer demand
4. a major change in technology for diagnosis and treatment, leading to demands by physicians and consumers for major service changes and capital expenditures

5. an attempt by one or more competitors to increase their market share for existing hospital services
6. an attempt by one or more competitors to diversify into services other than acute care that are likely to be highly profitable and grow quickly in volume
7. a competing hospital joining a multihospital system
8. combinations of the above

Revision of the Mission Statement and Development of Goals

An intense look at the present and likely future will suggest whether the initial mission statement will put the hospital in a condition considered desirable by its staff and supporters. While the hospital is unlikely to change its superordinate goals or what it considers essential elements of its mission (e.g., service to a community), changes in other parts of its mission statement should be seriously considered. A revised mission statement will describe what unmet needs can be met and what current activities are consistent with the hospital's future environment, resources, and capabilities.

Rather than being just a narrow statement of what the hospital can achieve, the mission statement can express the aspirations of the hospital; but it should then be followed by a detailed statement of the goals that will have to be achieved in order for the hospital to fulfill its mission. The level of performance that the hospital aspires to in various areas should be described.

The revision of the mission statement and the development of goals require answers to the following questions:

1. Does the initial mission statement reflect consumer and physician needs and demands?
2. Can it be achieved given the internal and external conditions that the hospital is likely to face?
3. What level of performance will be needed in order for the hospital to achieve its mission in terms of services and groups served, technologies utilized, growth rate and market share for services, the cost of services, revenue received and net profit, increases in assets, development of new sources of funds, and staff skills?

Development and Evaluation of Alternative Strategies

It is impossible to predict all the goals that a hospital might wish to achieve, but goals concerning the hospital's services and financial performance are likely to be given a high priority. Marketing concepts and techniques can be useful in evaluating whether the hospital should consider changes in services, market groups, and technology.

Abell categorizes market strategies as focused, differentiated, or undifferentiated.[9] A hospital might choose a focused strategy and narrow its scope to one or more functions (e.g., diagnosis), patient or physician groups, or technologies (e.g., ultrasound). A hospital with a differentiated market strategy would combine a broad scope with differentiation in one or all of the dimensions (i.e., needs and groups served, technology used) of its market. For example, population groups such as the elderly, young married couples and teenagers could be offered primary care services that fit their unique needs.

Alternatively, the hospital might choose an undifferentiated market strategy, with a broad scope of functions, groups, and technologies and no attempt to differentiate between the needs of specific market segments. The construction of an office building for physicians adjacent to the hospital is a common outgrowth of this type of market strategy.

The hospital must also be concerned with the response of competitors to changes. The competitor response profile compiled earlier will assist in evaluating the consequences of changes in needs served, market groups, and technology. A nearby hospital that defines itself as the regional center for cancer treatment might, for example, be successful in blocking the acquisition of therapeutic radiology equipment through its political contacts, acting to fend off what it perceives as a threat to its survival.

The support of important internal and external groups must also be evaluated. As Kotler has pointed out, organizations engage in numerous exchanges with individuals and groups.[10] The successful implementation of proposed changes will depend on the reaction of others—the balance between what they are being offered and what they must provide. For example, an important board member who serves out of loyalty to his life-long community may be unable to support the development of satellite clinics in adjacent communities.

Finally, the hospital must evaluate whether it has the resources to make the desired changes in its services. Those resources include not only cash, but staff, skills, and systems to support the changes. The financial models we will discuss in Chapters 10 and 11 can assist in selecting a strategy, but they must be supplemented by a careful evaluation of the less quantifiable considerations, for example, the clinical and management skills available.

A hospital may also wish to consider a change in its organizational structure as a way to meet its goals. Horizontal integration could allow the hospital to achieve economies of scale. Forward or backward vertical integration could lower the hospital's unit costs or secure markets for its services. The hospital industry has been particularly creative in developing multiinstitutional arrangements that allow horizontal or vertical integration without the changes in corporate structure required in other industries. Backward integration through cooperative ventures that do not require changing the structure of members is rare in most industries, but is now common among hospitals (e.g., shared data processing services).

Careful consideration must therefore be given to the need for actual changes in corporate structure.

Increasing the scope or scale of operations is not the only type of organizational change being considered by hospitals. Severing assets in order to obtain revenue is also being considered. This can occur through the separate incorporation of one or more of the hospital's activities or by the transfer of cash and other assets to a new corporate entity. A critical question is whether the skills, style, structure, and systems of the hospital are suited to the management of a diversified firm.

The development and evaluation of alternative strategies requires answers to the following questions:

1. Changes in functions, market groups, and technology:
   - Should the hospital adopt a focused, differentiated, or undifferentiated market strategy to meet its goals?
     a. Can specific unserved needs of particular segments of consumers and physicians be identified?
     b. Are there alternative technologies for providing services, and would their use stimulate greater demand for services or an improvement in net revenue?
     c. Are consumers price sensitive; do they value specific characteristics of hospitals that result in higher prices?
     d. Does the likely net revenue per unit of service require that the hospital increase the volume of services it provides in order to meet its financial goals?
   - What is likely to be the response of competitors?
     a. How vulnerable are competitors?
     b. Will the change provoke a response because of its threat to important values and goals of the competitor?
     c. How quickly and effectively can competitors retaliate?
     d. Are competitors likely to take offensive moves; how strongly, and what would be the likely consequences?
   - How will important internal groups react to the change?
     a. Does the change threaten the position of important staff or board members; is their cooperation essential for effective implementation?
     b. Does the change require active commitment, and has this been won?
   - What will be the reaction of important external groups?
     a. Is government approval needed, and is this likely?
     b. Will third party payers have to alter their reimbursement policies, or will the strategy trigger a change with negative consequences?
     c. Does the strategy alter formal or informal commitments made to community groups and political leaders? Is this likely to affect their level of financial or political support, and how serious would be the consequences?

- Can the hospital afford to make the change?
  a. Are assets required that the hospital will have difficulty obtaining?
  b. Will the hospital experience cash flow problems if growth rates are less than predicted; can financing be obtained to deal with the problem?
- Can the hospital obtain the needed management, staff, skills, and systems to support the change?

2. Changes in organizational structure:
   - Is the hospital likely to benefit from an increase in the scale of its operations?
     a. Is additional capital needed for necessary changes which the hospital doesn't have access to?
     b. Are there economies of scale in the production of services that the hospital cannot achieve?
     c. Are there economies in purchasing that the hospital cannot benefit from?
     d. Does the hospital's size and financial condition prohibit acquiring needed expertise?
   - What form of organizational change is likely to secure the required increase in scale and subsequent benefits?
     a. Are the hospital's problems shared by other hospitals in its service area; would combining institutions result in a beneficial change?
     b. Do the characteristics of the hospital's market suggest that only affiliation with an outside institution will produce the needed change?
     c. Does the needed change require cooperation or consolidation? Will important external and internal groups permit the change? Under what conditions?
   - Does the hospital possess assets in the form of money or expertise that are severable?
     a. Are there significant financial benefits from severing specific activities because of reimbursement policies or tax codes?
     b. Is the change likely to lead to actions by government and third party payers that would be detrimental to the hospital?
     c. Can the hospital retain sufficient control to ensure that the activities of the new entities will benefit the hospital now and in the future?
     d. Can the new entities that are created secure the resources they need without assistance from the hospital? Is such assistance barred by government regulations?
     e. Are the skills, style, structure, and systems of the new entities (or corporate umbrella) suited to the management of a diversified firm?

Selection of Strategies and Objectives

After completing an evaluation of the alternatives, the hospital must then select those strategies and objectives that, in the aggregate, it believes are consistent with its mission statement and will achieve the goals it has set.

The selection of strategies and objectives requires answers to the following questions:

1. What consumers and physicians will the hospital serve, with what services, using what technologies?
2. What approach will the hospital take in dealing with competitors?
3. How will the hospital secure the support of, or deal with opposition from, important internal and external groups?
4. How will the hospital finance the changes?
5. How will the necessary manpower and skills be obtained?
6. What changes in organizational structure will be made?
7. What is the time frame for making the changes?
8. What do we wish to accomplish during the first six months? In the first year? Within five years?

Development of Contingency Plans

In developing a strategic plan, a hospital will assume that some events or scenarios are less likely to occur than others. For example, a competing hospital may be unlikely to expand its services. If it did, however, it could have serious consequences for the hospital. Thus, while we cannot develop plans to deal with all the changes that might possibly occur, a hospital should be ready to cope with those that would have the most serious consequences. Rather than developing an alternative strategic plan for each such event, contingency planning should focus on the short-term actions that would have to be taken to neutralize or offset the most serious consequences (i.e., ''damage control''), thereby giving the hospital time to modify its strategic plan.[11]

A critical decision that has to be made is what warning signal or ''trigger point'' will be used to decide whether a contingency plan will be implemented. Returning to our example, reliance on informal networks to signal the expansion of a service may trigger unwarranted and costly moves as the hospital unnecessarily implements a contingency plan. Rumors are not always correct. On the other hand, waiting for construction or marketing materials to be released may cripple the hospital's ability to respond.

A process must be established for acquiring and evaluating information and for deciding who can make a decision to implement a contingency plan. The magnitude of the impact of the decisions—financially or in terms of the achievement of the hospital's mission and goals—will be an important factor. As we will discuss later, this increases the importance of an evaluation, monitoring, and control system for both internal and external events.

The development of contingency plans requires answers to the following questions:

1. Looking back at the alternative scenarios that have been developed, which of those not assumed in setting strategy could have serious consequences if not dealt with quickly?
2. What is the probability that these events could actually occur?
3. What would be the magnitude of the consequences in terms of our goals and mission?
4. What strategies would neutralize or offset the most serious consequences?
5. What actions would have to be taken, by whom, with what resources (and how would the resources be obtained)?
6. What warning signals or "trigger points" would signal that an unfavorable event has occurred?

Development and Implementation of Program Plans

The strategic plan that has been developed must now be translated into numerous managerial and operational decisions, which may or may not be collected in documents called plans. Some organizations produce a range of such documents, including marketing, new product, and financial plans. We will assume that midlevel managers must, at a minimum, develop budgets and financial plans that reflect the implications of the strategic decisions that have been made.

These documents will ask what changes in inputs (staff, equipment, etc.) will be needed, and at what point in time. This can then be translated into estimates of the capital, operating funds, and cash flow that will be needed. Since there are numerous uncertainties that surround the acquisition of resources and their utilization, numerous "what if" questions will need to be asked to test the sensitivity of the plans to specific assumptions. Chapters 10 and 11 examine some of the financial models that are available to estimate the impact of changes in utilization on individual cost centers within hospital departments and on other departments.

In the implementation of program plans, managers' decisions will focus on how to acquire and allocate resources in an effective and efficient way. The concern of numerous subordinates will be to see that the resources they are given are used to produce the intermediate and final products of the hospital—high-quality services and improved patient outcomes.

The development and implementation of program plans require answers to the following questions:

1. What changes will have to be made in the activities and resources of the major functional units of the hospital, including the clinical departments, finance, marketing and planning, and other administrative services? Over what time periods?
2. What are the staffing implications of the changes?
3. What funds will be available to make the changes?
4. Can department heads obtain the equipment and other capital assets in the desired time frame?
5. What effect will delays in one department have on plan implementation?

Development and Implementation of Operational Plans

Operational control is less likely to involve the use of a document called a plan, but it can still be complex and involve numerous decisions based on information and experience. Physical space must be prepared and used, staff must be trained and supervised, and inventory and other systems must be modified and used. The major difference between the program and operational levels is that at the operational level we are more likely to have already made the relevant decisions, or we can draw on the experience of others.

Yet it is important to remember that the efficiency and effectiveness of the decisions and actions taken at the operational level may determine the success of the strategic plan. As Hayes and Abernathy point out, business schools and the current style of American managers have tended to belittle the importance of understanding the operational level of organizations, which may partly explain the drop in quality that has made some American products uncompetitive.[12] In short, the importance of detailed operational planning should not be underestimated.

The development and implementation of operational plans requires answers to the following questions:

1. How will physical space be utilized in providing the new or changed services?
2. How will personnel be recruited and, if necessary, trained?
3. What changes in management systems, such as payroll and inventory, will be needed?
4. How will any new or changed services be marketed?
5. What legal procedures must be followed to implement the changes in services or organizational structure?
6. Will the changes in structure require changes in space, personnel, or systems?

Development of an Evaluation, Monitoring, and Control System

The planning process does not end with a document; it ends with the achievement of goals and progress in the fulfillment of a mission. The planning process should include the continual evaluation of progress. This requires the monitoring of internal and external data, both on the changes that the plan initiated and on the environment that affects the hospital.

The monitoring of such data requires the development of formal systems. The one usually already available is the budgeting process, which must now be used to measure the attainment of strategic, managerial, and operational objectives. Other systems will be needed, however, at all three levels. At the strategic level, "intelligence" (in the military sense) will be needed. Data will have to be gathered on the community and competitors and analyzed for their significance to the hospital.

The development of techniques for analysis is probably less important than the delegation of responsibility for the evaluation and monitoring function. The relevant individuals must be held accountable, much as we hold the hospital's chief financial officer accountable for evaluating, monitoring, and controlling revenues and expenditures. (How we do this is discussed in greater detail later in the chapter.)

The development of an evaluation, monitoring, and control system requires answers to the following questions:

1. Who will measure our progress in implementing the operational and program plans and in attaining our objectives?
2. What formal systems will be used to track progress? Will we use budget variance reports? Program Evaluation and Review Technique (PERT) charts?
3. What data and information will we need? How will it be obtained, stored, processed, retrieved? Who will get the information?

Plan Revision and Implementation of Contingency Plans

The planning process begins again when the projected goals have been achieved or the internal or external environment makes the current plan unusable. A formal review is usually initiated at least annually, or sometimes more frequently, regardless of events. The board and senior management will need to review the plan if only to ensure that the systems for implementation, tracking progress, and activating contingency plans are functioning effectively and to remind everyone of what the hospital's mission, goals, and objectives are.

As with contingency planning, it is important that responsibility be placed on one or more individuals to "trigger" the revision of the plan. Otherwise, an irrelevant plan is likely to lie on the shelf while the hospital lacks strategies and goals for the future.

Plan revision and the implementation of contingency plans require answers to the following questions:

1. How frequently will the plan be formally reviewed?
2. What system will be developed to learn of new opportunities and threats?
3. Who will be responsible for ordering the revision of strategies and the implementation of contingency plans?

DEVELOPMENT OF A STRATEGIC PLANNING CAPABILITY

In light of the numerous steps, decisions, and questions involved in the strategic planning process, some hospitals may conclude that strategic planning is an impossible task. A large amount of information is required that the hospital may not have, and that its decision makers may have no experience in using. If the hospital is doing strategic planning for the first time, it can be a formidable task. But it can be made easier by developing the systems needed to design and implement the process. Exhibit 2–2 shows the steps that should be taken to develop the capability to plan.

Peters,[13] Steiner,[14] and others have described in some detail the process and internal structure required for effective strategic planning. Our major concern now is with three questions: What information do we need? How do we get it?

Exhibit 2–2 Development of a Strategic Planning Capability

Major Questions	Major Steps
Are we ready to plan?	Assessment of the support for and understanding of the planning process
Who will plan?	Development of a planning structure
What is the planning process?	Development of planning guidelines, timetable, and principles
Who will provide the needed skills and knowledge?	Selection of staff, consultants and advisory groups
What information do we need to plan?	Development of a management information system for strategic planning
How do we get the information?	Collection of internal and external data
	Selection or development of ways to access data and procedures
	Development of procedures for processing data
How will we know if the situation is changing?	Development of an evaluation, monitoring, and control system linked to the planning process

How do we use it? The remainder of the book examines in detail how these questions might be answered in the strategic planning process.

REFERENCES

1. P.N. Reeves, *Strategic Planning for Hospitals* (Chicago: Foundation of the American College of Hospital Administrators, 1983).

2. J.B. Webber and J.P. Peters, *Strategic Thinking: New Frontier for Hospital Management* (Chicago: American Hospital Association, 1983).

3. J.P. Peters and S. Tseng, *Managing Strategic Change in Hospitals: Ten Success Stories* (Chicago: American Hospital Association, 1983).

4. R.T. Pascale and A.G. Athos, *The Art of Japanese Management: Applications for Executives* (New York: Simon and Schuster, 1981), p. 188.

5. Ibid., p. 178.

6. J.P. Peters, *A Guide to Strategic Planning for Hospitals* (Chicago: American Hospital Association, 1979), p. 70.

7. Pascale and Athos, *Art of Japanese Management,* p. 81.

8. M.E. Porter, *Competitive Strategy: Techniques for Analyzing Industries and Competitors* (New York: Free Press), p. 48.

9. D.F. Abell, *Defining the Business: The Starting Point of Strategic Planning* (Englewood Cliffs, N.J.: Prentice-Hall, 1980), p. 184.

10. P. Kotler, *Marketing for Nonprofit Organizations* (Englewood Cliffs, N.J.: Prentice-Hall, 1975), p. 22.

11. G.A. Steiner, *Strategic Planning: What Every Manager Must Know* (New York: Free Press, 1979), p. 231.

12. R. Hayes and W. Abernathy, "Managing Our Way to Economic Decline," *Harvard Business Review,* July-August 1980:67f.

13. Peters, *Guide to Strategic Planning,* pp. 43–86.

14. Steiner, *Strategic Planning,* pp. 53–310.

Part II

Sources of Data and Information

Chapter 3

Hospital Information Systems

Most hospital strategic planning tasks require data collected in the hospital. In order to fully describe the links between strategic decision making and hospital information systems, this chapter provides a basic outline of the hospital's information systems. Emphasis is put on computerized systems. The elements of an information system are defined, and the growth of hospital computerized information systems is described. Different methods of categorizing these systems are presented, and a brief sketch of the types of systems currently in use is offered. Two of these types are described in detail. Finally, the relationship between strategic planning and the hospital information system is discussed.

A number of information-system characteristics are not covered in this chapter. This is because they are well-described in other publications;[1–9] also they are not central to our main concern—strategic planning. Thus, there is here no description of specific technical details, such as the computer hardware or software needed to operate computerized information systems. Similarly, no attention is devoted to the design, evaluation, selection, installation, or maintenance of computerized systems.

OVERVIEW

The hospital is a complex institution in which medical and business functions are performed, and an enormous amount of data is required to support these functions. In fact, there is at least one type of data that is collected and processed separately in each unit in most hospitals (see Figure 3–1). These data are needed for purposes that can be divided into four groups: basic transactions; control reporting; operational planning; and strategic planning. In terms of Anthony's categories of management decisions, presented in Chapter 1, basic transactions and control reporting systems are used for operational decisions, operational planning systems for managerial decisions, and strategic planning systems for strategic decisions.

Figure 3–1 Hospital Information Systems

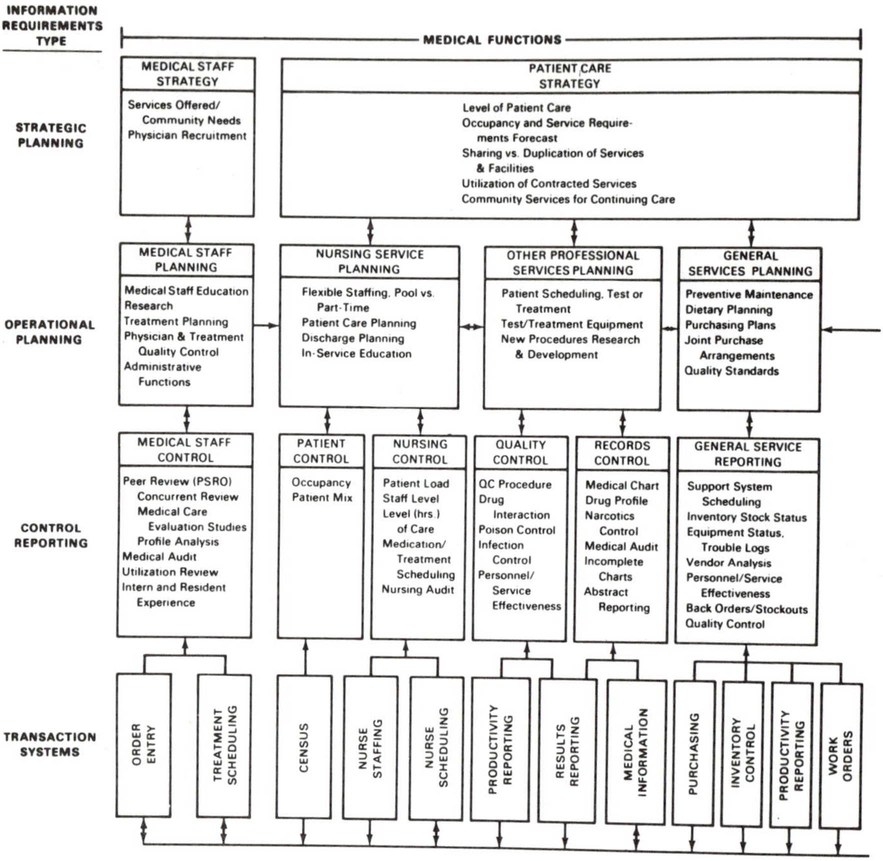

A hospital's information collection and processing activity is generally thought of as being made up of a number of information systems. In simple terms, each of these information systems is a separate self-contained process—either manual, computerized, or a combination of both. This process has raw data as its input, data collection and processing as its activity, and a data base and processed data as its output (see Figure 3–2).

Consider two examples. The first is a system for determining a hospital's daily census and occupancy rate. The input data are counts of the number of patients on each ward at a specified time (usually midnight) each day. The data processing would involve tabulating the raw number of patients and dividing it by the number of maintained beds to yield an occupancy rate (see Table 3–1). This would be done every day for each ward.

Figure 3–1 continued

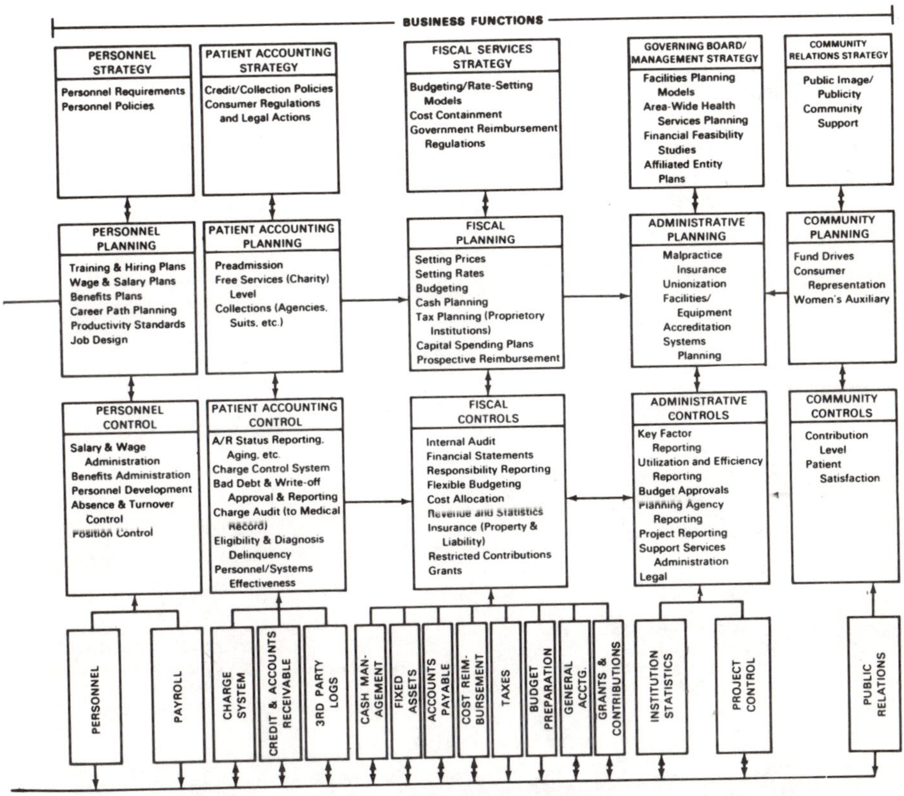

Source: T.K. Shaffert and C.E. McDowell, "Hospital Information Systems: An Overview," *Topics in Health Care Financing* 4, no. 4 (Summer 1978):pp. 6–7.

On a daily basis, the tabulations of the daily census (Table 3–2) would be of use to administrators for the operational planning of such items as temporary or floating nurse staffing levels on each ward. On a routine longer-term basis, a biannual basis for example, these data could be used for administrative purposes, such as planning permanent nurse-staffing and bed levels on each ward. On an even longer-term basis, say every five years, the data base—which might consist of the daily census and maintained bed and occupancy levels—could be used for strategic planning of bed levels in each department.

The second example is an information system for ordering and reporting the results of laboratory tests for hospital patients. The data input for this system includes (1) the type of test ordered, (2) the patient's location in the hospital, (3) an indication of whether the test was urgent, (4) the date and time the test

Figure 3–2 Basic Elements of an Information System

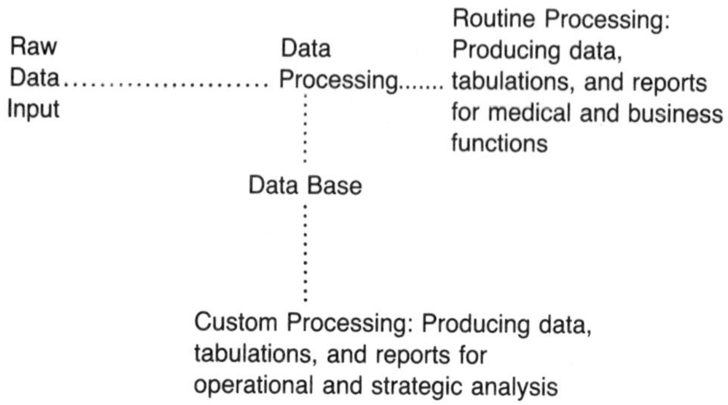

Table 3–1 Census Report

CENSUS

CITY HOSPITAL 03-21-83 MIDNIGHT

	BED CAPACITY	OCCUPANCY
MEDICINE-EAST	78	65
MEDICINE-WEST	62	50
SURGERY-EAST	57	51
SURGERY-WEST	52	47
OB	25	18
GYNECOLOGY	35	30
PEDIATRICS	40	30
NURSERY	28	22
MENTAL HEALTH	15	08
CORONARY CARE	15	11
MICU	10	09
SICU	10	07
TOTAL	427	348

PERCENTAGE OCCUPANCY: 81,498

Source: Reprinted with permission of Electronic Data Systems Corporation, Health Services Division, Dallas, Texas.

Table 3–2 Daily Census Variation Report

DAILY CENSUS VARIATION — PEDIATRICS
CAPACITY: 40
CITY HOSPITAL — APR-MAY 1983

APR 01	23	APR 22	35	MAY 12	33
APR 02	25	APR 23	35	MAY 13	33
APR 03	27	APR 24	36	MAY 14	35
APR 04	35	APR 25	37	MAY 15	34
APR 05	31	APR 26	37	MAY 16	33
APR 06	32	APR 27	35	MAY 17	33
APR 07	30	APR 28	32	MAY 18	32
APR 08	32	APR 29	31	MAY 19	31
APR 09	37	APR 30	29	MAY 20	33
APR 10	38	MAY 01	28	MAY 21	32
APR 11	35	MAY 02	30	MAY 22	35
APR 12	30	MAY 03	30	MAY 23	35
APR 13	32	MAY 04	33	MAY 24	37
APR 14	26	MAY 05	33	MAY 25	37
APR 15	29	MAY 06	35	MAY 26	36
APR 16	32	MAY 07	35	MAY 27	33
APR 17	33	MAY 08	32	MAY 28	30
APR 18	33	MAY 09	32	MAY 29	29
APR 19	32	MAY 10	32	MAY 30	28
APR 20	30	MAY 11	32	MAY 31	29
APR 21	31				

Source: Reprinted with permission of Electronic Data Systems Corporation, Health Services Division, Dallas, Texas.

results were reported, and (5) the ordering physician's identification code. These data items are needed for conducting and reporting the test. In other words, they are needed for the basic transactions involved in laboratory testing.

The resulting data base could be processed for a number of purposes. Operational planning purposes include the scheduling of laboratory personnel and the maintenance and upgrading or expansion of laboratory equipment. For the most part, the data processing for these purposes involves tabulations of the number of tests daily by machine (see Table 3–3) and/or employee, if codes for employees are included in the data base. A transaction-system example would be the entry on the patient's bill of the number and cost of each type of laboratory test performed by the hospital. An example of a control-reporting purpose would be the use of the data in this data base for either retrospective or concurrent medical audit. This would require the extraction of the number of each type of laboratory test conducted for each patient and the combination of this information with the data in the patient's chart abstract. An example of a strategic-planning use would

Table 3–3 Weekly Laboratory Test Report

WEEKLY LAB
TOTAL AUTOMATED TESTS RUN

CITY HOSPITAL — WEEK BEGINNING 03-13-83 — WEEK ENDING 03-19-83

MACHINE NO.	MACHINE TYPE	MACHINE USE BY DATE 13	14	15	16	17	18	19	WEEK TOTAL
01	AUTOMATED CELL COUNTER	103	168	182	171	197	185	122	1128
02	ASTRA-1	51	83	78	77	65	65	42	461
03	ASTRA-2	55	79	80	61	59	62	40	436
04	MULTI-CHANNEL AUTO ANALYZER	88	109	117	106	120	116	89	745
05	CENTRIFUGAL ANALYZER	45	59	56	56	53	60	42	371
06	COAGOMATE	16	32	30	27	22	28	19	174

Source: Reprinted with permission of Electronic Data Systems Corporation, Health Services Division, Dallas, Texas.

be the creation of tabulations of past laboratory-resource utilization trends for an analysis aimed at devising a long-term strategy for the provision of efficient, high-quality laboratory services in a hospital.

The above two information systems represent simple systems, involving data from one source. In practice, information systems are often more complex. Some information systems, for instance, extract data from data bases in different information systems and combine them to produce output that integrates the data. An example is a system that produces patient bills by extracting and then combining data from other information systems, such as a patient registration system, a laboratory-test system, and a radiology-department system. Other systems receive data from more than one source and integrate them into one combined data base. Figure 3–3 illustrates this type of system; Data Care's Patient Care Information System, described later in this chapter, is a specific example of such a system.

GROWTH OF COMPUTERIZED HOSPITAL INFORMATION SYSTEMS

The computerization of hospital information systems—which began in the late 1950s and has grown at an accelerating pace since then—has been driven by a number of factors. Probably the most important of these is the rapid development of relevant computer hardware and software. Another driving force is the in-

Figure 3–3 Patient Information System

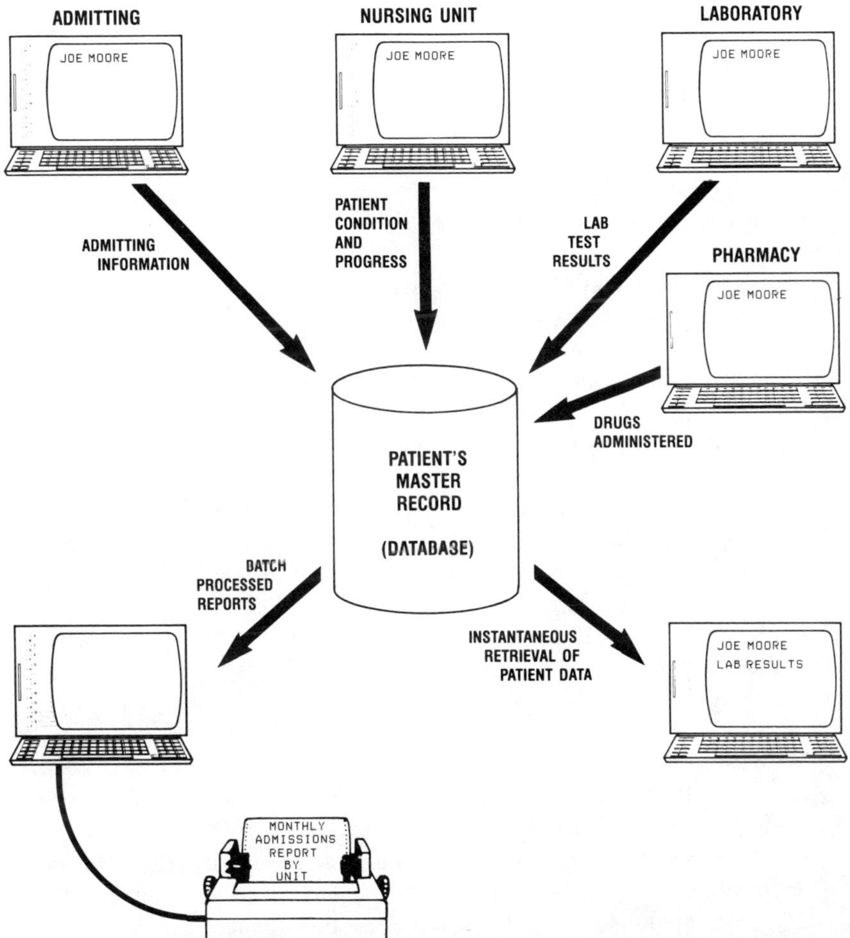

Source: Reprinted with permission of Electronic Data Systems Corporation, Health Services Division, Dallas, Texas.

creasing speed and sophistication and the decreasing cost of computer processing, which have given computerized systems significant cost advantages over manual systems. This is particularly true in the case of the complex hospital data reporting requirements of programs such as Medicaid, Medicare, PSROs, and health planning agencies. For example, computerization is virtually essential to enable hospitals to evaluate the impact on revenue of the prospective reimbursement system required by the Social Security Amendments of 1983.

The period prior to 1960 has been referred to as the "precomputer era."[10] During that period, the vast majority of hospital information systems were operated manually. In some applications, mechanical aids such as posting and bookkeeping machines and mechanical data recorders were used. Punched-card machines with capabilities for sorting, collating, and tabulating were available during the 1950s but were not widely used in hospitals.

The decade of the 1960s saw rapid progress in computer technology and its applications, spurred mainly by the development of faster, lower-cost, transistorized machines. This progress led to the computerization of many hospital information systems. Whereas a 1962 survey found less than 1 percent of U.S. hospitals using computers,[11] a similar survey conducted in 1970 found that the proportion using computers had increased to 45 percent.[12]

Hospitals vary widely in organizational structure, plant size, staffing patterns, personnel procedures, and clinical treatment patterns. Nevertheless, the basic software for certain hospital information systems is the same, or very similar, for all hospitals. This is true, for example, of the information system required for Medicare billing, which began in the mid-1960s. Shared computer services were therefore developed for these types of information systems. Such computer services take advantage of the economies of scale and the lower per-hospital software development and hardware acquisition costs available from sharing the same computer system. These services were initially used in the 1960s and are widespread today. A 1975 American Hospital Association survey, for example, found that 56 percent of all U.S. hospitals used outside, shared data processing services.[13]

The decade of the 1970s saw a continued computerization of hospital information systems. A survey by the Healthcare Financial Management Association, for example, showed that 80 percent of all U.S. hospitals used computerized data processing in 1976, compared with 45 percent in 1970.[14]

In addition to the increasing use of computer processing, there are other important ways in which hospital computer applications are changing. One is the development and spread of interactive, real-time processing. On-line processing involves two-way communication between the computer and person guiding the processing. It allows for, or facilitates, the performance of a number of data processing activities, such as word processing; the inputting and immediate editing of data or coded instructions; instantaneous retrieval of stored information, such as a patient's registration data (see Figure 3–4) or current inventory levels of medical supplies (see Figure 3–5); and the manipulation or updating of stored information, such as personnel pay scales and titles. The growth of interactive processing was undoubtedly hastened by the creation and use of time-sharing software that allows the computer to be used simultaneously by more than one person.

The other way in which hospital computer applications are changing is that

Figure 3–4 Request for Patient Registration Data

```
ALPHA LOCATOR FOR ADMISSION/INQUIRY HISTORY FILE

C-- SMITH, CAR

     ENTER FROM TWO TO THIRTY LETTERS OF THE
     PATIENT NAME AND SELECT C
```

The clerk types in "SMITH, CAR" and selects "C", by pushing the touch contact switch, causing the next screen to appear.

```
    PATIENT'S              BIRTH
    NAME                   DATE              MEDICAL RECORD NO.
C--SMITH, CARL             121348                 1800008
D--SMITH, CARL             012331                 1600001
E--SMITH, CAROL            032751                 1700002
F--SMITH, CAROL            121251                 1900001
G--SMITH, CAROLE           010170                 1500003
H--SMITH, CAROLINE         082662                 1300002
I--SMITH, CARROLL          050021                 1400006


S--RETURN TO INITIAL SCREEN
T--CONTINUE TO NEXT SCREEN
```

The clerk selects the correct patient by touching "F", causing the medical record history abstract screen for this patient to appear.

```
MEDICAL RECORD NUMBER 1900001 VISIT# 02

NAME:            SMITH, CAROL
ADDRESS:         102 MAIN STREET
CITY:            ELKTON STATE: MD. ZIP: 21921
PHONE#           301-828-5555

BIRTH DATE:      12-12-51

SOCIAL SECURITY: 200-50-6000

LAST ADMISSION DATE     11-16-74
       DISCHARGE DATE   11-30-74
ADMITTING DIAGNOSIS     DIABETES

ADMITTING PHYSICIAN:    DR. MARK REED

S--RETURN TO SELECT ANOTHER PATIENT
T--CONTINUE TO INITIATE READMISSION
```

Source: Reprinted with permission of Electronic Data Systems Corporation, Health Services Division, Dallas, Texas.

---

they are beginning to be integrated. Integration is an attempt to eliminate some of the duplication and unnecessary expense involved in operating numerous separate information systems in the hospital. An example of such integration is

Figure 3–5 Request for Inventory Level

```
FILE MAINTENANCE-BULK INVENTORY MGMT. SYSTEM

C-ADD LINE ITEM

E-CHANGE LINE ITEM                        (ENTER STOCK NUMBER)

G-INQUIRY 0101 CATHETER, SUCTION          (ENTER STOCK NUMBER)

I-DELETE LINE ITEM -                      (ENTER STOCK NUMBER)



T-EXIT
```

The clerk types in the inventory item and name, "0101 CATHETER, SUCTION," and then selects "G" by pushing the touch contact switch.

```
RECORD MAINTENANCE-BULK INVENTORY MGMT. SYSTEM

C-COMMON RECORD DATA

E-BULK RECORD DATA

G-BULK RECORD HISTORY DATA

I-VENDOR DATA (1st 3 VENDORS)

K-VENDOR DATA (LAST 2 VENDORS)


T-EXIT
```

The clerk selects the type of data required by touching "E", causing the requested data to appear on the following screen.

```
RECORD DATA-BULK INVENTORY MGMT. SYSTEM
ITEM NUMBER 0101
ITEM NAME   CATHETER, SUCTION
BULK LOCATION     AISLE 2       BULK STOCK BAL     0000001
PHYS INVEN DATE   821115        PHYS INVEN QTY     0000021
BULK AVG. COST    0002004       BULK AVG DATE      8211
BULK LAST COST    0002004       BULK LAST DATE     8210
BULK FYTD USAGE   00000034      BULK FYTD PURCH    000018375
DATE LAST ISSUE   821203        UNITS PER UNIT     00012
UNIT OF ISSUE     BOX           MAXIMUM LEVEL      0000200
MAX ISSUE QTY     0002          SAFETY LEVEL       00104

S-SELECT ANOTHER AREA-SAME ITEM
T-EXIT
```

Source: Reprinted with permission of Electronic Data Systems Corporation, Health Services Division, Dallas, Texas.

---

the blending of separate patient medical chart abstracting and billing systems into a combined chart-abstracting and billing system. This would eliminate a number of activities, including the double entry and storage of data such as the patient's name and address and admission and discharge dates.

It will probably be impossible to integrate all the different hospital computerized information systems depicted in Figure 3–1. However, it is entirely feasible, and even desirable, to integrate many of them. This is particularly true of the information systems related to, or derived from, the delivery of services to the patient, such as the allocation of nursing staff, patient chart abstracting, billing, medical audit, utilization review, and the requisitioning of ancillary services (see Figure 3–3). Several versions of information systems that integrate these different services have been developed and successfully deployed.[15] These systems generally create, continuously update, and use a comprehensive computerized record for each patient. It is anticipated that these types of integrated systems will be more widely used in the future, due to the decreasing costs and increasing sophistication of computer processing.

It is also anticipated that the future will bring an expanded use of computers in the hospital in general. There is currently a move to make computers, particularly microcomputers, more "user friendly." This means the instructions needed to use them are becoming more like common language and less like computer language. This development will help create more computer users among persons who are currently unwilling to learn computer languages. More generally, increases in computer memory capacity and the rapidly decreasing cost of inputting, storing, processing, and outputting information have already fostered, and will continue to foster, the spread of computerization.

All of these changes will inevitably spur the use of computerized data in strategic analyses. They will make the creation, maintenance, and processing of data bases that are important for strategic planning much simpler and less expensive than they are at present. In a similar vein, the creation and maintenance of such data bases over periods of time will facilitate the analysis of long-term trends that are so important for the strategic planner.

TYPES OF HOSPITAL INFORMATION SYSTEMS

Categories

There are many different ways of categorizing hospital information systems.[16–19] Shaffert and McDowell have presented a two-dimensional method of depicting and categorizing hospital information systems.[20] This method, shown in Figure 3–1, is used here because it is comprehensive and logically conceived. According to Shaffert and McDowell, information systems can be grouped on the basis of two factors: their functions and the purpose for which the information they generate is used. This latter factor is referred to as the information requirements type in Figure 3–1.

Shaffert and McDowell, along with Minch et al.,[21] recognize two groups of information system functions: medical functions and business functions. Shaffert and McDowell recognize four types of information requirements: transaction systems, control reporting, operational planning, and strategic planning. As can be seen from Figure 3–1, transaction systems provide information required for day-to-day clinical and business activities, such as treatment scheduling and payroll preparation. Control reporting and operational planning systems provide information that is derived, or aggregated, from transaction systems, usually on an ongoing, but less often than a daily, basis. Control reporting data are needed for monitoring and controlling activities such as medical audit and internal fiscal audits. Operational planning data are used to make, and monitor the implementation of, short-term plans covering internal operations—both medical and administrative. Strategic planning information is derived from data collected for, or produced by, any of the other three types of information systems.

Strategic planning is long-range in its orientation. Thus, a specific strategic planning issue, such as the services to be offered by a hospital, is addressed on a relatively infrequent basis, possibly once every few years. Consequently, data for a specific strategic planning analysis would be produced relatively infrequently, even though strategic planning is an ongoing activity. Strategic planning is different from operational planning, controlling, and transacting in that it is generally more externally focused. In other words, it considers factors that are outside the hospital, such as population growth and the need for services in the geographic area around the hospital. In a similar vein, it uses data that derive from outside, as well as inside, the hospital, whereas data for operational purposes are derived almost exclusively from internal information systems.

Applications

Hospital information systems now cover a large and increasing number of a hospital's data collection and processing activities.[22–30] Each entry or line in the boxes in Figure 3–1 represents a separate information collection and processing activity, that is, a separate information system in terms of the elements presented in Figure 3–2. Other terms also apply; the activity could be a separate component or application of a software package in the hospital's information systems. For example, the transaction system application entitled "census" in Figure 3–1 is an information system that collects data on the number of patients on each ward in the hospital each day.

There are a great number and variety of available application packages. Those in Figure 3–1 do not, by any means, represent a complete list. A more complete list, developed under contract to the National Center for Health Services Research, contains 280 applications, covering 31 units within the hospital.[31] And even this latter list is not assumed to be exhaustive.

Part of the reason for the great variety of available applications is the large number of persons and institutions involved in their development. Many hospitals, for instance, develop and operate some or all of their systems themselves. Such self-developed and operated systems are referred to as in-house systems. A great number of applications have also been developed by software vendors, who market their products to hospitals that operate them. These are called turnkey systems. In some instances, the vendor will develop and operate the applications for the hospital. Applications that are developed and operated for hospitals by vendors are usually designed to provide the same services to more than one hospital simultaneously and are therefore referred to as shared systems. These are described in Chapters 5, 10, and 11.

Some information system applications are more likely than others to yield data that are useful for strategic planning. One such application involves selecting information from the patient's medical chart and writing it on a separate computer record, known as the patient chart abstract (see Exhibit 3–1). This record is also

---

Exhibit 3–1 Data Items on the Chart Abstract Used for Prospective Reimbursement by the New Jersey State Department of Health

Hospital code	Primary service
Hospital type	Primary payer
Patient billing number	Transfer destination
Patient record number	Special Care Unit 1
Admission class	Days in Special Care Unit 1
Admission hour	Special Care Unit 2
Admission year	Days in Special Care Unit 2
Admission month	Year of principal procedure
Admission day	Month of principal procedure
Discharge year	Day of principal procedure
Discharge month	Consultation 1
Discharge day	Consultation 2
Residence code	Consultation 3
Sex	Consultation 4
Birth year	Attending physician code
Birth month	Principal surgeon code
Birth day	Major physician code
Age code	Zip code
Referral source	Major diagnosis
Principal diagnosis	Major procedure
Other diagnosis (7)	Major service
Principal procedure	Referral source code
Other procedure (6)	Transfer destination code
Discharge status	

Source: New Jersey State Department of Health, "A Prospective Reimbursement System Based on Patient Case-Mix for New Jersey Hospitals, 1978–1982" *Handbook for Bill/Abstract Merge* (Trenton, N.J.: New Jersey State Department of Health, 1979).

known as the discharge abstract because it contains information, such as discharge diagnoses, that is often not entered in the chart itself until after the patient is discharged.

Patient chart abstracts are collected in a substantial portion of acute-care general hospitals in the United States.[32] The process of abstracting information from the medical chart is done in a variety of ways. In some institutions, the creation of the chart abstract is a separate application whose sole purpose is the manual selection of data from the completed patient's chart to be used in the creation of a computerized chart abstract. In others, the abstract is created as a byproduct of applications, with objectives other than chart abstract creation. The Patient-Care Information System (PCIS), developed and marketed by Data Care, Inc., is one such application.[33] This application is an on-line interactive system that collects a large proportion of the information in the medical chart as it is entered in the chart. In addition to being used to create chart abstracts, this information can be made available for such purposes as the instantaneous ordering

Figure 3–6 Request for Patient Clinical History

```
ALPHA LOCATOR FOR CLINICAL HISTORY INQUIRY

PATIENT'S                    BIRTH       MEDICAL
NAME                         DATE        RECORD NO.

F-- JOHNSON, WILLIAM         080557      1100006
G-- JOHNSON, ALICE           022218      1200002
H-- JONES, MARGARET          123040      1000006
I-- JOSEPH, LEE              061645      2200008

S-- RETURN TO NEXT SCREEN
T-- CONTINUE TO NEXT SCREEN
```

The clerk locates clinical history information for WILLIAM JOHNSON by pushing the touch contact switch "F". The data appears on the next screen almost instantly.

```
MEDICAL RECORD NO. 1100006     VISIT #03
NAME: JOHNSON, WILLIAM
BIRTHDATE: 08-05-27
451-00-6667

VISIT #01: 09-22-77 -- 09-30-77
DIAGNOSIS: ANGINA
PHYSICIAN: DR. RICHARD MARTIN

VISIT #02: 03-15-82 -- 03-24-82
DIAGNOSIS: MYOCARDIAL INFARCTION
PHYSICIAN: DR. RICHARD MARTIN

R-- REQUEST DETAILED VISIT HISTORY
S-- RETURN TO SELECT ANOTHER PATIENT
T-- CONTINUE TO INITIATE READMISSION
```

If further clinical history data (lab values, etc.) is required, the clerk may select "R".

Source: Reprinted with permission of Electronic Data Systems Corporation, Health Services Division, Dallas, Texas.

of ancillary services and the monitoring of the patient's clinical progress. Figure 3–6, which is based on a system developed by the Electronic Data Systems Corporation, illustrates the instantaneous retrieval of a patient's computerized clinical history that is made possible by applications such as Data Care's PCIS.

The data in the chart abstract (Exhibit 3–1) are useful for a number of strategic planning applications, including patient origin studies (see Chapter 6), analysis of medical staff utilization patterns (see Table 3–4 and Chapter 8), and the projection of future demand for existing or proposed new services. Chart abstract

Table 3–4 Monthly Physician Profile

CITY HOSPITAL — MAY 1983 — PAGE 1 OF 6

	LOS IN DAYS	ANCILLARY CHARGES LAB	OR	PHARM	RADI	REHAB	TOTAL
DR. KYLE BATES							
PATIENTS:							
DALE MARTIN	8	$648	$588	$138	$125	$ 70	$1569
BETH STANFORD	4	$256	_	$ 86	$ 75	_	$ 417
JOE NAKAYAMA	6	$563	$381	$187	_	_	$1131
VIRGINIA MARTIN	6	$322	$832	$122	_	$ 35	$1311
DR. AL CHESTERTON							
PATIENTS:							
JANELLE PETERS	3	$203	$321-D	$ 45	_	_	$ 569
SARA MOFFETT	3	$186	$220-D	$ 49	_	_	$ 455
SHARON GRAHAM	2	$157	_	$ 38	_	_	$ 195
ELLEN HORTON	4	$538	$276	$ 59	_	$ 35	$ 908
NANCY SEAT	3	$422	$492	$ 50	_	_	$ 964
DR. SAMUEL HENDERSON							
PATIENTS:							
J.F. RICKELS	2	$155	_	$ 30	$ 35	_	$ 220
JAMES RODGERS	1	$ 58	_	$ 18	$ 42	_	$ 118
MARTIN STONE	6	$788	$544	$106	$100	$105	$1643
LEA GRAY	4	$350	_	$ 72	_	$ 35	$ 457
MARVIN LEE	6	$522	_	$121	_	$105	$ 748
SUZANNE LAFEY	5	$882	_	$101	$ 80	_	$1063
LESA BROWN	3	$349	_	$ 27	$ 33	_	$ 409
KEITH MICHAELSON	1	$107	_	$ 15	_	_	$ 122
AUDREY BRUNNER	1	$138	_	$ 29	_	_	$ 167
DOUGLAS SHERMAN	2	$206	_	$ 37	_	_	$ 243
DR. RAYMOND JONES							
PATIENTS:							
SANDRA RASTER	5	$681	$481	$ 88	_	_	$1250

CONTINUED

Source: Reprinted with permission of Electronic Data Systems Corporation, Health Services Division, Dallas, Texas.

data can also be collected and processed by a shared data system such as the Professional Activities Study of the Commission on Professional and Hospital Activities (PAS) (see Chapter 5).

The second application that yields data useful for strategic planning is the creation of the patient's bill. This record usually contains the charges for hospital services delivered to patients, broken down into categories representing the different departments responsible for delivering the services, such as radiology, laboratory, dietary, physical therapy, nursing, and special care units (see Exhibit 3–2).

The patient's bill is created by collecting data on the quantity of each separate service delivered to the patient and then multiplying it by the per-unit charge for the service. Data on the quantity of each separate service delivered to the patient are obtained in a number of ways, depending on the data collection and processing systems in the hospital. At the one extreme, these data are collected and compiled separately in each separate service delivery department. They are then sent to a billing unit for entry into each patient's bill. At the other extreme, data on services delivered to each patient, along with other clinical and patient information, are compiled on an ongoing, typically daily, basis. The bill for each patient is then created after discharge by means of software that abstracts the data on the quantity of services delivered and automatically multiplies it by the appropriate unit charge (see Figure 3–7).

The patient bill is useful for a wide range of strategic financial planning activities (see Chapter 10). When combined with the chart abstract, as is done in some institutions, usually for case-mix reimbursement purposes,[34] the data on the patient's bill become even more useful to the strategic planner. The merged abstract-bill provides data in a form convenient for examining specific charges, such as CT scanner charges by hospital department, physician or diagnosis (see Table 3–5), or region of the hospital's service area (see Chapters 6 and 7). The merging of the patient's chart abstract and bill permits easy determination of the profitability of, or the revenue that could be received from, serving specific markets (see Chapters 6 and 7).

CONCLUSION

Because it is long-range in orientation, strategic planning cannot rely solely on the data output of the hospital's information systems. Such output is designed for routine, short-range, sometimes daily, medical or business functions. Also, the strategic planner is future oriented, whereas data in the hospital's information system refer to past or current events or activities.

Typically, the strategic planner will abstract and summarize data from the output or data base of one or more of the hospital's information systems. If the

Exhibit 3–2 Example of a Patient's Bill for Hospital Services

INPATIENT HOSPITAL AND SKILLED NURSING FACILITY ADMISSION AND BILLING
HOSPITAL AND MEDICAL INSURANCE BENEFITS-SOCIAL SECURITY ACT

Form Approved
OMB No. 0938-0010

This report is authorized by 42 USC 1395n, 42CFR 405, 1660. Your cooperation is needed to keep proper beneficiary records and to make proper Medicare payments.
NOTICE: Anyone who misrepresents or falsifies essential information requested by this form may upon conviction be subject to fine and imprisonment under Federal law.

1. Patient's last name | First name | MI | 2. Sex ☐ M ☐ F | 3. Health Insurance claim number

4. Patient's address *(Street number, City, State)* | Zip Code | 5. Date of birth | 6. Medical record number

7. Date of this admission | 8. Provider name and address *(City and State)* | 9. Provider number | 10. Attending physician

11. Dates of qualifying stay FROM THRU | 12. Qualifying and other prior stay information

If any of your medical expenses may be paid by your insurance organization or State Agency, complete Items 13 and 14.
If you do not want information about this Medicare claim released to your insurance organization, check this block ☐

13. Name and address of organization or agency | 14. Policy or Identification Number

15. Patient's Certification, Authorization to Release Information, and Payment Request. I certify that the information given by me in applying for payment under Title XVIII of the Social Security Act is correct. I authorize any holder of medical or other information about me to release to the Social Security Administration and/or the Medicare Program or its intermediaries or carriers or to the Professional Standards Review Organizations any information needed for this or a related Medicare claim. I request that payment of authorized benefits be made on my behalf.

Signature *(Patient or authorized representative) (Signature by mark must be witnessed)* | ☐ Contained in provider's record | Date

16. Admitting diagnoses | Employment Related and/or Entitlement to Other Government Programs ☐ Yes ☐ No *(If Yes, Give Name and Address of Employer and/or Program)* | Do not use this space

17. (a) Principal diagnosis | (b) Other diagnoses

18. Surgical procedures *(Show date of each)*

19. STATEMENT OF SERVICES RENDERED | Total Charges | Non-covered Chg's.

Blood pints furnished | Pints replaced | Not replaced | Charge per pint

A.

Accommodation | Days | Rate

- B. 1-Bed
- C. 2-3-4 Bed
- D. 5 or more Beds
- FOR HOSPITAL ONLY: E. Intensive care; F. Coronary care; G.; H. Operating room; I. Anesthesia; J. Outpatient services
- K. Blood administration
- L. Pharmacy
- M. Radiology
- N. Laboratory
- O. Medical surgical and central supplies
- P. Physical therapy
- Q. Occupational therapy
- R. Speech pathology
- S. Inhalation therapy
- T. Other *(Describe)*
- U. TOTALS
- V. Inpatient deductible
- W. Blood deductible pts. @
- X. Coinsurance days ( ) ( )
- Y. TOTAL DEDUCTIONS

20. Statement covers period FROM | THRU

21. Date guarantee of payment began | 22. Date UR notice received

23. Date active care ended | 24. Date benefits exhausted

25. Patient status: A. Date discharged | B. Date of death | C. ☐ Still patient

26. Lifetime reserve days | 27. Non-covered days | 28. Covered days

30. Remarks

PIP
(a) ☐

31. Reimbursement amount $

FOR INTERMEDIARY USE

32. Verified non-covered stays From Thru | 33. Non-pmt code | 34. Days used

29. I certify that the required physician's certification and recertifications are on file

Signature of provider representative | Date Received | 35. Approved by | Date approved

Form **HCFA-1453 (C)** (5-80) (Formerly SSA-1453C)

Department of Health and Human Services
Health Care Financing Administration

Source: Health Care Financing Administration, Form SSA-1453(3): *Inpatient Hospital and Skilled Nursing Facility Admission and Billing*. Washington, D.C.: Department of Health, Education and Welfare, undated.

Figure 3–7 Production of an Inpatient's Bill

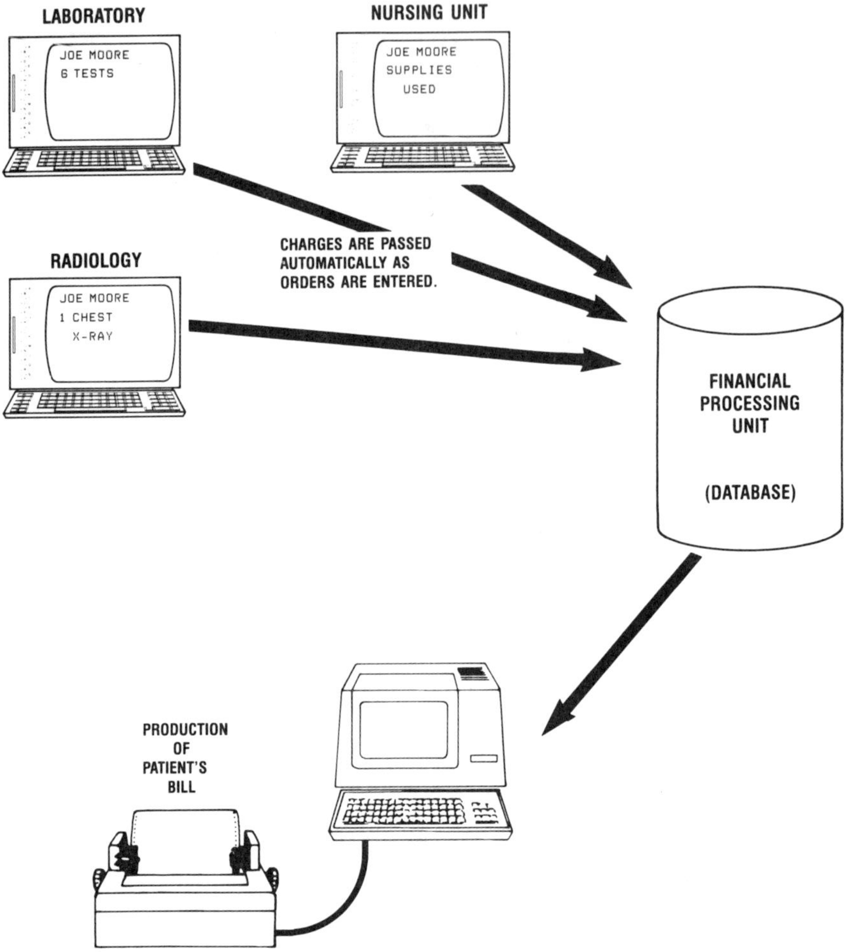

Source: Reprinted with permission of Electronic Data Systems Corporation, Health Services Division, Dallas, Texas.

---

necessary data are not available in any of the hospital's information systems, the strategic planner may have to collect them de novo. Once obtained, the data for strategic planning may be tabulated, used to make projections, or used as input to a quantitative decision-making model (Chapters 6 through 10 offer detailed illustrative examples; Figure 3–1 depicts the relationship between strategic planning and the other applications of hospital information systems).

Table 3–5 CT Scan Summary

CITY HOSPITAL							PAGE 1 OF 3 OCT 82-MAR 83
				DIAGNOSIS			
PHYSICIAN	MENIN-GIOMA	CBA	OBS	HERN. DISC	SUB-ARACH. HEMOR.	OTHER	TOTAL
DR. JAMES CARR	1	4	6	1	1	3	16
DR. GEORGE HOUSE	0	3	3	0	2	2	10
DR. LISA KENT	4	6	10	6	5	7	38
DR. CARL LANGE	12	26	33	15	12	42	140
DR. DOROTHY KING	1	5	4	2	2	4	18
DR. EUGENE PEABODY	3	8	8	5	4	4	32
DR. ROBERT RICH	5	7	6	6	5	3	32
DR. BELINDA HARDER	3	5	2	0	1	6	17
DR. STEVE DUNN	14	22	21	6	11	26	100
DR. EDWARD BURNS	4	6	11	6	5	10	42

CONTINUED

Source: Reprinted with permission of Electronic Data Systems Corporation, Health Services Division, Dallas, Texas.

The hospital strategic planner sometimes requires information on events or conditions outside the hospital. This information is obtained from other data systems or services. (Chapter 4 examines one of these sources: government data; Chapter 5 focuses on another outside source: shared information systems.)

REFERENCES

1. C.J. Austin, *Information Systems for Hospital Administration* (Ann Arbor, Mich.: Hospital Administration Press, 1979).

2. T.K. Shaffert, ed., "Hospital Information Systems," *Topics in Health Care Financing* 4, no. 4 (Summer 1978).

3. G. Thompson and I. Handelman, *Health Data and Information Management* (Boston: Butterworths, 1978).

4. E. Drazen and J. Metzger, *Methods for Evaluating Costs of Automated Hospital Information Systems,* Research Summary Series, National Center for Health Services Research (Hyattsville, Md.: U.S. Department of Health and Human Services, July 1981).

5. J.A. Balgrosky, D.W. Strum, and E. Bradley, ''Evaluation Helps Ensure an AHIS Performs to Its Potential,'' *Hospitals* 56, no. 9 (1982):82.

6. H.H. Schnitz, *Hospital Information Systems* (Germantown, Md.: Aspen Systems Corp., 1979).

7. M.H. Hodge, *Medical Information Systems* (Germantown, Md.: Aspen Systems Corp., 1977).

8. R.C. Koza, ed., *Health Information Systems Evaluation* (Boulder, Colo.: Colorado Associated University Press, 1974).

9. D.A. Minch et al., ''Information Systems: Audit Is a First Step in Planning,'' *Hospitals* 56, no. 9 (1982):85.

10. Austin, ''Information Systems,'' p. 36.

11. Ibid., p. 12.

12. A.G. Battle and D.A. Rey, ''Current Status and Trends of Hospital Information Systems,'' *Topics in Health Care Financing* 4, no. 4 (Summer 1978):12.

13. Frost and Sullivan, Inc., *Data Processing Systems and Services for the U.S. Health Care Industry* (New York: Frost and Sullivan, 1975).

14. Battle and Rey, ''Current Status and Trends,'' p. 12.

15. Data Care, Inc., *Patient Care Information Systems—Application Software* (Roanoke, Va.: Data Care, 1982).

16. Austin, ''Information Systems,'' pp. 161–242.

17. Minch et al., ''Information Systems,'' p. 86.

18. T.M. Ball, ''Computers: Prescription for Hospital Ills,'' *Datamation,* September 1975, pp. 50–51.

19. T.K. Shaffert and C.E. McDowell, ''Hospital Information Systems: An Overview,'' *Topics in Health Care Financing* 4, no. 4 (Summer 1978):5–7.

20. Ibid., pp. 6–7.

21. Minch et al., ''Information Systems,'' p. 86.

22. Austin, ''Information Systems,'' pp. 161–242.

23. Shaffert, ''Hospital Information Systems,'' pp. 5–7.

24. Thompson and Handelman, *Health Data.*

25. Schnitz, *Hospital Information Systems.*

26. Hodge, *Medical Information Systems.*

27. D. Lingberg, *The Growth of Medical Information Systems in the United States* (Lexington, MA: Lexington Books, 1979).

28. G.A. Bekey and M.D. Schwartz, eds., *Hospital Information Systems* (New York: Marcel Dekker, 1972).

29. R.R. Grams, ''The Current Status and Future Prospects for Computers in Hospitals,'' *Hospitals* 51 (October 1977):187.

30. Hospital Financial Management Association, *The State of Information Processing in the Health Care Industry* (Chicago: Hospital Financial Management Association, 1976).

31. E.M. Young, ed., *Automated Hospital Information Systems Workbook* (Los Angeles: University of Southern California, Center for Health Services Research, 1981).

32. National Academy of Sciences, Institute of Medicine, *Report of a Study: Reliability of National Hospital Discharge Survey Data* (Washington, D.C.: National Academy of Sciences, 1980), p. 6.

33. Data Care, Inc., *Patient Care Information Systems.*

34. New Jersey Department of Health, "A Prospective Reimbursement System Based on Patient Case-Mix for New Jersey Hospitals," *Third Annual Report of the Diagnosis Related Group Project* (Trenton, N.J.: New Jersey Department of Health, 1980).

Chapter 4

Government Data

OVERVIEW

A significant proportion of the data used in strategic planning derives from sources external to the hospital. In particular, government data are essential to a hospital's strategic planning. This is true for a number of reasons. First, government data are the main, often the only, source of information about a hospital's external environment. Also most government data cover large areas, usually the whole nation, and therefore allow for interarea comparisons, which is often important in strategic planning. In addition, government data are available over long periods of time, hence allowing for analyses of time trends and for projections into the future, both fundamental techniques for strategic analysis.

There are a large number of federal, state, and local government agencies involved in collecting and disseminating data on health and health care. A partial list of such agencies in the federal government is presented in Table 4–1. In this chapter the following government data systems are described: (1) the census, (2) the data collection program of the National Center for Health Statistics, (3) the Medicare system, (4) the Area Resource File, and (5) state government data systems. (Our descriptions of these systems are intended primarily for the practitioner who is not familiar with government data; other readers may wish to skim or skip this chapter.)

It is important to note that there are limitations to most of the data in these government systems. In some cases, the accuracy of the data varies from year to year; in other instances, it varies with geographic location. And often the level of accuracy of the data is undetermined. For example, cause of death, an item required legally to be reported on the death certificate, is notoriously unreliable; and no attempts are made to determine and correct for the errors. Similarly, the hospital data collected by the American Hospital Association are self-reported and unaudited.

Table 4–1 Selected Federal Government Agencies and the Health Data They Collect

Agency	*Data*
National Center for Health Statistics	Health Interview Survey Health resources statistics Health and Nutrition Examination Survey Vital and health statistics Health resources utilization
Bureau of the Census	Population census Social indicators
National Institute of Mental Health	Mental health statistics
Bureau of Labor Statistics	Health care components of the Consumer Price Index Health industry employment and earnings
Department of Agriculture	Nutrition data Federal food programs
Health Care Financing Administration	Medicare statistical system National medical costs and expenditures
Center for Disease Control	Abortion statistics Notifiable diseases

Source: Bureau of the Census, *Statistical Abstracts of the United States, 1978* (Washington, D.C.: Government Printing Office, 1978), pp. 981–983.

Another limitation in much of the data collected and/or disseminated by government agencies is that the data do not provide detail at the local (e.g., county) level, the level on which many hospital strategic decisions focus. For example, most of the surveys conducted by the National Center for Health Statistics do not generally yield county-level data; many of them do not even yield state-level data.

The information in this chapter is not sufficient for many strategic planning applications in other ways. We have devoted very little attention to the question of the accuracy of government data. Moreover, the information that is presented will probably become outdated in the not-too-distant future. This is because government data agencies, and the nature of the data they collect and disseminate, change in response to the inevitable changes in public policy and economic conditions in the nation. Finally, our descriptions are not comprehensive; there is, for example, no description of the data collected by three of the agencies listed in Table 4–1: the National Institute of Mental Health, the Bureau of Labor Statistics, and the Department of Agriculture.

An attempt is made to list the publications and computer tapes that the data agencies described in this chapter disseminate. It should also be noted that many government data agencies produce unpublished reports that are often available on request. In some instances, they will produce special reports or tabulations in response to specific requests. The strategic planner is advised to seek such unpublished or special reports if the published documents do not contain adequate data for their purposes.

CENSUS DATA

The Bureau of the Census, which was officially established as a permanent federal agency in 1902, is the principal source of data on the size, distribution, characteristics, and growth of the U.S. population.[1] The bureau uses three mechanisms for generating these data: (1) the decennial census, (2) the current population survey (CPS), and (3) population estimates and projections.

The original purpose of the decennial census of the U.S. population, which is required by the U.S. Constitution, was to yield data on which the apportionment of seats in the House of Representatives could be based.[2] The census has been conducted every ten years since 1790. Today it collects far more information than needed for the apportionment of legislative districts. In fact, as Table 4–2 indicates, the 1980 census attempted to collect 6 population and 9 housing items on 100 percent of the U.S. population and 26 population and 18 housing items on a sample basis. In areas of the country estimated to contain more than 2,500 persons, the sample was one in six households (16.7 percent); in areas estimated to contain 2,500 or fewer persons, the sample was three in six households (50 percent). The 50-percent sampling rate was needed to yield reliable statistics for participation in certain federal programs.[3,4] The overall 1980 national sampling rate was 19.7 percent,[5] a rate that is generally high enough to yield local-area data reliable enough for most hospital strategic analyses.

Processing of the data collected in the 1980 census will result in the publication of a number of documents (Table 4–3) and computer magnetic tapes (Table 4–4) containing tabulations of the census data. One series of these documents and computer tapes was released before the end of 1982; the rest were expected to be available in 1983 or 1984.[6] Figure 4–1 provides a graphic depiction of the geographic areas used in presenting census data tabulations.

The primary purpose of the current population survey (CPS) is the generation of monthly statistics on the labor force. However, it also provides information on other subjects, such as consumer income, which could be of use in strategic

Table 4–2 Subject Items Included in the 1980 Census

100-Percent Items

Population	Housing
Household relationship	Number of units at address
Sex	Complete plumbing facilities
Race	Number of rooms
Age	Tenure (whether unit is owned or rented)
Marital status	Condominium identification
Spanish/Hispanic origin or descent	Value of home (owner-occupied units and condominiums)
	Contract rent (renter-occupied units)
	Vacant for rent, for sale, etc.; and period of vacancy

Sample Items*

Population	Housing
School enrollment	Type of unit
Educational attainment	Stories in building and presence of elevator
State or foreign country of birth	Year built
Citizenship and year of immigration	Year moved into this house
Current language and English proficiency	Acreage and crop sales
Ancestry	Source of water
Place of residence five years ago	Sewage disposal
Activity five years ago	Heating equipment
Veteran status and period of service	Fuels used for house heating, water heating, and cooking
Presence of disability or handicap	Costs of utilities and fuels
Children ever born	Complete kitchen facilities
Marital history	Number of bedrooms
Employment status last week	Number of bathrooms
Hours worked last week	Telephone
Place of work	Air conditioning
Travel time to work	Number of automobiles
Means of transportation to work	Number of light trucks and vans
Persons in carpool	Homeowner shelter costs for mortgage, real estate taxes, and hazard insurance
Year last worked	
Industry	
Occupation	
Class of worker	
Weeks looking for work in 1979	
Amount of income in 1979 by source	

*To meet the aim of greater statistical reliability for small areas, there will be a 50% sample for governmental jurisdictions with a population of less than 2,500. The sample will be one-in-six (16.7%) in areas with a population of 2,500 or more, yielding a National sample rate of 19.7%.

Revised September, 1979

Source: Bureau of the Census, *1980 Census Basics* (Washington, D.C.: U.S. Government Printing Office, 1979).

Table 4–3 Major Report Series from the 1980 Census

Population

Series PC(1)-A (One per State)	**Number of Inhabitants.** Final official population counts are presented for States, counties, SMSA's, urbanized areas, minor civil divisions, census county divisions, all incorporated places, and census designated places of 1,000 inhabitants or more.
Series PC(1)-B (One per State)	**General Population Characteristics.** Statistics on age, sex, race, marital status, Spanish/Hispanic origin, and household relationships are presented for States, counties, SMSA's, urbanized areas, minor civil divisions, census county divisions, Indian reservations, and places of 1,000 inhabitants or more.
Series PC(1)-C (One per State)	**General Social and Economic Characteristics.** These reports focus on population items collected on a sample basis. Each subject is shown for the following areas: States, counties, SMSA's, urbanized areas, and places of 2,500 inhabitants or more.
Series PC(1)-D (One per State)	**Detailed Characteristics.** These reports cover most of the population subjects collected on a sample basis, presenting the data in considerable detail and cross-classified by age, race, and other characteristics. Each subject is shown for the following areas: States (by urban, rural-nonfarm, and rural-farm residence), large SMSA's, and large cities.

Housing

Series HC(1)-A (One per State)	**General Housing Characteristics.** Statistics on 100-percent housing items are presented for States, counties, SMSA's, urbanized areas, minor civil divisions, census county divisions, Indian reservations, and places of 1,000 inhabitants or more.
Series HC(1)-B (One per State)	**Detailed Housing Characteristics.** These reports focus on the housing items collected on a sample basis. Each subject is shown for the following areas: States, counties, SMSA's, urbanized areas, and places of 2,500 inhabitants or more.

Population & Housing

Series PHC(1) (One per SMSA and one for each State)	**Block Statistics.** Reports show data for individual blocks on selected 100-percent population and housing items. The series includes one report for each SMSA (presenting block statistics for the urbanized area, places of 10,000 inhabitants or more, and smaller communities which contracted with the Census Bureau to provide block statistics) and a "balance of State" report for each State (presenting block statistics for places of 10,000 inhabitants outside of SMSA's or more and smaller communities which contracted with the Census Bureau to provide block statistics).
Series PHC(2) (One per SMSA and one for each State)	**Census Tracts.** Reports present selected population and housing items (100-percent and sample) for individual census tracts. The series includes one report for each SMSA and a "balance of State" report for those tracted areas outside of SMSA's.
Series PHC(3) (One per State)	**Summary Characteristics for Governmental Units.** Reports present selected population and housing items (100-percent and sample) for counties, incorporated places, and "active" MCD's qualifying for revenue sharing purposes.

Source: Bureau of the Census, *1980 Census Basics* (Washington, D.C.: U.S. Government Printing Office, 1979).

Table 4–4 Major 1980 Census Summary Tape Files (STF)

STF	Tabulation Areas	Data Items	1970 Comparability
1	Blocks, ED's/BG's, census tracts, places, MCD's/CCD's, counties, U.S. Congressional Districts, States	Basic tabulations of 100% population and housing items (age, sex, tenure, etc.)	1st & 3rd counts
2	Census tracts, places (1,000 or more inhabitants), MCD's/CCD's, counties, SMSA's, States	Detailed tabulations of 100% data (age, sex, tenure, etc.). Separate summaries by selected race categories and Spanish/ Hispanic origin.	2nd count
3	ED's/BG's, census tracts, MCD's/CCD's, places, counties, ZIP Code areas, States	Basic tabulations of sample items (income, education, etc.) in combination with selected 100% items (age, race, etc.)	5th count
4	Census tracts, places (1,000 or more inhabitants), MCD's/CCD's, counties, SMSA's, States	Detailed tabulations of sample items (income, education, etc.) in combination with selected 100% items (age, race, etc.). Separate summaries by selected race categories and Spanish/Hispanic origin.	4th count
5	States, SMSA's, large counties and cities	More detailed tabulations of sample items (income, education, etc.) in combination with selected 100% items (age, race, etc.).	6th count

Other 1980 Census Computer Files

Master Area Reference File (MARF)—Contains numeric codes and names (where appropriate) of geographic areas, and population and housing counts for all geographic areas in the 1980 census.

"Special Population Summary Prepared in Accordance with Public Law 94-171"—Contains total population, race, and Spanish/ Hispanic origin counts for all geographic areas in the 1980 census. Used for legislative reapportionment/redistricting purposes.

GBF/DIME Files—Computerized versions of the Metropolitan Map Series. Available for the urbanized portions of SMSA's. Used to assign census geographic codes to addresses (geocoding).

Public-Use Microdata files—Disclosure-free information for sampled individual records allowing for special tabulations of data not otherwise provided.

Source: Bureau of the Census, *1980 Census Basics* (Washington, D.C.: U.S. Government Printing Office, 1979).

planning. The CPS is a monthly nationwide survey of the adult U.S. population living in a representative sample of about 70,000 housing units or other living quarters. The Bureau of the Census issues a series of publications based on CPS data under the general title *Current Population Reports*.

Estimates of the size of the population in the years between the decennial census (i.e., interdecennial census) are made annually on the first of July using the decennial census data as benchmarks. The projection method involves estimations of each of the three components of population change over the past year: (1) births, (2) deaths, and (3) net migration. These are then combined with the estimates of the size of the population on the first day of July in the previous year. These estimates are published for the nation as a whole, for states, and

Figure 4–1 Geographical Areas Used in Reporting Census Data (1980)

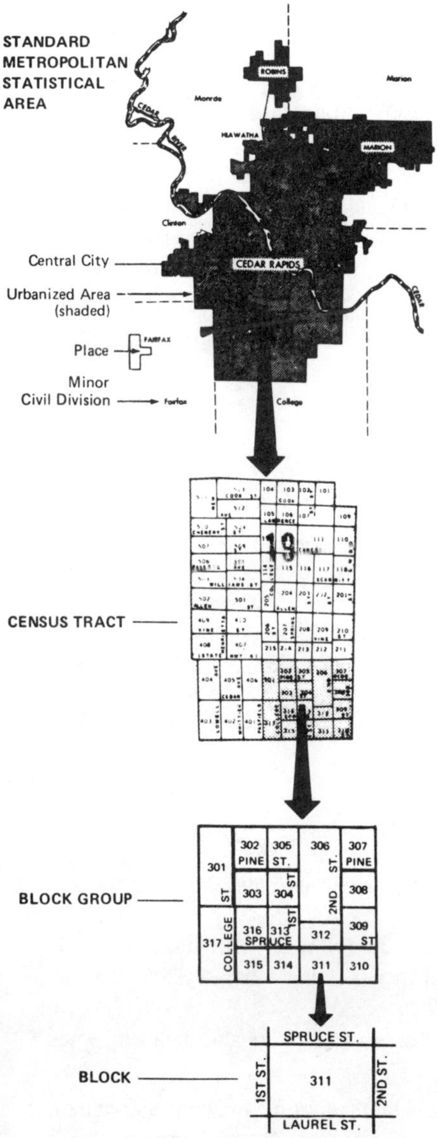

Governmental areas include: States, U.S. Congressional Districts, counties, minor civil divisions, and incorporated places (cities, villages, etc.).

Statistical areas include:

Standard Metropolitan Statistical Areas (SMSA)—As a rule consist of a city of 50,000 inhabitants or more together with the county or counties in which it is located. Contiguous counties are included in an SMSA if they are metropolitan in character and are socially and economically integrated with the central county. A county containing a city of 25,000 to 50,000 population may constitute an SMSA if the addition of densely settled adjacent places would bring the city up to the 50,000 level and the SMSA has a population of at least 75,000.

Urbanized Areas (UA)—Defined by population density, they comprise the central city of an SMSA plus the surrounding closely settled urban fringe (suburbs).

Census County Divisions (CCD)—For data reporting purposes, CCD's take the place of minor civil divisions (MCD) in States where MCD's are not adequately defined.

Census Designated Places (CDP)—A concentration of population, with a definite residential nucleus, which is not legally incorporated.

Census Tracts—Statistical subdivisions of SMSA's, each tract averages 4,000 inhabitants. Defined by local committees, tracts are frequently used to approximate neighborhoods.

Enumeration Districts(ED)—Administrative areas set up by the Census Bureau for census collection purposes, also used as tabulation areas. Each averages about 800 inhabitants.

Block Groups (BG)—Groups of city blocks, averaging 1,000 population, are used in areas where block statistics are tabulated.

Blocks—The smallest type of census geographic area, they average 100 people and are bounded by four streets or some over physical feature. They are used as tabulation areas in UA's, places of 10,000 population or more, and some additional areas.

Source: Bureau of the Census, *1980 Census Basics* (Washington, D.C.: U.S. Government Printing Office, 1979).

for metropolitan areas. The data on births and deaths are obtained from the National Center for Health Statistics. Net national immigration estimates are based on data from the Immigration and Naturalization Service, the Department of Defense, the Puerto Rico Planning Board, and the Civil Service Commission (federal employees abroad). Estimates for the states are based on these types of data and statistics from public and private schools. Some larger counties or cities, and in some instances regional agencies, may also prepare such estimates.

Unfortunately, the techniques for estimating population at the state level are not precise enough to allow a breakdown by age and other social and demographic variables that are useful in market analysis (discussed in Chapter 6). Breakdowns for areas smaller than counties and for a few of the large cities are also not undertaken because of the large potential error of the estimates. This makes the federal census an important event for strategic analyses in hospitals and many other industries.

Population estimates and projections are published in the P-25 series of *Current Population Reports*.

NATIONAL CENTER FOR HEALTH STATISTICS

The National Center for Health Statistics (NCHS) is the largest, most comprehensive source of reliable national data on health, sickness, and health care. Currently NCHS is organized into four data collection systems that are involved in the gathering, processing, and dissemination of data covering many aspects of health and health care. The four systems are:

1. vital statistics system
2. population survey system
3. health resources utilization statistics system
4. health resources statistics system

NCHS uses a number of mechanisms for releasing its data. These include:

- the *Vital and Health Statistics Series* (see Exhibit 4–1), which describes (1) the data collection methodologies used in the center's data system, (2) the data systems themselves, and (3) the data
- *Advance Data Reports,* which are brief summaries of recent data on topics of special interest
- *Monthly Vital Statistics Report,* which contains monthly and cumulative data on births, deaths, marriages, divorces, and infant deaths and provides brief analyses of these vital statistics[7]
- the *Catalog of Publications* of the National Center for Health Statistics, which contains a cumulative list of the center's publications,[8] and the quarterly Publication Note, which updates the catalog every three months

Exhibit 4–1 Vital and Health Statistics Series Descriptions (December, 1981)

SERIES 1. **Programs and Collection Procedures.**—Reports describing the general programs of the National Center for Health Statistics and its offices and divisions and the data collection methods used. They also include definitions and other material necessary for understanding the data.

SERIES 2. **Data Evaluation and Methods Research.**—Studies of new statistical methodology including experimental tests of new survey methods, studies of vital statistics collection methods, new analytical techniques, objective evaluations of reliability of collected data, and contributions to statistical theory.

SERIES 3. **Analytical and Epidemiological Studies.**—Reports presenting analytical or interpretive studies based on vital and health statistics, carrying the analysis further than the expository types of reports in the other series.

SERIES 4. **Documents and Committee Reports.**—Final reports of major committees concerned with vital and health statistics and documents such as recommended model vital registration laws and revised birth and death certificates.

SERIES 10. **Data From the National Health Interview Survey.**—Statistics on illness, accidental injuries, disability, use of hospital, medical, dental, and other services, and other health-related topics, all based on data collected in the continuing national household interview survey.

SERIES 11. **Data From the National Health Examination Survey and the National Health and Nutrition Examination Survey.**—Data from direct examination, testing, and measurement of national samples of the civilian noninstitutionalized population provide the basis for (1) estimates of the medically defined prevalence of specific diseases in the United States and the distributions of the population with respect to physical, physiological, and psychological characteristics and (2) analysis of relationships among the various measurements without reference to an explicit finite universe of persons.

SERIES 12. **Data From the Institutionalized Population Surveys.**—Discontinued in 1975. Reports from these surveys are included in Series 13.

SERIES 13. **Data on Health Resources Utilization.**—Statistics on the utilization of health manpower and facilities providing long-term care, ambulatory care, hospital care, and family planning services.

SERIES 14. **Data on Health Resources: Manpower and Facilities.**—Statistics on the numbers, geographic distribution, and characteristics of health resources including physicians, dentists, nurses, other health occupations, hospitals, nursing homes, and outpatient facilities.

SERIES 15. **Data From Special Surveys.**—Statistics on health and health-related topics collected in special surveys that are not a part of the continuing data systems of the National Center for Health Statistics.

SERIES 20. **Data on Mortality.**—Various statistics on mortality other than as included in regular annual or monthly reports. Special analyses by cause of death, age, and other demographic variables; geographic and time series analyses; and statistics on characteristics of deaths not available from the vital records based on sample surveys of those records.

Exhibit 4–1 continued

SERIES 21. **Data on Natality, Marriage, and Divorce.**—Various statistics on natality, marriage, and divorce other than as included in regular annual or monthly reports. Special analyses by demographic variables; geographic and time series analyses; studies of fertility; and statistics on characteristics of births not available from the vital records based on sample surveys of those records.

SERIES 22. **Data From the National Mortality and Natality Surveys.**—Discontinued in 1975. Reports from these sample surveys based on vital records are included in Series 20 and 21, respectively.

SERIES 23. **Data From the National Survey of Family Growth.**—Statistics on fertility, family formation and dissolution, family planning, and related maternal and infant health topics derived from a periodic study of a nationwide probability sample of ever-married women 15–44 years of age.

For a list of titles of reports published in these series, write to:

Scientific and Technical Information Branch
National Center for Health Statistics
Public Health Service
Hyattsville, Md. 20782

Source: National Center for Health Statistics, *Data Systems of the National Center for Health Statistics*, Vital and Health Statistics, series 1, no. 16 (Hyattsville, Md.: U.S: Department of Health and Human Services, December 1981).

- NCHS computer tapes, which contain some data otherwise available in hard-copy form (these tapes, particularly if they contain more detail than the hard copies, are sometimes valuable for strategic planning)
- the *Catalog of Public Use Data Tapes* from the National Center for Health Statistics, which describes the contents and availability of the tapes and provides information on how to acquire them

From the perspective of the strategic planner, it is important to note that almost none of the data available from NCHS provide information at the local or regional level. These data are, therefore, useful to the strategic planner primarily for establishing nationwide or statewide conditions or historical trends.

All of the NCHS data provide information at the federal level, some provide information at the state level, and a very small proportion provide information at the local level. For example, the data collected in NCHS's General Population Surveys, National Hospital Discharge Survey, National Ambulatory Medical Care Survey, and National Nursing Home Survey are all based on nationwide samples of 50,000 or less. This means that the maximum average sample in each state is about 1,000. In fact, the sample is very much smaller than 1,000 in states with small populations, particularly if the nationwide sample is less than 50,000 (as it is for almost all of NCHS's surveys). Estimates of the value of the survey items based on data in low-population states are therefore subject to large sampling errors. Hence, techniques have been developed for calculating synthetic estimates in low-population states. These estimates take into account not only the survey data but also the composition of the population in the state for which the synthetic estimates are being made.[9]

Following are descriptions of the four NCHS data systems and the Cooperative Health Statistics System.

Vital Statistics System

Vital statistics, which today cover deaths, births, marriages, divorces, notifiable diseases, and induced abortions are widely used in both the public and private sectors.[10] For example, they are used for developing marketing strategies for babies' toys, in actuarial assessments for life insurance policies, and in strategic planning of hospital services.[11–14]

The existing nationwide system for the collection of vital statistics can be traced historically to the development of the first standard death certificate by the federal census office and the adoption of this certificate by 17 states and the District of Columbia at the beginning of the 20th century.[15] Although state laws requiring the reporting of vital events, primarily to protect individual rights with respect to ownership of property, date back to 17th-century colonial days, the procedures for, and the quality of, enforcement of the laws was haphazard and uncoordinated until the mid-20th century.[16] The creation of a coordinated nationwide system for producing timely, high quality vital statistics was achieved through a cooperative federal, state, and local government effort, now spearheaded by the Division of Vital Statistics in NCHS.[17,18] Today, every state has a law requiring the continuous registration of births and deaths, and almost all of them have central registries for marriage and divorce records.[19]

Nationwide data on notifiable diseases have been collected under federal law since 1878, when an act of Congress mandated this collection for pestilential diseases, such as cholera, smallpox, plague, and yellow fever.[20] Today, federal law requires the reporting of 44 infectious diseases, including gonorrhea, hepatitis, syphilis, tuberculosis, salmonellosis, shigellosis, german measles, mumps, and chicken pox.[21] However, it is widely accepted that there is still significant underreporting of the numbers of these diseases. For instance, it is estimated that, just prior to the introduction of the measles vaccine in the mid-1960s, the rate of unreported cases of measles was about 90 percent.[22]

As a result of two U.S. Supreme Court rulings in the mid-1970s that declared that state laws restricting abortions were unconstitutional and that state laws that required reporting of abortions were constitutional, several states established mandatory induced-abortion reporting systems.[23] In an attempt to make these systems uniform and ensure high quality data, the Division of Vital Statistics, in cooperation with appropriate state health officers, registrars, and statisticians, has developed a standardized abortion reporting certificate and standardized completion procedures. The division has published this material and recommends its use by any state or local agency involved in collecting and processing abortion statistics.[24] The division has also been collecting, aggregating, and publishing data on induced abortions. One report, covering 13 states in 1979, has already been published; a second, covering 15 states in 1980, is forthcoming.

Today, almost all vital statistics are derived from certificates completed at the local, county, or city level (see the examples in Figure 4–2). Exhibit 4–2 shows the latest (1978) version of the standard certificate recommended by the Division of Vital Statistics for the recording of deaths. The federal government cannot require that uniform certificates and procedures be used throughout the country. This is because control of the registration of births, deaths, marriages, and divorces is guaranteed to the state under the police powers portion of the U.S. Constitution.[25] However, the certificates and procedures used in most states are very similar to those recommended by the Division of Vital Statistics.[26]

While birth and death data are currently of very high quality, the data on marriages and divorces are not yet as well developed.[27] For instance, approximately 15 states do not yet provide microfilm or computerized copies of their marriage and divorce certificates; they provide only counts of marriage by month and counts of marriages and divorces by county.[28] On the other hand, some states collect data on items that are not in the certificates recommended by the Division of Vital Statistics,[29] and these extra items could be of use to the strategic planner.

The Division of Vital Statistics disseminates data in two formats: publications and computer tapes. Vital statistics are issued in three publications: the *Monthly Vital Statistics Report* and its supplements; *Vital Statistics of the United States;* and *Vital and Health Statistics* reports.[30,31] The *Monthly Vital Statistics Report* contains monthly and cumulative tabulations and brief analyses.[32] Provisional crude monthly counts are issued with a 2-month lag, and final annual statistics are issued with an 18-month lag.[33] *Vital Statistics of the United States* contains tabulations and more detailed analyses of the vital statistics.[34] The lag time for this publication, which is bound annually, is about three years.[35] Series 20 of the publication contains tabulations and more detailed analyses of natality, marriage, and divorce statistics.[36,37] For example, Series 21, No. 36, provides data on trends and differentials in births to unmarried women between 1970 and 1976. This type of report and other special reports are issued as resources permit.

Of special interest to planners is a series of reports focused on health planning.[38] This series is referred to as *Statistical Notes for Health Planners*. Publications in the series are issued irregularly. They are intended as guides for health planners in the use of appropriate techniques in handling vital and health statistics. The series includes guides on the uses of vital statistics for planning

Figure 4–2 The Vital Statistics Registration System in the U.S.

RESPONSIBLE PERSON OR AGENCY	BIRTH CERTIFICATE	DEATH CERTIFICATE	FETAL DEATH CERTIFICATE (Stillbirth)
Hospital Authority	1. Completes entire certificate in consultation with parent(s) 2. Files certificate with local office or State office, per State law.	When death occurs in hospital, may initiate preparation of certificate: Completes name, date of death, and place of death information; obtains certification of cause of death from physician; and gives certificate to funeral director.	1. Completes entire report in consultation with parents(s) 2. Obtains cause of death from physician. 3. Obtains authorization for disposition of fetus. 4. Files report with local office or State office, per State law.
Funeral Director		1. Obtains personal facts about decedent and completes certificate. 2. Obtains certification of cause of death from physician or medical examiner or coroner. 3. Obtains authorization for disposition, per State law. 4. Files certificate with local office or State office, per State law.	If fetus is to be buried, the funeral director is responsible for obtaining the authorization for disposition. NOTE: In some States the funeral director, or person acting as such, is responsible for all duties shown above under hospital authority.
Physician or Other Professional Attendant	Verifies accuracy of medical information and signs certificate.	Completes certification of cause of death and signs certificate.	Provides cause of fetal death information.
Local Office* (may be Local Registrar or City or County Health Department)	1. Verifies completeness and accuracy of certificate and queries incomplete or inconsistent certificates. 2. If authorized, makes copy or index for local use. 3. Sends certificates to State registrar.	1. Verifies completeness and accuracy of certificate and queries incomplete or inconsistent certificates. 2. If authorized, makes copy or index for local use. 3. If authorized by State law, issues authorization for disposition upon receipt of completed certificate. 4. Sends certificates to State registrar.	If State law requires routing of fetal death reports through local office, the local office will perform the same functions as shown for the death certificate.
City and county health departments use data derived from these records in allocating medical and nursing services, followups on infectious diseases, planning programs, measuring effectiveness of services, and conducting research studies.			
State Registrar, Office of Vital Statistics	1. Queries incomplete or inconsistent information. 2. Maintains files for permanent reference and as the source of certified copies. 3. Develops vital statistics for use in planning, evaluating, and administering State and local health activities and for research studies. 4. Compiles health-related statistics for State and civil divisions of State for use of the health department and other agencies and groups interested in the fields of medical science, public health, demography, and social welfare. 5. Sends copies of records or data derived from records to the National Center for Health Statistics.		
Public Health Service—National Center for Health Statistics	1. Prepares and publishes national statistics of births, deaths, and fetal deaths; and constructs the official U.S. life tables and related actuarial tables. 2. Conducts health and social-research studies based on vital records and on sampling surveys linked to records. 3. Conducts research and methodological studies in vital statistics methods including the technical, administrative, and legal aspects of vital records registration and administration. 4. Maintains a continuing technical assistance program to improve the quality and usefulness of vital statistics.		

*Some States do not have local vital registration offices. In these States the certificates or reports are transmitted directly to the State office of vital statistics.

Source: National Center for Health Statistics, *Funeral Director's Handbook on Death Registration and Fetal Death Reporting* (Hyattsville, Md.: U.S. Department of Health, Education, and Welfare, July 1978).

Exhibit 4–2 U.S. Standard Certificate of Death: Combined Form for Physician, Medical Examiner, or Coroner

(PHYSICIAN, MEDICAL EXAMINER OR CORONER)
U.S. STANDARD
CERTIFICATE OF DEATH

Form Approved
OMB No. 68R 1901

LOCAL FILE NUMBER — STATE FILE NUMBER

TYPE OR PRINT IN **PERMANENT INK** **FOR INSTRUCTIONS SEE HANDBOOK**

DECEDENT

DECEDENT—NAME FIRST MIDDLE LAST 1.					SEX 2.	DATE OF DEATH *(Mo., Day, Yr.)* 3.
RACE—(e.g., White, Black, American Indian, etc.) *(Specify)* 4	AGE—Last Birthday *(Yrs.)* 5a.	UNDER 1 YEAR: MOS. / DAYS 5b.	UNDER 1 DAY: HOURS / MINS. 5c.	DATE OF BIRTH *(Mo., Day, Yr.)* 6.	COUNTY OF DEATH 7a.	
CITY, TOWN OR LOCATION OF DEATH 7b.		HOSPITAL OR OTHER INSTITUTION—Name *(If not in either, give street and number)* 7c.				IF HOSP. OR INST. Indicate DOA, OP/Emer. Rm., Inpatient *(Specify)* 7d.
STATE OF BIRTH *(If not in U.S.A., name country)* 8.	CITIZEN OF WHAT COUNTRY 9.	MARRIED, NEVER MARRIED, WIDOWED, DIVORCED *(Specify)* 10.		SURVIVING SPOUSE *(If wife, give maiden name)* 11.		WAS DECEDENT EVER IN U.S. ARMED FORCES? *(Specify Yes or No)* 12.
SOCIAL SECURITY NUMBER 13.		USUAL OCCUPATION *(Give kind of work done during most of working life, even if retired)* 14a.			KIND OF BUSINESS OR INDUSTRY 14b.	
RESIDENCE—STATE 15a.	COUNTY 15b.	CITY, TOWN OR LOCATION 15c.		STREET AND NUMBER 15d.		INSIDE CITY LIMITS *(Specify Yes or No)* 15e.

IF DEATH OCCURRED IN INSTITUTION, SEE HANDBOOK REGARDING COMPLETION OF RESIDENCE ITEMS.

PARENTS

FATHER—NAME FIRST MIDDLE LAST 16.	MOTHER—MAIDEN NAME FIRST MIDDLE LAST 17.

INFORMANT—NAME *(Type or Print)* 18a.	MAILING ADDRESS STREET OR R.F.D. NO. CITY OR TOWN STATE ZIP 18b.

DISPOSITION

BURIAL, CREMATION, REMOVAL, OTHER *(Specify)* 19a.	CEMETERY OR CREMATORY—NAME 19b.	LOCATION CITY OR TOWN STATE 19c.
FUNERAL SERVICE LICENSEE Or Person Acting As Such *(Signature)* 20a. ▶	NAME OF FACILITY 20b.	ADDRESS OF FACILITY 20c.

DEPARTMENT OF HEALTH, EDUCATION, AND WELFARE—PUBLIC HEALTH SERVICE—NATIONAL CENTER FOR HEALTH STATISTICS
1978 REVISION

CERTIFIER

To be Completed by CERTIFYING PHYSICIAN Only

21a. To the best of my knowledge, death occurred at the time, date and place and due to the cause(s) stated.

(Signature and Title) ▶

DATE SIGNED *(Mo., Day, Yr.)*	HOUR OF DEATH
21b.	21c. M

NAME OF ATTENDING PHYSICIAN IF OTHER THAN CERTIFIER *(Type or Print)*

21d.

To be Completed by MEDICAL EXAMINER or CORONER Only

22a. On the basis of examination and/or investigation, in my opinion death occurred at the time, date and place and due to the cause(s) stated.

(Signature and Title) ▶

DATE SIGNED *(Mo., Day, Yr.)*	HOUR OF DEATH
22b.	22c. M
PRONOUNCED DEAD *(Mo., Day, Yr.)*	PRONOUNCED DEAD *(Hour)*
22d. ON	22e. AT M

NAME AND ADDRESS OF CERTIFIER (PHYSICIAN, MEDICAL EXAMINER OR CORONER) *(Type or Print)*

23.

REGISTRAR	DATE RECEIVED BY REGISTRAR *(Mo., Day, Yr.)*
24a. *(Signature)* ▶	24b.

CAUSE OF DEATH

CONDITIONS IF ANY WHICH GAVE RISE TO IMMEDIATE CAUSE STATING THE UNDERLYING CAUSE LAST

25. IMMEDIATE CAUSE *[ENTER ONLY ONE CAUSE PER LINE FOR (a), (b), AND (c).]*

PART I

(a) — Interval between onset and death

DUE TO, OR AS A CONSEQUENCE OF:

(b) — Interval between onset and death

DUE TO, OR AS A CONSEQUENCE OF:

(c) — Interval between onset and death

PART II OTHER SIGNIFICANT CONDITIONS—Conditions contributing to death but not related to cause given in PART I (a)	AUTOPSY *(Specify Yes or No)* 26.	WAS CASE REFERRED TO MEDICAL EXAMINER OR CORONER *(Specify Yes or No)* 27.

ACC., SUICIDE, HOM., UNDET., OR PENDING INVEST. *(Specify)*	DATE OF INJURY *(Mo., Day, Yr.)*	HOUR OF INJURY	DESCRIBE HOW INJURY OCCURRED
28a.	28b.	28c. M	28d

INJURY AT WORK *(Specify Yes or No)*	PLACE OF INJURY—At home, farm, street, factory, office building, etc. *(Specify)*	LOCATION STREET OR R.F.D. No. CITY OR TOWN STATE
28e.	28f.	28g.

HRA-162-1
Rev. 1/78

Source: National Center for Health Statistics, *Funeral Director's Handbook on Death Registration and Fetal Death Reporting* (Hyattsville, Md.: U.S. Department of Health, Education, and Welfare, July 1978).

purposes. One such publication is entitled *Using Natality Data in Health Planning*.[39] The series also includes a number of reports containing tabulations and analyses of death statistics broken down by health service area.[40] One such report presents death rates from ischemic heart disease and other related diseases by health service area from 1968 to 1972.[41] Health service areas are areas (usually containing several counties) for health planning, designated under Public Law 93–641.

The vital statistics data tapes for public use are issued annually, and can be procured from the National Technical Information Service (NTIS-Computer Products Office, 5285 Port Royal Road, Springfield, Virginia, 20161). They are usually available within 2½ years of the data year.[42] These tapes are potentially very useful for local area strategic planning because of the large amount of detail they contain (see Exhibit 4–3) and because they allow the planner to custom produce tabulations and analyses to address specific planning issues. However, it should be mentioned that the data tapes listed in Table 4–4 are of limited use for large-city planners who wish to perform analyses on the local neighborhood level because the place of residence is not coded for areas with less than 250,000 persons. This is one of several steps taken to protect the confidentiality of the persons on whom the vital data are obtained. For the same reason, data from localities with populations smaller than 250,000 persons are aggregated so as to reflect the size of the population without revealing specific residential locations, names and addresses do not appear on tabulations or data tapes, and vital certificate numbers are not released without written permission from the states whose records are involved.[43]

There are, however, computerized geocoding systems that can aggregate address-specific data to areas such as census tracts.[44] These geocoding systems represent powerful tools for large-city strategic analyses because these types of analyses usually focus on conditions at the local neighborhood level.

The Division of Vital Statistics also conducts follow-back surveys that generate more statistical detail than is normally provided by vital records. These surveys are also used to evaluate the quality of the data derived from the vital records. They collect data on samples of vital events registered during the sample year.[45] The follow-back surveys conducted to date have been focused on natality and mortality.[46] Mortality follow-back surveys were performed annually between 1961 and 1968, and natality follow-back surveys were performed in the years from 1963 to 1968 and again in 1972. Infant mortality follow-back surveys were performed annually from 1964 to 1966. A natality follow-back survey that covered fetal mortality was conducted in 1980. The data produced by the follow-back surveys are released through the *Monthly Vital Statistics Report* (supplements), the *Vital and Health Statistics* reports, and public use data tapes.[47,48]

Exhibit 4–3 Description of the 1968–1977 Mortality Data Tapes

Items on Tapes

Data year
Residence of decedent:
  State
  County
  City (250,000 persons or more)
  Population size
  SMSA
  Metropolitan/nonmetropolitan
Age at death (single years)
Month of death
Day of death (1972-77)
Place of death (State, county)
Race:
  1968 (7 categories)
  1969-75 (9 categories)
Sex
Underlying cause of death:
  Each cause
Whether autopsy performed (1972-77)
Whether findings used (1972-77)

Record length	160
Block size	3,200
Approximate number of records	2,000,000
Number of reels:	
1968	10
1969	10
1970	10
1971	10
1972	5
1973	10
1974	10
1975	10
1976	10
1977	10

Source: National Center for Health Statistics, *Catalog of Public Use Data Tapes from the National Center for Health Statistics* (Hyattsville, Md.: U.S. Department of Health and Human Services, November 1980).

Population Survey System

The National Health Survey Act of 1956 called for ongoing surveys and special studies to obtain data on the amount, distribution, and effects of illness in the United States. It also called for the collection of data on the health care services rendered for, or because of, these illnesses. Pursuant to this act, a survey, known to many as the National Health Survey, was initiated in July 1957. Since then, this survey has become established as the National Health Interview Survey (NHIS). The term *national health survey* now refers generally to the survey activities within NCHS.[49]

The purpose and scope of the NHIS is "to provide national data on the incidence of acute illness and accidental injuries, the prevalence of chronic conditions and impairments, the extent of disability, the utilization of health care services, and other related topics."[50] NHIS data cover socioeconomic and demographic variables as well as health, disability and health care utilization. They are collected in direct interviews in a cross-sectional sample of about 40,000 U.S. households annually.

The National Medical Care Utilization and Expenditure Survey (NMCUES) is an offshoot of the NHIS. It generates detailed national data on the utilization of, and expenditures for, various types of medical care. This survey is intended to provide information on how much of what type of medical care different population subgroups are using, and at what cost. It is also intended to yield baseline data against which the effects of future changes in medical care financing and delivery can be measured.

The first part (Cycle I) of the NMCUES was conducted in 1980; a second cycle is planned for the mid-1980s. Cycle I consisted of three separate surveys. The first was a survey of persons in about 6,000 households in a multistage-area, probability sample of all U.S. households. The second was a survey of persons in about 10,000 households in a probability sample of all Medicaid households in four states: New York, California, Texas, and Michigan.

The National Health and Nutrition Examination Survey (NHANES) is another population survey sponsored by NCHS. The purpose of the survey is the measurement and monitoring over time of the health and nutritional status of the U.S. population. The first three programs in this survey, conducted in the 1960s, involved only examinations of the population's health status; these were called Health Examination Surveys (HES I, HES II and HES III). Starting in 1970, the NHANES was expanded to reflect the assignment to NCHS of an additional responsibility: the measurement of the population's nutritional status. NHANES I was initiated in 1970, NHANES II in 1976, and NHANES III is scheduled to begin in 1987. Each of the NHANESs has taken three to four years to complete and yield data.

The samples of the HES and NHANES programs have all been multistage, clustered, probability samples of U.S. residents. Each of the three HES sample sizes was about 7,500. The two NHANES samples contained close to 30,000 in their health segment and about 20,000 in their nutritional segment.

Health Resources Utilization Statistics System

There are three NCHS surveys that collect data on health resources utilization: the National Hospital Discharge Survey, the National Ambulatory Medical Care Survey, and the National Nursing Home Survey.

National Hospital Discharge Survey

The National Hospital Discharge Survey (NHDS) has provided data on the utilization of inpatient services in most short-stay U.S. hospitals since 1964. The data include information on length of stay, diagnoses and surgical operations, patient characteristics, and hospital address and ownership. The NHDS sample is a two-level stratified sample, the first level being hospital, and the second being discharge. It includes about seven percent of all short-stay hospitals and approximately one percent of all discharges in short-stay hospitals in the United States. The data are abstracted from the patients' charts. The abstracted items are very similar to those specified in NCHS's Uniform Hospital Discharge Data Set (see the section following on the Cooperative Health Statistics System). These data are the only national data on hospital discharges by diagnosis covering all hospitals and all patients.

National Ambulatory Medical Care Survey

The National Ambulatory Medical Care Survey (NAMCS) has been operating since 1973. It collects and disseminates data on the utilization of physician-office-based ambulatory medical care, which currently represents about 70 percent of all direct ambulatory medical care in the United States. It is anticipated that the NAMCS will eventually cover all ambulatory medical care, including that delivered in neighborhood health centers, hospital outpatient facilities, and health maintenance organizations.

A modified probability-proportional-to-size sampling procedure is used in the NAMCS.[51] This procedure treats standard metropolitan statistical areas differently than nonmetropolitan areas and yields a nationwide sample of about 3,000 physicians in office-based practice. Each physician is asked to report data on a sample of patients treated during a specific week of the year; the reporting week is randomly assigned in the physician sample. This procedure yields data on a sample of about 50,000 patient visits per year.

Data collected by the NAMCS vary slightly from year to year, but they generally cover the following types of information for each sample visit: date and duration of visit, patient characteristics, reason for visit, duration of the problem, diagnoses, diagnostic and therapeutic procedures, and disposition. These items are collected on a form called the patient record. Each sample physician is responsible for using NAMCS procedures to select a sample of patients, and for having patient records completed for each sample patient.

National Nursing Home Survey

The National Nursing Home Survey (NNHS) began formally in 1972. It was preceded by several ad hoc NCHS surveys of nursing homes and their residents between 1963 and 1969. The advent of Medicaid and Medicare in the mid-1960s led to large and increasing expenditures of government funds on nursing home services. This generated the need for the ongoing collection of data on nursing home patients, utilization, costs, and resources to provide information on the use of public funds in the nursing home industry. The NNHS attempts to fill this need.

Two surveys have been conducted so far: the first in 1973–1974, and the second in 1977. Both surveys used four questionnaires: (1) a facility questionnaire covering such items as the number of beds and the service provided; (2) an expense questionnaire that collected expenses by category, including labor, operating and fixed; (3) a staff questionnaire on employee characteristics, such as work experience, salary, sex, and age; and (4) a residents' questionnaire with questions on residents' demographic characteristics, health, participation in social activities, monthly charge, and source of payment. The 1977 survey used an additional questionnaire on discharged patients. This covered some of the items on the resident questionnaire. The 1973–1974 survey covered a nationally representative sample of 2,100 nursing homes and a subsample of 25,100 staff and 19,400 residents. The 1977 survey sample included 1,700 nursing homes and subsamples of 16,800 staff, 7,100 residents, and 5,300 discharged residents.

Health Resources Statistics System

NCHS collects data on two categories of health care providers: facilities and personnel. For this purpose, it maintains the National Master Facility Inventory (NMFI) and inventories on the 13 health occupations licensed at the state level. In addition, NCHS conducts surveys to gather information on nonlicensed health workers.

The NMFI is a bank of data on the 33,000 inpatient health care facilities in the United States. Its data are described in Exhibit 4–4. The bank was first assembled in 1962. Three techniques are used to keep its data current. The first, used for facilities other than hospitals, is a series of biennial mail surveys. These surveys are used to eliminate from the NMFI those facilities that are no longer operating and to ensure that the data on each of the facilities in the inventory are accurate and current. The second technique, also used for facilities other than hospitals, is the regular acquisition of lists of new facilities from state government licensure agencies, national voluntary associations, and other appropriate sources. These lists are used to add new facilities to the inventory.

Since 1968, NCHS has collaborated with the American Hospital Association (AHA) in gathering data on U.S. hospitals for the NMFI. Currently the AHA

Exhibit 4–4 Types of Data Collected in the National Master Facility Inventory

Hospitals: Ownership; major types of services offered; whether various facilities and services are offered; number of beds, admissions, inpatient days of care; discharges; patient census; number of bassinets, live births and newborn days of care; outpatient utilization; number of surgical operations; reserves, expenses, and assets; and staffing.

Nursing homes: Ownership; major types of service; licensed and staffed beds: beds certified for Medicare and Medicaid; admission policy with regard to age, sex, and various conditions; patient census by age and sex; inpatient days of care; number of admissions; discharges; deaths; staffing; who is in charge of nursing care; number of patients receiving nursing care; services routinely provided; basic monthly charge; and operating expenses.

Other facilities: Ownership; major types of service; licensed and staffed beds; beds certified as intermediate care beds; admissions policy regarding age and sex; patient census by age and sex; inpatient days of care; number of admissions, discharges, and deaths; staffing; basic monthly charge; and operating expenses.

Source: National Center for Health Statistics, *Data Systems of the National Center for Health Statistics: Programs and Collection Procedures* (Hyattsville, Md.: U.S. Department of Health, Education, and Welfare, December, 1981).

collects and computerizes hospital data annually on all hospitals in the United States, and NCHS purchases these data from the association. The association publishes the results of its annual survey. For many strategic planning applications, the AHA publication is a more convenient source of information on hospitals. The association's *Guide to the Health Care Field,* which is based on the survey and is published annually, does not aggregate the data by county as the NMFI does. However, it does present a large amount of information on each listed hospital, including the number of beds and admissions, occupancy rates, and the types of services available in each hospital.

NMFI data are released in two forms: reports and computer tapes. Preliminary data from NMFI surveys are published in the biennial edition of NCHS's *Health Resources Statistics*. Final data are published in Series 14 of NCHS's *Vital and Health Statistics* and in two special reports. One of these is for hospitals, and the other is for nursing homes. Both provide data by county and standard metropolitan statistical area.[52] Special reports and tabulations in response to individual requests are prepared subject to availability of funds. NMFI data tapes can be purchased from NCHS. It should be mentioned, however, that some of the data on the original NMFI tapes can be released only in aggregated form or with facility identification codes removed because portions of the facility data are collected under a pledge of confidentiality.[53]

During the years 1976 through 1980, several state cooperative health statistics system contractors (see the following section) collected and edited health facilities data for their states. These data were given to NCHS for inclusion in the NMFI.

NCHS has maintained inventories on health care workers since 1964. The objective of this data collection activity is "to produce reliable statistics on distribution; availability; and demographic, educational, and professional characteristics of persons employed in the health occupations."[54] Thirteen health-care occupations are licensed in all 50 states. NCHS has agreements with some states to provide data on these occupations; the states collect these data in conjunction with each state's licensing system. The information has been obtained by means of a self-administered questionnaire, either attached to or enclosed with the mailed application for license. Mail and telephone follow-up procedures have been used with nonrespondents. The 13 health-care occupations licensed in all 50 states are doctors of medicine, doctors of osteopathy, pharmacists, chiropractors, dentists, dental hygienists, registered nurses, licensed practical nurses, nursing home administrators, optometrists, physical therapists, podiatrists, and veterinarians.[55]

Data on health workers not licensed in all 50 states have been collected by means of two types of NCHS mail surveys of health care facilities. The first gathers data on the number of each type of health worker in facilities such as hospitals, nursing homes, group practices, and clinics. The second gathers more detailed data on "specific types of health workers, such as nursing personnel in hospitals, health-care administration personnel and public health personnel."[56]

Cooperative Health Statistics System

As described in the previous section, the federal government collects and disseminates data on health status and the utilization, cost, and availability of health care services and manpower. All of these data are available on these topics at the federal level, some of them are available at the state level, and a small proportion are available at the local level.

The cooperative health statistics system that operated in the late 1970s had four main purposes:

1. to increase the size of the sample of data collected so as to yield useful information on the local, state, and regional levels as well as the federal level
2. to increase the topics covered to include health status; availability, utilization, and cost of health services and manpower; and environmental, social, and other health hazards
3. to provide technical assistance and material incentives in the form of contracts to help ensure that the data collected at the local and state levels were timely, of high quality, and based on uniform definitions and collection procedures throughout the country
4. to aggregate the data collected on the state and local levels to yield information on the nation as a whole

The need for cooperation between local, state, regional, and federal data collection activities to ensure the availability of high quality comparable data without unnecessary duplication of effort has long been appreciated. NCHS and other interested parties began working toward the creation of a cooperative system in the early 1970s.[57] In 1974, their efforts resulted in the inclusion of legislative authority for the Cooperative Health Statistics System (CHSS) in Public Law 93–353, the Health Services Research, Health Statistics, and Medical Libraries Act.[58] The objectives and functions of the system and its products were further enunciated in Public Law 92–603, the Professional Standards Review Organization legislation, and in Public Law 93–641, the National Health Planning and Resources Development Act of 1975.

The CHSS is housed administratively within NCHS. The mechanisms used to achieve its objectives include advisory committees and agreements and working arrangements with other relevant federal agencies, state and local governments, and some health professional organizations. However, in 1983 federal fiscal austerity forced the CHSS to be disbanded. The only component of the program that currently exists is that dealing with vital statistics. This activity is based administratively in NCHS's Division of Vital Statistics. By the end of 1982, its budget had not been significantly reduced by the Reagan administration's austerity measures. This is probably due to the widely accepted significance of vital statistics; the historically long and productive cooperative effort in collecting and disseminating vital statistics, involving all levels of government; and the fact that the vital statistics system serves as a model or ideal for the cooperative system, since it is the only existing, successful, long-standing, federally sponsored cooperative health data collection activity (see the earlier section on the vital statistics system).

The future of the cooperative system, and more generally of any federally initiated program to achieve goals similar to those of the cooperative system, is uncertain. What is fairly certain is that most of the other pre-CHSS data collection and dissemination activities of NCHS described in previous sections will continue to exist. Unfortunately, from a strategic planning perspective, most of its data-collection programs, other than the vital statistics system, do not provide information at the regional and local level. However, the federal and statewide statistics that they do provide are extremely useful in establishing national and statewide trends over time. They also make possible the quantification of current conditions in the nation and in specific states. This type of information can be valuable for hospital strategic planning because trends and current conditions at the local level can often be estimated or inferred from national or statewide data.

THE MEDICARE STATISTICAL SYSTEM

The Medicare Statistical System (MSS) is a potentially important and useful source of data for strategic planning. The MSS collects and processes large amounts of information on Medicare providers, patients, utilization, and costs. Many of these data are made available in the form of tables, reports, and computer data tapes.[59] The MSS is significant to planners for a number of reasons: (1) The Medicare-eligible population consumes a substantial and growing proportion of U.S. health care resources;[60,61] (2) MSS data from different geographic regions are collected and processed using uniform definitions and procedures in an attempt to ensure that the resulting data are comparable; and (3) MSS data cover many aspects of the Medicare treatment system, such as patients' clinical diagnoses, provider physicians' specialties, and services available in provider hospitals.

Data and Products

The federal Health Care Financing Administration (HCFA) was created in 1977 to bring health financing and quality assurance programs into a single agency.[62] HCFA's Office of Research, Demonstrations, and Statistics (ORDS) has prime responsibility for HCFA's research and statistical activities.[63] As one of its activities, ORDS operates the MSS, which has the overall purpose of providing information for monitoring, evaluating, and improving the efficiency, quality, utilization, and costs of the Medicare program.

MSS data are derived from three separate administrative components of the Medicare program: enrollment, claims processing, and provider certification (see Figure 4–3). More specifically, MSS data are derived from data collected by, and used in, the ongoing administration of these three components of the Medicare program. The HCFA publication *A Guide to ORDS Publications*, provides a brief but comprehensive description of the tables, series, and reports produced by MSS.[64] As can be seen from Figure 4–3, the MSS is a series of processes involving the extraction of computerized data, the merging of computerized data, and the creation of both published and unpublished tables and reports from various computerized data files.

Uses in Planning

The MSS's published annual tabulations of the number of Medicare enrollees by county have been extremely useful for planning purposes.[65] This is because these data are thought to be very accurate estimates of the 65-year-and-older population—even more accurate in some instances than Bureau of the Census noncensus year estimates.[66] They are derived from the MSS Health Insurance Skeleton Eligibility Write-Off File, which contains such information as claim numbers, demographic characteristics, areas of residence, and enrollment status. This file is produced from the Health Insurance Master Record file, an administrative file containing a record for each person enrolled in either Part A or Part

Figure 4–3 Overview of the Medicare Statistical System (1980 Data)

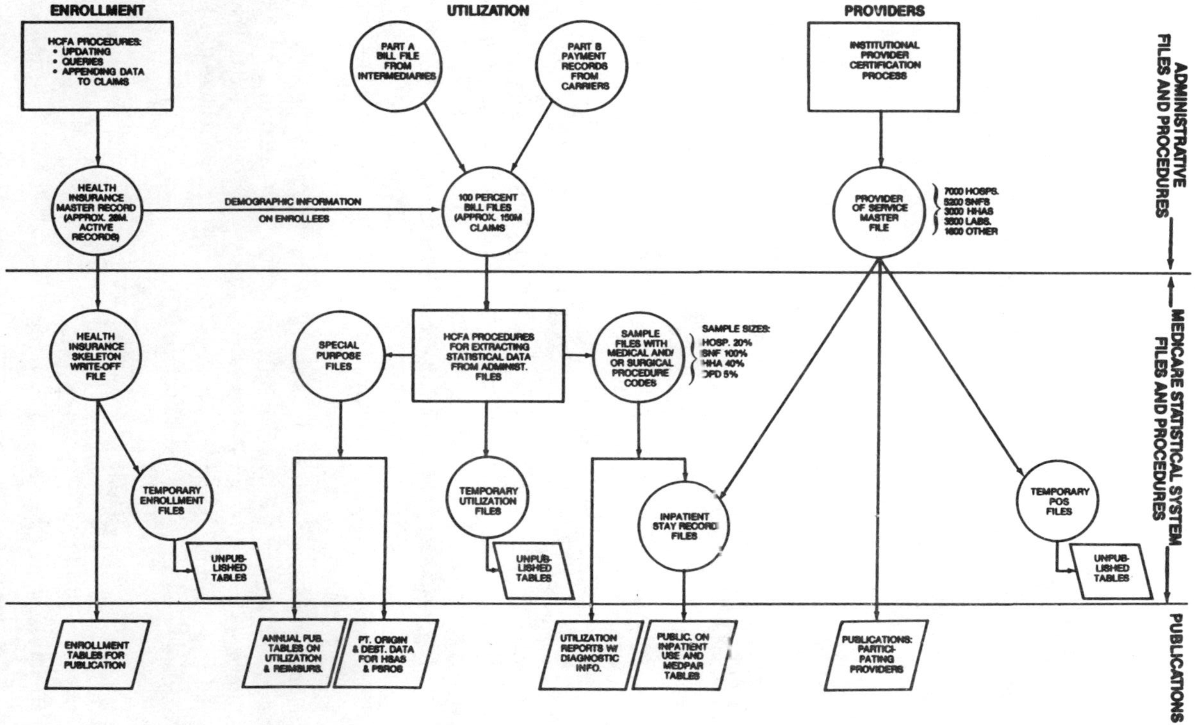

Source: Alpha Center for Health Planning, *A Planner's Guide to the Medicare Statistical System* (Bethesda, Md.: Alpha Center for Health Planning, October 1981).

B, or both parts, of Medicare (see Figure 4–3). MSS publications on enrollment are listed in Table 4–5. A significant number of unpublished tabulations of enrollment are also produced by the MSS.[67] One of them provides data broken down by zip code, which could be extremely useful for strategic planning at the local level.[68]

The master file on providers of service contains the following type of information on every hospital, skilled nursing facility, home health agency, independent laboratory, and other institutional provider certified for participation in the Medicare program:[69]

- type of facility
- fiscal intermediary
- geographic location
- types of services available
- how specific services (e.g., blood bank and physical therapy) are provided (e.g., in-house, by outside contractor, or not provided)
- dates of certification, review, or termination
- number of employees by type
- number of beds (hospital and skilled nursing facilities)

Besides being useful in assessing the need for services, the published tables of Medicare providers (Table 4–5) can be used in preparing or checking inventories of providers at the local level. It is important to note, however, that the MSS way of counting providers is different from that of other institutions such as the American Hospital Association and the Joint Commission for the Accreditation of Hospitals (JCAH).[70] For instance, Medicare certifies osteopathic hospitals but does not certify Veterans Administration hospitals, while the Joint Commission certifies Veterans Administration hospitals but does not certify osteopathic hospitals.[71]

Information on the utilization of health care resources by Medicare beneficiaries derives predominantly from bills for services rendered to those beneficiaries under both Part A and Part B of Medicare (see Figure 4–3). The information in the administrative 100-percent bill files, from which the MSS utilization data bases are abstracted, includes:

- beneficiary's demographic characteristics
- provider's identification
- beneficiary's geographic area of residence
- provider's geographic area of location
- beneficiary's diagnosis

- major clinical procedures performed for beneficiary
- treatment dates
- charges by services, total, and reimbursed by Medicare
- units of service (patient days for hospitals and skilled nursing facilities, and visits for home health agencies and clinics)
- ancillary services used, by type

As can be seen in Figure 4–3, several utilization data files are created by the MSS for the purposes of producing various tables and reports. Some of these files contain all bills and others contain samples of all bills—generally 20-percent samples for hospitals, 100-percent samples for skilled nursing facilities, 5-percent samples for outpatient treatment, and 40-percent samples for home health agencies.[72] In addition, while most MSS utilization data files are derived solely from the administrative 100-percent bill files, some also include data from the Health Insurance Master Record file and the Provider Master File (see Figure 4–3). The MSS utilization data files are used to produce the reports listed in Table 4–5.

One MSS data file that is of particular significance for planning is the Medical Provider Analysis and Review (MEDPAR) file. This file was originally produced for research purposes and then used to generate tabulations for Professional Standards Review Organizations (PSROs) and Health Systems Agencies (HSAs). The MEDPAR file contains a 20-percent sample of hospitalized Medicare beneficiaries and contains the information listed in Exhibit 4–5. In the years 1974 through 1978, 21 different tabulations containing data for planning, broken down by health service area, were produced and distributed to the nation's HSAs and statewide planning agencies (see Exhibit 4–6). In addition, there are several other tables, prepared specifically for health planning purposes, that provide information at the health services area level.[73–75] This information includes enrollment data, data on hospital patient origin and destination, and information on average hospital charges for the 25 most frequent diagnoses.

Interviews and discussions with planners suggest that the enrollment data (Table 4–6) and the patient's county-of-residence and hospital-of-discharge tables (Table 4–7) have been particularly useful.[76] The enrollment data, which are generally considered to be the most accurate measure of the interdecennial-census elderly population in many areas of the country, have been used for such planning activities as assessing hospital-bed need and the need for other medical services used by the elderly; and identifying geographic concentrations of the frail elderly—those over 75 years of age. The patient origin data are important in defining and analyzing secular trends in hospital service areas and in identifying potential markets for hospital services. There is evidence that hospital service areas defined by means of MEDPAR data are very close to those based on whole-population data,[77] but this is probably not true for all local areas.[78]

Table 4–5 Summary of MSS-Published Data by Topic

Topic & Year	*Title of Publication*	*Series*	*Publ. #*
Enrollment			
1979	Medicare: Persons Enrolled	Notes	HCFA 03079
1978	Medicare: Persons Enrolled	Notes	HCFA 03065
1976–1977	Medicare: Persons Enrolled in the Health Insurance Program	Proj. Stat.	HCFA 03076
1975	Section 2: Persons Enrolled in the Health Insurance Program	M:HIA*	HCFA 062
1974	Section 2: Persons Enrolled in the Health Insurance Program	M:HIA*	SSA
1970	Section 2: Persons Enrolled in the Health Insurance Program	M:HIA*	SSA
1969	Section 2: Persons Enrolled in the Health Insurance Program	M:HIA*	SSA
1968	Section 2: Persons Enrolled in the Health Insurance Program	M:HIA*	SSA
Providers			
1980	Medicare: Participating Providers & Suppliers of Health Serv.	Notes	HCFA 03088
1979	Medicare: Participating Health Facilities	Prog. Stat.	HCFA 03060
1979	Medicare: Participating Providers & Suppliers of Health Serv.	Notes	HCFA 03066
1972–1974	Section 3: Participating Providers	M:HIA*	SSA
1971	Section 3: Participating Providers	M:HIA*	SSA 76-11706
Reimbursement			
1978–1979	Reimbursement by State and County	Prog. Stat.	HCFA 03106
1977	Section 1.1: Reimbursement by State and County	M:HIA*	HCFA 03001
1976	Section 1.1: Reimbursement by State and County	M:HIA*	
1974–1975	Section 1.1: Reimbursement by State and County	M:HIA*	SSA 77-11717
1972	Section 1.1: Reimbursement by State and County	M:HIA*	
Utilization			
1978	Medicare: Summary of Use and Reimbursement by Person	Notes	HCFA 03116
1975	Summary—Utilization and Reimbursement by Person	Prog. Stat.	HCFA 03084
1973–1974	Section 1.2: Summary of Utilization and Reimbursement by Person	M:HIA*	HCFA 03000
Hospital Utilization			
1978	Medicare: Inpatient Use of Short-Stay Hospitals	Notes	HCFA 03087
1977	Medicare: Use of Short-Stay Hospitals by Aged Inpatients	Prog. Stat.	HCFA 03096

Table 4–5 continued

Topic & Year	*Title of Publication*	*Series*	*Publ. #*
1977	Medicare: Use of Short-Stay Hospitals	Notes	HCFA 03022
1967	Section 4.1: Short-Stay Hospital Utilization	M:HIA*	
Long-Stay Hospitals and Skilled Nursing Facilities			
1977	Medicare: Use of Long-Stay Hospitals	Notes	HCFA 03026
1967–1977	Medicare: Use of Skilled Nursing Facilities	Notes	HCFA 03021
Hospital Outpatient Services			
1974–1978	Medicare: Use of Hospital Outpatient Services	Notes	HCFA 03058
1974–1977	Medicare: Use of Hospital Outpatient Services	Notes	HCFA 03023
1975	Medicare: Use of Hospital Outpatient Services by the Disabled	Prog. Stat.	HCFA 03092
Home Health Services			
1978	Medicare: Use of Home Health Services	Notes	HCFA 03025
1977	Medicare: Use of Home Health Services	Notes	HCFA 03024
1977	Medicare: Use of Home Health Services	Prog. Stat.	HCFA 03064
1976	Medicare: Use of Home Health Services	Prog. Stat.	HCFA 03040
Selected State Data			
1973–1977	Medicare: Selected State Data	Prog. Stat.	HCFA 03059
1968–1972	Medicare: Selected State Data	M:HIA*	SSA 76-11711
Miscellaneous Reports			
1981	Medicare Data System	Monogr.	HCFA 03111
1980	Hospital Patient Origin & Destination Data	Monogr.	HCFA 03063
1980	Medicare Enrollment Data for Health Planners	Monogr.	HCFA 03064
1978	The MEDPAR Report, April 1978	Misc.	HCFA 7
1972	Section 1.3: Geographic Index of Reimb. by State & County	M:HIA*	SSA 76-11709

*Medicare: Health Insurance for the Aged and Disabled

Source: Alpha Center for Health Planning, *A Planner's Guide to the Medicare Statistical System* (Bethesda, Md.: Alpha Center for Health Planning, October 1981).

Exhibit 4–5 MEDPAR File Data Items

1. HI claim number
2. Provider number
3. State and county of residence
4. PSRO service area number
5. Discharge date
6. Principal diagnosis
7. Length of stay
8. Age
9. Sex
10. Race
11. Additional diagnoses indicator
12. Surgical indication
13. Discharge status
14. Day of admission
15. Additional surgery indicator
16. Amount reimbursed
17. Intensive and coronary care charges
18. Operating room charges
19. Pharmacy charges
20. Laboratory charges
21. Radiology charges
22. Supply charges
23. Anesthesia charges
24. Inhalation therapy charges
25. PSRO state code
26. Type of hospital
27. Total charges
28. Coinsurance days
29. ZIP code of beneficiary residence
30. Number of facilities and services
31. Medical school affiliation
32. Bed capacity (adult)
33. Covered days
34. Lifetime reserve days
35. Type of control
36. Periodic interim payment indicator
37. Date of admission
38. Date of surgery
39. Surgery code
40. Blood furnished
41. Intensive and coronary care days
42. Total accommodation charges
43. Type of entitlement
44. Total departmental charges
45. Covered charges

Source: Alpha Center for Health Planning, *A Planner's Guide to the Medicare Statistical System* (Bethesda, Md.: Alpha Center for Health Planning, October 1981).

Many of the MSS unpublished reports and tables also have potential planning applications. These reports and tables have been described elsewhere,[79] and most of them are available on request. For further information, or to make a request for these data, contact the agency directly. Communications should be addressed to Director, Office of Research, Demonstration, and Statistics, Division of Information Analysis, Room 2-B-14, 6340 Security Boulevard, Baltimore, Md. 21207. Similarly, requests for special tabulations derived from any of the MSS data files or for computer tapes containing data from those files should be addressed to Director, Office of Statistics and Data Management, 1-F-2 Oak Meadows Building, 6340 Security Boulevard, Baltimore, Md. 21207. The agency's current policy is to levy a fee for such requests. It attempts to satisfy all requests that do not threaten patient or hospital confidentiality and can be achieved within the agency's normally limited means.

Exhibit 4–6 Tables from the MEDPAR File

Table No.	Title
1	HSA Summary Table: Short-Stay Hospital Discharges for a 20-Percent Sample of Medicare Enrollees Aged 65 Years and Over
2	Selected Hospital Characteristics from the Medicare/Medicaid Automated Certification System, as of 12/77
3	Short-Stay Hospital Discharges for a 20-Percent Sample of Medicare Enrollees Aged 65 and Over: Number of Discharges, Average Length of Stay, and Percentile Stays for Selected Discharge Diagnoses
4	Short-Stay Hospital Discharges for a 20-Percent Sample of Medicare Enrollees Aged 65 and Over: Number of Discharges, Average Length of Stay, and Percentile Stays for Selected Surgical Procedures
5	Short-Stay Hospital Discharges for a 20-Percent Sample of Medicare Enrollees Aged 65 Years and Over: Number of Discharges and Average Length of Stay (ALOS) for Selected Primary Discharge Diagnoses (1-40 Day Stays Only)
6	Short-Stay Hospital Discharges for a 20-Percent Sample of Medicare Enrollees Aged 65 Years and Over: Percentage Distribution of Total Discharges and Total Days of Care by Length of Stay
7	Short-Stay Hospital Discharges for a 20-Percent Sample of Medicare Enrollees Aged 65 Years and Over: Percentage Distribution of Live Discharges and Live Days of Care by Length of Stay
8	Short-Stay Hospital Discharges for a 20-Percent Sample of Medicare Enrollees Aged 65 Years and Over: Percentage Distribution of Dead Discharges and Dead Days of Care by Length of Stay
9	Short-Stay Hospital Discharges for a 20-Percent Sample of Medicare Enrollees Aged 65 Years and Over: Percentage Distribution of Live Discharges by Day of Week of Admission (1-40 Day Stays Only)
10	Short-Stay Hospital Discharges for a 20-Percent Sample of Medicare Enrollees Aged 65 Years and Over: Average Length of Stay of Live Discharges by Day of Week of Admission (1-40 Day Stays Only)
11	Short-Stay Hospital Discharges for a 20-Percent Sample of Medicare Enrollees Aged 65 Years and Over: Percentage Distribution of Live Discharges by Day of Week of Discharge (1-40 Day Stays Only)
12	Short-Stay Hospital Discharges for a 20-Percent Sample of Medicare Enrollees Aged 65 Years and Over: Average Length of Stay of Live Discharges by Day of Week of Discharge (1-40 Day Stays Only)
13	Short-Stay Hospital Discharges for a 20-Percent Sample of Medicare Enrollees Aged 65 Year and Over: Average Length of Stay for Nonsurgical Discharges and Surgical Discharges and Percent of All Discharges with Surgery (1-40 Day Stays Only)

Exhibit 4–6 continued

Table No.	Title
14	Short-Stay Hospital Discharges for a 20-Percent Sample of Medicare Enrollees Aged 65 Years and Over: Average Length of Stay, Preoperative and Postoperative for Nonendoscopic Surgical Discharges (1-40 Day Stays Only)
15	Short-Stay Hospital Discharges for a 20-Percent Sample of Medicare Enrollees Aged 65 and Over: Number and Average Length of Stay for All Surgical Discharges by Single and Multiple Diagnoses (1-40 Day Stays Only)
16	Short-Stay Hospital Discharges for a 20-Percent Sample of Medicare Enrollees Aged 65 and Over: Number and Average Length of Stay for Nonsurgical Discharges by Single and Multiple Diagnoses (1-40 Day Stays Only)
17	Short-Stay Hospital Discharges for a 20-Percent Sample of Medicare Enrollees Aged 65 and Over: Percentage Distribution of Discharges and Average Length of Stay by Age (1-40 Day Stays Only)
18	Short-Stay Hospital Discharges for a 20-Percent Sample of Medicare Enrollees Aged 65 and Over: Percentage Distribution of Discharges and Average Length of Stay, by Sex and Race (1-40 Day Stays Only)
19	Short-Stay Hospital Discharges for a 20-Percent Sample of Medicare Enrollees Aged 65 Years and Over: Average Hospital Charges per Discharge and per Day (1-40 Day Stays Only)
20	Short-Stay Hospital Discharges for a 20-Percent Sample of Medicare Enrollees Aged 65 Years and Over: Long-Stay Discharges (29 Days or More)
21	Short-Stay Hospital Discharges for a 20-Percent Sample of Medicare Enrollees Aged 65 Years and Over: Pre and Postoperative Length of Stay by Day of Week of Admission for Nonendoscopic Surgical Discharges (Live Discharges of 1-40 Days Only)

Source: Alpha Center for Health Planning, *A Planner's Guide to the Medicare Statistical System* (Bethesda, Md.: Alpha Center for Health Planning, October 1981).

Limitations

It is important to note that the data, tables, and reports produced by the MSS are subject to certain limitations from a planning perspective.[80] These limitations include the following:

- The MSS data cover only Medicare-eligible patients, Medicare-reimbursed services, and Medicare-certified providers.
- Most of the MSS data items abstracted from patients' charts are subject to coding errors. This is particularly true for such items as diagnoses and clinical procedures.[81]

Table 4–6 Medicare Hospital Insurance Enrollees by Age, Race, Sex, County, and HSA, as of 07/01/78

STATE—MARYLAND **HSA NAME**—EASTERN SHORE

		All Persons			*Men*			*Women*			*Race*	
HSA Area	*Name of County*	*65 & Over*	*65-74*	*75 & Over*	*65 & Over*	*65-74*	*75 & Over*	*65 & Over*	*65-74*	*75 & Over*	*White*	*Other Known*
MD005	**HSA TOTAL**	35320	21334	13986	14812	9648	5164	20508	11686	8822	28431	6139
	MD CAROLINE	3277	1960	1317	1416	897	519	1861	1063	798	2768	467
	MD CECIL	4532	2874	1658	1940	1307	633	2592	1567	1025	4060	241
	MD DORCHESTER	4265	2559	1706	1775	1145	630	2490	1414	1076	3257	940
	MD KENT	2705	1607	1098	1182	748	434	1523	859	664	2132	526
	MD QUEEN ANNES	2393	1492	901	1104	730	374	1289	762	527	1909	438
	MD SOMERSET . . .	3013	1780	1233	1263	810	453	1750	970	780	2173	794
	MD TALBOT	4264	2530	1734	1799	1172	627	2465	1358	1107	3445	742
	MD WICOMICO. . . .	6906	4121	2785	2710	1763	947	4196	2358	1838	5590	1196
	MD WORCESTER. .	3965	2411	1554	1623	1076	547	2342	1335	1007	3097	795

Source: Alpha Center for Health Planning, *A Planner's Guide to the Medicare Statistical System* (Bethesda, Md.: Alpha Center for Health Planning, October 1981).

Table 4–7 Medicare Patient Origin Data, 1977

1977 MEDICARE PATIENT ORIGIN DATA FOR HSAS—HSA CA007

DISTRIBUTION OF DISCHARGES OF MEDICARE BENEFICIARIES AGE 65 AND OVER HOSPITALIZED IN CA007 HSA, BY HOSPITAL WHERE DISCHARGE OCCURRED AND COUNTY OF RESIDENCE, 1977

Hospital	*Discharges Number*	*Discharges Percent*	*Days of Care Number*	*Days of Care Percent*	*Hospital*	*Discharges Number*	*Discharges Percent*	*Days of Care Number*	*Days of Care Percent*
O Connor Hosp	3572	100.00	31134	100.00	Comm Los Gatos Sar	1925	100.00	14558	100.00
Provider No-050153					Provider No-050188				
County—CA Santa Clara					County—CA Santa Clara				
County of Residence					County of Residence				
CA Santa Clara	3243	90.79	28220	90.64	CA Santa Clara	1734	90.08	13091	89.92
CA Santa Cruz	34	.95	261	.84	CA Los Angeles	19	.99	120	.82
CA Monterey	27	.76	264	.85	CA Santa Cruz	14	.73	160	1.10
CA San Mateo	22	.62	166	.53	CA Sn Francisco	7	.36	54	.37
CA Alameda	21	.59	163	.52	CA Alameda	7	.36	85	.58
CA Sn Francisco	18	.50	179	.57	CA San Mateo	6	.31	59	.41
CA Los Angeles	14	.39	152	.49	CA Riverside	5	.26	42	.29
CA San Benito	12	.34	109	.35	CA Mendocino	4	.21	31	.21
CA Stanislaus	10	.28	130	.42	NV Washoe	4	.21	30	.21
CA Merced	9	.25	91	.29	CA Sacramento	3	.16	11	.08
CA Mendocino	6	.17	23	.07	CA Sonoma	3	.16	38	.26
CA San Joaquin	6	.17	53	.17	CA Monterey	3	.16	14	.10
CA Fresno	6	.17	39	.13	CA San Benito	3	.16	15	.10
AZ Maricopa	5	.14	25	.08	CA S' Luis Obspo	3	.16	36	.25
CA Butte	5	.14	31	.10	MN Ramsey	3	.16	15	.10
CA Shasta	3	.08	44	.14	NJ Monmouth	3	.16	34	.23
CA Tehama	3	.08	34	.11	NY Kings	3	.16	26	.18

Table 4–7 continued

Hospital	*Discharges*		*Days of Care*		*Hospital*	*Discharges*		*Days of Care*	
	Number	*Percent*	*Number*	*Percent*		*Number*	*Percent*	*Number*	*Percent*
CA Solano	3	.08	16	.05	PA Blair	3	.16	20	.14
NY Erie	3	.08	32	.10	TX Navarro	3	.16	10	.07
NY New York	3	.08	29	.09	All others	76	3.95	550	3.78
UT Salt Lake	3	.08	36	.12	Unknown county	19	.99	117	.80
All others	86	2.41	821	2.64					
Unknown county	30	.84	216	.69					

Note: Data reflect hospital bills received and processed in the Medicare statistical system as of September, 1978. Counties having 2 or less discharges are not listed. Listing ends either when 37 counties are listed or when 98 percent of discharges of a hospital are covered in the table.

Source: Alpha Center for Health Planning, *A Planner's Guide to the Medicare Statistical System* (Bethesda, Md.: Alpha Center for Health Planning, October 1981).

- The MEDPAR file contains a sample of only 20 percent of all hospitalized Medicare beneficiaries.

Despite these limitations, however, MSS data have proven useful for planning and they could become even more valuable in the future.

AREA RESOURCE FILE

The Area Resource File (ARF) is a computerized data base containing a wide range of detailed information on health professionals and health care facilities in each county in the United States.[82] It was initially created by the federal Bureau of Health Professions in 1971. Since then, the bureau has revised and updated the ARF on a continuing basis. The ARF could be useful for strategic planning because it attempts to bring together data from a number of different sources. However, the planner should note that the ARF data are no more reliable, complete, or accurate than the data in the sources from which they were obtained. ARF data currently consist of about 3,000 data items covering:

- *The number and type of health professionals in each county.* This includes physicians, dentists, osteopaths, veterinarians, optometrists, pharmacists, podiatrists, registered nurses, nurse practitioners, licensed practical nurses, and licensed hygienists. These data, particularly the data on physicians, are broken down by variables, such as age, specialty, and sex.
- *The number and type of health care facilities in each county.* This includes hospitals and nursing homes, with the data broken down by type of facility. In addition, the hospital data are broken down by the number of beds in, and the types of services (such as ICU and blood bank) offered by, the hospital.
- *Expenditures for health care services in each county.* These include total expenditures for hospital services, total Medicare expenditures for hospital services, total and per capita expenditures under Part A of Medicare for hospital services, total and per capita expenditures under Medicare Part B for outpatient services, number and age-sex characteristics of enrollees under Medicare Part A and Part B, and prevailing Medicare charges for a wide variety of physician and ancillary services.
- *The size, health, and socioeconomic characteristics of the population in each county.* This includes the number of persons broken down by age, sex, race, and ethnic origin. It also covers the number and types of births, and infant and fetal deaths. Adult deaths are broken down by race, cause, and age. Other population characteristics covered are crime, income, education, and employment levels and poverty and welfare status.

- *Environmental conditions in each county*. These include land area, population density, number of large animals, latitude and longitude, elevation, water hardness, crop season span, and temperature and rainfall statistics.
- *Utilization of health care resources in each county*. This covers inpatient days, outpatient visits, emergency room visits, and surgical procedures, by type of hospital.
- *Health professional education in each county*. This includes the number of each type of health professional training institution (such as medical school, nursing school, and licensed practical nursing school). The data also cover the number and level of students in each training institution and hospital internship, residency, and traineeship program, broken down by sex in most cases.

Many of the data in the ARF cover more than one year.[83] The total number of annual deaths in each county, for instance, is available for each year from 1970 through 1977. Similarly, the data on total annual expenditures for hospital services cover 1975, 1977, and 1978.

The data in the ARF are collected from a variety of sources.[84] The number of active physicians, for example, is obtained from *Physician Distribution and Medical Licensure in the U.S.*, Center for Health Services Research and Development, published by the American Medical Association. Mortality statistics are obtained from the mortality data tapes of the National Center for Health Statistics. ARF data are uniform for all parts of the U.S. and can be compared across counties, however, they also contain errors that should be recognized and accounted for when the data are used.

The ARF data are a useful source of information for strategic planning for several reasons. First, they cover a number of topics central to most strategic planning: the availability of health care facilities, expenditures for health care services, population characteristics, and health manpower. Second, they provide detail at the county level, which is often the lowest geographic level of aggregation available to the planner. Third, many ARF data items cover a number of years, which allows for historical trend analyses that are central to strategic planning. Finally, the uniformity of ARF data in all parts of the U.S. means that these data can be used to compare local trends across counties (see Table 4–8), regions, and states or in the nation as a whole. These types of comparisons help establish local historical trends that are important in strategic planning.

ARF data are available in the computerized Master Area Resource File and released in the form of published reports.[85] The Bureau of Health Professions has produced a number of such reports containing data that are useful for health planning. These include tabulations and rankings at the county (Table 4–8), health service area, and state level. These reports and the Master Area Resource

Table 4–8 Area Resource File Tabulation of Counties, Ranked by Ratio of 1978 Active, Nonfederal Physicians per 100,000 Population

State Name	*County Name*	*1978 Pop (In 100's)*	*1978 MD's*	*Ratio MD's/Pop*	*County Ranking*
Wisconsin	Dane	3,188	1,287	403.7	3,056
Maryland	Montgomery	5,750	2,349	408.5	3,057
Georgia	Fulton	5,596	2,299	410.8	3,058
Vermont	Chittenden	1,119	479	428.1	3,059
Georgia	Richmond	1,634	750	459.0	3,060
Kentucky	Fayette	1,907	895	469.3	3,061
Minnesota	Olmsted	920	1,372	491.3	3,062
Dist of Columbia	The District	6,710	3,322	495.1	3,063
Maryland	Baltimore City	7,919	4,201	530.5	3,064
Colorado	Denver	4,746	2,678	564.3	3,065
Pennsylvania	Montour	166	262	578.3	3,066
West Virginia	Monongalia	682	399	585.0	3,067
Florida	Alachua	1,308	792	605.5	3,068
Missouri	St Louis City	5,045	3,091	612.7	3,069
California	San Francisco	6,493	3,998	615.7	3,070
Michigan	Washtenaw	2,536	1,595	628.9	3,071
New Hampshire	Grafton	614	401	653.1	3,072
Massachusetts	Suffolk	6,826	4,657	682.2	3,073
Missouri	Boone	901	656	728.1	3,074
Virginia	Albemarle	890	724	813.5	3,075
North Carolina	Durham	1,451	1,187	818.1	3,076
New York	New York	13,537	11,646	860.3	3,077

Source: Bureau of Health Professions, *The Area Resources File: A Health Profession Planning and Research Tool* (Hyattsville, Md.: U.S. Department of Health and Human Services, November 1980).

File itself (NTIS Accession No. 0902485) can be purchased from the National Technical Information Service, U.S. Department of Commerce, 5285 Port Royal Road, Springfield, Virginia, 22161.

STATE GOVERNMENT DATA

State governments are involved in collecting, processing, and disseminating several types of data that are useful for strategic planning. In fact, as noted earlier, state governments are generally the primary agents in the collection of vital statistics and data on health manpower and health care facilities. In addition, they are involved, in collaboration with the federal Bureau of the Census, in producing interdecennial year estimates of the population within their borders. Also, as the principal administrators of Medicaid, state governments maintain management information systems for that program. These information systems could be used to produce the type of data for the Medicaid system that the Medicare Statistical System produces for the Medicare program. In fact, they are being used to produce statistics on utilization and costs in the Medicaid system. While some of these data may currently be useful in some states for strategic planning, there has not yet been any successful effort to create a uniform, nationwide Medicaid statistical system.

The federal government also plays a role in the state government collection and distribution of vital statistics, of data on health manpower, and health care facilities, and of population estimates. It provides revenue to subsidize all of these efforts. It also provides technical assistance for some of them and acts as the nationwide collator and disseminator of the data for all of them. If the cooperative health statistics system had continued to expand, it is conceivable that the federal government would have been able to continue to improve the uniformity and quality of these state data collection programs.

In general, the state government collection of data on health manpower and facilities is less uniform across state boundaries than the state government collection of vital statistics. This is primarily due to the fact that the federal government does not coordinate the state collection of manpower and facilities data as well as it does that of vital statistics.

There are currently several states, including New York and New Jersey, that have hospital rate-setting programs that collect such hospital data as patient bills, patient chart abstracts, and hospital cost reports. These data are potentially very important for strategic planning, because they provide information on such items as hospital resource utilization, patient characteristics, and the cost of treatment. Strategic planners are well-advised to explore the possibility of acquiring and using such data if there is a rate-setting program in their area.

The current federal budgetary crisis already has led, and will probably continue to lead, to reductions of federal support for, and influence over, the states' collection of vital statistics, data on health manpower, data on health facilities, Medicaid data, and population estimates. This is most clearly evidenced by the elimination in 1982 of the federal cooperative health statistics system. However, there is reason to believe that the collection of such data by state governments will continue, even if federal support diminishes. The reason is that each of the separate state data collection efforts has its own raison d'être that appears to be more durable than federal support. The collection of vital statistics and data on the health professions' licensure and health facilities certification, for instance, is mandated by state laws that are not likely to be changed in the foreseeable future. Similarly, the Medicaid program is not seriously threatened with elimination, even though federal support for the program is currently being reduced. Finally, the state interdecennial census year population estimates are needed for the allocation of federal monies to individual states on the basis of formulae that include the size of the state's population.

It is conceivable, however, that reductions in federal support to the states could prompt state austerity measures that could, in turn, cause reductions in the comprehensiveness or quality of the data collected and produced by these state programs. Such reductions would probably also lead to a loosening of the uniformity of state-collected data across state boundaries. This could cause difficulties for strategic planning, particularly if the planning focuses on an area that covers more than one state.

REFERENCES

1. Bureau of the Census, *Statistical Abstracts of the United States, 1978* (Washington, D.C.: U.S. Government Printing Office, 1978), p. 1.

2. Ibid., p. 1.

3. Bureau of the Census, "Tentative Publication and Computer Tape Program—Revised February 1982," *1980 Census of Population and Housing* (Washington, D.C.: U.S. Government Printing Office, 1982), p. 8.

4. Bureau of the Census, *1980 Census Basics* (Washington, D.C.: U.S. Government Printing Office, 1979), pp. 1–4.

5. Ibid., p. 1.

6. Bureau of the Census, "Tentative Publication," pp. 1–6.

7. National Center for Health Statistics, *Catalog of Publications of the National Center for Health Statistics 1977–81* (Hyattsville, Md.: U.S. Department of Health and Human Services, May 1982), pp. 8–9.

8. Ibid.

9. W.L. Schaible et al., *Small Area Estimation: An Empirical Comparison of Conventional and Synthetic Estimators for States,* Vital and Health Statistics, Data Evaluation and Methods Research, series 2, no. 82 (Hyattsville, Md.: U.S. Department of Health, Education, and Welfare, December 1979), pp. 1–4.

10. National Center for Health Statistics, *Data Systems of the National Center for Health Statistics: Programs and Collection Procedure,* Vital and Health Statistics Series 7, no. 16 (Hyattsville, Md.: U.S. Department of Health and Human Services, December 1981), pp. 4–8.

11. National Center for Health Statistics, *Funeral Director's Handbook on Death Registration and Fetal Death Reporting* (Hyattsville, Md.: U.S. Department of Health, Education, and Welfare, July 1978), p. 1.

12. National Center for Health Statistics, *Handbook on Marriage Registration* (Hyattsville, Md.: U.S. Department of Health, Education, and Welfare, August 1978), p. 2.

13. National Center for Health Statistics, *Hospital Handbook on Birth Registration and Fetal Death Reporting* (Hyattsville, Md.: U.S. Department of Health, Education, and Welfare, February 1978), p. 1.

14. National Center for Health Statistics, *Handbook on Divorce Registration* (Hyattsville, Md.: U.S. Department of Health, Education, and Welfare, August 1979), p. 1.

15. Public Health Service, National Vital Statistics Division, "History and Organization of the Vital Statistics System," *Vital Statistics of the United States* (Washington, D.C.: U.S. Department of Health, Education, and Welfare, 1950), pp. 2–19.

16. Ibid., pp. 1–19.

17. National Center for Health Statistics, Division of Vital Statistics, "Supporting Statement: The 1978 Revision of the United States Standard Certificates." Unpublished document supporting the division's request for approval of the revised standard vital statistics certificates (Hyattsville, Md.: Division of Vital Statistics, 1976).

18. Public Health Service, National Vital Statistics Division, "History and Organization," pp. 17–19.

19. National Center for Health Statistics, *Data Systems,* p. 4.

20. Public Health Service, National Vital Statistics Division, "History and Organization," pp. 15–16.

21. S. Jonas, "Population Data for Health and Health Care," in *Health Care Delivery in the United States,* ed. S. Jonas (New York, N.Y.: Springer, 1981), p. 48.

22. Ibid., p. 49.

23. National Center for Health Statistics, *Handbook on the Reporting of Induced Termination of Pregnancy* (Hyattsville, Md.: U.S. Department of Health, Education, and Welfare, 1979), pp. 1–2.

24. Ibid.

25. National Center for Health Statistics, Division of Vital Statistics, "1978 Revision," p. 1.

26. National Center for Health Statistics, *Data Systems,* pp. 4–5.

27. Ibid., p. 4.

28. Ibid., p. 4.

29. Director, Division of Vital Statistics, National Center for Health Statistics, April 1983: personal communication.

30. National Center for Health Statistics, *Data Systems,* p. 5.

31. National Center for Health Statistics, *Catalog of Publications,* pp. 8–9.

32. National Center for Health Statistics, *Data Systems,* p. 5.

33. Ibid., p. 5.

34. Ibid., p. 5.

35. Ibid., p. 5.

36. Ibid., p. 5.

37. National Center for Health Statistics, *Catalog of Publications,* p. 6.

38. Ibid., p. 9.

39. National Center for Health Statistics, *Using Natality Data in Health Planning* (Hyattsville, Md.: U.S. Department of Health and Human Services, November 1980).

40. National Center for Health Statistics, *Catalog of Publications,* p. 9.

41. National Center for Health Statistics, *Death Rates from Ischemic Heart Disease and Other Related Diseases by Health Service Area, 1968-72* (Hyattsville, Md.: U.S. Department of Health and Human Services, November 1979).

42. National Center for Health Statistics, *Data Systems,* p. 5.

43. Ibid., p. 5.

44. G.F. Pyle, *Applied Medical Geography* (Washington, D.C.: V.H. Winston & Sons, 1979).

45. National Center for Health Statistics, *Data Systems,* pp. 6–8.

46. Ibid., p. 6.

47. Ibid., pp. 7–8.

48. National Center for Health Statistics, *Catalog of Publications,* pp. 1–9.

49. National Center for Health Statistics, *Data Systems,* p. 11.

50. Ibid., p. 11.

51. Ibid., p. 22.

52. Ibid., p. 27.

53. Ibid., p. 27.

54. Ibid., p. 28.

55. Ibid., p. 28.

56. Ibid., p. 28.

57. National Center for Health Statistics, *The Cooperative Health Statistics System: Its Mission and Program,* Final report from the Task Force on Definitions to the Cooperative Health Statistics Advisory Committee, Vital and Health Statistics series 4, no. 19 (Rockville, Md.: U.S. Department of Health, Education, and Welfare, April 1977), p. 1.

58. Ibid., pp. 1–2.

59. Alpha Center for Health Planning, *A Planner's Guide to the Medicare Statistical System* (Bethesda, Md.: Alpha Center for Health Planning, October 1981).

60. K. Davis and R. Reynolds, "Medicare and the Utilization of Health Care Services by the Elderly," *Journal of Human Resources,* Summer 1975, pp. 361–377.

61. C.R. Fisher, "Differences by Age Group in Health Care Spending," *Health Care Financing Review* (Spring 1980).

62. J. Lubitz, *Medicare Enrollment Data for Health Planners,* Health Care Financing Monograph (Baltimore, Md.: Health Care Financing Administration, 1980), p. 1.

63. J. Lubitz, C. Walton, M. Newton, and S. Hadley, *Hospital Patient Origin and Destination Data for Medicare Patients 65 Years and Over,* Health Care Financing Monograph (Baltimore, Md.: Health Care Financing Administration, 1980), p. 1.

64. Office of Research, Demonstrations, and Statistics, *A Guide to ORDS Publications* (Baltimore, Md.: Health Care Financing Administration).

65. Alpha Center for Health Planning, *A Planner's Guide,* p. 5.

66. J. Hatten, "Medicare's Common Denominator: The Covered Population," *Health Care Financing Review* 2 (Fall 1980).

67. Alpha Center for Health Planning, *A Planner's Guide,* pp. 51–53.

68. Ibid., p. 13.

69. Ibid., pp. 14–18.

70. Ibid., p. 16.

71. Ibid., p. 16.

72. Ibid., pp. 20–31.

73. Ibid., pp. 31–42.

74. J. Lubitz, *Medicare Enrollment.*

75. J. Lubitz et al., *Hospital Patient Origin.*

76. Alpha Center for Health Planning, *A Planner's Guide,* pp. 4–5.

77. J.E. Wennberg and A.M. Gittlesohn, *A Small-Area Approach to the Analysis of Health System Performance,* Health Planning Methods and Technology Series, no. 21 (Washington, D.C.: Department of Health and Human Services, August 1980).

78. Alpha Center for Health Planning, *A Planner's Guide,* pp. 90–91.

79. Ibid., pp. 51–54.

80. Ibid., pp. 45–48; 104–105.

81. National Academy of Sciences, Institute of Medicine. *Report of a Study: Reliability of National Hospital Discharge Survey Data* (Washington, D.C.: National Academy of Sciences, 1980), pp. 98–101.

82. Bureau of Health Professions, *The Area Resources File: A Health Profession Planning and Research Tool* (Hyattsville, Md.: U.S. Department of Health and Human Services, November 1980).

83. Ibid., pp. 18–212.

84. Ibid., pp. 18–212.

85. Ibid., pp. 7–8.

Chapter 5

Shared Information Systems

INTRODUCTION

The hospital's information system and government data sources are usually unable to provide all the data that are needed for strategic planning. The data that are captured and stored by the hospital's information system concern what is happening within the hospital. The examination of the hospital's external environment and the evaluation of alternative strategies are just two of the tasks that require data on events outside of the hospital.

While government can provide much useful information, its circumscribed role in the U.S. health care system (e.g., as third party payer rather than provider of services for most people) limits the data to which it has access. A general fear of government intrusion in the lives of Americans, cynicism about the competence of government, and providers' fear of regulation have led to restrictions on the data that government can collect. For example, only a few states now require the submission of discharge abstracts for all hospital patients, although considerable knowledge could be gained from such documents about how hospitals expend their resources, which would assist in the setting of rates of payment for Medicaid services and the granting of certificates of need. The federal government also restricts its mandatory collection of discharge data to Medicare patients.

Caught in the position of needing external data but without a way to get it, some hospitals have moved to develop systems that put data in a central location and allow other organizations access to them. Hospitals have done this themselves, through professional associations, or in consortia that include a range of other organizations, including state government. To distinguish these arrangements from other types of shared data processing, we will define a shared information system as an arrangement in which:

- Data from individual hospitals reside in a central location.
- Hospitals have access to the data of other hospitals, although the data may or may not be aggregated to prevent identification of individual institutions, physicians, and patients.
- Hospitals are provided with one or more of the following: a common set of reports, the opportunity to purchase customized reports, or access to the data itself in order to prepare reports in a fixed or variable format.

Shared information systems are not the same as shared service arrangements for data processing, which usually do not allow a hospital access to data from other hospitals.

It is important for hospital managers to have access to data from other hospitals in their region. For example, access to such data allows hospital managers to determine their market share in their region, to describe the characteristics of consumers and physicians who are not being served, and to establish rates of utilization for the hospital's desired service area and market groups. Such rates are necessary if the potential demand in the region is to be estimated and then used in making forecasts of the hospital's own future volume of services.

Access to data from other hospitals also allows the hospital to compare its performance in order to assess its position in relation to competitors. The strengths and weaknesses of the hospital's internal operations can also be assessed through comparisons of staffing ratios, unit costs, and other measures of productivity and cost structure.

Of course, these benefits are realized only if the appropriate hospitals are included in the data base. This often means inclusion of all the hospitals that serve the hospital's service area and markets. For the purpose of productivity and cost analysis, it may also mean inclusion of hospitals that are similar in sponsorship, size, services, and mission. Obtaining the participation of the appropriate hospitals in the absence of a government requirement that the data be submitted is the major challenge facing the developers of shared data systems, and they are by no means always successful in meeting this challenge.

In addition to the benefits derived from obtaining access to external data, hospitals can also lower the cost of data processing, acquire access to computer resources at a lower cost, and obtain staff expertise that might otherwise be unavailable or unaffordable. These additional benefits will not be discussed here, since the relevant economies apply to most shared hospital services, not only to shared data systems, and because much has already been written about the advantages of shared hospital services.

In the following sections, we describe the characteristics of shared information systems now in operation, elaborate on why they are important to strategic planning, and identify the characteristics of shared information systems which are likely to improve and support strategic planning.

CHARACTERISTICS OF SHARED INFORMATION SYSTEMS

Rather than provide an inventory of shared information systems that would quickly become outdated, we examine here the primary forms of sponsorship for shared information systems today, what data are being stored, and what services are being provided.[1] This will suggest the available options for those hospitals that are considering participating in or developing a system. The structure, membership, data bases, and services provided by shared information systems reflect political conditions (i.e., both the power relationships among hospitals and their relationships with government), the funds available, and the level of competition among the hospitals. Other options are likely to emerge as hospitals seek to obtain similar benefits within the constraints of their own environments.

Sponsorship

Table 5–1 shows the current types of sponsorship of shared information systems at the state and national level. In many cases, the sponsors of shared

Table 5–1 Shared Information Systems: Types of Sponsorship

Type of Sponsorship	*Examples* *State*	*National*
Hospital association	Iowa Servi-Share[a,i]	HAS[c]
Professional association	—	HFMA[b]
Consortium	Missouri Health Data Corp.	CPHA[e]
State government	So. Carolina OCHS[f]	—
Other third party payer	Indiana BC/BS[g]	—
Other nonprofit[h]	Vermont CHICV[d]	—

[a]Now part of the activities of a separate corporation
[b]Healthcare Financial Management Association's Financial Analysis Service
[c]American Hospital Association's Hospital Administrative Services
[d]Cooperative Health Information Center for Vermont
[e]Commission on Professional and Hospital Activities
[f]Office of Cooperative Health Statistics
[g]Some Blue Cross/Blue Shield plans sponsor systems that cover only parts of states.
[h]These organizations have boards of directors that are not selected by constituent groups (e.g., hospitals) or from nominations by such groups.
[i]The Council of Community Hospitals has developed "Datasystem," which covers metropolitan Minneapolis. Statewide systems are more common.

information systems are individual organizations that can build on a specific strength. For example, hospital and professional associations draw on the trust of their members that the information will be held confidential and shared only according to agreed-upon rules. State government can require by law or regulation that data be submitted. Third party payers have data processing expertise that can reduce their costs, and to varying degrees they have also earned the trust of hospitals.

Consortia may have none of these strengths. Each consortium constituent signs an agreement that is expected to protect its rights, but such an agreement is initially untested and may lack specificity. The release of sensitive data may be left to committees that have not worked together, leaving open the possibility of embarrassing disclosures or bottlenecks in the flow of information. While the agreements may legally protect members, a sense of risk can hang over the consortium because other members stand to gain from the disclosure of information. This is especially true if a state government is a member.

The consortium also lacks the legal right to require the submission of data, although members may participate in order to head off a threat by a state government to require submission if voluntary efforts fail. The consortium also cannot rely entirely on the staff and resources of an existing organization if it is to avoid the charge that it has been captured by a constituent group.

The strengths of consortia lie in the opportunity to pool expertise, and in the creation of a neutral staff. Hospital representatives are given the opportunity to sit in the same room with state government representatives and other users of the data and learn what the data will be used for. They can explain the data's strengths and weaknesses, and then return to their hospitals to work to eliminate potential problems. This procedure could be invaluable if states choose to implement a reimbursement system that relies on case-mix measures based on data from patient discharge abstracts. A consortium can assemble a neutral staff to work with each of the constituents, learn each of their applications, and win their trust. This can avoid debates and even legal actions based on mistrust.

This discussion has assumed that the consortium includes a wide spectrum of users. In some cases, however, the constituent groups may be limited to a number of professional associations (e.g., representing hospitals and physicians). The purpose of such consortia may be both to pool resources and to avoid continual criticism of the shared information system by a group, such as a physicians' group, that has much to gain or lose from the use of the data. Hospitals might, for example, include representatives of the medical society on the board of a consortium to develop and disseminate data on DRGs, thereby hoping to avoid the criticism that such data cannot be analyzed without the advice of the physicians who supply the underlying data (e.g., diagnosis) to the hospitals.

We do not mean to imply that consortia developed by the hospitals themselves will not stimulate anxiety. This would be particularly true if competition between hospitals continues to grow. Information about the markets served by the hospitals can offer a competitive advantage that could lead to restrictions on the use of the data that severely limit their usefulness, or even to the end of the consortium. For example, requiring each hospital to approve all reports that are derived from its own data and given to another hospital would make data on hospital market share difficult to disseminate. Without an outside force pressing for the collection of the data (e.g., state government), shared information systems sponsored solely by hospitals may be very difficult to start.

The type of sponsorship for shared information systems is likely to be determined in the future by the external forces pressing on hospitals. These include the demands of third party payers, including government, for data on which to base reimbursement and other decisions. In such cases, hospitals are likely to press for the establishment of consortia in order to have some influence on the methods of data collection and analysis.

If the data are considered primarily useful to hospitals, the issue of cost will be a major concern, and hospital associations and third party payers may be the major sponsors. The former are likely to have both the trust of their members and experience in developing and operating shared service arrangements. The latter have experience in data processing and may already have the requisite equipment and staff. Government may then ask for, or require the submission of, the data for its own use.

Data Bases

The data bases to which shared information systems provide access can be described most simply by referring to the source documents from which the data are obtained. These include:

- patient discharge abstracts
- patient bills
- hospital financial statements (e.g., auditors' reports, reports to third party payers)
- surveys on staffing, manpower productivity, and available services

In addition, data collected by the state and federal government—especially U.S. census data and state population estimates—are likely to be stored in order to permit the calculation of rates of utilization.

Some data bases of shared information systems have a very narrow scope (e.g., they may contain only patient discharge data), while others contain data from several sources. Exhibit 5–1 describes the data bases of several shared information systems and illustrates the variation in scope.

The variation may result from a division of labor. The shared information system may itself be a source of data for separate information systems maintained by users. For example, the PAS system developed by the Commission on Profes-

Exhibit 5–1 Data Bases of Shared Information Systems: Selected Examples

1. Healthcare Financial Management Association's Financial Analysis Service
   Data base: Audited financial statements and facility data (e.g., bed size, sponsorship) submitted by hospitals
2. Massachusetts Health Data Consortium
   Data base: Patient discharge abstracts submitted by hospitals and U.S. census data
3. Servi-Share of Iowa
   Data base: Patient discharge abstracts, AHA annual survey data, data on incidence of infections seen in hospitals
4. South Carolina Office of Cooperative Health Statistics
   Data base: Patient discharge abstracts, AHA annual survey data, Medicaid bills, professional licensure data, U.S. census data

sional and Hospital Activities (CPHA) collects data from discharge abstracts and provides member hospitals with reports. The member hospitals may also receive computer tapes of their own data, which can be used internally or submitted to the state government if, as in New York and several other states, they are required to do so.

Other shared information systems serve as the primary resource for one or more users, and their data bases therefore have a wider scope. The Office of Cooperative Health Statistics (OCHS) of the South Carolina state government has a data base that includes hospital discharge abstracts, data from the AHA annual survey (which are collected in a joint effort between the South Carolina Hospital Association and the South Carolina Department of Health), and the other data listed in Exhibit 5–1. OCHS then serves the health data needs of the state government, while providing periodic routine reports to hospitals.

The future scope of the data bases of shared information systems is likely to depend on the extent to which they function in lieu of a separate information system for the user. At one extreme, they could offer the user access to all necessary resources—hardware, software, and data bases—of a management information system. At the other extreme, they may simply provide an economical and politically viable way of acquiring a single data file (e.g., data from all the discharge abstracts in a region). The scope will depend to a great extent on whether the staff, boards, and sponsors of the shared information systems have an interest in exploiting the computer technology now being developed, and the expertise and business ability to make such ventures financially viable. For political, economic, or other reasons, some existing systems may not choose to offer a wide variety of services, while other systems will prosper while they do so.

The age of the data being stored by shared information systems will also vary. Some shared information systems are integrated with the hospital's day-to-day management. The data they collect may be used by hospital management for utilization review and financial management. Such data must be up-to-date; they must therefore be transmitted by mail or over the telephone at short intervals or as they are recorded by hospital personnel.

Some shared information systems provide the hospital with data that are needed less frequently. A shared information system that collects data annually to fulfill the hospital's obligations to the state government or to prepare market share and other reports for strategic planning may have data for only one or more previous years. The timeliness of the data stored by a shared information system will thus be determined by the use of the data and the method of collection.

Services Provided

Shared information systems provide access to data that have been tested for accuracy (at least to the extent of identifying the direction and magnitude of errors). Users can sometimes have direct access, allowing them to transfer data to their own computers or to use the data through a timesharing service from terminals in their offices. This presents many problems for the shared information system, since the data are usually collected voluntarily under agreements that stipulate the uses to which the data can be put and/or the form in which they can appear in reports. Direct access to the data of other hospitals usually requires their consent, which may not be granted for all uses of the data.

Access to data from other hospitals is therefore usually provided through printed reports, which are either in a fixed format or custom designed for the user. Fixed format reports may come to the user routinely, or they may be provided on request. Exhibit 5–2 illustrates the variation in the ways access to data is currently provided in shared information systems.

Confidentiality

The issue of confidentiality of data is critical for the survival and expansion of shared information systems. The current trend in computer technology is to provide the user with greater flexibility in retrieving and manipulating data to produce useful information. If the information must be provided through a central office, much of this flexibility is lost.

A number of solutions are being tried. As we mentioned earlier, some shared information systems are granting access to data if the prior consent of the hospitals involved is received. This could develop into standing agreements among groups of hospitals to share data. Such agreements could be limited in time, allowing hospitals to withdraw at a later date if they felt that they had been harmed.

Exhibit 5–2 Access to Data Bases in Shared Information Systems: Selected Examples

1. Commission on Professional and Hospital Activities (CPHA)
   Access:
   a. PAS+ provides hospitals with a number of routine fixed-format reports.
   b. PAS+ Basic allows hospitals to submit data and retrieve fixed-format reports through an Apple microcomputer.
   c. DATA EXPRESS provides custom-designed reports generated by CPHA staff in 24-48 hours.
   d. PAS+/REPORTER allows hospitals to retrieve their own discharge data and generate reports interactively on-site. The degree of control the hospital has over the format of the reports depends on which of three versions of REPORTER it selects.
   e. EXPLOR is an interactive data-base management system. Clients can access the data of other hospitals that have been encrypted to ensure confidentiality. Hospital identification is allowed if a prior agreement has been reached. EXPLOR contains billing, manpower, and other data not collected through PAS.
2. Maine Health Information Center
   Access: Fixed-format reports are routinely prepared from patient discharge data. User-defined reports are also prepared by the center on request. Maine state law allows the center to provide data to users that identify individual hospitals, but it cannot disclose the names of patients or physicians. Groups of Maine hospitals may request and receive a computer tape of their data that they can then share. Most reports, however, are prepared by the center's staff.
3. Healthcare Financial Management Association's Financial Analysis Service (FAS)
   Access: Hospitals participating in the FAS receive an annual report comparing the financial performance of members, using only aggregated data. No other access to data is provided.

Another possible solution has been used by the U.S. Census Bureau, which allows access to tapes but prevents disclosure of the tapes' data on individuals. The software used to obtain access to the data does not permit a report on even a small number of individuals. While this restriction does not allow a comparison of the performance of specific hospitals, it does allow the planner to produce aggregate information on a region and to compare a hospital against specific groups of hospitals.

Confidentiality is less of an issue when the data are collected under a state law or regulation. In this case, the names of the hospitals are frequently made available with the data, while the names of the physicians and patients are usually considered confidential. This may raise complex issues, since state statutes may vary and hospital, physician, and consumer groups may win suits in the courts that require or bar the disclosure of identifying information.

While the required submission of hospital discharge and billing data to third party payers is considered a threat by some hospitals, it opens up possibilities for analyzing the data to assist hospitals in highly competitive environments to assess their performance and evaluate alternative strategies.

Shared information systems also conduct special surveys for users and provide access to data that are not collected by the system itself. The Maine Health Information Center provides access to a file of ambulance run reports. It also has prepared for the state government a file on instances of catastrophic illness. Servi-Share in Iowa maintains a file on incidence of infections seen in Iowa hospitals. The data that are collected by other organizations and most commonly included in data bases are from the U.S. Census and the AHA annual survey.

Shared information systems may move to compete with the vendors of hospital information systems and hospital consulting firms to provide access to new computer technology, including data-base management systems and microcomputer-based management information systems. Even without permission to provide unlimited access to the data, shared information systems have the advantage of understanding the data they collect and store.

If a hospital's data remain confidential, shared information systems may have a monopoly on the analysis of the data they store, allowing them to sell a wider range of services. However, the development of new solutions to the problem of hospital confidentiality will offer shared information systems the opportunity to expand their services to include the provision of software and data for on-site analysis of their data bases. The confidentiality issue will thus determine to a great extent the range of services that shared information systems will offer in the future.

IMPORTANCE OF SHARED INFORMATION SYSTEMS FOR STRATEGIC PLANNING

The primary benefit for strategic planning from a shared information system derives from the access to external data. In the assessment of its present position and the development and evaluation of alternative strategies, it is especially important that a hospital obtain data on all the consumers, physicians, and other health care providers in its service or market area.

Exhibit 5–3 shows a community-based, small-area analysis of community use rates available from the Massachusetts Health Data Consortium. The analysis indicates the number of discharge days and the number of discharges per 1,000 residents for Massachusetts communities and HSA areas. These data are provided for a number of age groups and hospital services. For each service area defined by the hospital, the analysis identifies the total level of utilization for hospital inpatient services in the area's towns and cities.

Exhibit 5–3 Community-Based, Small-Area Analysis of Community Use Rates

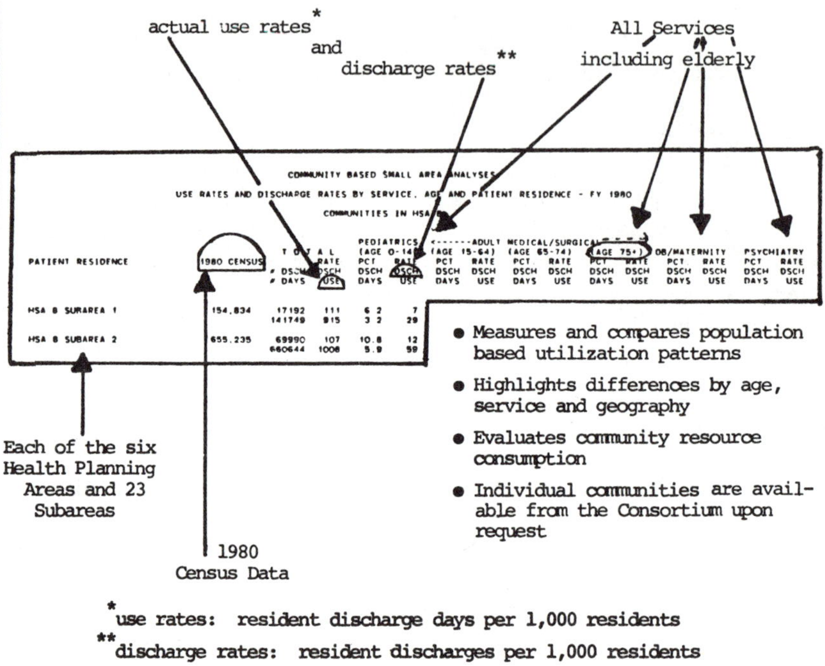

Source: Reprinted with permission of the Massachusetts Health Data Consortium, Inc., 400-1 Totten Pond Road, Waltham, Mass., 02154.

Exhibit 5–4 presents a report on the market share of individual hospitals. This standard report allows the hospital to identify its market share by age group and hospital service for up to 15 communities. User-specified reports can be requested to identify market share by payer and to give the market shares of each hospital serving community residents.

Two other series of standard reports show market share by diagnosis related grouping (DRG), groups of DRGs, and major diagnostic categories (MDC).[2] Descriptions of these reports appear in Chapter 6. Another series allows the hospital to calculate its market share for specific clinical subspecialties (e.g., cardiology). (A description of this series appears in Chapter 8.)

All of these variables can be used to define the hospital's market and to assess its level of performance in serving the existing demand. These data on the hospital's market and service area can also be used to evaluate alternative strat-

Exhibit 5–4 Market Share Report

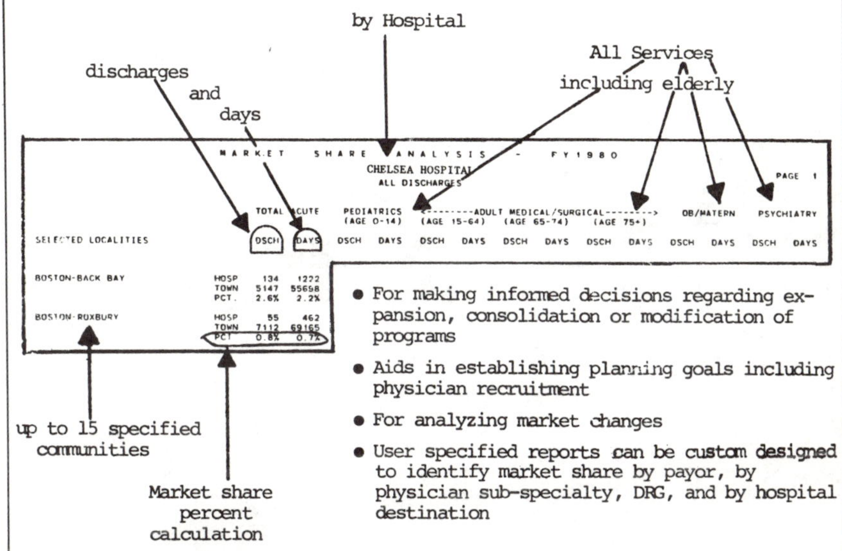

Source: Reprinted with permission of the Massachusetts Health Data Consortium, Inc., 400-1 Totten Pond Road, Waltham, Mass., 02154.

egies. The current level of utilization suggests the possibilities for an expansion of services. The current market share of competing hospitals suggests the difficulty the hospital will have in improving its current position.

This information can also be presented in graphic form. Figure 5–1 shows the changes between 1975 and 1980 in market share for hospitals serving Boston residents.

While a comparison of a hospital's performance with that of other hospitals that seek to serve the same service area and market is important for strategic planning, the strengths and weaknesses of the hospital may not be evident from the data. While the other hospitals may be competitors, they may not be peers. Differences in size, sponsorship, teaching programs, and other factors may make a comparison of performance misleading.

Exhibit 5–5 shows the formats of two reports in MONITREND, a management information system offered by the American Hospital Association's Hospital Administrative Services (HAS). For purposes of these reports, the hospital may stipulate a special group of hospitals that they consider peers (e.g., teaching hospitals with more than 800 beds).

Figure 5–1 Trends in Market Share: Boston Residents, 1975 vs. 1980

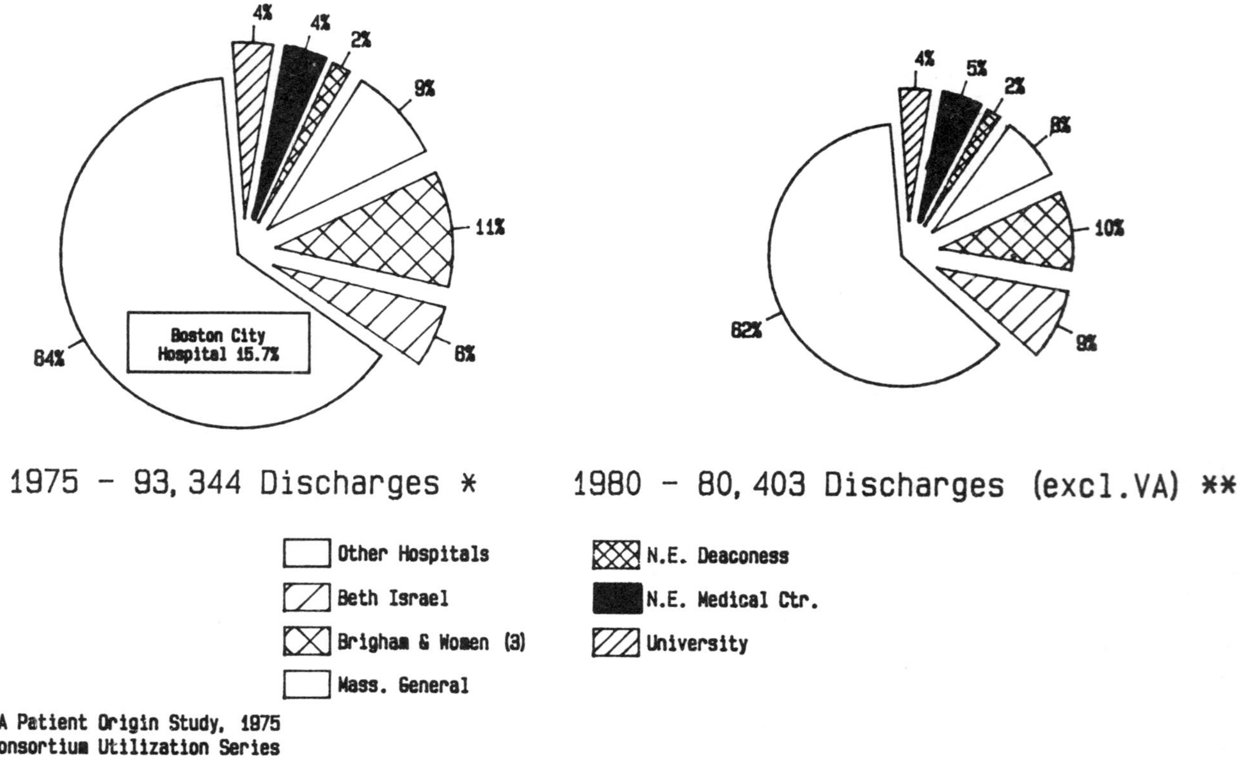

Source: Reprinted with permission of the Massachusetts Health Data Consortium, Inc., 400-1 Totten Pond Road, Waltham, Mass., 02154.

Exhibit 5–5 Two Monthly Reports from the American Hospital Association's MONITREND Service

1. This column indicates the average of the previous three months for the specific institution.
2. These are averages of the group median data for three prior months. Hospitals are automatically placed in the national and state (or regional) groups. Hospitals select which special groups (e.g., metropolitan, ownership, rate review group) they wish to participate in. The numbers 1, 2, 3, and 4 indicate in which quarter of the group data the hospital's data appeared. The letters L and H mean the hospital's indicator amount was in the lowest or highest five percent of the group, respectively.

   When an L or H appears here, the word "CHECK" will appear in the variance column . . . a clue to the participant to verify that data are correct.
3. The variances are calculated by subtracting the designated median (as shown in the Code column) from the hospital's indicator value. For example, the hospital's paid hours per diagnostic radiology procedure of 1.07 minus the national median of 1.22 equals a −.15 paid hours per procedure variance. A negative sign in the variance column indicates that the hospital's productivity is higher or expense is lower than the median.
4. The extension is always calculated by multiplying the variance times the divisor used in calculating the indicator.
5. Two new trend data columns: same three months prior year and same twelve months last year.
6. This percent change column is calculated by subtracting the average of the same three months last year from this year and then dividing this by the value of the average of the same three months last year.

MONITREND
For Hospitals

Ancillary Services Section	YOUR INST 3 MONTH AVERAGE (1)	GROUP MEDIAN DATA — GROUP MEDIANS (THREE MONTH AVERAGE) (2): NATIONAL (A)		STATE (B)		SPECIAL (C)		VARIANCE FROM MEDIAN (3)	CODE	EXTENSION (4)
Radiology - Diagnostic										
Procedures/Adj. Discharge	2.06	2.41	2	2.17	1	2.27	1			
Revenue/Procedure	26.10	30.70	2	26.07	3	26.09	3			
Direct Expense/Procedure	10.62	13.02	1	10.80	2	10.62	2			
Salary Expense/Procedure	6.44	6.89	2	6.02	3	6.12	3			
Physician Remuneration/Procedure	9.09	7.23	3	5.57	H	8.74	3	CHECK		
Ratio Total Direct Expense/Revenue	.76	.51	4	.51	4	.59	4			
Direct Expense Percent	3.96	3.65	3	3.63	3	4.13	2			
Outpatient Revenue Percent	52.13	39.67	4	40.63	4	47.08	4			
Paid Hours/Procedure	1.07	1.22	1	1.09	2	1.08	2	−.15	A	

	INTERNAL TREND DATA: CURRENT MONTH	AVG PRIOR 3 MONTHS: INDICATOR (5)	AVG PRIOR 3 MONTHS: RAW DATA	SAME 3 MONTHS LAST YEAR	PERCENT CHANGE (6)	AVERAGE PRIOR 12 MONTHS	SAME MONTHS LAST YEAR (5)
Radiology - Diagnostic							
Procedures/Adj. Discharge	2.10	2.06	3,046	2.17	− 5.0	2.10	2.06
Revenue/Procedure	26.21	26.10	79,497	22.79	14.5	23.79	22.14
Direct Expense/Procedure	9.93	10.62	32,346	7.58	40.1	9.64	8.02
Salary Expense/Procedure	6.27	6.44	19,614	5.05	27.5	5.96	5.17
Physician Remuneration/Procedure	9.12	9.09		7.94	14.4	8.28	7.72
Ratio Total Direct Expense/Revenue	.71	.76		.68	11.7	.75	.71
Direct Expense Percent	3.59	3.96	32,346	3.31	19.6	3.75	3.38
Outpatient Revenue Percent	52.43	52.13	41,442	53.47	− 2.5	53.61	53.93
Paid Hours/Procedure	1.05	1.07	3,254	.92	16.3	1.05	.99

Source: Reprinted from *HAS/MONITREND for Hospitals: Administrator's Guide*, with the permission of the American Hospital Association, © 1982.

MONITREND reports focus on short-term trends and are primarily intended to assist in management and operational-level planning and control rather than in strategic planning. In the absence of other comparative information, however, they can be useful in assessing the hospital's current position and the direction of change.

This brief discussion does not adequately describe all the available products and services being offered by shared information systems and their uses in strategic planning. However, it does emphasize the importance of shared information systems in strategic planning.

REFERENCES

1. A computer search of the literature on hospital and health services administration revealed that little has been written on shared information systems. To gather relevant information, telephone and personal interviews were conducted with the directors and staff of the shared information systems cited in the chapter. The authors also relied on knowledge gained while working with data consortia in New York and Massachusetts and with systems for collecting discharge-abstract and bill data that have been developed by the New York and New Jersey Departments of Health.

2. For a description of DRGs and MDCs, see L.K. Lichtig, "Data Systems For Case Mix," *Topics in Health Care Financing* 8, no. 4 (Summer 1982):13–15.

Part III

Improving Planning Analyses and Decisions

Chapter 6

Analysis of Service Areas and Markets

INTRODUCTION

Defining the population to be served is an essential component of planning and marketing, but it is also a subject of considerable controversy. Hospitals have traditionally designated one or more geographic and political units (e.g., a city or county) as their service area. This is sometimes a reflection of community loyalties and the fund-raising that started most nonprofit hospitals. Within the service area, specific population groups may be identified on the basis of income, religion, race, major health problems, and other characteristics relevant to the hospital's perceived mission.

The current situation facing hospitals, which we reviewed in Chapter 1, has led to considerable interest in the application of marketing techniques to hospitals. From a marketing perspective, a decision to begin with a geographic definition of the scope of a hospital's market is both limiting and potentially damaging. The needs of patients, physicians, and the hospital itself are the logical starting points. Geography is only one of many ways of defining the customers (i.e., consumers and physicians) to be served.

Consumer and physician needs and demands can change, and the hospital can also alter its services, organizational structure, and other characteristics. There are many possible changes the hospital can make that would alter the markets it serves and make a service area map obsolete, for example:

- relocation through a new facility or merger
- establishment of satellite clinics in distant communities
- development of the hospital as a regional or statewide center for specific services

On the other hand, many hospitals will give priority to their commitment to the community, having been founded with the resources of that community. A hospital may need the base of political and financial support in its community. It may feel that it has no separate existence apart from the community whose residents serve as its board members, employees, and medical staff.

There is thus no universal answer to the question of whether a hospital should begin with a geographic definition of a service area and market. Certainly most hospitals will find it difficult to ignore the population adjacent to its facilities. No hospital can afford, however, to limit its examination of the question, Who do we serve?, to a listing of towns, counties, and cities. Regardless of the starting assumption, market and service area analysis must include an in-depth examination of who is being served, what the hospital's opportunities are, and who remains unserved.

This chapter explores in some detail the techniques for such an analysis and suggests how some decisions in the strategic planning process can be improved by a careful analysis of markets and service areas. The focus is on marketing information rather than market research,[1] since a major concern of this book is how routinely maintained data bases can be exploited to support strategic planning. At the end of the chapter, we discuss briefly the need for market research.

DEFINING MARKETS AND SERVICE AREAS

The defining of markets and service areas requires that we make numerous decisions about boundaries and divisions. We must divide or segment geographic areas, people, the people's needs, services, and technologies. While these may seem to be merely "technical" decisions best left to planning and marketing professionals, they are critical because they determine the context in which decisions on mission, goals, and resource allocation are made. Once service areas and markets are determined, certain consumer and physician needs may go undetected.

We could, for example, define a hospital's market by selecting a group of counties, then dividing the population into age groups, and finally defining which hospital services consumers currently use. One market might be "Cardiac care for the over-65 in Hudson and Morris counties." However, this method of defining a market is unlikely to lead to the detection of other potential markets, such as:

- hospice care (not currently offered) for Medicare patients currently residing at home or with their families
- health education, promotion and prevention programs for local industries

The determination of markets is an essential step in defining the hospital's mission and the business it is in. Poor judgment could result not only in the loss of revenue to the hospital but also in a loss of services to groups of patients and physicians. Because they have predominated for so long in the hospital industry, we begin first with geographic definitions of service areas, returning later to the question of how we can define current and potential markets.

Service Area Definition

Service areas can be based either on communities (to which we assign hospitals or hospital beds) or on hospitals (to which we assign either all or part of the communities). The former approach, sometimes called a population-based approach, might at first seem to offer nothing of value to hospitals, yet political and other factors may require it. A municipal or county hospital must view a political jurisdiction as its service area. State and local planning organizations may utilize political jurisdictions (e.g., towns and counties) in making decisions on service expansion and reimbursement.

Depending on the approach chosen, the communities or hospitals must be allocated. The methods that have been developed to do this fall into three general categories: normative, administrative, and empirical:[2]

1. Normative methods utilize accessibility or other criteria to determine what the boundaries around the hospitals or communities should be. We might, for example, decide that all members of the community should be within 30 minutes of travel time to emergency facilities for the treatment of heart attacks. If our approach is hospital-based, we can allocate to the hospital those communities within 30 minutes of travel time.[3] If our approach is population-based, we can divide the region or state into service areas based on travel time along existing roads, assigning hospitals to each service area where they exist, and noting the new facilities that will be needed to meet the criteria.[4] In either case, alternatives such as mobile ICUs and air evacuation can be considered to fill the gaps detected in services.
2. Administratively determined methods involve the assignment of communities or hospitals by some authority, usually public. A hospital may be assigned a community and told that it will be held accountable for the health care provided to that community.[5] A foundation or other funding source may offer the hospital positive, financial rewards for assuming this responsibility. In a population-based approach, hospitals or parts of hospitals may be allocated to serve a community.[6]
3. Empirical methods involve the analysis of existing patterns of movement between patient residence (and more rarely physician location) and hospital location. This requires what is called a patient origin study (described later in this chapter). A physician origin study (described in Chapter 8) is also needed if the service area is based on physician location and movement.

In the hospital-based approach, the flow of patients is used to assign communities or groups of patients to specific hospitals.[7]

In a population-based approach, hospitals or parts of hospitals can be assigned to the population in a particular geographic area.[8] The rules for assignment can become critical, however. It is highly unlikely that all patients in a geographic area will utilize a single hospital. Thus, if the entire area is assigned to the hospital, reality is distorted. (Different methods of assignment are examined in a later section.)

Combinations of the three methods (normative, administrative, and empirical) can be used. A city may be administratively defined as the service area, but subareas may be determined by empirical methods.[9] Service areas could be defined empirically, but then changes could be suggested to meet normative criteria.[10]

Considerable work has been done by operations researchers in developing population-based methods that are both empirical and normative. Models have been developed in attempts to achieve several objectives: selection of locations for facilities so that average travel time is minimized, determination of the smallest number of facilities (and their locations) that will meet specified travel time criteria, and selection of the best locations for a specified number of facilities. ReVelle and his colleagues have prepared a review of these models for Emergency Medical System (EMS) services.[11]

We cannot hope to describe all of the methods that have been used for service area determination. (Readers may wish to consult an annotated bibliography and critique prepared by Government Studies and Systems in 1978.[12]) However, there are several specific methods of defining service areas that can be utilized by hospitals with varying levels of access to data, which is often the most critical problem in selecting a method. For some methods, data collected by the hospital itself (internal data) will suffice. Other methods require that hospitals have access to data on all patients or physicians—data that can be provided only by other hospitals or all payers in the hospital's service area (external data).

Methods Using Internal Data

Hospitals can use data captured on bills and patient discharge abstracts to calculate an "index of commitment" or hospital dependency.[13] The index is a simple measure of the extent to which the hospital (hospital Y in the formula below) has committed resources to a community (area X in the formula below). The index is calculated by dividing the number of admissions or discharges for a particular geographic area by the hospital's total number of admissions or discharges:

$$\text{Index of commitment} = \frac{\text{Admissions or discharges in area X}}{\text{Total admissions or discharges for hospital Y}}$$

Table 6–1 shows the commitment index for a hospital. The geographic area should be the smallest mutually exclusive area on which data are captured (e.g., towns and cities). This permits later aggregations during the planning process.

There are a number of ways in which this index can be used to define a service area. Geographic areas could be ranked in descending order according to the percentage of admissions or discharges they provide. The service area can then be defined as comprising those geographic areas that cumulatively provide a large proportion of the hospital's admissions or discharges, for example, 90 percent. Table 6–1 shows the towns that would be included in the hospital's service area under this definition.

The cut-off point is, of course, arbitrary, and exceptions should be made if one or more towns excluded from the service area have almost the same index value as those included. The cut-off point should be set so that the great majority of the hospital's admissions and discharges are included; it should represent a break between areas with significantly different contributions to the hospital's total patient load (e.g., five percent vs. ten percent).

The most serious weakness of this method is that the geographic areas that are included may be sending only a small percentage of their population to the hospital. A geographic area might send only 5 percent of its patients to the hospital but represent 20 percent of the hospital's admissions. By allocating the

Table 6–1 Calculation of an Index of Commitment

		Index Values	
Town	*Admissions to Memorial Hospital*	*Percentage of Hospital Admissions*	*Cumulative Percent*
1	5330	54.41	54.41
2	1387	14.15	68.56
3	893	9.12	77.68
4	762	7.79	85.47
5	488	4.98	90.45[a]
6	336	3.43	93.88
7	178	1.82	95.70
8	89	.91	96.61
All others	332	3.39	100.00
Total	9795	100.00	

[a]Towns 1 to 5 would comprise Memorial Hospital's service area if a cut-off of 90 percent is used. However, Town 6 might-be included because its index value is close to that of Town 5 and the index drops rapidly with Town 7. Even if Towns 1 to 6 are included, the service area would not include all the people who use Memorial Hospital.

area to that hospital, we could be ignoring the fact that another hospital receives 85 percent of the area's admissions.

Methods Using External Data

One way to avoid the above problem is to calculate an "index of relevance" or community dependence.[14] This is a simple measure of the extent to which communities use a hospital. The place of residence of all patients admitted or discharged during a particular time period is obtained through a cooperative effort with other hospitals or from government agencies (see Chapters 4 and 5). The number of patients from each geographic area (area X in the formula below) who go to each hospital (hospital Y in the formula below) is then divided by the total number from that area:

$$\text{Index of relevance} = \frac{\text{Admissions or discharges for hospital Y}}{\text{Total admissions or discharges in area X}}$$

The index of relevance is another name for the hospital's market share, that is, the proportion of the market (measured in this case by the number of admissions or discharges) that the hospital receives. If market share is multiplied by the use rate in the area (e.g., admissions per 1,000 population), the "draw rate" is determined. This is the proportion of utilization in the area that the hospital serves.

While different terms may be used, the objective remains much the same: to express the importance of the hospital in serving the demand that exists in various communities. In using the number of admissions and discharges, we make the assumption that demand (which is a function of consumer values and preferences, among other factors) can be accurately measured by prior patterns of utilization. When a hospital begins to ask how markets might be changed, it is important that its managers remember that the use of current or past admissions and/or discharges may not accurately reflect where consumers would like to receive services in the future. Table 6–2 shows the index of relevance for the communities that utilize the hospital represented in Table 6–1.

A service area can be determined in several ways. Griffith suggests designating areas of high, medium, and low relevance. He uses index values of 75 percent or more for high, 40 to 74 percent for moderate, and less than 40 percent for low.[15] The service area of the hospital could thus be defined as communities with a high or moderate relevance. A primary service area could be defined in several ways, for example, by including those areas with high relevance. A secondary service area could then be defined as those areas with moderate relevance.

The Massachusetts state government uses an alternative method that requires both hospital dependency (i.e., the index of commitment) and community de-

Table 6–2 Calculation of an Index of Relevance

Town	Total Admissions to All Hospitals	Total Admissions to Memorial Hospital	Index Values: Percentage of Admissions to Memorial Hospital
1	12,565	5,330	42.42
2	6,815	1,387	20.35
3	3,367	893	26.52
4	1,380	762	55.22
5	7,123	488	6.85
6	2,874	336	11.69
7	310	178	57.42
8	551	89	16.15

pendency (i.e., the index of relevance) to define service areas. It defines service areas separately for medical/surgical, pediatric, and obstetrical services. A primary service area consists of those communities that, when ranked ordinally, account for 90 percent of the facility's service-specific annual admissions. Also, each community must send 5 percent or more of its patients to the facility.[16]

If the data in Tables 6–1 and 6–2 were for the hospital's medical/surgical patients, the Massachusetts definition would put Towns 1 to 5 in the hospital's medical/surgical service area. This method does not solve the problem of including in a hospital's service areas those communities that send a larger proportion of their patients elsewhere. Massachusetts is less concerned with the development of mutually exclusive boundaries between service areas than it is with the appropriate allocation of the population to each facility. The population of each community is therefore allocated by multiplying the total population by the percentage of patients who go to a particular hospital. This calculation is illustrated in Table 6–3.[17] The result is a set of overlapping service area boundaries. Still, the method avoids making the assumption that all of a community's population should be allocated to a hospital even when the hospital does not serve all of that population's patients.

Some other methods that have been developed to create mutually exclusive service area maps make the same assumption. Poland and Lembcke, for example, developed a procedure that allocates to a hospital's service area all communities that send a majority of their patients to the hospital (i.e., they have an index of relevance of more than 50 percent).[18] However, their study was undertaken in parts of Kansas with a low population density and in which "63% of the short-term general and allied special hospitals had less than 50 beds."[19] These conditions (which are unlikely to exist in urban and suburban areas) would reduce

Table 6–3 Calculation of Service Area Population

Town	*1980 Pop. (15 Yrs +)*		*Percentage of Admissions to Memorial Hospital*		*Service Area Population*
1	97,918	×	42.42	=	41,537
2	54,118		20.35		11,013
3	21,799		26.52		5,781
4	16,798		55.22		9,276
5	57,752		6.85		3,956
6	29,367		11.69		3,433
				Total	74,996

Note: The service area population would vary depending on which towns were included, i.e., which criteria were used to define the service area.

the chance that the communities would be served by more than one hospital and that allocating all of a community's population to one hospital would seriously misrepresent the situation.

Wennberg and Gittelsohn conducted a number of studies in New England that involved the development of mutually exclusive service areas.[20,21] They used a plurality rule, assigning communities to the hospital that received the largest percentage of the community's patients. Again, however, their work focused on rural areas in which the overwhelming number of residents went to hospitals near their homes.

The Boundary Problem

If the term *service area* carries the connotation of a zone in which one hospital has exclusive responsibility for the care of a population, some unsolved problems remain. With the exception of some very rural areas and perhaps small pockets of urban areas, the movement of patients creates a far more complex situation. A more useful approach is to view each hospital as having a varying attraction (the origin of the term *draw rate*) for people and physicians in various geographic areas.[22]

If service areas are not mutually exclusive, hospitals cannot be held accountable for meeting all of a community's health care needs, and communities cannot claim exclusive jurisdiction over a hospital. If a map is drawn that represents the actual flow of patients, we are left with multiple zones of attraction, pull, or drawing power. Hospital zones will overlap. In urban areas, patients may be attracted to many different hospitals, making a service area map complex and misleading. It would be extremely difficult, for example, to draw the service area of a major teaching hospital in Boston, New York City, Chicago, or other metropolitan area in which hospitals tend to be close together and to draw their patients and physicians from a large geographic area. In such situations, it may be more useful to abandon the idea of individual hospital service areas and instead examine nongeographic patterns of use within the urban area (e.g., differential use by income or religious affiliation).

This is not to say that maps are not useful or that listing the communities that the hospital serves is misleading. Community identification can serve the same purpose for the hospital that it serves for citizens and government—as a way of declaring commitment and responsibility to a group of people. What we cannot lose sight of, however, is that many hospitals allocate their resources in complex ways, meeting some of the needs of some people with some of the available technology. The identification of a service area composed of communities should not mask this fact, thereby leading the hospital and the community away from the hard task of delineating exactly what the hospital can do and for what it can be held accountable.

Defining Markets

Abell, Hammond, and others have suggested that marketing and strategic planning can and should be combined.[23] The term *strategic market planning* has been used to describe a process that merges the analysis of markets, implementation of a marketing plan, and planning for the attainment of the desired future of an organization.[24] We will not attempt to describe all of the areas in which marketing and strategic planning should overlap. A critical first step, however, is to define the organization's market.

One question that is frequently posed early in the strategic planning process is, What business are we in? Using somewhat different terms, the marketing professional begins by asking who the organization's customers are and what products are sold. While the more general strategic planning question should be raised first, answering it requires consideration of the same information that the marketing professional is seeking. To say that a hospital is in the health care business is true (and may suggest opportunities that a more narrow definition would not), but it will not itself lead to the development of strategy. Using Abell's three components for defining a business, we must also examine what customer groups are served, what needs of those customers are satisfied, and what technologies are utilized. We can then begin looking at the opportunities available to the hospital.

We will call this early, common task of both strategic planning and marketing *market definition*. This results in a description of what business the organization is in, but in terms that are more precise than "health care" or "acute inpatient care.'' First, the hospital's current market is defined; then, as the hospital develops its mission statement, goals, and objectives, the hospital's future desired market is described.

Unlike the service areas we have examined, markets may or may not be defined geographically. While location or residence may be used to describe physician or consumer groups, other characteristics, such as age, may be chosen instead. The criterion used in determining how markets are defined is the extent to which the definition is useful in describing consumer and physician needs and demands in a way that suggests the hospital's opportunities for service.

Needs, demands, and opportunities are not static; they change over time. Needs and demands change for many reasons, including changing economic conditions and shifts in values and attitudes. For example, birthing rooms (homelike rooms in a hospital where women can give birth with their family present) are the result of a consumer demand that grew out of both changed economic conditions (the high cost of regular hospital services) and shifts in values and attitudes (the desire of women and their spouses to have more control over the birth process). Hospital opportunities also change as the hospital changes, for example, when new physicians arrive or the hospital alters its mission.

Market definition must be ongoing if the hospital is to plan for, rather than simply react to, the changes that are occurring internally and externally. Markets can be changed as well as defined. The necessity for such change is determined by the assessment of the hospital's position, as described in Chapter 2. Later in this chapter we describe the types of information that provide support to the hospital's decision makers as they move through the strategic planning process.

Strategic Business Units and Multiple Markets

Market definition will vary according to the level we are examining in the organization: the entire hospital, a unit (e.g., pediatrics), or a program (e.g., hypertension screening). For example, the differences between a cancer management center and an emergency room in the patient and physician groups that are served, the functions and needs that are served, and the technologies that are used are so great that a single market definition for the entire hospital is likely to hinder rather than assist planning and marketing.

This situation is not unique to hospitals. Indeed, the concept of a strategic business unit (SBU) has been developed to aid all types of managers in defining the multiple businesses and markets for their organizations. Kotler defines an SBU as ideally having the following characteristics:[25]

- It is a single business or collection of related businesses.
- It has a distinct mission.
- It has its own competitors.
- It has a responsible manager.

- It consists of one or more program units and functional units.
- It can benefit from strategic planning.
- It can be planned independently of the other businesses.

Program units are segments of a business that represent specific functions or needs or consumer and physician groups served. Functional units are resources used to implement programs (e.g., the radiology department). As Kotler notes, there is considerable variation in how SBUs, program units, and functional units are defined in the business literature.

> For example, at General Electric some "Strategic Business Units" (SBUs) encompass several divisions and have annual sales of in excess of $500 million. In other companies, business units are defined much more narrowly—either representing a product department or even a product line or major market segment.[26]

Each hospital has to ask whether a unit or program in the hospital would profit by being treated as autonomous. Autonomous here does not necessarily imply separate incorporation; it means rather being provided with the opportunity to plan separately for the future and being provided with the authority and resources to implement the resulting plan.

Some program or functional units can be more easily defined as SBUs than others. A network of free-standing primary care centers will more easily fit the definition of an SBU than the hospital's laboratory. Utilization, revenues, and expenditures may be so completely controlled by the hospital that the lab manager may not be easily held accountable for achieving a number of goals, including profitability. On the other hand, hospital management may wish to expand the services its lab offers to physicians and other providers; this may necessitate giving considerable freedom to the lab manager to meet the competition.

After designating the lab as an SBU, hospital management must then consider the possible limits of autonomy. Should the lab manager be allowed to purchase supplies separately from other units? Can the hospital itself be given a lower priority at certain times to provide services to others? These are not easy questions, but the answers will determine whether the concept of an SBU is meaningful for a particular hospital.

Regardless of whether SBU designations are used, a single market definition for an entire hospital would be too long and complex to be useful. A hospital serves more than one market; the question is, how should those markets be defined?

Three Dimensions of Market Definition

A market is a combination of patients and physicians, needs, and technologies. This definition is essentially the same as that used by Abell, who believes that market boundaries can be defined in terms of customer groups, customer functions, and technologies.[27] To appreciate the importance of using all three dimensions when defining a market, consider the following two market definitions for City Hospital:

1. The provision of acute inpatient services to residents of Adams, Schuyler, Morris, and Jefferson counties.
2. City Hospital receives 85 percent of the population hospitalized in Adams and Schuyler counties, providing services in most medical specialties. Physicians and patients from Morris and Jefferson county come to City Hospital primarily for cancer treatment, since the hospital has the only medical oncology department in the four-county area.

The second definition of City Hospital's market would be far more useful in developing and revising a mission statement and evaluating alternative changes in services. The first definition suggests that the hospital provides a homogeneous set of services, has no advantages over other hospitals, and meets the needs of patients and physicians in identical ways. It does not identify the differences in technology that give City Hospital a competitive advantage.

A major dilemma in defining markets arises from the numerous ways in which patients and physicians, needs, and technologies can be divided or segmented to suggest differences in how the hospital is used. For example, further investigation might reveal to City Hospital three additional factors:

1. City Hospital's cancer patients from Morris and Jefferson counties are almost entirely Medicare patients. Younger patients tend to use University Hospital, about 30 miles away.
2. Morris and Jefferson county physicians under 40 years of age use University Hospital for cancer referrals.
3. Patients from Morris and Jefferson counties who require radiation therapy are treated at University Hospital and hospitals in an adjacent metropolitan area.

To uncover this information, we would have to segment or divide (1) physicians by office location, age, referral hospital, patient diagnosis, and type of procedure; and (2) patients by place of residence, hospital location, payer, diagnosis, and type of procedure.

Of course, these are not the only ways in which patients and physicians can be segmented. Also, we have not specified the way in which diagnoses, procedures, and technologies can be segmented to yield useful information. Ultimately, each patient and physician could be viewed as unique. With many physicians and patients, a hospital must choose a limited number of market segments for examination. Such a choice carries with it, however, the risk that important opportunities or threats will be overlooked.

If City Hospital in the above example did not examine its patients by age or payer, it might, based on growth in the population, plan an expansion in services that would never occur because it is not attracting patients from younger age groups. Similarly, if it did not differentiate the various modes of treatment or technologies, it might not realize that it is failing to capture patients who require radiation therapy.

Segmenting Consumers

In order to segment consumers, we need information on those factors that affect their use of health services. This will allow us to predict more accurately the current and future response of consumers to the services offered. (The segmenting of physicians is examined in Chapter 8.)

Kotler defines the bases for segmentation of customer markets as "customer product requirements" and "customers' responses to marketing stimuli."[28] Both variables might be measured by examining past buying behavior or through contact with customers. Kotler points out that some "segmenters" go right to the use of "market descriptors" because "good data exist and the segments are more definable."[29] Market descriptors are the geographic, demographic, psychographic, and behavioristic variables used in segmenting consumer markets.

> In psychographic segmentation, buyers are divided into different groups on the basis of lifestyle or personality differences . . . In behavioristic segmentation, buyers are divided into different groups on the basis of their knowledge, attitude, use, or response to the actual product or its attributes.[30]

Table 6–4 shows some of the major segmentation variables for consumer markets.

A considerable body of research is already available to hospitals for use in predicting differences in the use of health services by consumers.[31–33] Table 6–5 lists some of the variables that have been shown to be related to the use of services for acute conditions and preventive services, based on a large number of studies of factors that affect the utilization of such services.

These factors have been categorized according to the model suggested by Andersen, who believes that need and predisposing and enabling variables explain much of the variation in the utilization of health services.[34] Need can be measured by the amount of illness perceived by the individual or the physician, both of whom affect the actual use of services. Thus, consumer-defined need can be distinguished from the need for services as defined by physicians and other providers. Some consumers have a propensity to use more health services. This propensity can be predicted by looking at characteristics that exist prior to

Table 6–4 Major Segmentation Variables for Consumer Markets

Variables	*Typical Breakdowns*
Geographic	
Region	Pacific, Mountain, West North Central, West South Central, East North Central, East South Central, South Atlantic, Middle Atlantic, New England
County size	A, B, C, D
City or SMSA size	Under 5,000, 5,000–19,999, 20,000–49,999, 50,000–99,999, 100,000–249,999, 250,000–499,999, 500,000–999,999, 1,000,000–3,999,999, 4,000,000 or over
Density	Urban, suburban, rural
Climate	Northern, southern
Demographic	
Age	Under 6, 6–11, 12–19, 20–34, 35–49, 50–64, 65+
Sex	Male, female
Family size	1–2, 3–4, 5+
Family life cycle	Young, single; young, married, no children; young, married, youngest child under six; young, married, youngest child six or over; older, married, with children; older, married, no children under 18; older, single; other
Income	Under $3,000, $3,000–$5,000, $5,000–$7,000, $7,000–$10,000, $10,000–$15,000, $15,000–$25,000, $25,000 and over
Occupation	Professional and technical; managers, officials and proprietors; clerical, sales; craftsmen, foremen; operatives; farmers; retired; students; housewives; unemployed
Education	Grade school or less; some high school; graduated high school; some college; graduated college
Religion	Catholic, Protestant, Jewish, other
Race	White, black, oriental
Nationality	American, British, French, German, Scandinavian, Italian, Latin American, Middle Eastern, Japanese
Social class	Lower-lower, upper-lower, lower-middle, upper-middle, lower-upper, upper-upper
Psychographic	
Life style	Straights, swingers, longhairs
Personality	Compulsive, gregarious, authoritarian, ambitious
Behavioristic	
Purchase occasion	Regular occasion, special occasion
Benefits sought	Economy, convenience, prestige
User status	Nonuser, exuser, potential user, first-time user, regular user
Usage rate	Light user, medium user, heavy user
Loyalty status	None, medium, strong, absolute
Readiness stage	Unaware, aware, informed, interested, desirous, intending to buy
Marketing-factor sensitivity	Quality, price, service, advertising, sales promotion

Source: Philip Kotler, *Marketing Management: Analysis, Planning, and Control,* 4th ed., © 1980, p. 199. Reprinted by permission of Prentice-Hall, Inc., Englewood Cliffs, N.J.

Table 6–5 Variables That Affect Consumer Use of Health Services

Variable Classification	*Specific Variable*
I. Need	
A. Indicators of health status	Perceived seriousness Chronic activity limitation Disability days
II. Predisposing	
A. Sociodemographic	Age, sex, education, marital status, race
B. Sociopsychological	Previous health behavior
III. Enabling	
A. Economic	Income, price,[a] employment
B. Organization	Alternative organization[b]
C. Availability of services	Urban-rural residence Distance to services Regular source of care Supply of services[c]

[a]The out-of-pocket cost to the consumer rather than the price or charge.
[b]HMOs and other organizations that offer comprehensive health services. The effect of prepayment has not been separated from type of organization as an explanatory variable.
[c]The use of health services is affected by the supply of hospital beds (measured by beds per 1,000 population and occupancy) and the supply of physicians (measured by physicians per 1,000 population).

the onset of illness—characteristics that Andersen calls predisposing factors. Factors that affect the ability of the individual to respond to the perception of need are enabling factors.

It is essential that all three factors—need, predisposing variables, and enabling variables—be carefully considered; serious errors in planning can be made by assuming that only one of the factors is important. In developing a new service, some individuals in the hospital could point out that a need for a service exists, but fail to think about whether patients have access to the economic resources to make use of the service. The development of a preventive service could be advocated based on provider-defined need, the resources available, and patients' ability to pay. But if the question of whether patients perceive a need for the service is disregarded, the service could be underutilized.

The variables listed in Table 6–5 could be used in any first effort by the hospital to segment consumers. Table 6–6 shows how one hospital's patients were segmented by age and trends examined over time. Lack of data will limit many hospitals to just a few variables. However, additional variables may be important, especially when specific services that were not the focus of the reported research are examined. Many hospitals have access to much more specific data on their patients than are usually available to researchers on the general

Table 6–6 Historical Discharges by Age Component at Western Hospital

1976–1979

Age Component	*1976[1] Discharge*	*Percent*	*1977 Discharge*	*Percent*	*1978 Discharge*	*Percent*	*1979[2] Discharge*	*Percent*	*Percent Change 1976–1979*
65 years and older	2,027	20.4%	2,004	21.5%	1,877	20.6%	2,136	24.1%	5.4%
15–64 years	5,178	52.1	4,837	51.9	4,686	51.5	4,576	51.6	(11.6)
15–64 years (female[3])	685	6.9	618	6.6	700	7.7	625	7.0	(8.8)
15–44 years (female[4])	848	8.5	844	9.0	848	9.3	811	9.1	(4.4)
14 years and younger	1,200	12.1	1,026	11.0	995	10.9	725	8.2	(39.6)
Total	9,938	100.0%	9,329	100.0%	9,106	100.0%	8,873	100.0%	(10.7)

[1]Actual breakdowns not available for medical/surgical 15–64, obstetrics or gynecology discharges in 1976—estimates are based on historical distribution.
[2]Estimates based on annualized PAS data.
[3]Discharges from the gynecology service only.
[4]Discharges from the obstetrics service only.

Notes: As shown, the 0–14 years age group has declined as a percent of total admissions by 39.6%. This decrease is clearly reflected in the decreasing rate of pediatric utilization. The total number of patients aged 15–64 years has also decreased during the period under analysis. However, the female component of this age group, the users of obstetric and gynecological services, has decreased at a lower rate.

In contrast to the 0–14 years age group, this table indicates that the 65 years and over component of the patient mix is growing as a proportion of total patients, as well as increasing in absolute terms. This growth in utilization by the older age group has significant implications for planning since this population has a tendency to utilize hospital inpatient services at a higher rate than the younger age groups and to need a greater intensity of care during hospitalization.

Source: 1976–1979 PAS reports. Reprinted by permission of Amherst Associates, Inc., Chicago, Ill.

population. These data would include information from chart abstracts, medical records, and patient bills.

It is important that the hospital examine variables that together adequately explain variations in the use of services. Statistical techniques have been developed to aid the hospital in evaluating the adequacy of the variables it has selected. (In Chapter 7 we present a case study that demonstrates how one of those techniques, multiple regression analysis, can be used.)

Segmenting Needs

Consumers and physicians utilize a hospital because they believe that it can satisfy certain of their needs. Consumers want to eliminate, avoid or reduce what have been called the five Ds—disease, discomfort, dissatisfaction, disability, and death. For instance, consumer-perceived severity of illness and limitation of activity has been shown to affect the use of services (see Table 6–5). (Physician needs are discussed in Chapter 8.)

One way to segment consumer needs is according to the functions that the hospital is expected to perform, either primary prevention (the total avoidance of a problem) or secondary prevention (reducing the consequences of a problem). These functions are carried out by providing a range of specific services. Exhibit 6–1 presents a system for categorizing the range of health services that can be provided.[35] These services can be provided in various settings, as defined in Exhibit 6–2.[36] Exhibit 6–3 presents a matrix that a hospital may use to show the range of options in the services it is providing.

There has been considerable discussion in the hospital industry of the need for hospitals to expand the services they offer to include additional services and settings, thereby filling in more of the Exhibit 6–3 matrix. Day hospital services for the elderly and health promotion in the workplace are two examples. Exhibit 6–4 provides a set of characteristics of the health system (the combination of services and settings) that could be used to develop criteria for performance evaluation and market analysis.[37]

The hospital performs a number of functions in the community, often for the same individuals at various stages of an actual or potential problem. The hospital may first screen the population for hypertension, provide treatment to lower blood pressure, stabilize those who have a stroke, and then provide speech and physical therapy.

There are a number of ways the medical profession has developed to categorize patients according to their problems or illnesses. Some hospitals utilize a problem-oriented medical record that categorizes patients on the basis of their descriptions of their sensations, limitations in activity, and concerns.[38] Most hospitals categorize patients on the basis of physician diagnoses, utilizing the ICD-9-CM system *(International Classification of Diseases,* 9th edition, *Clinical Modifi-*

Exhibit 6–1 Categories of Health Services

1. Community health promotion and protection:

   Those services directed at the community level toward improving the personal health behavior of residents and improving the quality of environmental factors affecting their health.

2. Prevention and detection services:

   Those services delivered to individuals in order to promote optimal physical and mental well-being, including protection from the development of disease and ill health, or those services which identify disease or ill health at the presymptomatic or unrecognized symptomatic stage.

3. Diagnosis and treatment services:

   Diagnosis and treatment services are those which identify and/or alleviate specific diseases and conditions of their symptoms once they have become symptomatic.

4. Habilitation and rehabilitation services:

   Services designed to assist the ill, injured, or disabled individual to achieve, or be restored to the fullest physical, mental, social, vocational, and economic usefulness of which that individual is capable.

5. Maintenance services:

   Services provided to individuals with chronic physical and/or mental conditions in order to prevent deterioration of those conditions, as well as services provided to those in need of assistance in activities of daily living. The purpose of such services is to enable an individual to participate in the community to the fullest degree of which that individual is capable. Maintenance services do not include habilitation or rehabilitative services, since the primary purpose of the latter services is to *increase* functional ability rather than maintain an existing level of functions.

6. Support services:

   Services provided to ensure adequate management of medical care resources and patient care environment, which assist the delivery of services without the provision of direct patient care (as in pharmacy, tissue, and social services) and which contribute to continuity of care (as in referral and discharge planning services).

7. Enabling services:

   Organized activities designed to influence the means by which health system services are delivered. These may include the concerns of:

   - health planning (such as data assembly and analysis, goal determination, action recommendation, implementation strategy)
   - resources development (manpower, facilities, equipment)
   - financing (third party reimbursement, public grants, and expenditures for services)
   - regulations (certificate of need and 1122 agreements, manpower and facility licensure, rate and insurance regulation)

Exhibit 6–1 continued

- research (biomedical, behavioral, technological, organizational, and services delivery).

Source: Bureau of Health Planning, Health Resources Administration, U.S. Department of Health, Education, and Welfare, *Program Policy Notice: Guidelines for the Development of Health Systems Plans and Annual Implementation Plans* (Washington, D.C.: BHP, HRA, DHEW, February 23, 1979), pp. 30–31.

cations) that is now required by the federal government for Medicare and Medicaid patients.[39] However, the ICD-9-CM system segments patients in hundreds of categories; some hospitals therefore choose to look at the most common diagnoses.

A number of more complex techniques for clustering patients into groups have been developed. These are often called case-mix techniques, since they attempt to describe the distribution of patients with similar problems within the hospital. The most widely known is the diagnosis related group or DRG technique first developed at Yale for use in utilization review.[40] The DRG technique groups patients according to similarities in length of stay. A number of other techniques have been developed that group patients according to the stage of illness they have reached[41] or the services they require.[42] A review of these techniques has been prepared by the American Hospital Association.[43]

Besides the problem of obtaining the necessary data, the most serious problem a hospital faces is how to avoid becoming hopelessly confused by the mass of numbers that segmentation by need or function can produce. The detailed classifications useful in clinical treatment are too detailed for the initial stages of planning.

One strategy to deal with this problem is to determine whether the hospital has a high or low market share (based on the hospital's mission and goals) for patients in a particular category, and then focus attention on that category to determine whether the hospital might be able to improve (or needs to protect) its market position. Exhibit 6–5 shows a Massachusetts Health Data Consortium report on market share by DRG that could be used to make this determination. The consortium also prepares a report that shows market share by hospital service and patient age (see Chapter 5) and by the clinical subspecialty of the physician (see Chapter 8).

The Social Security Amendments of 1983 provide an additional reason for focusing attention on specific types of patients, since the amendments require that hospitals be reimbursed for Medicare beneficiaries on the basis of a prospectively determined rate of payment per case. A rate is set for patients in each DRG. Hospitals can now lose money by incurring expenses that exceed the prospective rate, and they can make a profit when expenses are less. Hospitals

Exhibit 6–2 Settings in Which Health Services May Be Delivered

- **Community setting:**

  Settings in which community health promotion and health systems enabling services, rather than personal health care services or patient-related support services are provided.

- **Home setting:**

  Providing health care services in the patient's residence with the result that the patient does not travel in order to receive services.

- **Mobile setting:**

  Providing health care services at temporary locations (selected for their convenience to a geographically selected target population) using a movable vehicle or facility, or providing health care services during transportation of patients.

- **Ambulatory setting:**

  Providing health care services to patients who travel to the provider to receive services. An ambulatory setting has no regular provision for patients to stay overnight.

- **Short-stay setting:**

  Providing health care services to patients who stay overnight in the institution, fifty percent or more of whom return to their normal place of residence within less than thirty days of entering the institution.

- **Long-stay setting:**

  Providing health care services to patients who stay overnight in the institution, fifty percent or more of whom remain in the institution thirty days or longer. A long-stay setting may be the usual place of residence of some or all of its patients.

- **Free-standing support setting:**

  A location where health services are provided which support the delivery of personal health care services without providing direct patient care, and which is not a component of an organization which delivers personal health services in another setting. Free-standing support settings include: (1) medical laboratories; (2) dental laboratories; (3) pharmacies; (4) tissue banks; and (5) health information centers.

Source: Bureau of Health Planning, Health Resources Administration, U.S. Department of Health, Education, and Welfare, *Program Policy Notice: Guidelines for the Development of Health Systems Plans and Annual Implementation Plans* (Washington, D.C.: BHP, HRA, DHEW, February 23, 1979), p. 32.

may wish to focus their attention on DRGs with high or low operating margins, and on the most frequent DRGs. These DRGs will suggest the greatest opportunities and threats for a hospital.

Table 6–7, produced using Shared Medical Systems' Command Patient Information Reporting System, shows a hospital's operating margins for two DRGs. This standard report helps the hospital analyze its Case Mix Profile in terms of

Exhibit 6–3 A Matrix for Displaying the Range of Options for Health Service Providers

Service Type	*Settings*						
	Community	*Home*	*Mobile*	*Ambulatory*	*Short-Stay*	*Long-Stay*	*Free-Standing Support*
Community Health Promotion and Protection							
Prevention and Detection							
Diagnosis and Treatment							
Habilitation and Rehabilitation							
Maintenance							
Support							
Enabling							

each DRG (using Medicare's definition of a DRG—"MCARE" in the table). It can be used to point out areas where profitability might be increased, or areas that might be used to offset losses in other necessary areas.

The figures in the upper right indicate the total number of patients included (18,788), their total patient days (143,814), and the total of their charges ($58,774,981). Next appears the estimated reimbursement expected for these patients ($47,465,450), followed by the costs for these patients ($46,766,144). Finally, profit for these patients is projected at $699,306. This represents the difference between costs and estimated reimbursement, a profit margin of 1.47 percent (calculated by dividing profit by estimated reimbursement). In addition, these figures are broken down in terms of average per patient and average per patient day.

For DRG 107, Coronary Bypass, there were 137 patients. Each patient had an average stay of 18.2 days. Patients in this DRG incurred charges of $2,468,324, or 4.2 percent of the $58,774,981 in total charges. The average charges per patient were $18,010. The estimated reimbursement per patient amounts to $14,916. The average costs per patient amounted to $13,653. The average total profit for each patient in DRG 107 amounts to $1,263, yielding a profit margin of 8.47

Exhibit 6–4 Characteristics of the Health System

- **Availability:**

  The supply and types of health services that can be produced given the supply and feasible alternative allocations of resources (personnel, equipment, facilities, and finances) to produce those services.

- **Accessibility:**

  The ability of a population or a segment of a population to obtain available health services. This ability is determined by economic, temporal, locational, architectural, cultural, organizational, and informational factors, which may be barriers or facilitators to obtaining services.

- **Continuity:**

  The extent of effective coordination of services provided to individual patients and the community over time, within and among health care settings.

- **Acceptability:**

  The level of satisfaction expressed by consumers of services and providers of services with the availability, accessibility, cost, quality, continuity, and courtesy and consideration of the health system.

- **Quality:**

  The degree to which services provided are properly matched to the needs of the population, are technically correct, and achieve beneficial impact. Quality can be considered in three dimensions: (1) the structural aspects of resources and services; (2) the process of producing and delivering services; and (3) the outcomes of services on health status, environment, and/or behavior.

- **Cost:**

  All expenses incurred in producing and delivering health services.

Source: Bureau of Health Planning, Health Resources Administration, U.S. Department of Health, Education, and Welfare, *Program Policy Notice: Guidelines for the Development of Health Systems Plans and Annual Implementation Plans* (Washington, D.C.: BHP, HRA, DHEW, February 23, 1979), p. 33.

percent for that DRG. Note that, by comparison, DRG 122 yields an average $520 loss per patient, with a profit (loss) margin of −10.20 percent.

In order to understand why the treatment of some patients is or is not profitable, the resources they consume need to be examined.

Table 6–8, which was also developed using Command, allows one to analyze further the hospital resource consumption of patients in DRG 107, Coronary Bypass, in terms of charges and costs of ancillary and routine services.

The figures in the upper right indicate a total number of patients of 137 (.73 percent of all hospital patients), averaging 18.2 patient days each. Average charges per patient were $18,010, with reimbursement estimated averaging at

Exhibit 6–5 Hospital Market Share Analysis Using DRGs

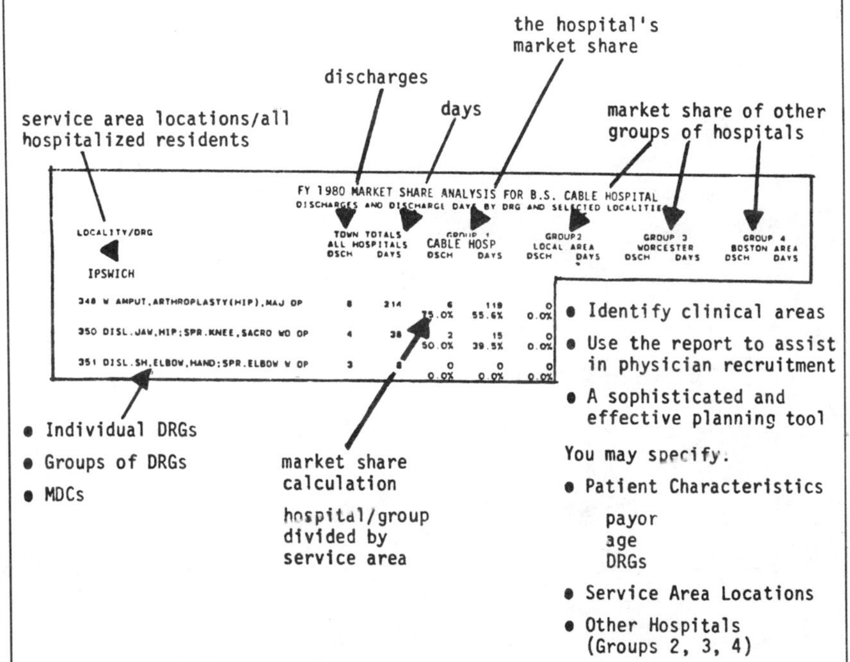

Source: Reprinted with permission of the Massachusetts Health Data Consortium, Inc., 400-1 Totten Pond Road, Waltham, Mass., 02154.

$14,916 per patient, and costs averaging $13,653 per patient. Average per patient profit is $1,263.

The greatest amount of ancillary charges come from Cost Center 13, Respiratory Therapy. For all 137 patients RT charges totalled $453,668, or 18.38 percent of all charges, averaging $3,311 per patient. Costs for these services totalled $190,077, 10.16 percent of all costs, averaging $1,387 per patient.

Note that the report also points out that Operating Room charges for one patient have been lost! Only 136 patients are indicated. The accuracy of this analysis depends on the accuracy and completeness of medical and charge records.

In terms of all routine hospital services, charges amounted to $554,491, or 22.46 percent of all charges. Average charge per patient was $4,047. Cost for these services was $597,510, 31.94 percent of all costs, with average cost per patient amounting to $4,361.

Table 6–7 Case Mix Profile by DRG—Discharges for Jan.–Dec. 1982

	TOTAL	PCT	AVG/PT	AVG/PD
PTS	18,788			
PT DAYS	143,814		7.7	
CHARGES	58,774,981		3,128	409
EST REIMB	47,465,450		2,526	330
COST	46,766,144		2,489	325
PROFIT	699,306	1.47	37	5

DRG	MCARE NO	[<-PATIENTS->] TOTAL	[<--PT DAYS-->] TOTAL AVG/PT	[<--CHARGES-->] TOTAL AVG/PT	PCT	[<--EST REIMB-->] TOTAL AVG/PT	PCT	[<----COST---->] TOTAL AVG/PT	PCT	[<---PROFIT---->] TOTAL AVG/PT	PCT MARGIN
107	CORONARY BYPASS	137	2,496 18.2	2,468,324 18,010	4.20%	2,043,545 14,916	4.30%	1,870,521 13,653	4.00%	173,024 1,263	8.47%
122	CIRCU-LATORY DISORDERS W/AMI	181	2,420 13.3	1,052,957 5,817	1.79%	922,760 5,098	1.94%	1,016,840 5,618	2.17%	-94,080 -520	-10.20%

Source: Produced by SMS's Command Patient Information Reporting System. Reprinted with permission of Shared Medical Systems © 1983.

Table 6–8 Resource Consumption Profile by DRG—Discharges for Jan.–Dec. 1982

DRG MCARE NO: 107

CORONARY BYPASS (W AND W/O CATHETERIZATION)

	TOTAL	PCT	AVG/PT
PTS	137	0.73	
PT DAYS	2,496	1.74	18.2
CHARGES	2,468,324	4.20	18,010
EST REIMB	2,043,545	4.30	14,916
COST	1,870,521	4.00	13,653
PROFIT	173,024	8.47	1,263

		[<--PTS-->]		[<-----CHARGES----->]			[<-------COST------->]		
	COST CENTER	NBR	PCT	TOTAL	PCT	AVG/PT	TOTAL	PCT	AVG/PT
ANCILLARY									
	1 O.R.	136	99.3%	298,363	12.09%	2,194	256,964	13.74%	1,889
	5 ANESTH	137	100.00%	14,254	0.58%	104	6,776	0.36%	49
	6 LAB	137	100.00%	218,276	8.34%	1,593	148,389	7.93%	1,083
	8 XRAY-D	137	100.00%	75,020	3.04%	548	55,205	2.95%	403
	10 DRUGS	137	100.00%	116,438	4.72%	850	87,294	4.67%	637
	13 RESP TH	137	100.00%	453,668	18.38%	3,311	190,077	10.16%	1,387
	21 OR SUP	136	99.3%	394,061	15.96%	2,898	187,290	10.01%	1,377
ROUTINE	ALL	137	100.00%	554,491	22.46%	4,047	597,510	31.94%	4,361

Source: Produced by SMS's Command Patient Information Reporting System. Reprinted with permission of Shared Medical Systems © 1983.

A hospital may also wish to focus on certain consumer needs when consumers and physicians perceive that there is an unmet need that the hospital might serve. This requires a type of market research that is discussed at the end of the chapter.

Segmenting Technology

Finally, we need to segment the available technologies. This requires descriptions of the technologies that the hospital currently uses, the opportunities for changes, and the threats to its current market position.

Since technologies represent alternative ways of addressing patient or physician needs, a hospital should begin with those needs rather than segment technologies on the basis of its current organizational structure or available equipment. Rather than ask what technologies it uses in medical/surgical or pediatric services, for example, the hospital should ask what functions it performs and what services it provides, in what settings, and how it treats particular diagnoses or problems. This will help to avoid the error of assuming that technology consists of major equipment (in our broad definition, chemotherapy is a technology) and that the hospital uses technologies primarily in inpatient services.

A useful way to begin to define technologies is to array the most important services, diagnoses, problems, and procedures in terms of volume and revenue received. The question that can then be posed to the medical staff or an outside consultant is, What alternative technologies now exist, or can be expected in the near future? Changes resulting from serving new populations and demographic and other changes in the hospital's current market should then be considered. What should result is a definition of the range of technologies that the hospital currently uses and the alternatives to those technologies, now and in the future, based in part on the hospital's access to reimbursement for capital and operating expenses.

Three-Dimensional Market Definition

The hospital's market (and the business it is in) should be defined along three dimensions: patient and physician groups, functions and needs served, and technologies utilized. If it neglects to use this three-dimensional definition, the hospital risks missing an opportunity or ignoring a competitive threat, and may fail to provide some needed services in the community.

Using the example of City Hospital discussed earlier, one of that hospital's markets could be described in these three dimensions:

1. Patient group: Medicare beneficiaries from Morris and Jefferson counties
2. Function/need: Cancer therapy
3. Technology: Surgery (including implantation of radioisotopes) and chemotherapy

In light of our discussion of market differentiation in Chapter 2, it appears that City Hospital has a focused market strategy for cancer services, at least in Morris and Jefferson counties. It serves (or focuses on) a single segment of the population (the basis of segmentation being place of residence, payer, and age). Its function in the two counties is primarily to meet the need for treatment in one major diagnostic category, cancer. While it uses more than one technology, it does not offer a major one—radiation therapy.

This situation is not the result of active market planning. It is the unplanned result of actions and circumstances City Hospital may never have considered (e.g., competition with hospitals in Morris and Jefferson counties, and with University Hospital).

City Hospital has not designated an SBU that incorporates its services to cancer patients. Services are provided by several program and functional units: hematology, medical oncology, surgery, gynecologic oncology, pediatric oncology, social services, laboratory, blood bank, physical therapy, and diagnostic radiology. Creation of a cancer treatment center as an SBU, with an administrative staff responsible for planning and coordination, could help to increase the volume and quality of the services being provided, but this also involves determining who will be responsible and accountable for achieving the goals of the center and for determining what markets it should serve.

Figure 6–1 shows the current situation and three options of City Hospital. The hospital could choose to continue its focus on cancer therapy, but broaden its scope of patients, making an effort to attract patients with Blue Cross, commercial insurance, and Medicaid coverage. This is Option 1, in which the three-dimensional figure representing the hospital's current market expands to the right along the axis that represents patient groups (in this instance segmented by payer).

Alternatively, the hospital could broaden the scope of the technologies it uses. This is Option 2, in which the three-dimensional figure representing the hospital's current market expands along the axis that represents the technologies used. Finally, the functions and needs of consumers related to cancer could be expanded (which requires adding some technologies), as shown in Option 3. Or the hospital might combine all three options, changing along all three dimensions: functions/needs, technologies, and patient groups served.

The purpose of this three-dimensional representation is to underscore the necessity for hospitals to be concerned about all three dimensions of the markets it serves, rather than focus on only one. By placing the hospital's current position along a scale that shows alternatives, the things the hospital is not doing (and may not wish to do) are also highlighted.

City Hospital may also improve its position by differentiation, that is, by treating one or more segments of its market differently or by differentiating itself from its competitors in some way. For example, it might offer transfer services to and from local hospitals at a reduced rate to patients (differentiating itself

Figure 6–1 Market Strategies for City Hospital in Morris and Jefferson Counties

A. CURRENT MARKET

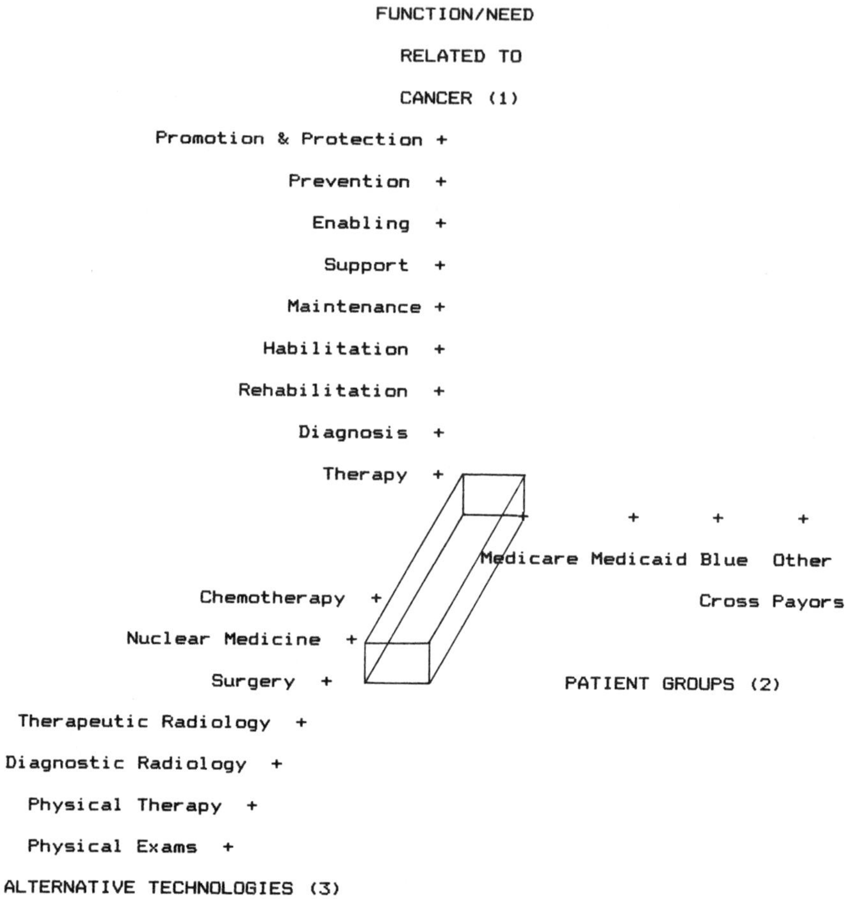

Figure 6–1 continued

B. OPTION 1: BROADEN SCOPE OF PATIENT GROUPS SERVED

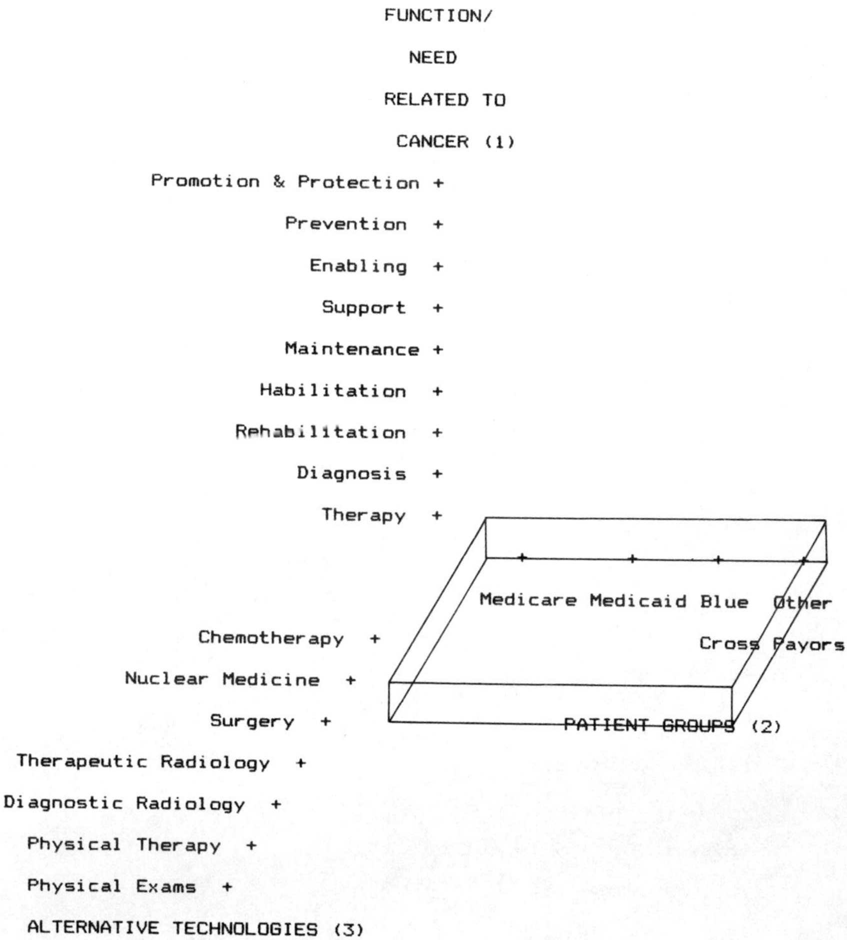

Figure 6–1 continued

B. OPTION 2: BROADEN SCOPE OF TECHNOLOGIES USED

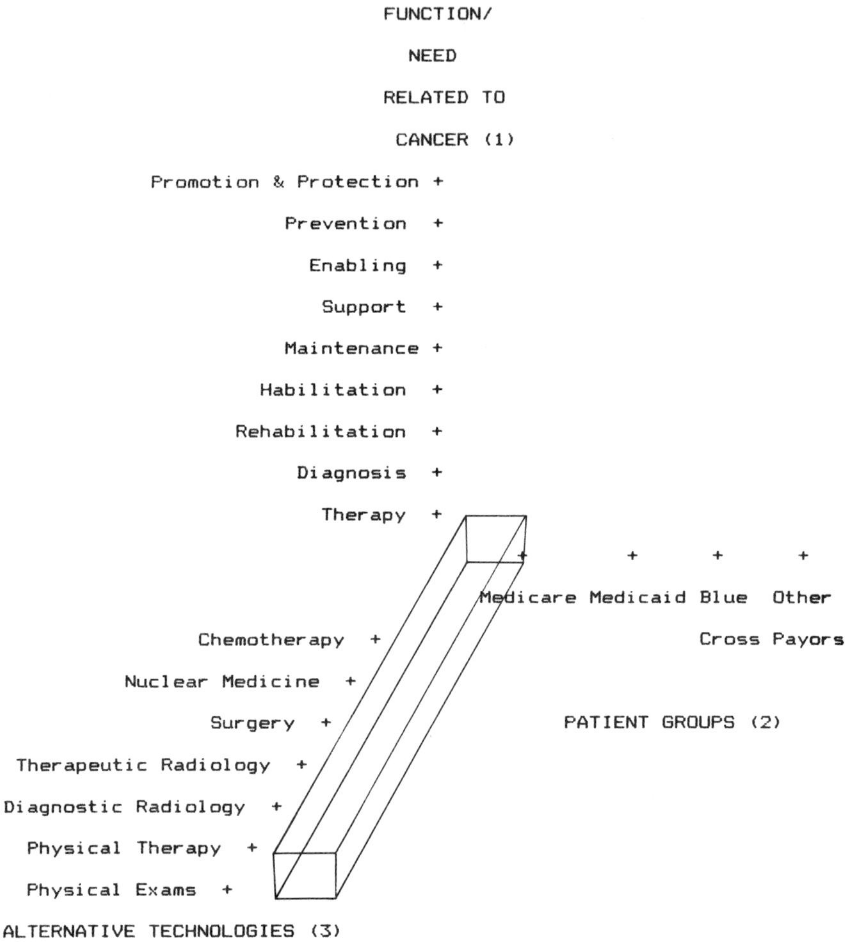

Figure 6–1 continued

C. OPTION 3: BROADEN SCOPE OF FUNCTIONS AND NEEDS SERVED

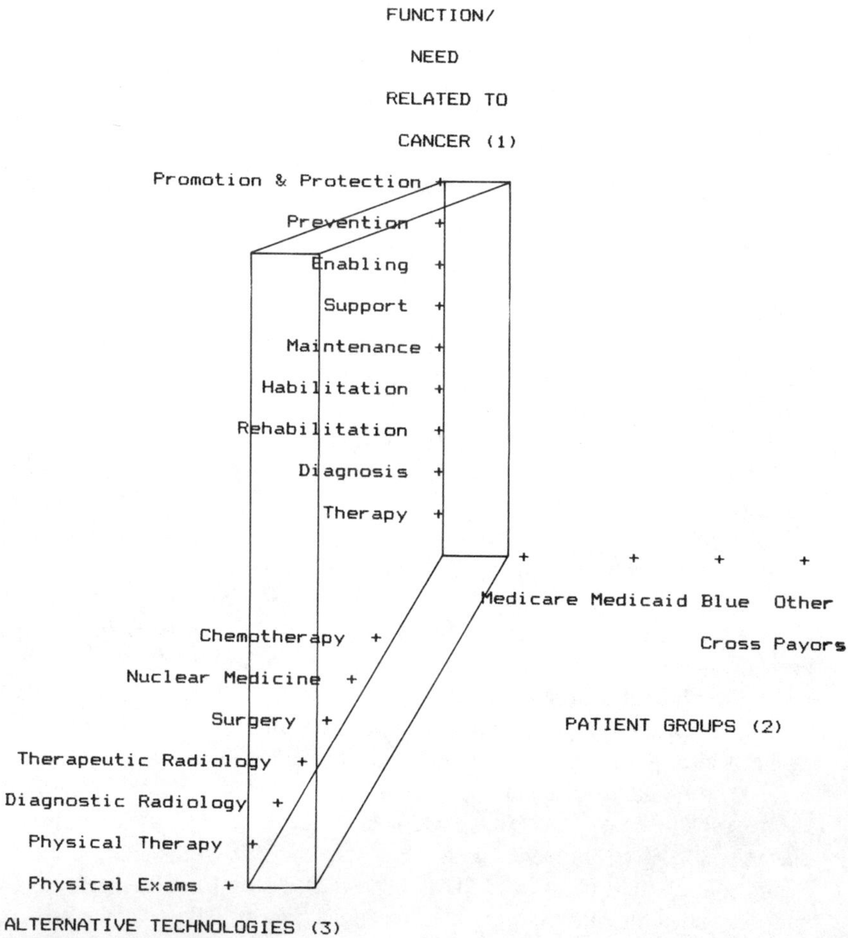

[1]Most services could also be provided in alternative settings. Also, problems other than cancer could be dealt with.

[2]Other bases of segmentation include patient diagnosis, age, and sex.

[3]Each category could also be subdivided according to type of equipment or other resources required.

Source: Adapted from Derek F. Abell, *Defining the Business: The Starting Point of Strategic Planning.* Englewood Cliffs, N.J.: Prentice-Hall, Inc. 1980, Ex. 3-4, p. 31, by permission of the Harvard Business School on behalf of the copyright holder, the President and Fellows of Harvard College.

from University Hospital). Or it might develop a subspecialty in a particular type of cancer (e.g., childhood leukemia), thereby giving differential treatment to a particular segment of patients.

Hospitals can significantly improve the chances of both surviving and achieving their goals if they take the time and effort to define the market they serve and then ask how that market could be redefined for the benefit of the hospital and the community.

Portfolio Analysis

If a hospital is composed of a number of separate businesses, it is appropriate to ask how resources will be divided up among these businesses. To what extent should City Hospital, for example, devote resources to developing services for cancer patients, instead of the growing number of patients with cardiovascular problems?

Some SBUs and programs may be provided with additional resources with which to grow, while others without such additional resources may be able to provide the capital for growth in other units. A hospital may also decide to eliminate a unit and use its resources elsewhere. These decisions are made in a complex environment in which physicians, consumers, the hospital board, administrators, and government regulators each possess some power to influence the decisions. In any case, health needs and the requirements of high quality clinical practice are likely to remain important considerations in many hospitals.

Techniques have been developed that emphasize other factors considered in making investment decisions. These are the techniques of *portfolio analysis,* the term that describes the analytic process used by investors to make decisions about their holdings of stocks, bonds, and other types of investment. With the growth of multiproduct and multifirm corporations, the term has also been applied to the decision-making process used by corporations to determine which businesses and products to retain or invest in.

One such technique has been developed by the Boston Consulting Group. It places emphasis on the demands for cash that result from operating a dynamic organization with a number of SBUs. Those SBUs with a high market growth rate demand more and more cash to fuel that growth. SBUs with a relatively high share of the market generate cash. The Boston Consulting Group (BCG) has identified four types of SBUs in terms that indicate the desirable courses of action for each type. High-growth/high-share SBUs are "stars," since, while they require cash, they also generate it. Low-growth/high-share SBUs are "cash cows," since while they generate cash, they also have low cash requirements; the cash that is produced can be sent elsewhere. Stars are expected to become cash cows and fuel growth for the organization. High-growth/low-share SBUs are "question marks;" they require cash to fuel their growth, but generate less than is needed. Management has to decide which of the question marks will become stars and which will never achieve sufficient market share to assist the organization in meeting its cash needs and growth objectives. Finally, low-growth/low-share SBUs are "dogs;" they may generate enough cash to support themselves, but they are unlikely to provide cash for company growth.[44,45]

While it does focus attention on the need for cash to begin offering new services, use of the BCG growth-share matrix (services are located on a matrix with market share on the rows and growth rate in the columns) as the sole technique for decision making leads to numerous problems. The matrix focuses on current, short-term conditions rather than on future trends. Its underlying theory is based on the "product life-cycle," which assumes that products move along a curve from rapid growth to maturity to decline.[46]

The notion of the "product-life-cycle" is not always appropriate for hospitals. If, for example, we apply that theory to obstetrics, we can see the problems it poses. Because of a downturn in the number of births in the 1970s, obstetrics is often a declining service in hospitals. On the other hand, demographic forecasts show an increase in the near future in the number of births among women who have delayed childbirth until their 30s. Also, there are services in a hospital that cannot be divested because of community needs. Pediatrics could be a low-growth/low-share service, but a hospital might have to retain it because it serves a group of people with few other alternatives.

Another technique that is useful in portfolio analysis is market-attractiveness and business-position assessment.[47,48] Milch and Martinelli have used this technique to assess the position of hospitals in Baltimore, Maryland.[49] While it is useful in examining consumer markets, this technique is presented in Chapter 8, where we focus on the hospital's medical staff.

Market Research

Our focus in this chapter is on the use of routinely collected data for market definition (e.g., data from discharge abstracts). When the necessary data are not routinely collected, market research is needed. Market research is "original, objective, systematized (and usually professionally performed) research."[50] It requires skills in sampling, survey design, and analytical techniques. These skills have been well-defined,[51–53] but many managers have little or no experience in using them.

This does not mean that market research should not be conducted. On the contrary, surveys of consumers and physicians that are properly written, administered, and analyzed offer a number of advantages over routinely collected data from clinical and administrative records. The questions in such surveys can be written to provide the hospital with specific information on perceptions, preferences, potential demand, and actual usage of services.[54] The hospital may be interested in developing health promotion services for local industries at the worksite. In this case, hospital records will suggest what the important health problems are in the community, but they will not identify health behaviors, assess consumer knowledge, or reveal preferences concerning such services or perceptions of the hospital among employees and employers. Special surveys also offer the opportunity to probe into the reasons for responses, and allow people who may not use current services to be included in the research.

However, before becoming involved in market research, we would urge hospitals to examine carefully the data they already have and to make use of data collected by the government and the shared information systems discussed in Chapter 5. The expense of market research has to be weighed against the impact the resulting information is likely to have. This may limit the use of surveys to specific target groups. Their use for the community as a whole may not be feasible because the cost of obtaining a sample of all community residents may be prohibitive. Still, advances in the use of telephone surveys may offer a solution to the problem of high cost. Cooperative arrangements with other hospitals may also be a solution.

In any event, hospitals should review the substantial literature on surveys and market research and contact local experts in universities and industry before becoming involved in costly surveys. Consulting firms also offer surveys, which may appear expensive but may produce more valid information because of the expertise such firms possess.[55]

SERVICE AREA AND MARKET ANALYSIS IN THE STRATEGIC PLANNING PROCESS

Service area and market analysis contributes to performing all of the tasks in the strategic planning process. Table 6–9 shows the types of analysis required for each of the tasks in the strategic planning process.

The hospital must arrive at an assessment of its present position by examining both its current and potential service area and market. It must understand how its position in that potential market has changed over time, and then ask what will happen if it makes no change in what it provides and to whom. This is essential for revising its mission statement and developing goals that will fulfill its mission. The hospital can then move on to develop, evaluate, and set strategies and objectives.

Service areas or markets will always be in a state of change. A hospital should be prepared to deal with the most damaging possible changes by developing contingency plans with defined "trigger points" that will signal the need to act. The hospital can then develop and implement program and operational plans and move toward meeting its objectives and goals. Also, needs and technologies are

Table 6–9 Service Area and Market Analysis in the Strategic Planning Process

Planning Tasks	*Analysis Required*
1. Internal analysis	Identify consumer and physician groups served, services provided, needs met, and technologies used.
2. External analysis	Identify total potential market, served and unserved. Identify potential competitors.
3. Assessment of present position	Determine change over time in the portion of potential market served and the impact of that change on the hospital.
4. Development and evaluation of alternative scenarios	Forecast utilization and financial conditions, assuming no change in markets served, and then assuming decreases or increases in markets served due to competition and other factors.
5. Revision of mission statement and development of goals	Compare current and future markets with those in initial mission statement. Assess impact of market goals.
6. Development and evaluation of alternative strategies	Assess impact of alternative changes in market groups served, functions performed, and technologies used. Estimate use, financial impact, and competitor response.
7. Determination of strategies and objectives	Describe market groups, functions, and technologies over the time frame of the plan.
8. Development of contingency plans	Determine what changes in markets would have the most serious negative consequences. Assess the impact of alternative strategies for limiting their impact. Set "trigger points" for signaling a need to act.
9. Development and implementation of program and operational plans	Specify characteristics of consumer markets to be served.
10. Development of evaluation, monitoring, and control system	Monitor changes in use of services by markets selected. Compare changes with goals in plan. Explain and determine impact of variances.
11. Revision and implementation of contingency plans	Reexamine assumptions about market groups, their needs, and the technologies to be used.

Exhibit 6–6 Market and Service Area Information to Support Selected Strategic Planning Decisions

1. **Task: Internal Analysis**
   - *Decision/question:* Is there a need and/or demand for other services and technologies in the consumer or physician groups we now serve? Should we provide additional services or use other technologies?
   - *Information:*
     a. use of other hospitals or providers for specific services
     b. differences in the technologies used by these alternative providers
     c. strong growth rates for alternative providers
     d. third party payment available for services and technologies not offered by the hospital
     e. lower than expected use rates for specific services
     f. demand for services and technologies revealed in surveys
2. **Task: External Analysis**
   - *Decision/question:* What other providers wish to serve the same needs and demands? What should be our response?
   - *Information on other providers:*
     a. volume of services provided in total market
     b. changes in technology, types of services, and volumes
     c. changes in patient and physician characteristics
     d. market share for consumer and physician groups
     e. market share for new technologies
     f. changes in market share
     g. marketing surveys and research conducted
3. **Task: Assessment of Present Position**
   - *Decision/question:* What has been the rate of change in the hospital's market position? What actions might be taken to change any negative trends?
   - *Information concerning changes over 2–5 years:*
     a. services or technologies that the hospital has not been able to provide but for which there has been a need or demand by consumers or physicians
     b. consumer and physician groups in its market that the hospital has not been able to serve
     c. change in the hospital's growth rate and market share
     d. change in the hospital's relative market share
     e. change in market attractiveness and the hospital's market position
4. **Task: Development and Evaluation of Alternative Scenarios**
   - *Decision/question:* What would be the impact on the hospital's services and financial condition of an attempt by one or more competitors to increase market share for existing hospital services? What should be the hospital's response?
   - *Information:*
     a. consumer and physician groups that competitors wish to attract; needs they wish to serve; technologies they will use
     b. resources in which competitors are likely to invest
     c. hospital dependence on the targeted consumer and physician groups in terms of service volume and revenues
     d. consumer and physician characteristics related to the use of services: needs, perceptions, preferences, satisfaction

Exhibit 6–6 continued

e. estimate of annual market share loss if no change is made; resulting decrease in utilization and revenues

5. **Task: Revision of Mission Statement and Development of Goals**
   - *Decision/question:* What level of performance will be needed in order for the hospital to achieve its mission? How should the mission statement be revised to reflect projected performance?
   - *Information:*
     a. volume of services, consumers and physicians served, and technologies needed to fulfill the hospital's mission statement
     b. if mission is not stated in financial terms, the revenue, expense, and cash flow implications of the market objectives
6. **Task: Development and Evaluation of Alternative Strategies**
   - *Decision/question:* Do the characteristics of the hospital's market suggest that only affiliation with an outside institution will produce the needed changes? Should the hospital establish that affiliation?
   - *Information:*
     a. expected need and demand for services and technologies
     b. resource requirements to meet expected need and demand; an estimate of the impact of scale and experience effects on expenses per unit of service
     c. hospital capability to secure the required resources and to support the services financially
     d. estimate of joint service utilization, costs, and revenues if services are provided with another organization (e.g., hospital, physician group practice)
7. **Task: Setting of Strategies and Objectives**
   - *Decision/question:* What consumers and physicians will the hospital serve? With what services? Using what technologies?
   - *Information:*
     a. annual estimates of groups served, volume and type of services provided, and technologies used to meet goals
     b. estimates of resources required for market changes, and their source
8. **Task: Development of Contingency Plans**
   - *Decision/question:* With regard to the alternative scenarios developed, which of those not assumed in setting strategy could have serious consequences if not dealt with quickly?
   - *Information:*
     a. estimate of impact of alternative market assumptions on goals in the plan
     b. ranking of characteristics of consumers and physicians, technology, and competition in terms of the rapidity of possible changes
     c. ranking of alternative scenarios in order of the seriousness of impact and the rapidity of change

constantly changing in the health care field. Thus, the hospital must develop systems for tracking its progress and reexamining the assumptions it has made about market groups, their needs, and the technologies to be used.

SUPPORT FOR SPECIFIC PLANNING DECISIONS

Each of the tasks in strategic planning involves numerous decisions. Service area and market analysis can provide information that will improve the chances of making the right decisions. Each decision must be based on assumptions concerning the current situation, historic trends, and the future. If information is available that increases the probability that those assumptions are correct, the likelihood of making correct decisions is increased.

For example, a hospital may want to know whether there is a need or demand for additional services in its current market. An affirmative answer could result in a decision to develop a new service. If the hospital obtains information on the use of services in other hospitals by a population group that it considers to be in its own market, the assumptions used in making the decision to offer the services are more likely to be correct. If it has no information on the use of that service, its assumptions (e.g., that there is a need or demand it can meet) are more likely to be wrong.

Exhibit 6–6 lists some of the information we believe is needed to support the decision-making process in strategic planning. Readers are encouraged to add to the list by including other information that their organizations are capable of producing and by extending the table to include other decisions. How much information is produced will depend on the data available, the priority of the decision, the level of understanding of relevant factors, and the degree of risk the decision maker is willing to tolerate.[56]

REFERENCES

1. R.N. Clarke and L. Shyavitz, "Marketing Information and Market Research—Valuable Tools for Managers," *Strategic Planning in Health Care Management,* ed. W.A. Flexner, E.N. Berkowitz, and M. Brown (Rockville, Md.: Aspen Systems Corp., 1981), p. 99.

2. W. Shonick, *Elements of Planning for Area-Wide Personal Health Services* (Saint Louis: C.V. Mosby, 1976), p. 62.

3. For a discussion of this method, see R. Marrinson, "Hospital Service Areas: Time Replaces Space," *Hospitals* 38, no. 2 (January 1964):52–54.

4. For an example of this method, see R. Church and C. ReVelle, "The Maximal Covering Location Problem," Papers of the Regional Science Association, vol. 32 (1974):101–118.

5. G.W. Shannon and G.E.A. Dever, *Health Care Delivery—Spatial Perspectives* (New York: McGraw-Hill, 1974), p. 16.

6. Ibid., p. 21.

7. An example is the Poland-Lembcke method described in Shonick, *Elements,* pp. 65–67.

8. An example can be found in J. Wennberg and A. Gittelsohn, "Small Area Variations in Health Care Delivery," *Science* 182 (December 14, 1973):1102–1108.

9. For an example at the state level, see J.D. Taliaferro and W.W. Remmer, "Identifying Integrated Regions for Health Care Delivery," *Health Service Reports* 88, no. 4 (April 1973):337–343.

10. For an example, see R.L. Morrill and P. Kelley, "Optimum Allocation of Services: A Hospital Example," *Annals of Regional Science* 3 (1969):55–66.

11. C. ReVelle, D. Bigman, D. Shilling, J. Cohon, and R. Church, "Facility Location: A Review of Context-Free and EMS Models," *Health Services Research* 12 (1977):129–145.

12. Government Studies and Systems, *Methods to Determine Geographic/Population Boundaries for Specific Health Services: State-of-the-Art Report* (Washington, D.C.: U.S. Department of Health, Education, and Welfare, Health Resources Administration, Bureau of Health Planning and Resources Development, 1978).

13. J.R. Griffith, *Quantitative Methods for Hospital Planning and Control* (Lexington, Mass.: Lexington Books, 1972), p. 76.

14. Ibid., p. 76.

15. Ibid., p. 77.

16. Commonwealth of Massachusetts, Department of Public Health, Office of State Planning, *1979 State Health Plan* (Boston: Department of Public Health, Office of State Health Planning, 1979), p. 415.

17. This technique is suggested by Griffith, *Quantitative Methods,* p. 73.

18. For a description of the method, see Shonick, *Elements,* pp. 65–67, and Griffith, *Quantitative Methods,* p. 71.

19. Shonick, *Elements,* p. 65.

20. J. Wennberg and A. Gittelsohn, "Small Area Variations in Health Care Delivery," *Science* 182 (December 14, 1973):1103.

21. J. Wennberg and A. Gittelsohn, "Health Care Delivery in Maine I: Patterns of Use of Common Surgical Procedures," *Journal of the Maine Medical Association* 66, no. 5 (May 1975):123.

22. R.L. Morrill, "Locational Efficiency of Chicago Hospitals: An Experimental Model," *Health Services Research* 4, no. 2 (Summer 1969):128–141.

23. D.F. Abell and J.S. Hammond, *Strategic Market Planning* (Englewood Cliffs, N.J.: Prentice-Hall, 1979), p. xi.

24. Ibid., p. 9.

25. P. Kotler, *Marketing Management: Analysis, Planning and Control* (Englewood Cliffs, N.J.: Prentice-Hall, 1980), p. 76.

26. Abell and Hammond, *Strategic Market Planning,* p. 8.

27. D. Abell, *Defining the Business: The Starting Point of Strategic Planning* (Englewood Cliffs, N.J.: Prentice-Hall, 1980), p. 17.

28. Kotler, *Marketing Management,* p. 198.

29. Ibid.

30. Ibid., pp. 201–202.

31. L.A. Aday and R. Eichhorn, *The Utilization of Health Services: Indices and Correlates, A Research Bibliography* (Washington, D.C.: National Center for Health Services Research and Development, 1972).

32. A. Donabedian, *Aspects of Medical Care Administration: Specifying Requirements for Health Care* (Cambridge, Mass.: Harvard University Press, 1973), pp. 77–88, 513–543.

33. R. Andersen, J. Lion, and O.W. Anderson, *Two Decades of Health Services: Social Survey Trends in Use and Expenditure* (Cambridge, Mass.: Ballinger, 1976), pp. 5–64.

34. R. Andersen, *A Behavioral Model of Families' Use of Health Services* (Chicago: University of Chicago, Center for Health Administration Studies, 1968), pp. 14–19. Andersen's model focuses on families' use of health services.

35. U.S. Department of Health, Education, and Welfare, Health Resources Administration, Bureau of Health Planning, *Program Policy Notice: Guidelines for the Development of Health Systems Plans and Annual Implementation Plans* (Washington, D.C.: BHP, HRA, DHEW, February 23, 1979), pp. 30–31.

36. Ibid., p. 32.

37. Ibid., p. 33.

38. L.L. Weed, *Medical Records, Medical Education and Patient Care* (Cleveland: Case Western Reserve University Press, 1969), p. 25.

39. Health Care Financing Administration, *International Classification of Diseases,* 9th ed. *Clinical Modifications,* vols. 1–3 (Washington, D.C.: Government Printing Office, 1981).

40. J. Thompson, R. Fetter, and C. Mross, "Case Mix and Resource Use," *Inquiry* 12 (December 1975):300–312.

41. M.L. Garg et al., "Evaluating Patient Costs: The Staging Mechanism," *Medical Care* 16 (1978):191.

42. W.W. Young, R.B. Swinkola, and D.M. Zorn, "The Measurement of Hospital Case Mix," *Medical Care* 20, no. 5 (May 1982):501.

43. M.P. Plomann, *Case Mix Classification Systems: Development, Description and Testing* (Chicago: American Hospital Association, 1982).

44. Kotler, *Marketing Management,* pp. 76–78.

45. B. Henderson, *The Experience Curve Reviewed: IV. The Growth Share Matrix of the Product Portfolio,* Perspectives no. 135. (Boston: Boston Consulting Group, 1973).

46. Abell and Hammond, *Strategic Market Planning,* p. 60.

47. Ibid., pp. 211–227.

48. Kotler, *Marketing Management,* pp. 78–79.

49. R. Milch and P. Martinelli, "Community Health Markets: A Portfolio Perspective," *Health Care Management Review* (Fall 1978).

50. Clarke and Shyavitz, *Marketing Information,* p. 99.

51. T.C. Kinnear and J.R. Taylor, *Marketing Research: An Applied Approach* (New York: McGraw-Hill, 1979).

52. P. Green and D.S. Tull, *Research For Marketing Decisions* (Englewood Cliffs, N.J.: Prentice-Hall, 1975).

53. W.A. Flexner, C.P. McLaughlin, and J.E. Littlefield, "Discovering What The Consumer Really Wants," in *Health Care Marketing: Issues and Trends,* ed. P.D. Cooper (Rockville, Md.: Aspen Systems Corp., 1979), pp. 219–228.

54. Clarke and Shyavitz, *Marketing Information,* p. 104.

55. For example, Messner Healthcare Marketing in Grand Rapids, Michigan, will supply a hospital with patient questionnaires, tabulate the results by computer, and provide reports to management.

56. H. Raiffa, *Decision Analysis: Introductory Lectures on Choices Under Uncertainty* (Reading, Mass.: Addison-Wesley, 1970), p. 8.

Chapter 7

Case Studies of Service Area and Market Analysis

INTRODUCTION

In this chapter, we offer three case studies of how information can be used to assist managers in making decisions in the strategic planning process and how analytical techniques can be used to produce that information. These case studies demonstrate that data analysis does not always lead to clear-cut answers. The analysis usually assists or supports decision makers instead of replacing their judgment and experience.

In the first case study, the hospital's management and board begin a strategic planning process. Staff are instructed to gather and manipulate mostly internal data. Data are retrieved from a number of separate computer and manual files. Many of the tables are prepared by hand.

The analysis in this case focuses on the population now being served by the hospital, that population's needs, the services being provided, and the technologies being used. The hospital begins by defining its market share in various geographic areas, then segments the population it now serves by age, sex, and need (defined by patient diagnosis). After looking at data on population trends in the area it serves and the limited data on the services provided by other hospitals, decisions are made on which services to add over the next five years. This first case study demonstrates that hospitals can begin to use the concepts described in Chapter 6 to examine their service areas and markets without making a large investment in computer technology.

In the second case study, a hospital consulting firm makes use of a computer-based model to provide a hospital with a utilization forecast. The consultants and hospital decision makers are required to make a series of assumptions about the hospital and the population it serves. If those assumptions are changed, the forecasting model quickly recalculates a new forecast. The output of the analysis in this case study is more precise than that in the first case study, but it is no less dependent on the judgment and experience of the users. This case demonstrates how computers can be used in the analysis of service areas and markets, (a subject discussed more fully in Chapter 11).

In the third case study, an integrated set of computer programs widely available in university computer centers is used to analyze a statewide data base of hospital discharge abstracts in an attempt to identify the factors that determine the use of a hospital service—the coronary care unit or CCU. The focus is on the characteristics of hospitals and the communities they serve that might affect utilization.

Rather than assume that the consumer characteristics listed in Table 6–5 are the most important, hospitals with access to the necessary data (through the shared information systems described in Chapter 5) can begin to examine the specific communities and populations they serve. The results can be used in segmenting consumers and defining markets, as well as in developing strategies to increase the use of the hospital's services. A hospital cannot begin to develop this type of information unless a shared information system has already been developed—a resource that was not available in the first case study.

None of the three case studies is an ideal illustration of the concepts and techniques described in Chapter 6. However, rather than formulate one or more ideal cases, we have chosen to describe in these cases three analyses that have actually been carried out to support decision making by hospitals (and, in the last case study, by state regulators and planners). The three studies demonstrate that hospitals can start immediately to improve the way they make decisions, though how much analysis they can do will depend on the data and computer resources available.

URBAN HOSPITAL

Urban Hospital is a not-for-profit 370-bed community hospital located in a medium-sized metropolitan area. (The hospital name has been changed and its identity concealed at its request.) It is located in the central city of that metropolitan area, which, like many in the eastern United States, has seen significant changes occur in the racial, income, and age composition of its population. As part of its strategic planning process, Urban Hospital undertook an assessment of its current position by conducting an internal and external analysis. We present here those parts of that analysis that focused on the hospital's service area and market.

Utilization of Hospital Services

Table 7–1 shows the changes that occurred in the use of Urban Hospital beds between 1974 and 1978. The total number of staffed beds increased by 11 during

Table 7–1 Urban Hospital: Patient Day Summary, 1974–1978

	1974	*1975*	*1976*	*1977*	*1978*
Adult med-surgical:					
Patient days	75,420	79,206	80,423	78,237	73,174
Staffed beds	252	268	264	264	253
Unit occupancy	82.0%	81.0%	83.2%	81.2%	79.2%
Daycare:					
Patient days	3,053	3,571	3,887	4,121	4,314
Staffed beds	10	10	14	14	14
Unit occupancy	84.0%	98.0%	75.7%	80.7%	84.2%
Pediatrics:					
Patient days	5,559	5,256	5,080	4,580	4,679
Staffed beds	27	27	25	25	25
Unit occupancy	56.7%	53.3%	55.6%	50.0%	51.2%
Psychiatric:					
Patient days	267	2,812	5,480	6,639	9,270
Staffed beds	12	12	19	19	30
Unit occupancy	42.5%	64.2%	78.9%	95.8%	84.7%
OBS:					
Patient days	5,395	5,860	5,645	6,026	6,966
Staffed beds	20	20	20	20	20
Unit occupancy	74.0%	80.5%	77.0%	82.5%	95.5%
Nursery:					
Patient days	5,455	6,347	6,188	7,251	7,530
Staffed beds	38	38	28	28	28
Unit occupancy	39.5%	45.5%	60.4%	71.1%	73.6%
Total:					
Patient days	95,149	103,052	106,703	106,854	105,933
Staffed beds	359	375	370	370	370
Unit occupancy	72.6%	75.3%	78.5%	79.1%	78.4%

Source: Confidential communication with the hospital.

this period, and the mix of beds also changed. The hospital added 4 ambulatory surgery (or "daycare") beds and 18 psychiatric beds. It reduced the number of staffed nursery beds by 10 and the number of pediatric beds by 2. During the period, the number of adult medical surgical beds rose by 16 to 268, only to drop again to 253 by 1978.

The hospital attributed its improvement in total patient days and occupancy during the 1974–1978 period partly to "fine-tuning" staffed beds to patient demand. For example, the staffed bed complement in pediatrics was reduced from 25 in 1978 to 20 in 1979 because of low utilization. The five beds were allocated to the CAPS unit (child adolescent psychiatric service), which had previously been utilized at 98 percent.

Table 7–2 shows the changes in the volume of special services that occurred during the 1974–1978 period. Clinic visits and visits by privately referred patients more than doubled. There was also substantial growth in the lab and for most diagnostic and therapeutic procedures. Operating room use showed a more modest increase.

The hospital saw itself as an efficient provider that had been able to increase its utilization. It decided, however, to take a look at the population it was serving to determine whether any changes would occur that would affect its future.

Population Served

Table 7–3 shows the changes between 1974 and 1978 in Urban Hospital's market share in cities and towns that provided 83 percent of the hospital's admissions in 1978. Urban Hospital gained market share in each city and town (with the exception of Town 14) and captured a greater share of a slightly increasing number of admissions. The total number of admissions in these cities and towns increased from 78,886 in 1974 to 81,549 in 1978, or by 3.4 percent.

An important question was whether Urban Hospital would have to rely on increases in market share for growth, or whether increases in population would suffice. Table 7–4 shows the projected increase from 1980 to 1985 in the population of the cities and towns in the HSA region it serves and the resulting increase in service area population. The hospital receives 90 percent of its patients from this region. Service area population is calculated by multiplying the hospital's 1978 market share (or index of relevance) by the projected population. If Urban Hospital's market share remains constant, the population it serves will increase by only 2,473 people, or 2.1 percent, by 1985.

It is possible that the rate of utilization will increase as well. The age and sex distribution of the population are both related to the use of hospital services. Table 7–5 shows the projected age and sex distribution of the total area population. Since the hospital does not have its market share for each age and sex group, it cannot calculate the age and sex distribution of its service area population. However, Table 7–5 does indicate the general trend in the region. Increases in population age groups 0–4, 25–49, and 60+ are expected between 1980 and 1985. Since hospital utilization is considerably higher for the 60+ population, Urban Hospital may see increasing utilization if its patient population becomes older. The increase in the 0–4 age group suggests that an increase in the use of obstetrical services will occur. Reductions in age groups 5–24 and 50–59 will counterbalance these increases.

An increase in the over-65 population is likely to increase Urban Hospital's dependence on government programs. Table 7–6 shows the change in the distribution of patients by financial status between 1975 and 1979. While the hospital's dependence on Medicare patients did not substantially increase in that

Table 7–2 Urban Hospital: Statistical Summary, 1974–1978

	Statistic	FY 74	FY 75	FY 76	FY 77	FY 78	FY 74-FY 78 Increase (Decrease)	FY 74-FY 78 % Change
Special Services								
Operating room	No. of operations	7,682	8,525	8,707	8,556	8,579	897	11.7%
Laboratory	No. of tests	427,712	650,345	740,335	789,520	881,305	453,593	106.1%
Radiology	No. of exams	45,383	54,962	61,754	62,443	62,441	17,058	37.6%
Nuclear medicine	No. of exams	3,610	3,935	4,751	5,307	5,274	1,664	46.1%
Rehabilitative med.	No. of modalities	—	18,864	20,887	26,065	30,824	11,960	63.4%
EKG	No. of exams	14,506	16,714	18,034	17,020	21,558	7,052	48.6%
Cardiac catheterization lab	No. of procedures	—	—	—	248	383	135	54.4%[b]
Inhalation therapy	No. of treatments	44,766[a]	40,501[a]	201,392	270,319	299,242	97,850	48.6%[b]
Pulmonary lab	No. of tests	4,372	6,221	13,950	21,741	22,267	17,895	409.3%
IV therapy	No. of units	194,990	195,155	221,058	222,001	223,182	28,192	14.5%
Outpatient Services								
Emergency room	Visits	32,118	40,467	44,321	46,858	49,996	17,878	55.7%
Clinics	Visits	9,849	20,426	20,125	19,997	20,532	10,683	108.5%
Private referred	Visits	8,020	12,888	13,177	13,725	18,071	10,051	125.3%
Other Statistics								
Births	—	1,161	1,376	1,397	1,529	1,740	579	49.9%
Deaths	—	255	253	264	254	245	(10)	(3.9%)

[a]Not comparable to FY 76–78.
[b]Incomplete trend

Source: Confidential communication with the hospital.

Table 7–3 Urban Hospital: Market Share Index Change, 1974–1978, for Selected Towns in HSA Region

Town	*Market Share % 1978*	*Market Share % 1974*	*% Increase (Decrease) in Market Share 1974–1978*
1	31.32	24.57	6.75
2	9.86	8.40	1.82
3	29.68	19.68	10.00
4	6.82	4.47	2.35
5	31.22	22.74	8.48
6	7.08	5.11	1.97
7	27.46	23.29	4.17
8	20.56	10.43	10.13
9	45.10	39.16	5.94
10	9.55	6.91	2.64
11	12.89	10.78	2.11
12	11.05	9.43	1.62
13	16.11	13.85	2.26
14	18.63	18.70	(.07)
15	4.22	1.96	2.26
16	7.64	6.37	1.27
17	8.38	5.16	3.22
18	17.97	16.54	1.43

Source: Confidential communication with the hospital.

period, government sources were responsible for paying the bills of 46.1 percent of the hospital's patients in 1979. Because of its inner-city location, the hospital serves a large number of patients who are recipients of Medicaid and city welfare. Cutbacks in funding for these programs could increase the hospital's bad debts and charity care and/or force the hospital to refer these patients to other institutions. Yet, in the past, the higher utilization of services by the poor may have assisted the hospital to maintain adequate occupancy rates.

Case Mix

In order to identify trends in the needs it serves, Urban Hospital divided its patients into major diagnostic groups for two years, 1973 and 1978. Tables 7–7 and 7–8 show the number of patients and patient days in each diagnostic group for those two years. Table 7–9 shows the diagnostic groups ranked in descending order according to their contribution to the hospital's total number of patient days.

Table 7–4 Urban Hospital: Projected Population in Service Area and HSA Region, 1980–1985

Town	*Projected 1980 Population*	*Projected 1980 Service Area*	*Projected 1985 Population*	*Projected 1985 Service Area*	*Population Increase (Decrease)*	*Service Area Increase (Decrease)*
1	146,833	45,988	147,490	46,194	657	206
13	67,466	10,484	67,384	10,472	(82)	(12)
9	20,659	9,318	21,493	9,694	834	376
11	54,778	7,061	55,362	7,137	584	76
3	24,892	7,388	25,979	7,711	1,087	323
12	45,617	5,041	47,757	5,278	2,140	237
5	14,592	4,556	14,819	4,627	227	71
6	27,756	1,963	28,030	1,982	274	19
20	79,705	1,523	79,798	1,525	93	2
14	9,268	1,729	9,616	1,792	348	63
21	28,360	1,685	28,894	1,717	534	32
2	16,615	1,639	17,543	1,730	928	91
10	22,302	2,130	22,702	2,169	400	39
22	29,044	1,331	29,748	1,363	704	32
4	25,554	1,743	27,550	1,879	1,996	136
18	7,497	1,348	8,264	1,486	767	138
23	55,560	745	57,070	765	1,510	20
8	10,407	2,140	10,669	2,194	262	54
16	13,671	1,045	14,214	1,086	543	41
7	4,430	1,217	4,634	1,273	204	56
24	36,757	603	37,647	618	890	15
17	10,549	884	11,457	961	908	77
25	16,808	809	17,098	823	290	14
26	1,531	216	1,574	222	43	6
27	9,483	403	10,130	430	647	27
28	5,551	179	6,263	202	712	23
29	17,025	275	17,521	283	496	8
30	2,365	58	2,564	63	199	5
31	15,659	257	16,059	264	400	7
15/19	52,453	2,188	53,402	2,227	949	39
32	5,339	243	5,648	257	309	14
33	7,837	508	8,166	529	329	21
34	4,427	390	4,937	435	510	45
35	11,270	239	11,617	247	347	8
36	7,735	509	8,088	533	353	24
37	10,251	294	10,842	311	591	17
38	10,162	521	11,255	577	1,093	56
Total	930,208	118,650	953,284	121,056		2,406

Source: Confidential communication with the hospital.

Table 7–5 Projected Population by Age Group, 1975–1985, in Urban Hospital's HSA Region

Age	*1975*			*1980*			*1985*		
	Male	*Female*	*Total*	*Male*	*Female*	*Total*	*Male*	*Female*	*Total*
Total (all)	442,981	467,651	910,632	454,141	476,067	930,208	466,241	487,043	953,284
0–4	32,639	31,308	63,947	28,682	27,416	56,098	33,646	32,099	65,745
5–9	38,302	37,579	75,881	32,837	31,456	64,293	28,934	27,704	56,638
10–14	44,395	43,091	87,486	38,422	37,723	76,145	33,087	31,794	64,881
15–19	44,848	44,163	89,011	43,788	42,817	86,605	38,236	37,783	76,019
20–24	37,084	37,598	74,682	44,182	44,004	88,186	43,513	42,747	86,260
25–29	30,449	36,104	66,553	38,155	37,804	75,959	44,544	44,101	88,645
30–34	31,894	31,040	62,934	31,980	36,412	68,392	38,662	38,054	76,716
35–39	25,426	25,559	50,985	32,058	31,262	63,320	32,071	36,644	68,715
40–44	23,972	25,707	49,679	25,212	25,595	50,807	31,778	31,238	63,016
45–49	26,610	28,338	54,948	23,746	25,709	49,455	24,680	25,345	50,025
50–54	26,655	29,003	55,658	25,471	27,853	53,324	22,558	25,131	47,689
55–59	23,346	25,282	48,628	24,414	27,665	52,079	23,472	26,669	50,141
60–64	20,023	21,394	41,417	21,673	24,283	45,956	22,522	26,379	48,901
65–69	15,483	18,285	33,768	18,220	20,348	38,568	19,353	22,665	42,018
70–75	9,953	13,801	23,754	12,948	16,168	29,116	15,198	17,880	33,078
75+	11,902	19,399	31,301	12,353	19,552	31,905	13,987	20,810	34,797

Source: Confidential communication with the hospital.

Table 7–6 Urban Hospital: Percentage of Occupancy by Financial Status, Fiscal Years 1975–1979

	FY 1975	*FY 1976*	*FY 1977*	*FY 1978*	*FY 1979*	*1975–1979 % Increase (Decrease)*
Blue Cross	29.2%	27.6%	26.0%	24.6%	23.2%	(6.0%)
Commercial	19.8	20.7	20.5	22.0	23.0	3.2
Subtotal	49.0	48.3	46.5	46.6	46.2	(2.8)
Medicare	25.5	26.7	27.2	26.3	25.9	.4
Medicaid/city welfare	18.9	18.7	18.6	19.5	20.2	1.3
Subtotal	44.4	45.4	45.8	45.8	46.1	1.7
Self-pay	5.4	5.0	5.4	5.8	6.0	.6
Other	1.2	1.3	2.3	1.8	1.7	.5

Source: Confidential communication with the hospital.

The hospital noted that its dependence on obstetrics and gynecology, newborn, female genital, normal delivery, and complicated OB accounted for 18.87 percent of total patient days in 1973 and 19.07 percent in 1978. Table 7–5 shows that the number of females 15–44 is expected to increase by 5.8 percent between 1980 and 1985 in the hospital's region, while the total population grows by 2.5 percent. The hospital allowed newborn, normal delivery, and complicated OB to rise from 12.6 to 15.2 percent of its total patient days between 1973 and 1978. While the increase in the female population of child-bearing age does not suggest that a downturn in births will occur, the hospital needs to examine the population it now actually serves, rather than the regional population. Continuing growth may require the hospital to attract a different population (e.g., in terms of residence, income, etc.). Cutbacks in Medicaid and city welfare may leave the hospital vulnerable, and other sources of income may be needed to fund the services that the hospital is now providing to the low-income population adjacent to the hospital.

Mental diagnoses rose from 1.68 percent of patient days in 1973 to 9.56 percent of patient days in 1978. They contributed the highest proportion of patient days of any diagnostic group in 1978. Table 7–10 shows that length of stay for mental disorders increased by 235 percent to an average of 22.33 days between 1973 and 1978. During this period, the hospital developed an acute psychiatric unit for adults and a separate, longer-term unit for children and adolescents. Patients in all other diagnostic categories showed a decrease in length of stay. Table 7–11 shows, however, that Urban Hospital's adult and child psychiatry patients have significantly different average lengths of stay (9.2 days and 61.0

Table 7–7 Urban Hospital: Diagnostic Group Analysis, FY 1973

Diagnostic Group	*Patients*	*% Patients*	*Patient Days*	*% Patient Days*
Infective	242	1.65	1607.2	1.78
Malignant neoplasm	853	5.82	7536.1	8.37
Mental	227	1.55	1513.1	1.68
Diabetes	199	1.36	2368.1	2.63
Hypertension	158	1.08	1189.2	1.32
Acute/Other heart	669	4.56	9370.1	10.41
Cerebro/Other vascular	459	3.13	5728.3	6.36
Pneumonia & Bronchitis	253	1.73	2511.2	2.79
Hypertrophy of T & A	509	3.47	1272.5	1.41
Other respiratory	336	2.29	2118.8	2.35
Hernia	347	2.37	2413.9	2.68
GI	445	3.04	4728.6	5.25
Genitourinary	585	3.99	3984.9	4.43
Female genital	1,185	8.08	5644.5	6.27
Normal delivery	868	5.92	3390.0	3.76
Complicated OB	452	3.08	2172.6	2.41
Skin	225	1.53	1638.8	1.82
Musculoskeletal	410	2.80	3935.8	4.37
Fractures/Trauma	537	3.66	4431.9	4.92
Newborn	1,170	7.98	5791.3	6.43
Other	4,531	30.91	16,696.0	18.54
Total patients	14,660			
Total patient days	90,043			

Source: Confidential communication with the hospital.

days, respectively, in 1978). Blue Cross and commercial insurance coverage for psychiatric care is frequently limited. Again, in order to pay for such long stays, the hospital must be relying on government insurance or self-pay patients (whose income would be considerably higher than that of the population adjacent to the hospital).

Table 7–5 shows that the population age group 5–19 in the hospital's region is expected to decrease by 29,505 or 15.9 percent between 1980 and 1985. However, the use of psychiatric services is far more sensitive to sources of payment, supply of services, and attitudes concerning its usefulness and acceptability than are other health services, so that population size is not the most critical factor.

The hospital's increasing dependence on child psychiatry offers both threats and opportunities that need to be closely examined. The hospital may be meeting

Table 7–8 Urban Hospital: Diagnostic Group Analysis, FY 1978

Diagnostic Group	*Patients*	*% Patients*	*Patient Days*	*% Patient Days*
Infective	305	1.57	1609.6	1.55
Malignant neoplasm	1,042	5.37	8931.6	8.61
Mental	444	2.29	9913.2	9.56
Diabetes	225	1.16	2204.6	2.13
Acute/Other heart	754	3.89	7454.5	7.19
Cerebro/Other vascular	515	2.65	5793.3	5.59
Pneumonia & Bronchitis	432	2.23	2878.0	2.77
Other respiratory	374	1.93	2051.4	1.98
Hernia	312	1.61	1919.0	1.85
GI	623	3.21	6346.5	6.12
Genitourinary	589	3.04	3787.7	3.65
Female genital	1,179	6.08	4047.8	3.90
Normal delivery	1,137	5.86	3910.8	3.77
Complicated OB	930	4.79	4277.5	4.12
Musculoskeletal	628	3.24	4147.0	4.00
Fractures/Trauma	704	4.04	6211.6	5.99
Newborn	1,760	9.07	7554.8	7.28
Other	7,368	37.98	20,680.0	19.94
Total patients	19,401			
Total patient days	103,719			

Source: Confidential communication with the hospital.

the needs of a previously unserved population at a time when the demand for other services is falling. There are fewer norms that can be used to regulate the provision and cost of psychiatric care, thus permitting the hospital to set charges more freely; it may face less competition. However, Table 7–12 shows that the two hospitals that are viewed as the most important competitors both offer inpatient psychiatric services.

Table 7–9 shows that heart conditions decreased significantly, from 10.41 to 7.19 as a percentage of total patient days, between 1973 and 1978. While the number of patients increased by 85, average length of stay decreased by 4.15 days (Table 7–10). The result was a drop of 1,916 patient days.

This may be the result of not using an available technology. As Table 7–12 shows, Urban Hospital, unlike its two competitors, does not perform open heart surgery. Thus, the drop in length of stay may be due to the loss of the most seriously ill patients to other hospitals. It also may be due to changing attitudes in its medical staff concerning the required hospital stay following a heart attack. While there may not be a need for a third open heart unit in the area, Urban

Table 7–9 Urban Hospital: Case-Mix Composition, Groups by Relative Rank, 1973 and 1978

Rank	*Diagnostic Group*	*1973 % Pt. Days*	*Rank*	*Diagnostic Group*	*1978 % Pt. Days*
1	Acute/Other heart	10.41	1	Mental	9.56
2	Malignant neoplasms	8.37	2	Malignant neoplasm	8.61
3	Newborn	6.43	3	Newborn	7.28
4	Cerebro/Other vascular	6.36	4	Acute/Other heart	7.19
5	Female genital	6.27	5	Gastrointestinal	6.12
6	Gastrointestinal	5.25	6	Fractures/Trauma	5.99
7	Fractures/Trauma	4.92	7	Cerebro/Other vascular	5.59
8	Genitourinary	4.43	8	Complicated OB	4.12
9	Musculoskeletal	4.37	9	Musculoskeletal	4.00
10	Normal delivery	3.76	10	Female genital	3.90
11	Pneumonia & Bronchitis	2.79	11	Normal delivery	3.77
12	Hernia	2.68	12	Genitourinary	3.65
13	Diabetes	2.63	13	Pneumonia & Bronchitis	2.77
14	Complicated OB	2.41	14	Diabetes	2.13
15	Other respiratory	2.35	15	Other respiratory	1.98
	Total	73.43		Total	76.66

Source: Confidential communication with the hospital.

Hospital's inability to utilize this technology will affect its ability to capture the increase in demand for services that results from the aging of the population in its region.

Table 7–12 raises some questions about alternative services to be considered in light of what we know about the hospital's population. None of the three hospitals in the area operates a long-term care unit. None of them operates inpatient or outpatient alcoholism or drug units. Inadequate sources of reimbursement and competition from other providers may make the development of these services impractical, but the development of them would be consistent with demographic trends and the hospital's current position as an inner-city hospital.

Urban Hospital needs to consider expanding the needs it meets to include long-term care for the elderly and treatment of alcohol and drug problems. This would involve a change in the consumer groups it serves. Changes in technology are not a major concern in either of these two areas.

Table 7–10 Urban Hospital: Average Length of Stay (ALOS) by Diagnostic Group, 1973 and 1978

Diagnostic Group	*ALOS 1973*	*ALOS 1978*	*Increase (Decrease)*	*% Change*
Infective	6.64	5.28	(1.36)	−20.5
Malignant neoplasm	8.84	8.57	(.27)	−3.1
Mental	6.67	22.33	15.66	+234.8
Diabetes	11.90	9.80	(2.10)	−17.6
Acute/Other heart	14.01	9.89	(4.12)	−29.4
Cerebro/Other vascular	12.48	11.25	(1.23)	−9.9
Pneumonia & Bronchitis	9.93	6.67	(3.26)	−32.8
Other respiratory	6.31	5.48	(.83)	−13.2
Hernia	6.96	6.15	(.81)	−11.6
GI	10.63	10.19	(.44)	−4.1
Genitourinary	6.81	6.43	(.38)	−5.6
Female genital	4.76	3.43	(1.33)	−27.9
Normal delivery	3.91	3.44	(.47)	−12.0
Complicated OB	4.81	4.60	(.21)	−4.4
Musculoskeletal	9.60	6.60	(3.00)	−31.3
Fractures/Trauma	8.25	7.92	(.33)	−4.0
Newborn	4.95	4.29	(.66)	−13.3

Source: Confidential communication with the hospital.

The Hospital's Own Assessment

Urban Hospital's long-range plan also included an assessment of its medical staff and financial condition. In its long-range plan, the hospital set the objectives for each of its departments, as shown in Table 7–13.

The hospital's decision makers decided to respond to the assessment of its current position in a number of ways. They chose to broaden the scope of the consumer needs the hospital can meet by adding services, particularly those related to cardiac and psychiatric problems. This will involve a change in technologies (e.g., cardiac catheterization). While many services will be available to the entire population, the hospital has a more focused strategy for others. New psychiatric services will be developed for children, and geriatric evaluative and outreach services will also be developed. The purpose of this market differentiation is to increase the use of its services by tailoring them to meet the needs of these particular consumer groups. The hospital will also be able to differentiate itself from competitors, none of whom currently offers these services.

Table 7–11 Urban Hospital: Average Length of Stay by Unit, 1974–1978

Unit	*1974*	*1975*	*1976*	*1977*	*1978*	*1974–1978 % Increase (Decrease)*	*1974–1978 % Increase (Decrease)*
Adult med-surg.	7.9	7.6	7.5	7.5	6.5	(1.4)	(17.72)
Daycare surgery	1.0	1.0	1.0	1.0	1.0	0.0	0.0
Pediatrics	3.9	3.8	3.9	3.9	4.9	1.0	25.64
Psychiatric	38.1[a]	42.6[a]	49.6[a]	57.7[a]	9.2[b]	0.0	Inc.
CAPS	—	—	—	—	61.0[c]	0.0	Inc.
Obstetrics	3.9	3.8	3.6	3.7	4.5	0.6	15.38
Nursery	4.7	4.7	4.3	4.7	4.7	0.0	0.0

[a]Combined adult/child adolescent psychiatry
[b]Adult psychiatry only
[c]Child psychiatry only
— = Not available
Inc. = Incomplete trend

Source: Confidential communication with the hospital.

Conclusion

Much more information about Urban Hospital's service area and market would have been desirable, and indeed may have been available to the hospital as it wrote its plan. This case study illustrates the position most hospitals are in. They have a limited amount of information that they must examine in the context of the desires of important groups in and outside of the organization. The Table 7–13 list of services was not generated automatically by a computer model. The information we have provided adds support for moving in several directions—particularly, toward services for the elderly and maternity services. It also suggests that the hospital cannot rely just on population growth, but must rather be creative in finding needs to meet, populations to serve, and technologies to utilize.

By first defining its markets, Urban Hospital can begin to understand where it is going. By analyzing the external environment—particularly trends in the population (both served and unserved)—it can begin to see what its markets should be. This leads to the development of specific plans to make changes in technologies used, needs met, and market groups served that will allow the Hospital to survive in the coming turbulent times.

Table 7–12 Urban Hospital: Services Available in Area Hospitals, 1979

Unit/Service	*Urban Hospital*	*Memorial Hospital*	*City Hospital*
1. Postoperative recovery room	X	X	X
2. Cardiac care unit	X	X	X
3. Intensive care unit	X	X	X
4. Open heart surgery		X	X
5. Pharmacy/Full-time pharmacist	X	X	X
6. Pharmacy/Part-time pharmacist			
7. X-ray therapy		X	X
8. Cobalt therapy		X	X
9. Radium therapy	X	X	X
10. Diagnostic radioisotope facility	X	X	X
11. Therapeutic radioisotope facility	X	X	X
12. Histopathology laboratory	X	X	X
13. Organ bank		X	
14. Blood bank	X	X	X
15. Electroencephalography	X	X	X
16. Respiratory therapy dept.	X	X	X
17. Premature nursery	X	X	X
18. Self-care unit			
19. Long-term care unit			
20. Inpatient hemodialysis	X	X	X
21. Outpatient hemodialysis		X	X
22. Burn care unit			
23. Physical therapy dept.	X	X	X
24. Rehabilitation inpatient unit	X		
25. Occupational therapy dept.		X	X
26. Rehabilitation outpatient dept.	X	X	X
27. Psychiatric inpatient unit	X	X	X
28. Psychiatric outpatient services	X	X	X
29. Psychiatric partial hospitalization program	X		X
30. Psychiatric emergency services	X	X	X
31. Psychiatric home care			
32. Psychiatric consultation education services	X	X	X
33. Clinical psychology services	X	X	X
34. Organized outpatient dept.	X	X	X
35. Emergency department	X	X	X
36. Social work department	X	X	X
37. Family planning service	X		X
38. Genetic counseling service	X		
39. Inpatient abortion service	X		X
40. Outpatient abortion service	X		X
41. Home care department	X	X	
42. Dental services	X	X	X
43. Podiatric services			X
44. Speech pathology services	X	X	X

Table 7–12 continued

Unit/Service	*Urban Hospital*	*Memorial Hospital*	*City Hospital*
45. Hospital auxiliary	X	X	X
46. Volunteer services dept.	X	X	X
47. Patient representative services	X	X	
48. Alcoholism/Drug inpatient unit			
49. Alcoholism/Drug outpatient unit			
50. Respiratory disease unit			
51. Neonatal intensive care unit		X	X
52. Pediatric inpatient unit	X	X	X

Source: Confidential communication with the hospital.

Table 7–13 Proposed Changes in Services at Urban Hospital, 1980–1984

Unit or Service Developed	*Year(s)*
1. Department of Medicine	
• An outpatient dialysis unit	1980
• An inpatient respiratory intensive care unit	1981–1983
• A cardiac rehabilitation service (inpatient and outpatient)	1980–1983
• Cardiac catheterization services	1980–1983
2. Department of Surgery	
• Consolidated ambulatory surgery complex	1980–1983
• Shock unit for medical and surgical patients	1980–1981
• Cardiovascular and thoracic and peripheralvascular surgery	1980
3. Department of Rehabilitation Medicine	
• Inpatient rehabilitation unit of five to eight beds	1980
• An outpatient stroke and amputee service for rehabilitative care	1980
• A pain clinic	1981
• Integrated satellite rehabilitative care centers	1981–1984
4. Department of Pediatrics	
• An expanded acute behavioral crisis program in concert with child/adolescent psychiatry	1980
• A day treatment CAPS program developed with a school curriculum	1981–1984
• A group home for CAPS day treatment patients	1981–1984
• A long-term care facility for disturbed children and adolescents	1982–1984
5. Department of Adult Psychiatry	
• Behavioral diagnostic services for patients on other services	1980–1981
• Extended stabilization service	1981–1984
• A network for provision of follow-up care	1981–1984
6. Department of Ambulatory and Community Medicine	
• Geriatric evaluative and outreach services	1980–1984
• Evaluative physical assessment service for screening in government and private sector settings	1980–1984
7. Department of Obstetrics and Gynecology	
• A free-standing, five-bed, low-risk birthing center	1980–1981

WESTERN HOSPITAL

While the analysis conducted for Urban Hospital provides important information for decision makers, it does not yield specific service volumes that can be used in financial planning. To determine what the flow of revenue is likely to be in the future, we need forecasts of patient days, lab procedures, and other service volumes. A range of models that vary in mathematical sophistication and data requirements is available that can provide these forecasts.

The following forecast, prepared by Amherst Associates for Western Hospital (the name is changed to protect the hospital's confidentiality), is an example of a utilization forecasting model for inpatient days that relies on a series of mathematical relationships between population size, the rate at which the population uses services, and the hospital's market share. (More complex forecasting models that require more data are discussed elsewhere in the literature.[1–3])

The Forecasting Model

Amherst Associates' model is based on the following three relationships:

1. $\dfrac{\text{Admissions to hospital}}{\text{Population}} = \text{Draw rate}$
   (If the population is expressed in 1,000s, the draw rate is expressed as admissions per 1,000 population).

2. Draw rate × Projected population (in 1,000s) = Forecasted admissions

3. Forecasted admissions × Forecasted average length of stay = Forecasted patient days

The Amherst model has been further refined in the following three ways:

1. Separate forecasts are prepared for the medical/surgical, obstetrics, gynecology, and pediatric units.

2. Separate forecasts are prepared for medical/surgical patients over 65 and those between 15 and 64, recognizing the higher rate at which the older group uses services.

3. Rather than just using historic draw rates, Amherst Associates prepared separate forecasts that reflected trends in utilization.

Projected Draw Rates

Table 7–14 shows the calculation of historic draw rates for Western Hospital as well as the total use rates for the hospital's primary and secondary service areas. Service areas were calculated by using a patient origin study; the primary area provided 88.2 percent of the hospital's total admissions in 1979. The area hospital use rate was calculated by dividing the total number of admissions to all hospitals by the area's population. Table 7–14 shows that Western Hospital's draw rate from its primary service area decreased by 10.2 percent, while the total use rate in the area declined by 7.5 percent. In other words, the use of Western Hospital declined faster than the use of all area hospitals. The reverse was true in Western's secondary service area.

Table 7–15 shows the historical draw rate by age group, service, and residence. Age group and residence were determined from data on patient discharge abstracts submitted to PAS. The distribution of patients between the primary and secondary service areas was determined by applying the percentage for all age groups in that year (i.e., 88.2 percent of the admissions from each age and service group were assumed to come from the primary service area in 1979). This assumption allowed the hospital to use PAS reports already prepared rather than tabulate the information from discharge abstracts.

Exhibit 7–1 describes how projected draw rates were determined, using information on trends in utilization. The projected draw rates were then multiplied by the projected population in a particular year (obtained from the state government) to yield the forecast of admissions shown in Table 7–16.

Pending further investigation of the appropriateness of the hospital's average length of stay, current levels were used. Forecasted admissions were then multiplied by the average length of stay to yield the forecasted patient days shown in Table 7–17. Table 7–18 shows the historic trends.

Based on this forecast, the hospital faces a stable or declining occupancy in all services except psychiatry. This forecast can now be used in conjunction with forecasts of the distribution and amount of revenue by type of payer to prepare a forecast of revenues for Western Hospital.

Conclusion

Amherst Associates' model uses an empirically defined geographic service area. Some of the consumer characteristics listed in Table 6–5 are then examined to determine whether current demand is likely to continue in the future. The model is a good example of how service area and market analysis concepts can be combined and used.

Table 7–14 Historical Draw Rates for Western Hospital

Historical draw rates for the medical/surgical, obstetric, gynecological, and pediatric age groups from the primary and secondary service areas are shown. Age-related admissions were determined by using PAS Reports. Admissions from each age group in each service area have been estimated by applying the appropriate annual patient origin percentages to the annual historical admissions for each age group. The population estimates have been derived from the total service area population estimates and the age distribution estimates which are presented in previous tables. Draw rates are calculated by dividing the estimated number of admissions by the estimated population figures.

As shown in Table 7–15 the draw rates for most Hospital services have decreased over the historical period 1976 to 1979. The draw rates for the medical/surgical patients aged 65 years and over have not decreased as consistently as the rates for other services, and in fact, the number of admissions from this age group has increased. This trend has implications for possible new service alternatives such as gerontology and selected psychiatric services. Table 7–14 presents a comparison of historical draw rates by service area and area hospital use rates for the period 1975 to 1978.

COMPARISON OF WESTERN'S DRAW RATES[1]
WITH AREA HOSPITAL USE RATES[2]
1975 to 1978

Service Areas	*1975*	*1976*	*1977*	*1978*	*Percent Change 1975–1978*
Primary					
Admissions From Western	8,887	8,845	8,303	8,105	(8.8)%
Population	121,465	122,109	122,755	123,400	1.6
Western's Draw Rate	73.17	72.44	67.64	65.68	(10.2)
Area Hospital Use Rate	194.39	192.30	182.25	179.71	(7.5)
Secondary					
Admissions From Western	599	606	570	556	(7.2)%
Population	69,285	69,403	69,520	69,639	0.5
Western's Draw Rate	8.65	8.73	8.20	7.98	(7.7)
Area Hospital Use Rate	160.70	158.74	151.25	146.04	(9.1)

[1]Defined as admissions of patients to Western Hospital residing in the service areas, per 1,000 population of those areas.

[2]Defined as admissions of patients residing in the service areas to area hospitals, per 1,000 population of those areas.

Western has experienced a decreasing draw rate in both service areas which, in part, reflects a decline in the overall area hospital use rate. However, Western's 10.2% decrease in the primary service area is significantly greater than the area use rate decrease of 7.5%. These statistics indicate the need to focus Hospital marketing efforts. In the secondary service area, Western's performance is better than the overall average, since the decline in its draw rate is only 7.2% as compared with the decrease in the area use rate of 9.1%. The secondary service area statistics may indicate success in establishing referral networks outside of the immediate area.

Source: PAS Reports; Urban Decision Systems, Population Estimates; American Hospital Association, Guide to the Health Care Field, 1976–1979 editions; State Department of Health, Hospital Reports, 1977–1978. Reprinted by permission of Amherst Associates, Inc., Chicago, Ill.

Table 7–15 Historical Draw Rates for Western Hospital, by Age Component, 1976–1979

Age Component	*Admissions*			
	1976	*1977*	*1978*	*1979*[2]
Medical/Surgical[1] (65+ Years)				
Primary Service Area				
Admissions	1,804	1,784	1,671	1,901
Population	12,821	13,258	13,574	14,018
Draw Rate	140.71	134.56	123.10	135.61
Secondary Service Area				
Admissions	124	122	115	130
Population	10,411	10,637	10,794	11,022
Draw Rate	11.91	11.47	10.65	11.79
Medical/Surgical[1] (15–64 Years)				
Primary Service Area				
Admissions	4,608	4,305	4,170	4,073
Population	78,150	78,563	79,099	79,514
Draw Rate	58.96	54.80	52.72	51.22
Secondary Service Area				
Admissions	316	295	286	279
Population	41,503	41,503	41,575	41,576
Draw Rate	7.61	7.11	6.88	6.71
Obstetrics (15–44 Female)				
Primary Service Area				
Admissions	755	751	755	722
Population	27,352	27,743	28,012	28,407
Draw Rate	27.60	27.07	26.95	25.42
Secondary Service Area				
Admissions	52	52	52	50
Population	13,742	13,834	13,997	14,091
Draw Rate	3.78	3.76	3.72	3.55
Gynecology (15–64 Female)				
Primary Service Area				
Admissions	610	550	623	557
Population	39,807	40,141	40,475	40,811
Draw Rate	15.32	13.70	15.39	13.65
Secondary Service Area				
Admissions	41	38	43	38
Population	21,098	21,134	21,240	21,276
Draw Rate	1.94	1.80	2.02	1.79

Table 7–15 continued

Age Component	Admissions 1976	1977	1978	1979[2]
Pediatrics[3] (0–14 Years)				
Primary Service Area				
Admissions	1,068	913	886	645
Population	31,138	30,934	30,727	30,515
Draw Rate	34.30	29.51	28.83	21.14
Secondary Service Area				
Admissions	73	63	60	44
Population	17,489	17,380	17,270	17,160
Draw Rate	4.17	3.62	3.47	2.56

[1]Includes psychiatry.
[2]Annualized from 1978 PAS Reports (through February).
[3]Includes psychiatry, obstetrics and gynecology.

Source: Compiled from PAS Reports, 1976–1978 (February). Reprinted by permission of Amherst Associates, Inc., Chicago, Ill.

The Western Hospital case study demonstrates some of the advantages of using a computer-based model. A Western Hospital administrator or board member could have requested that any one of the assumptions listed be changed to determine the effect of the change on the final forecast. The Amherst model is capable of recalculating the forecast in a matter of minutes. The savings in time and money involved in using computer models are likely to result in their widespread use in the next few years, especially as hospitals face the pressures and constraints outlined in Chapter 1.

Exhibit 7–1 Projected Draw Rates for Western Hospital

Draw rate projections for fiscal years 1980 through 1985 are based upon separate forecasts of the draw rates for each patient service area for each age grouping. In addition, the present and projected availability of service area physicians and hospital resources, interviews with area health care professionals, and present and proposed utilization review programs were analyzed in preparing the forecasts. Admissions of area residents have been forecast reflecting the respective trends in draw rates and availability of facilities and services at Western Hospital. Admissions were based on the following admitting patterns from the patient service areas.

Primary Service Area:

— Medical/surgical admissions for patients 65 years of age or older are assumed to remain constant at 133.5 per 1,000 population 65 and older.

Exhibit 7–1 continued

— Medical/surgical admissions for patients 15 to 64 years of age are forecast to decrease from 48.7 to 46.5 per 1,000 population between 1980 and 1981, and to remain constant for the remainder of the forecast period.

— Pediatric admissions (patients 0–14 years of age, excluding newborns) are assumed to decrease from 19.4 to 14.4 per 1,000 population 0–14 between 1980 and 1982, then to remain constant thereafter, reflecting the current trends.

— Obstetric admissions are anticipated to decrease from 24.8 per 1,000 female population 15–44 years of age in 1980 to a constant 22.8 in 1983–1985 per 1,000 population, 1985 reflecting the stabilization of the decreasing trend in fertility rates.

— Gynecological admissions are anticipated to remain stable at 14.5 per 1,000 female population 15–64 years of age.

— Newborn admissions (births) are forecast to change proportionately with the obstetric admissions at 80% of obstetric admissions.

Secondary Service Area:

— Medical/surgical admissions for patients 65 years of age and older are forecast to remain constant at 11.5 per 1,000 population 65 and older.

— Medical/surgical admissions for patients between 15 and 64 years of age are expected to decrease slightly from 6.4 per 1,000 population in 1980 to 6.2 in the 1981–1985 period.

— Pediatric admissions are forecast to decrease from 2.3 in 1980 to 1.7 in 1982 per 1,000 relevant population, and to remain at that level in subsequent years, reflecting the increased use of outpatient services by the pediatric population.

— Obstetric admissions are expected to decrease slightly from 3.5 in 1980 to 3.3 in 1983–1985, per 1,000 of the female population 15–44 years of age.

— Gynecological admissions are expected to remain constant between 1980 and 1985 at 1.9 per 1,000 of the female population 15–64 years of age.

— Newborn admissions (births) are forecast to change in proportion to obstetric admissions over the six-year period.

Admissions from other areas are likely to increase over the period due to expansion of referral networks, through the establishment of linkages in specific specialties. Because this referral base is so difficult to define in terms of population, estimates were based on expected utilization from this area and include a stable component for trauma cases.

Source: Reprinted by permission of Amherst Associates, Inc., Chicago, Ill.

Table 7–16 Distribution of Western Hospital Admissions to Service Categories

The forecast of admissions by age component to Western Hospital based on the draw rate assumptions in Exhibit 7–1 appears below. To complete this forecast of the status quo, the age-related admissions are distributed among the various clinical services including

Table 7–16 continued

medical/surgical, psychiatry, obstetrics/gynecology, pediatrics, and nursery based on historical trends. The medical/surgical admissions are primarily from patients aged 15 years and over, less admissions to psychiatry from patients in that age group, plus admissions from the pediatric age group that are not placed in the pediatrics unit. Obstetric and gynecological admissions are estimated from their respective female age projections plus an addition from the 0–14 age group. Pediatric unit admissions are those patients 0–14 years of age who do not go to the adolescent psychiatry, OB/GYN, or medical/surgical floors. Newborns are estimated at 80% of obstetric admissions.

Forecast Admissions[1] By Age Component
and Service Area[2]
1980–1985

Age Component	*Admissions*					
	1980	*1981*	*1982*	*1983*	*1984*	*1985*
65+ (Medical/Surgical)[3]						
Primary	1,912	1,953	1,977	2,018	2,043	2,085
Secondary	128	129	130	131	133	134
Other	98	105	110	115	120	125
Total	2,138	2,187	2,217	2,264	2,296	2,344
15–64 (Medical/Surgical, Psychiatry)[4]						
Primary	3,894	3,715	3,718	3,714	3,717	3,714
Secondary	267	258	257	257	256	255
Other	220	230	240	250	260	270
Total	4,381	4,203	4,215	4,221	4,233	4,239
15–44 Female (Obstetrics)						
Primary	713	696	681	666	672	674
Secondary	50	49	49	48	48	49
Other	39	39	39	39	39	39
Total	802	784	769	753	759	762
15–64 Female (Gynecology)						
Primary	596	596	597	599	600	600
Secondary	40	40	40	40	40	40
Other	32	32	32	32	32	32
Total	668	668	669	671	672	672

Table 7-16 continued

Age Component	*Admissions* 1980	1981	1982	1983	1984	1985
0–14 (Pediatrics, Psychiatry, Obstetrics, Gynecology)						
Primary	586	510	444	447	451	454
Secondary	40	35	30	30	30	31
Other	34	32	30	29	27	26
Total	660	577	504	506	508	511
Total Primary Service area	7,701	7,470	7,417	7,444	7,483	7,527
Total Secondary Service Area	525	511	506	506	507	509
Total Other Service Area	423	438	451	465	478	492
Total All Service Areas	8,649	8,419	8,374	8,415	8,468	8,528

[1]Admissions do not include newborns.

[2]Forecast admissions = projected draw rates × projected population estimates for each age component in each service area.

[3]Includes psychiatry.

[4]Includes psychiatry, obstetrics, and gynecology.

Source: Reprinted by permission of Amherst Associates, Inc., Chicago, Ill.

Table 7–17 Forecast Utilization for Western Hospital, Fiscal Years 1980–1985

Inpatient Service	*1980*[1]	*1981*	*1982*	*1983*	*1984*[1]	*1985*
Medical/Surgical[2]						
Admissions	6,046	5,877	5,896	5,926	5,963	5,978
Average Length of Stay	8.7	8.7	8.7	8.7	8.7	8.7
Patient Days	52,596	51,130	51,295	51,556	51,881	52,009
Average Daily Census	143.7	140.1	140.5	141.3	141.7	142.5
Available Beds	201	201	201	201	201	201
Percent Occupancy	71.5	69.7	69.9	70.3	70.5	70.9
Psychiatry						
Admissions	602	625	650	675	702	725
Average Length of Stay	16.1	16.1	16.1	16.1	16.1	16.1
Patient Days	9,692	10,062	10,465	10,868	11,301	11,673

Table 7–17 continued

Inpatient Service	*1980*[1]	*1981*	*1982*	*1983*	*1984*[1]	*1985*
Average Daily Census	26.5	27.6	28.7	29.8	31.0	32.0
Available Beds	31	31	31	31	31	31
Percent Occupancy	85.4	88.9	92.5	96.0	99.6	103.2
Obstetrics/Gynecology						
Admissions	1,484	1,462	1,448	1,434	1,438	1,444
Average Length of Stay	3.7	3.7	3.7	3.7	3.7	3.7
Patient Days	5,491	5,409	5,358	5,306	5,321	5,343
Average Daily Census	15.0	14.8	14.7	14.5	14.6	14.6
Available Beds	20	20	20	20	20	20
Percent Occupancy	75.0	74.1	73.4	72.7	72.7	73.2
Pediatrics						
Admissions	541	455	380	380	381	381
Average Length of Stay	5.0	5.0	5.0	5.0	5.0	5.0
Patient Days	2,707	2,275	1,900	1,900	1,905	1,905
Average Daily Census	7.4	6.2	5.2	5.2	5.2	5.2
Available Beds	23	23	23	23	23	23
Percent Occupancy	32.2	27.1	22.6	22.6	22.6	22.7
Total Adult and Pediatrics						
Admissions	8,673	8,419	8,374	8,415	8,484	8,528
Average Length of Stay	8.1	8.2	8.2	8.3	8.3	8.3
Patient Days	70,486	68,876	69,018	69,630	70,408	70,930
Average Daily Census	193.1	188.7	189.1	190.8	192.9	194.3
Available Beds	275	275	275	275	275	275
Percent Occupancy	70.0	68.6	68.8	69.4	70.0	70.7
Newborns						
Admissions	643	627	615	602	609	610
Average Length of Stay	3.5	3.5	3.5	3.5	3.5	3.5
Patient Days	2,251	2,195	2,153	2,108	2,131	2,134
Average Daily Census	6.2	6.0	5.9	5.8	5.8	5.8
Available Beds	17	17	17	17	17	17
Percent Occupancy	36.2	35.4	34.7	34.0	34.2	34.4

[1]Adjusted for leap year.
[2]Includes admissions to medical/surgical, critical care, orthopedic and neurological units.

Source: Reprinted by permission of Amherst Associates, Inc., Chicago, Ill.

Table 7–18 Historical Utilization for Western Hospital, Fiscal Years 1976–1979

Inpatient Service	*1976*	*1977*	*1978*	*1979*[1]
Medical/Surgical[2]				
Discharges	6,756	6,389	6,233	6,119
Average Length of Stay	8.8	8.7	8.6	8.8
Patient Days	59,155	55,797	53,911	53,951
Average Daily Census	161.6	152.9	147.7	147.8
Available Beds	201	201	201	201
Percent Occupancy	80.4	76.1	73.5	73.5
Psychiatry				
Discharges	456[3]	516	512	593
Average Length of Stay	16.0	16.9	16.4	16.1
Patient Days	7,296	8,732	8,404	9,570
Average Daily Census	19.9	23.9	23.0	26.2
Available Beds	31	31	31	31
Percent Occupancy	64.3	77.2	74.3	84.6
Obstetric/Gynecological				
Discharges	1,533	1,492	1,580	1,450
Average Length of Stay	3.9	3.9	3.6	3.7
Patient Days	5,930	5,752	5,732	5,319
Average Daily Census	16.2	15.7	15.7	14.6
Available Beds	20	20	20	20
Percent Occupancy	81.0	78.8	78.5	72.9
Pediatrics				
Discharges	1,193	932	781	711
Average Length of Stay	5.7	4.8	5.2	5.0
Patient Days	6,836	4,442	4,036	3,565
Average Daily Census	18.7	12.2	11.1	9.8
Available Beds	23	23	23	23
Percent Occupancy	81.2	52.9	48.1	42.5
Total Adult and Pediatrics				
Discharges	9,938	9,329	9,106	8,873
Average Length of Stay	8.0	8.0	7.9	8.1
Patient Days	79,217	74,723	72,083	72,405
Average Daily Census	216.4	204.7	197.5	198.4
Available Beds	275	275	275	275
Percent Occupancy	78.7	74.4	71.8	72.1
Newborns				
Discharges	737	680	692	602
Average Length of Stay	4.4	3.7	3.6	3.5

Table 7–18 continued

Inpatient Service	*1976*	*1977*	*1978*	*1979*[1]
Patient Days	3,282	2,540	2,490	2,135
Average Daily Census	9.0	7.0	6.8	5.8
Available Beds	17	17	17	17
Percent Occupancy	52.7	40.9	40.1	34.4

[1]Annualized from PAS Reports from July, 1978–February, 1979.
[2]Includes discharges from medical/surgical, critical care, orthopedic and neurological units.
[3]Psychiatry not broken out in PAS Reports in 1976. Estimates from internal sources.

Source: PAS Reports, 1976–1979 (February); Hospital Census Records, 1976. Reprinted by permission of Amherst Associates, Inc., Chicago, Ill.

CARDIAC CARE UNITS IN NEW JERSEY

In the two case studies we have examined, no attempt was made to determine which specific consumer characteristics are related to variations in the use of health services in a specific community. However, some of the consumer characteristics listed in Table 6–5 (e.g., age and sex) have been shown in numerous research studies to be related to variations in utilization.

In this third case study, a state-wide data base consisting of patient discharge abstracts and a statistical software package are used to explore factors that are related to variations in utilization in specific service areas. This knowledge can then be used in segmenting consumer groups and in the development of forecasting models.

As noted in Chapter 6, variations in the utilization of health services are explained by predisposing, enabling, and need variables. The two previous case studies used a number of these variables in attempts to examine and forecast utilization—for example, patient diagnosis (a need variable), patient age and sex (predisposing variables), and insurance coverage (an enabling variable). Other factors were not considered—for example, the availability of services, measured by the supply available; whether the services were accessible; and the relative weights that should be assigned to each variable (e.g., whether the level of insurance coverage or the availability of a service should be given more importance in forecasting utilization).

As part of a research project (funded by the National Center for Health Services Research and the Bureau of Health Planning in the U.S. Department of Health and Human Services) to develop better planning criteria, we examined the importance of a range of variables in explaining variations in the demand for cardiac care units (CCUs).[4–7] The state of New Jersey provided us with a computer tape that contained all discharge abstracts for all hospitals in New Jersey for 1977. We selected 19 hospitals for the study because they had separate CCUs, rather than CCUs combined with ICUs, and because of their accuracy in reporting CCU treatment in their chart-abstract data.

A fundamental principle underlying our research was that the need for CCU beds depends primarily on case mix or diagnosis. In order to utilize diagnosis as a basis for studying CCU utilization, we required a list of diagnoses that are eligible for treatment in a CCU. A list of such diagnoses was developed based on a review of the literature, the opinions of a panel of cardiologists, and an examination of the actual patterns of utilization in the 19 hospitals. The resulting list of CCU-eligible diagnoses was divided into seven categories (see Table 7–19). Each category was considered distinct in terms of its clinical characteristics and CCU resource utilization.

Using the information on town of residence on each discharge abstract, a patient origin study was conducted, and hospital service areas were established. As one part of our analysis, we then attempted to identify the variables that were strongly related to the hospital-to-hospital variations in the proportion of hospitalized patients with CCU-eligible diagnoses who were treated in the CCU, that is, the variables that explained the differences in the proportion of eligible patients who actually got treated in the CCU. As Table 7–20 shows, that proportion differed significantly among the 19 hospitals.

Table 7–21 shows the variables that a review of the literature suggested were important and on which we had data. The first four and the last are enabling variables. Age, sex, and race are predisposing variables (although race is highly correlated with income and source of payment, both enabling variables). The diagnostic severity variable is a measure of need.

The multiple regression procedure from the software package *Statistical Package for the Social Sciences*[8] was used to determine which of the variables best explained the variation in (1) the percentage of discharges with acute myocardial infarction (i.e., diagnostic categories (DICAT) 1 + 2) that were CCU treated and (2) the percentage of discharges with a CCU-eligible diagnosis (DICATs 1–7) that were CCU treated.

Tables 7–22 and 7–23 show that the proportion of eligible patients actually treated in the CCUs is strongly and negatively related to the CCU occupancy rate. In other words, either, (1) CCU admission criteria were tighter in hospitals with high-occupancy, or (2) CCU admission criteria were looser in hospitals with low-occupancy CCUs. This could be explained by the following hypothesis: Cardiologists in hospitals with high-occupancy CCUs are often left with little choice but to adopt stringent CCU admission criteria because their CCUs are full most of the time. Cardiologists in hospitals with low-occupancy CCUs, on

Table 7–19 Categories of Diagnoses Treatable in Cardiac Care Units (CCU)

DICAT[a] *No.*	*Diagnoses in DICAT*[a]
1	Simple acute myocardial infarction (AMI)
2	Complicated AMI
3	Intermediate syndrome
4	Rule-out MI
5	Cardiac arrhythmia problems
6	Intensive cardiac conditions treatable in a regular intensive care unit
7	Other CCU-eligible cardiac conditions not often seen in the CCU
8	Diagnoses that are not eligible for CCU treatment

[a]Diagnostic category

Source: Reprinted with permission from *Social Science and Medicine* 16 (1982), James Greenberg and Roger Kropf, "Adjusting Planning Guidelines for Cardiac-Care Units," © 1982, Pergamon Press, Ltd.

the other hand, are able to use more liberal CCU admission criteria because there are usually some empty beds in their CCUs.

Similarly, CCU treatment is negatively related to the number of CCU-eligible discharges per bed for both acute myocardial infarction and all CCU-eligible discharges. This suggests that CCU admission criteria were more stringent in hospitals with more eligible patients for each CCU bed. The same hypothesis described above could explain this result.

The proportion of eligible discharges that were treated in the CCUs is also negatively related to CCU bed availability, defined as the number of maintained CCU beds in the hospital per 100,000 service area population. In other words, either (1) as the supply of beds increases, the proportion of eligible patients treated in the CCU decreases, or (2) as the supply decreases, the proportion of eligible patients treated increases.

While these conclusions might appear to contradict the findings reported earlier, it should be noted that the number of maintained CCU beds per 100,000 service area population is really a measure of supply rather than accessibility. It relates the amount of a resource to the total size of the population rather than to the magnitude of the need. Because of age distributions and variations in other risk factors, equal-sized populations may produce different numbers of people eligible for CCU treatment. Also, this independent variable is not as strongly associated with the dependent variable we are trying to explain as the others are

Table 7–20 Percentage of CCU-Treated Discharges in 19 Selected Hospitals by DICAT (1977)

	Percentage of Discharges with CCU-Eligible Diagnoses in the Following DICATs That Were CCU Treated									
Hosp. No.[a]	*DICAT 1*	*DICAT 2*	*DICAT 1+2*	*DICAT 3*	*DICAT 4*	*DICAT 1–4*	*DICAT 5*	*DICAT 6*	*DICAT 7*	*DICAT 1–7*
3	49.0	29.3	40.9	25.0	4.4	12.6	12.3	11.2	1.0	10.2
12	84.3	70.6	80.2	63.7	22.2	34.9	21.3	11.9	2.6	26.1
14	64.1	54.9	59.7	45.7	11.1	23.6	16.5	8.0	1.5	16.8
16	45.9	49.3	47.0	27.0	5.8	13.5	13.8	7.9	1.7	11.4
20	83.3	63.5	73.4	50.0	11.5	20.8	12.0	7.8	.8	14.7
26	85.1	66.2	77.9	69.9	12.4	28.0	16.4	14.3	1.4	19.7
29	83.2	75.5	81.0	51.6	16.8	26.0	26.1	31.3	4.8	21.6
39	34.9	25.3	32.5	13.1	1.7	7.6	3.7	2.9	.7	5.2
47	79.0	86.7	81.3	53.2	11.9	28.7	21.1	6.7	1.0	20.6
48	82.7	86.0	83.4	69.0	11.3	22.4	25.7	22.9	4.8	20.4
51	61.0	40.8	54.7	39.3	11.2	19.4	15.1	4.8	1.3	14.1
56	63.0	50.0	58.7	46.2	10.5	26.5	18.5	9.1	3.4	19.5
57	59.7	79.6	64.3	61.3	7.8	23.2	29.8	18.4	2.0	18.8
58	77.1	76.5	76.9	77.8	25.6	30.3	34.3	15.6	2.9	23.5
78	85.2	84.1	92.4	72.0	10.3	22.4	26.1	22.1	1.9	18.2
80	73.3	75.6	74.4	29.0	5.7	12.8	14.5	12.7	.4	6.9
85	64.1	66.7	65.3	43.3	3.4	12.7	20.2	15.5	.8	12.0
92	73.1	91.9	81.4	61.7	10.8	26.1	41.9	24.7	2.3	24.6
112	43.8	56.8	47.7	27.0	7.1	15.9	12.8	17.1	2.3	13.9
Mean	68.0	64.7	67.0	48.7	10.6	21.4	20.1	13.9	2.0	16.8
Std. Dev.	15.8	19.3	16.6	18.5	6.0	7.3	9.0	7.5	1.3	5.8

[a]Hospital numbers used in data processing

Source: Reprinted with permission from *Social Science and Medicine* 16 (1982), James Greenberg and Roger Kropf, "Adjusting Planning Guidelines for Cardiac-Care Units," © 1982, Pergamon Press, Ltd.

in Table 7–22; and it is not significantly related to the percentage of acute-myocardial-infarction discharges that are CCU treated (see Table 7–23).

Tables 7–22 and 7–23 also show that the proportion of eligible discharges treated in the CCU is positively related to the percentage of eligible patients who are nonwhite. In other words, either (1) hospitals with more stringent CCU admission criteria tend to treat smaller proportions of nonwhite patients with CCU-eligible diagnoses, or (2) hospitals with looser CCU admission criteria tend to treat larger proportions of nonwhite patients with CCU-eligible diagnoses.

Table 7–21 Possibly Significant Independent Variables for Phase-2 Analysis of Cardiac Care Units in 19 Selected Hospitals

Variable	*Quantitative Indicators*
Type of hospital	Teaching or nonteaching (VAR02, D1 and E1)[a]
Extent to which the CCU is filled	CCU occupancy rate (VAR03)
Availability of CCU beds in the CCU-service area	Number of maintained CCU beds in the hospital per 100,000 service-area population (VAR04)
Socioeconomic characteristics of CCU-treated patients	Per capita income of the service-area population (VAR12)
CCU patient's age	Percentage of CCU-treated discharges with diagnoses in DICATs 1+2 and 1–7 that are over 65 years of age (VAR46 and VAR53)
CCU patient's sex	Percentage of CCU-treated discharges with diagnoses in DICATs 1+2 and 1–7 which are female (VAR66 and VAR73)
CCU patient's race	Percent of CCU-treated discharges with diagnoses in DICATs 1+2 and 1–7 that are nonwhite (VAR86 and VAR93)
Diagnostic severity of hospitalized patients with CCU-eligible diagnoses	Percentage of discharges with diagnoses in DICAT 1–7 that have diagnoses in DICATs 1, 2, 1+2, 3, 4, 1–4, 5, 6, and 7 (VAR104 thru VAR112)
In-hospital demand for CCU beds	Number of discharges with diagnoses in DICATs 1, 2, 1+2, 3, 4, 1–4, 5, 6, 7, and 1–7 per CCU bed (VAR143 thru VAR152)

[a]The names in parentheses were used in data processing.

Source: James Greenberg, Jacob Haft, Gayle Budke, and James Roth, *A Diagnosis-Based Study of the Planning of Cardiac-Care Units,* Final Report for DHEW Grant No. 1-R03-HS03538-01 (Brooklyn College, 1979), p. 219.

Table 7–22 Phase-2 Regression Results for Discharges with CCU-Eligible Diagnoses in 19 Selected Hospitals

Dependent variable:
VAR103—% discharges with DICAT 1–7 diagnoses that are CCU treated

Independent variables:
VAR03—CCU occupancy rate
VAR04—CCU bed availability
VAR93—% CCU-treated discharges with DICAT 1–7 diagnoses that are nonwhite
VAR152—No. of discharges with DICAT 1–7 diagnoses per CCU bed

Table 7–22 continued

Regression Statistics:

Multiple R	0.90208		F = 15.3, df = 14/4	
R Square	0.81375			
Adjusted R Square	0.76053			
Standard Error	2.84901			

Variable	*B*	*Beta*	*Std. Error B*	*F*[a]
VAR03	–0.1504566	–0.61051	0.03179	22.400
VAR04	–0.7788721	–0.75818	0.26584	8.584
VAR93	0.7521701	1.00574	0.17517	18.439
VAR152	–0.2086798D-03	–1.04611	0.00004	32.682
(Constant)	40.90463			

[a]All values of F are significant at the five-percent level.

Source: Reprinted with permission from *Social Science and Medicine* 16 (1982), James Greenberg and Roger Kropf, "Adjusting Planning Guidelines for Cardiac-Care Units," © 1982, Pergamon Press, Ltd.

Table 7–23 Phase-2 Regression Results for Discharges with Acute Myocardial Infarctions in 19 Selected Hospitals

Dependent variable:
VAR96—% discharges with DICAT 1 + 2 diagnoses that are CCU treated

Independent variables:
VAR03—CCU occupancy rate
VAR86—% CCU-treated discharges with DICAT 1 + 2 diagnoses that are nonwhite
VAR145—No. of admissions with DICAT 1 + 2 diagnoses per CCU bed

Regression statistics:

Multiple R	0.89162		F = 19.4, df = 15/3	
R Square	0.79498			
Adjusted R Square	0.75398			
Standard Error	8.21931			

Variable	*B*	*Beta*	*Std. Error B*	*F*[a]
VAR03	–0.3837978	–0.54715	0.08215	21.825
VAR86	1.464285	0.49606	0.34517	17.996
VAR145	–0.3535193D-02	–0.48413	0.00086	17.090
(Constant)	101.4198			

[a]All values of F are significant at the one-percent level.

Source: Reprinted with permission from *Social Science and Medicine* 16 (1982), James Greenberg and Roger Kropf, "Adjusting Planning Guidelines for Cardiac-Care Units," © 1982, Pergamon Press, Ltd.

The four variables together explain 90 percent of the variance between the 19 hospitals in the percentage of eligible discharges that are CCU treated. The regression equation can be used to predict the effect of changes in any one of the variables on the proportion of patients treated. This allows decision makers to ask the type of "what if" questions so important to planning. It also focuses attention away from variables that do not significantly explain the situation at hand.

At one time, this type of analysis would have been considered impossible in most hospitals. As we have seen, however, the requisite data resources and computer hardware and software are becoming less expensive and more accessible. For at least some hospitals, this type of analysis has now become a real possibility and could improve the base of information used to make decisions.

REFERENCES

1. J.R. Griffith, *Quantitative Methods for Hospital Planning and Control* (Lexington, Mass.: Lexington Books, 1972), pp. 37–64.

2. D. Warner and D. Holloway, *Decision-making and Control for Health Administration* (Ann Arbor, Mich.: Health Administration Press, 1978), pp. 239–284.

3. M. Warner, J. Steinberg, and M. Brown, "A Strategic Planning Model for Multihospital Systems," *Inquiry* 18, no. 3 (Fall 1981):214–223.

4. J. Greenberg and R. Kropf, "Adjusting Planning Guidelines for Cardiac-Care Units," *Social Science and Medicine* 16 (1982):1157–1167.

5. J. Greenberg et al., *A Diagnosis-Based Study of the Planning of Cardiac-Care Units*, Final Report of DHEW Grant No. HS03538 (Brooklyn, N.Y.: Brooklyn College, Department of Health Science, 1979), pp. 206–242.

6. J. Greenberg and R. Kropf, "A Case-Mix Method for Developing Health Planning Criteria for Hospital Services," *Medical Care* 19, no. 11 (November 1981):1083–1094.

7. J. Greenberg and R. Kropf, "The Economic Impact of Alternative Cardiac Care Unit Treatment Practices," *Health Services Research* 17, no. 1 (Spring 1982):45–59.

8. Norman Nie et al., *Statistical Package for the Social Sciences*, 2nd ed. (New York: McGraw-Hill, 1975), pp. 320–367.

Chapter 8

Medical Staff Analysis

INTRODUCTION

Physicians could be viewed as the hospital's primary consumers because of their influence on patients' decisions concerning medical care. Physicians have a major influence on whether patients enter the hospital. If the resources exist and the patient can afford them, the type and volume of resources used are largely determined by physicians.

Physicians are also potentially serious competitors for hospitals. Free-standing ambulatory surgery units can compete with hospital-based units. Emergi-Centers and other types of free-standing ambulatory care centers aimed at providing immediate access to medical care can compete with hospital emergency rooms and outpatient clinics. Hospitals can no longer assume that the arrival of additional physicians in the community will automatically mean higher occupancies.

A limiting factor on physicians' autonomy as consumers and competitors is their need for the hospital as a place to work that is equipped with expensive equipment and human resources. Physicians are therefore compelled to not only work regularly in the hospital but to become involved in its management. Without physician involvement, the hospital's board, administrators, and staff cannot be expected to make the many decisions regarding the acquisition and use of resources.

Some physicians devote themselves solely to their patients and neither seek nor obtain formal or informal positions of authority and influence. Others develop and seek to preserve such positions, giving them the ability to influence the services the hospital provides and the expenditures that are made.

Because physicians are partly consumers, partly competitors, and also participate in hospital management, medical staff analysis must shift among several viewpoints. It must look at physicians as both part of the internal environment, affecting the utilization and cost of resources, and as part of the external environment, determining the hospital's opportunities and threatening its current position in the community.

As part of the internal environment, physicians can affect the volume of patients in the hospital, the use of resources (e.g., lab tests, patients' length of stay), and therefore occupancy levels. The medical specialties and training of physicians will determine the technologies that the hospital utilizes, many of the services offered, and therefore the needs served in the community. In states where rate setting and other controls on hospital revenue are in effect, physicians in their dual roles as consumers and hospital managers may represent a distinct threat to the hospital's survival because of the impact of their decisions on the cost of care and the revenues received.

As part of the external environment, physicians in the community can affect the hospital by becoming direct competitors or by serving the interests of competing hospitals. In addition to establishing facilities that offer services usually provided in the hospital, physicians can join HMOs or enter into contracts with third party payers with the aim of reducing hospitalization (e.g., by joining a "primary care network" in which physicians are at risk for the cost of medical care). Since even physicians with staff privileges can choose to utilize other hospitals, their shifting allegiances among individual hospitals represent both threats and opportunities for hospitals that wish to retain or increase their current market share.

In this chapter, we describe some of the information and analytical techniques for describing and evaluating the impact of physicians on the hospital. First, techniques for defining physician service areas and markets are examined. Then several techniques for evaluating physician markets are presented. Finally, the role of medical staff analysis in the strategic planning process is described, and an attempt is made to define the information that can assist managers in making some important decisions in that process.

DEFINING PHYSICIAN SERVICE AREAS

Based on our own review of hospital plans,[1] we must conclude that maps are not commonly used to define the physician population hospitals serve. Yet, at the same time, hospitals show a great deal of concern about whether the distance between the hospital and physicians' offices has a negative impact.

The number of physicians' office buildings constructed adjacent to hospitals is testimony to the belief of hospital boards and administrators that proximity encourages use. However, this belief is based more on cursory observation rather than on empirical research. Many physicians appear highly concerned with the use of their time, especially about time spent in unproductive ways (e.g., in traveling, especially on crowded urban and suburban highways). Before examining some of the ways of defining physician service areas, we should look at some of the research concerning the effect of distance on physicians' use of the hospital.[2]

Distance and Hospital Use

A few studies have shown that distance is a factor in the use of particular hospitals by physicians. Some have shown that the farther a physician's office is from a hospital, the less likely the physician is to use the hospital,[3] or to make referrals to it.[4,5]

In some communities, estimating the effect that distance has on hospital use is complicated by the fact that some physicians have multiple offices. A group of obstetricians/gynecologists may have an office near an urban teaching hospital and also one or more offices in suburban locations. Routine deliveries may be performed at a nearby suburban community hospital, while high risk deliveries are performed at the teaching hospital. In addition to the severity of the problem, the use of a particular hospital may depend on the location of the physicians' residences, amenities for the physicians and patients, and other factors. Market research of the type described in Chapter 6 may be needed to ascertain how and why such choices are made.

If the physician has a formal (e.g., chairman of a department) or informal leadership position in a hospital, distance may be less important. The physician may then be compensated for the additional travel time by the esteem and respect of colleagues and members of the community. Providing physicians with teaching or consulting positions in their medical specialty may have the same effect.

The empirical evidence on whether distance affects the use of hospitals by physicians is limited. The evidence does support the conclusion that physicians, like consumers, alter their behavior as the distance to a hospital increases.

Distance may be less of a factor if the physician is knowledgeable concerning the specific advantages of utilizing a distant hospital.[6] Rather than simply reduce distance by relocation or by purchase of another hospital or a satellite clinic, some hospitals have begun to realize the importance of working with local physicians to increase the physicians' knowledge about the hospital, thus diminishing distance as a determining factor.

Defining Service Areas Using Internal Data

In order to understand the potential impact of distance on physician behavior, the current location of the physicians should be examined. The techniques for this purpose are similar to those used for patients, but the sources of data are different. The hospital will need to acquire a list of physician office addresses that includes the county, minor civil division (i.e., city or town), and zip code.

To this can be added information on the physicians' use of services as expressed in admissions, discharges, patient days, revenues, and other measures. An "index of hospital dependence" can then be calculated. For example, the number of discharges attributed to physicians in each geographic area can be divided by the total number of discharges from the hospital during a particular period of time. Table 8–1 shows the index of hospital dependence for Metro Hospital. Other measures of dependence (e.g., revenues) could be used. The geographic areas can be ranked in descending order or clustered in zones at various distances from the hospital.

The hospital can then define its physician service area as the combined geographic areas that contain the physicians on which it is dependent for most of its service volume or revenue. Establishment of a boundary by setting an arbitrary cut-off point (e.g., 90 percent of discharges) is not as important as the determination of the level of dependence of the hospital on particular groups of physicians. By adding the location of competing hospitals to the map or examining the rate of population growth in each geographic area, the hospital can begin to explore both the opportunities and the threats in its current situation.

Methods Using External Data

Table 8–1 shows that a single town contains 27.1 percent of Metro Hospital's physicians and that the patients of those physicians represented 31.2 percent of the hospital's discharges in 1980. However, some important information is miss-

Table 8–1 Calculation of an Index of Hospital Dependence for Metro Hospital, Total Acute Care Service, 1980

Office Location (Town/City)	*Participating Staff*[a] *No.*	*%*	*No. of Metro Hospital Discharges*	*Index of Hospital Dependence*[b]
A	15	21.4	2233	26.7
B	14	20.0	1175	14.1
C	3	4.3	201	2.4
D	16	22.9	1988	23.8
E	19	27.1	2609	31.2
F	3	4.3	154	1.8
Total	70	100.0	8360	100.0

[a]Participating staff are those physicians who had a patient discharged from the hospital during the year.
[b]Index of hospital dependence = number of Metro Hospital discharges from office location area divided by total hospital discharges.

ing. We do not know the extent to which these physicians utilized other hospitals. If Metro Hospital served only a small proportion of their needs, it may be vulnerable to a shift in their admissions to other hospitals. If Metro provided services to a large majority of their patients, it might expect that a shift to other hospitals would be less likely. To obtain this information, we might calculate an "index of physician investment."[7] This would be a measure of the extent to which physicians have grown dependent on the hospital. Table 8–2 shows the index of physician investment for physicians in each office location area, that is, the number of discharges from each office location area divided by the total number of discharges generated by physicians in that office location area.

To calculate the index, data on discharges, admissions, patient days, or other measures of physician dependence on the hospital must be combined with data on physician location. Physician office addresses can be obtained from the American Medical Association's Medical Directory,[8] from the Directory of Medical Specialists,[9] or from companies specializing in direct mail advertising to physicians.[10] Since some physicians maintain more than one office location, assistance from the local medical society, planning agency, or other local source would also be helpful.[11]

Data on the total number of discharges (or other measures) for all physicians might be obtained through cooperative efforts with other hospitals or from government agencies (see Chapters 4 and 5). While data on the activities of individual physicians would be useful, legal requirements to maintain the confidentiality of physicians may make these data impossible to obtain. In particular, maintaining confidentiality could become a problem if the hospital wishes to calculate the index for geographic areas that contain only a few physicians. As Table 8–2 shows, however, information on individual physicians is not absolutely es-

Table 8–2 Calculation of an Index of Physician Investment for Southern Hospital

Office Location (Town/City)	*Total Physician Discharges*	*No. of Southern Hospital Discharges*	*Index of Physician Investment*[a]
A	4325	2054	47.5
B	5489	2567	46.8
C	3356	1002	29.9
D	4206	899	21.4
E	2078	346	16.7
Total	19454	6868	35.3

[a]Index of physician investment = number of Southern Hospital discharges from an office location area divided by total physician discharges from that office location area.

sential to determine the extent to which physicians as a group have made an investment in the hospital.

Again, drawing a boundary on a map to define a physician service area seems less useful than looking at the index values and assessing their significance. Table 8–2 shows, for example, that the physicians who serve Southern Hospital have made a limited investment. In none of the geographic areas does the hospital receive a majority of physicians' discharges. Physician investment is strongest in Towns A and B. The hospital should now ask why this is so and evaluate over time the strength of its attractiveness to physicians.

DEFINING PHYSICIAN MARKETS

The same three-dimensional definition of a market used in Chapter 6 can be applied to define physician markets. Physicians are now the "customer group." Our first task is to segment them in a way that yields information useful in explaining and predicting their behavior.

Segmenting Physicians

Table 8–3 shows some of the variables that may affect physician use of hospital services. The hospital can serve a number of functions for the physician, some of which are directly related to specialty. Anesthesiologists must depend on the hospital to do their work, while many pediatricians can see the majority of their patients outside of the hospital. Type of practice can also affect use; the solo practitioner is more dependent on the hospital's equipment and staff than the physician in a large, multidisciplinary group practice that may be able to replicate on-site some of the hospital's resources, to perform outpatient surgery, and to provide evening and weekend care that is often provided by hospitals. For example, group practice HMOs have been shown to decrease the use of hospital services.[12]

Physicians recognize the cycles in which their careers move. Younger physicians may enter into partnerships because of their limited ability to attract patients; older physicians may do the same in order to phase down a practice as retirement approaches without denying services to patients.[13] The number of physicians at each stage of the career cycle is important information in determining the utilization of hospital services. Also important is the length of time physicians have practiced in the community, since that affects the size of their practices.

The geographic region in which the physician practices affects the use of hospital services. For reasons that are not fully understood, the use of hospital services is lower in the West than in any other area of the country.[14] As noted earlier, there is evidence that distance between the physician's office and the hospital can affect utilization.

Table 8–3 Variables That May Affect Physicians' Use of Hospital Services

	Variable Classification	*Specific Variable*
1.	Function served by hospital	Medical specialty Type of practice
2.	Stage in career	Age Year of graduation from medical school Years of practice in the community
3.	Location	Geographic region of practice Distance to hospital
4.	Peer relations	Medical staff appointment and rank Formal position of authority Informal position of influence on decisions made Attendance at medical conferences and continuing medical education
5.	Supply	Access to beds, staff, and other resources Ratio of physicians to population
6.	Patient need, predisposing and enabling factors	See Table 6–5

Physicians' use of a hospital is also affected by their relationships with their peers. First, the physician needs peer approval to use the hospital. Then the physician will have varying access to the hospital's beds and services, depending on relationships with chiefs of staff and administrators and their rank in the medical staff (i.e., "attending" or "consultant" ranks as distinguished from "courtesy" privileges for those expected to use the hospital only infrequently). Physicians may also need referrals from their colleagues, which may or may not be provided.

Formal leadership positions, such as committee memberships, can also influence whether a physician uses a hospital. The holding of such positions can increase the extent to which the physician views the success of the hospital as a reflection of personal success and competence. Similarly, the holding of an informal position of influence may result in the same kind of identification with the hospital's interests and carry with it the respect and esteem of colleagues that the physician might not obtain elsewhere.

From their formal education and informal exposure to medical education as teacher or learner, physicians develop values and beliefs concerning the efficacy of hospital services. Procedures that were once common and whose efficacy was rarely questioned (e.g., tonsillectomies) can quickly come into disrepute, with a resulting drop in utilization.

Obviously, physicians' use of services is affected by access to resources. This includes beds, equipment, and staff. Also, the growing supply of physicians in the United States may limit the number of patients available to each physician, reducing hospital use per physician. However, the extent to which physicians will react to competition by providing more services to each patient and by serving previously unmet needs is unknown. Finally, the factors that affect consumer use of services, discussed in Chapter 6, will also have an impact on physicians and their use of hospital services. The inability of consumers to pay for hospital services because of cutbacks in Medicare and other insurance programs, for example, could limit the use of both physician and hospital services.

Segmenting Physician Needs

To a great extent, physician needs overlap those of the patients they serve. Physicians are interested in eliminating or avoiding for their patients the "five Ds"—disease, discomfort, dissatisfaction, disability, and death. They are also interested in both primary and secondary prevention of health problems. We can therefore segment physician needs with the same classification schemes used in Chapter 6 for segmenting consumer needs, that is, by service provided, setting, and patient diagnosis or problem.

We must remember, however, that physicians have both professional and administrative functions in the hospital setting. While the hospital is not expected to meet the job-related needs of consumers, it must, to some extent, meet such needs for physicians. These needs might involve such services as lounge or overnight accommodations, message services, and even food. In addition, physicians expect that their needs for professional respect and rewards will be gratified. They expect that hospital personnel will comply with their orders and show respect and that administrators will listen to and follow their recommendations.

In the hospital's attempt to attract and retain physicians, these physical and psychological needs and preferences may be far more important than the quality of the resources hospitals have to offer. Indeed, physician needs and preferences are often the subject of market research through special interviews and surveys of physicians. However, unless the hospital can differentiate groups of physicians according to their needs and preferences, such needs and preferences are not useful criteria for segmenting physicians.

Three-Dimensional Market Definition

The techniques for segmenting technologies described in Chapter 6 can also be applied to the definition of physician markets. A three-dimensional definition is as important for physician markets as it is for consumer markets. To illustrate, we will continue with the example of City Hospital in Chapter 6. As noted there, physicians in Morris and Jefferson counties under 40 years of age use University

Hospital, about 30 miles away, for cancer referrals. The current physician market for City Hospital in Morris and Jefferson counties is presented in Figure 8–1. The physicians have been segmented by age and location of practice.

To expand its physician market, a number of options are available to City Hospital. Three of them are indicated by the arrows in Figure 8–1: (1) The hospital could attempt to meet additional needs of the physicians it now services. (2) It could attempt to make available alternative technologies to these physicians. (3) It could seek to increase the scope of the physician group it now serves.

A survey of younger physicians could reveal a number of reasons for bypassing City Hospital:

- an inability to obtain admitting privileges
- difficulty for a new physician in getting beds
- unfamiliarity with specialists at City
- lack of knowledge about services at City
- a feeling that City is "second rate"

A description of the hospital's current physician market can suggest the questions that the hospital should be asking at this point.

EVALUATING PHYSICIAN MARKETS

Markets need to be evaluated as well as defined. Our three-dimensional market definition does not suggest which alternative strategy would be preferable. Its primary usefulness is to trigger thinking about the hospital's current position and the alternative strategies that are available. In this section we describe two techniques that can be useful in evaluating physician markets.

Business-position/market-attractiveness analysis is a technique for conducting a portfolio analysis. It is similar to the growth-share matrix described in Chapter 6 but expands the number of variables to be considered. Risk analysis is a technique for evaluating the accuracy of the assumptions made in preparing projections (e.g., of patient days and hospital revenue). In Chapters 10 and 11, we discuss the use of financial models that allow the user to carry out "sensitivity" analyses, in which the assumptions made (including those about the medical staff and utilization) are varied and their differential impact on the hospital's financial condition is estimated. None of these techniques was created for the purpose of evaluating physician markets. They can, however, be applied to decisions that hospitals must make concerning their present and future medical staffs.

Figure 8–1 Physician Market Strategies for City Hospital in Morris and Jefferson Counties

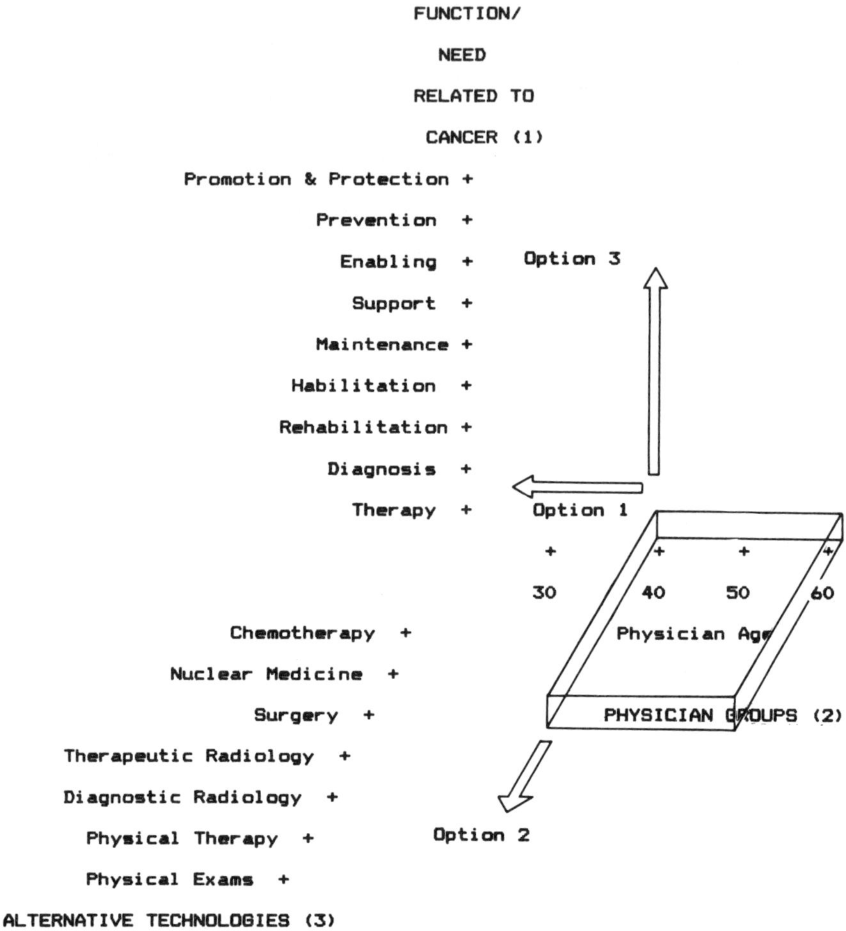

[1]Most services could also be provided in alternative settings. Also, problems other than cancer could be dealt with.

[2]Other bases for segmentation include specialty and type of practice.

[3]Each category could also be subdivided according to type of equipment or other resources required.

Source: Adapted from Derek F. Abell, *Defining the Business: The Starting Point of Strategic Planning.* Englewood Cliffs, N.J.: Prentice-Hall, Inc., 1980, Ex. 3-4, p. 31, by permission of the Harvard Business School on behalf of the copyright holder, the President and Fellows of Harvard College.

Business-Position/Market-Attractiveness Analysis

As noted earlier, physicians have several roles to play in the hospital. They are major customers, yet they also work in the hospital and have decision-making authority. Earlier, we treated physicians as customer groups. We asked what functions and needs the hospital served, and with what technologies, in order to define markets. We now turn to the physician's other role in the hospital, as a resource that attracts patients and influences expenditures, and ask how groups of physicians, classified as strategic business units (SBUs) (as defined in Chapter 6), can be evaluated prior to making investment decisions.

Of course, a hospital requires more than physicians to provide services. A hospital SBU must include the entire set of resources that contribute to the provision of services (i.e., staff, equipment, facilities). We assume here that the physician is the most important resource. In a few specialized services, the cost of equipment may be a more important concern (e.g., nuclear and radiation therapy, cardiac surgery, burn units). For most hospital services, however, the key to success is the number, quality, and medical practice patterns of the physicians who work in the hospital. While the dollars may flow for nurses, equipment, and facilities, the hospital's primary investment is in its medical staff.

What information would help in making decisions on which groups of physicians to invest in, how much, and how quickly? Which physicians should receive a steady but unchanged level of investment? Which physicians should receive fewer funds in the future?

Hospitals make investments in a service for a number of reasons. We hope that the major reason is the need for the service in the hospital's community. Other hospitals may be able to provide the service, however, and the question that must be raised then is whether the hospital's unique strengths (or business position) in providing that service justify the investment.

The attractiveness of the market must also be considered. If the demand for the service is growing slowly, for example, a quick and major investment may not be justified. This suggests that business position and market attractiveness could be used as criteria for making investment decisions.

The technique of business-position/market-attractiveness analysis was developed to consider simultaneously both of these variables.[15,16] The technique involves several tasks:[17,18]

- The factors that contribute to market attractiveness or business position are identified.
- The direction and form of the resulting relationships are determined.
- Each of the contributing factors is weighted in a composite measure of attractiveness or position, depending on its relative importance.

- A matrix is drawn with the measure of attractiveness on one axis and the measure of position on the other. The matrix is then divided into zones or cells. The most desirable SBUs for investment are in the areas that indicate both high attractiveness and strong position; the least desirable SBUs are in the areas that indicate both low attractiveness and weak position.

Figure 8–2 shows a 2 × 2 matrix prepared by Milch to analyze the relative product-market attractiveness and competitive position (business strength) of the SBUs that comprise a "large, diversified hospital located in a southeastern rural setting."[19] The position of each SBU (e.g., obstetrics) is indicated by a number on a matrix, with the number of admissions on one axis (business position) and the charges per admission (market attractiveness) on the other. Composite indices are not used. Milch recognizes the limitations of this approach and notes some of the other factors that need to be considered. His matrix illustrates the dilemma we face in finding adequate measures of position and attractiveness.

Figure 8–2 A Business-Position/Market-Attractiveness Matrix for a Hospital

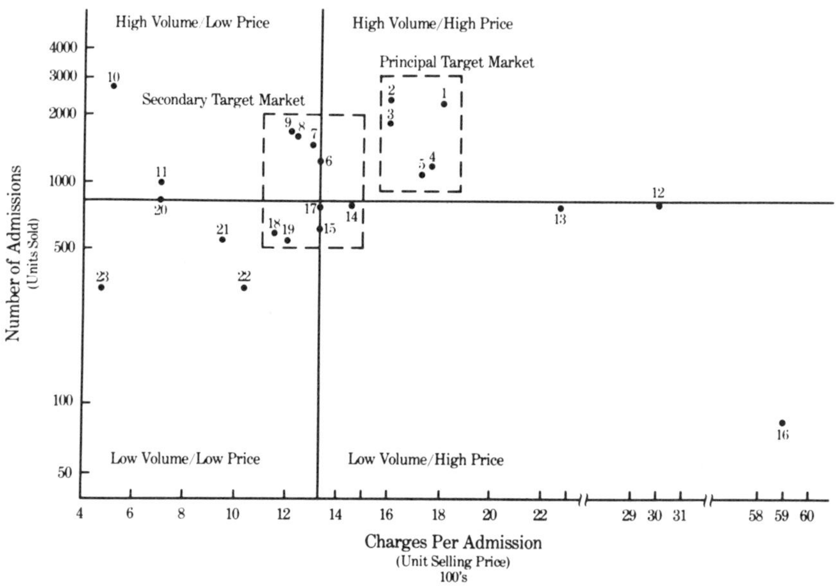

Source: Reprinted from "Product-Market Differentiation: A Strategic Planning Model for Community Hospitals" by Robert A. Milch, in *Strategic Planning in Health Care Management,* ed. W.A. Flexner, E.N. Berkowitz, and M. Brown, with permission of Aspen Systems Corp., Rockville, Md., © 1981.

High volume is not necessarily an adequate measure of the strength of a hospital's position in a market. The hospital may in fact have a small share of the market, be losing physicians to other hospitals and unable to replace them, and have an aging medical staff and inadequate equipment and facilities. The charge per admission may be an inadequate measure of market attractiveness. The market may be shrinking, third party discounts and allowances may be growing, competition from other hospitals may be accelerating, and regulation may be on the increase. The hospital runs a substantial risk of making a poor decision on investment by proceeding on the basis of the information provided in the Figure 8–2 matrix (e.g., by concentrating its funds on SBUs 1 to 5).

Identification of the factors that contribute to position and attractiveness involves judgment combined with accurate information. To this end, techniques are available that use groups of experts to arrive at an agreement on the factors to be included.[20] Each hospital needs to reach agreement on what those factors are by involving the board, administration, medical staff and others.

Table 8–4 presents a list of factors that might contribute to market attractiveness and business position. Based on such a list, the direction and form of the relevant relationships have to be determined. For example, a high proportion of board-certified specialists on the medical staff may be viewed as improving the hospital's position, while the high average age of the staff may be regarded as decreasing it.

Each SBU is given a score for each factor, and the factors are then combined into a single composite score.[21] Decisions about which factors in the Table 8–4 list are relevant and which scores and weights should be assigned to those factors to create a composite score are questions of judgment, depending on management's philosophy and strategy and the situation of the hospital. Relevant information will of course play an important role in the making of those judgments.

Table 8–5 shows a measure of the total size of the market for the services of various subspecialties. The table provides information on the patients treated by physicians in various clinical subspecialties in Worcester, Massachusetts, during 1980. Data from patient discharge abstracts are used to assign patients to a single clinical subspecialty. The subspecialties are then ranked according to the number of discharges.

Table 8–6 shows the market share for cardiology for various Worcester area hospitals. The table indicates the strength of each hospital's position. St. Vincent's Hospital is in a strong position, with 31 percent of the discharges. It is not dominant in the total market, however, since Memorial Hospital has 28 percent of the cardiology discharges.

Hospital management would also want to look at the revenues, expenses, and operating margins associated with each physician SBU. Table 6–7 shows the operating margin by DRG. By aggregating the DRGs associated with each SBU,

Table 8–4 Factors Contributing to the Market Attractiveness and Business Position of a Hospital

Attractiveness of Market	*Position of SBU*
1. Market factors:	
• size	share of market
• growth rate	annual growth rate
• sensitivity to price	price and influence on prices
• sensitivity to service features	features offered and dominance in market
• bargaining power of:	bargaining power of:
a. third party payers	third party payers
b. consumers	consumers
c. physicians	physicians
2. Competition:	
• degree of concentration	relative rank among competitors
• rapidness of entry and exit from markets	competitiveness in markets entered and exited
• changes in share	changes in relative share
• likelihood of technology substitution	vulnerability to new technology
• degree and types of integration	level of integration
3. Financial and economic factors:	
• economies of scale and experience	scale and experience
• barriers to entry or exit	barriers to entry or exit
• capacity utilization	capacity utilized
4. Technological factors:	
• maturity and volatility	ability to cope with change
• complexity	depth of skills
• differentiation	types of skills
• protection from diffusion	approval to use by government or other authority
5. Sociopolitical factors in the environment:	
• changes in attitudes and tastes	responsiveness and flexibility
• laws and government regulations	ability to cope
• influence with government and interest groups	political resources
• influence of community groups	responsiveness, flexibility, and current relationships

Source: From Derek F. Abell/John S. Hammond, *Strategic Market Planning: Problems and Analytical Approaches,* © 1979, p. 214. Adapted by permission of Prentice-Hall, Inc., Englewood Cliffs, N.J.

Table 8–5 Clinical Subspecialty Summary Report for Worcester, Massachusetts, by Town, Age, and Payer, FY 1980

WORCESTER TOTAL

RANK AND SUBSPECIALTY	# OF DSCH	% OF DSCH	# OF DAYS	% OF DAYS	AGE GROUPS 00-14	15-21	22-44	45-64	65-74	75+	PAYOR GROUPS COMM	BC	MCARE	MCAID	OTHER
1 GENERAL SURGERY	2711	10%	31238	14%	8%	8%	26%	27%	16%	15%	10%	40%	30%	10%	10%
2 CARDIOLOGY	2574	9%	26108	11%	1%	1%	6%	30%	26%	36%	4%	26%	61%	4%	4%
3 OBSTETRICS	2522	9%	9503	4%	0%	32%	67%	0%	0%	0%	16%	44%	0%	29%	12%
4 ORTHOPEDICS	2455	9%	28280	12%	5%	8%	30%	27%	13%	17%	10%	36%	30%	9%	15%
5 NEONATOLOGY	2184	8%	10744	5%	100%	0%	0%	0%	0%	0%	15%	47%	0%	26%	12%
6 GASTROENTEROLOGY	2095	8%	14884	6%	16%	5%	19%	23%	16%	20%	8%	35%	36%	15%	5%
7 PSYCHIATRY	1747	6%	21701	9%	1%	5%	45%	34%	10%	4%	9%	40%	21%	21%	10%
8 PULMONARY	1613	6%	14658	6%	23%	2%	10%	20%	19%	25%	5%	25%	45%	20%	4%
9 GYNECOLOGY	1604	6%	6655	3%	1%	8%	61%	23%	4%	3%	16%	50%	8%	22%	4%
10 NEUROLOGY	1194	4%	13058	6%	12%	8%	16%	20%	18%	27%	6%	28%	44%	11%	10%
11 OTOLARYNGOLOGY	1160	4%	3797	2%	41%	14%	22%	13%	7%	4%	14%	47%	12%	22%	5%
12 UROLOGY	964	3%	7861	3%	11%	4%	18%	26%	25%	17%	10%	36%	41%	8%	5%
13 ONCOLOGY	652	2%	8768	4%	2%	2%	6%	29%	32%	29%	7%	24%	59%	6%	3%
14 OPHTHALMOLOGY	648	2%	2578	1%	9%	4%	6%	22%	27%	32%	6%	26%	57%	7%	3%
15 GENERAL MEDICINE	624	2%	3537	2%	21%	12%	29%	14%	9%	15%	7%	36%	23%	22%	12%
16 NEPHROLOGY	528	2%	5041	2%	12%	7%	16%	20%	15%	31%	6%	26%	48%	16%	4%
17 DENTISTRY	519	2%	936	0%	9%	24%	35%	21%	4%	6%	14%	59%	11%	11%	6%
18 ENDOCRINE	487	2%	4873	2%	6%	3%	12%	27%	22%	31%	5%	31%	53%	8%	4%
19 NEUROSURGERY	288	1%	4236	2%	15%	7%	23%	31%	15%	11%	6%	43%	27%	9%	15%
20 THORACIC SURGERY	219	1%	3794	2%	5%	5%	13%	44%	27%	6%	8%	49%	32%	5%	5%
21 HEMATOLOGY	208	1%	1464	1%	29%	5%	15%	9%	11%	31%	5%	17%	47%	24%	7%
22 RHEUMATOLOGY	204	1%	1656	1%	8%	8%	18%	26%	15%	25%	9%	35%	41%	6%	9%
23 VASCULAR SURGERY	197	1%	3756	2%	2%	2%	18%	36%	21%	21%	13%	35%	44%	5%	4%
24 DERMATOLOGY	185	1%	1446	1%	11%	10%	18%	27%	14%	20%	8%	37%	34%	15%	6%
TOTAL GROUPABLE RECORDS	27582	100%	230572	100%	16%	8%	26%	21%	13%	16%	10%	37%	29%	16%	8%

NOTE:
TOTAL UNGROUPABLE RECORDS 1892

Source: Reprinted with permission of the Massachusetts Health Data Consortium, 400-1 Totten Pond Road, Waltham, Mass., 02154, © 1983.

Table 8–6 Clinical Subspecialty Town Report for Worcester, Massachusetts, by Hospital, Age and Payer, FY 1980

WORCESTER TOTAL

CARDIOLOGY

RANK AND HOSPITAL	# OF DSCH	% OF DSCH	# OF DAYS	% OF DAYS	<----------- AGE GROUPS					---------->	<------- PAYOR GROUPS				------>
					00-14	15-21	22-44	45-64	65-74	75+	COMM	BC	MCARE	MCAID	OTHER
1 ST VINCENT HOSPITAL	802	31%	8966	34%	1%	1%	6%	30%	30%	32%	3%	28%	62%	3%	4%
2 MEMORIAL HOSPITAL	715	28%	7359	28%	0%	0%	7%	28%	26%	39%	6%	25%	62%	3%	4%
3 WORCESTER HAHNEMANN HOSPITAL	398	15%	3758	14%	2%	1%	9%	30%	28%	30%	5%	28%	60%	5%	3%
4 FAIRLAWN HOSPITAL	296	11%	3018	12%	0%	0%	3%	18%	17%	62%	2%	14%	78%	3%	3%
5 UNIV. OF MASS. MEDICAL CENTER	155	6%	1076	4%	5%	1%	7%	47%	19%	21%	4%	42%	31%	17%	6%
6 DOCTORS HOSP. OF WORCESTER	104	4%	1139	4%	0%	1%	8%	30%	22%	39%	3%	17%	67%	10%	3%
7 HOLDEN DISTRICT HOSPITAL	32	1%	253	1%	0%	0%	3%	28%	13%	56%	3%	31%	63%	3%	0%
8 MASSACHUSETTS GENERAL HOSPITAL	13	1%	83	0%	15%	8%	8%	38%	15%	15%	0%	62%	38%	0%	0%
9 BRIGHAM AND WOMEN'S HOSPITAL	10	0%	91	0%	0%	0%	0%	50%	40%	10%	10%	10%	50%	0%	30%
10 CLINTON HOSPITAL	7	0%	50	0%	0%	0%	0%	86%	14%	0%	14%	29%	14%	0%	43%
11 CHILDREN'S HOSP MEDICAL CENTER	6	0%	25	0%	100%	0%	0%	0%	0%	0%	17%	50%	0%	17%	17%
12 CAPE COD HOSPITAL	5	0%	36	0%	0%	0%	0%	40%	40%	20%	20%	20%	60%	0%	0%
13 HENRY HEYWOOD MEMORIAL HOSP.	4	0%	26	0%	0%	0%	0%	100%	0%	0%	0%	75%	0%	0%	25%
13 NEW ENGLAND MEDICAL CENTR HOSP	4	0%	17	0%	0%	0%	0%	75%	0%	25%	0%	75%	25%	0%	0%
13 FRAMINGHAM UNION HOSPITAL	4	0%	12	0%	0%	0%	0%	100%	0%	0%	25%	75%	0%	0%	0%
16 MILFORD-WHITINSVILLE REG.HOSP	2	0%	11	0%	0%	0%	0%	0%	100%	0%	0%	0%	100%	0%	0%
16 HARRINGTON MEMORIAL HOSPITAL	2	0%	10	0%	0%	0%	0%	0%	0%	100%	0%	0%	100%	0%	0%
16 FALMOUTH HOSPITAL	2	0%	3	0%	0%	0%	0%	0%	100%	0%	0%	0%	100%	0%	0%
19 BETH ISRAEL HOSPITAL	1	0%	113	0%	0%	0%	0%	100%	0%	0%	0%	0%	0%	100%	0%
19 ALBANY COUNTY HOSPITALS (NY)	1	0%	12	0%	0%	0%	0%	0%	100%	0%	100%	0%	0%	0%	0%
19 GODDARD MEMORIAL HOSPITAL	1	0%	8	0%	0%	0%	0%	100%	0%	0%	100%	0%	0%	0%	0%
19 NEW ENGLAND DEACONESS HOSPITAL	1	0%	8	0%	0%	0%	0%	100%	0%	0%	0%	100%	0%	0%	0%
19 FAULKNER HOSPITAL	1	0%	7	0%	0%	0%	0%	0%	0%	100%	0%	0%	100%	0%	0%
19 LEOMINSTER HOSPITAL	1	0%	7	0%	0%	0%	0%	0%	100%	0%	0%	0%	100%	0%	0%
19 LEONARD MORSE HOSPITAL	1	0%	5	0%	0%	0%	0%	100%	0%	0%	0%	100%	0%	0%	0%
19 ADDISON GILBERT HOSPITAL	1	0%	4	0%	0%	0%	0%	0%	100%	0%	0%	0%	100%	0%	0%
19 LAHEY CLINIC HOSPITAL	1	0%	4	0%	0%	0%	0%	100%	0%	0%	0%	100%	0%	0%	0%
19 ST. JOSEPH'S HOSPITAL	1	0%	3	0%	0%	0%	0%	100%	0%	0%	0%	100%	0%	0%	0%
19 NEW ENGLAND BAPTIST HOSPITAL	1	0%	2	0%	0%	0%	0%	100%	0%	0%	100%	0%	0%	0%	0%
OTHER HOSPITALS	2	0%	2	0%	0%	0%	0%	100%	0%	0%	0%	50%	0%	0%	50%
TOTAL	2574	100%	26108	100%	1%	1%	6%	30%	26%	36%	4%	26%	61%	4%	4%

Source: Reprinted with permission of the Massachusetts Health Data Consortium, 400-1 Totten Pond Road, Waltham, Mass., 02154, © 1983.

the hospital is able to judge its position in each market. By estimating its prospective Medicare rate of payment and projected costs, it can also judge the magnitude of the barrier that the Medicare prospective payment system presents to its entry to various markets.

To determine some of the reasons for high or low operating margins, the hospital needs to examine the operating margin for each physician in a clinical subspecialty (see Table 8–7) and then search for the reasons for positive or negative margins by examining the cost and volume of ancillary and routine services provided to patients.

The consensus developed among hospital managers and board members in the process of carrying out this type of analysis is critical for the development of hospital strategy. The explicitness of the criteria used to rank groups of physicians will stimulate the kind of discussion and debate necessary for effective strategic planning. This type of analysis can be repeated for a number of possible areas of growth or retrenchment, and the hospital can then begin to view its future as one that involves a continual selection among alternatives.

Risk Analysis

Physicians have a major influence on the use of hospital services and therefore affect both the revenues and expenses of the hospital. This makes medical staff

Table 8–7 Operating Margins for Physicians, by Subspecialty

Date: 30-Nov-82
Time: 18:48

Any Hospital—12 Months
Report 4: Operating Margin by Physician

Subspecialty	*Patient Count*	*Direct Revenue*	*Direct Expenses*	*Operating Margin*	*% Margin*
Internal Med-Cardiology:					
925 Dr. #74	276	460,916	320,687	140,229	30.42
183 Dr. #14	165	243,856	260,049	–16,193	–6.64
745 Dr. #59	164	322,406	266,758	55,648	17.26
170 Dr. #12	133	176,640	140,451	36,189	20.49
333 Dr. #23	105	174,452	134,892	39,560	22.68
Subtotal	843	1,378,270	1,122,837	255,433	18.53

Source: Reprinted from "Case-Mix Management Information Systems," Chicago: Amherst Associates, Inc., 1983 with the permission of Amherst Associates, Inc., Chicago, Ill.

analysis essential in financial planning. The accuracy of financial projections is affected by the accuracy of projections of utilization, which in turn depend on projections of the supply and admitting practices of physicians. A change in the characteristics of the hospital's medical staff (e.g., a reduction in the number of family-practice physicians) or their behavior (e.g., a change in the percentage of their patients they admit to a hospital) will affect the accuracy of such projections. A risk analysis can be undertaken to assess the likelihood of such changes. Risk analyses are conducted by hospital staff, consultants, investment bankers, government agencies providing grants or loans, and by agencies like Moodys and Standard and Poors that rate bonds for capital financing.[22]

Of course, not all changes in the medical staff will have the same effect on the hospital. The loss of five physicians could be a disaster, or it could have only a limited impact. Among other factors, the result will depend on the volume of patients that the physicians admitted and the likelihood that that volume can be rapidly replaced. A sensitivity analysis is therefore also important. Such an analysis seeks to measure the size of the impact of a change on utilization, revenues, expenses, and other important variables.

While the computations required for a sensitivity analysis could be carried out by hand, computer models (some of which we describe in Chapters 10 & 11) have been developed to reduce considerably the human effort required. Sensitivity analysis requires the determination of the quantitative relationship between variables, an essential part of the development of a model. In contrast, risk analysis is frequently done by asking questions about the reasonableness of the assumptions being made. For this purpose, a model is useful, but not essential.

Exhibit 8–1 lists some of the information useful in assessing the risk that the characteristics or behavior of the medical staff will adversely affect projections of hospital utilization.

A Risk Analysis for Memorial Hospital

Medical Staff Characteristics

To illustrate how a risk analysis can be carried out, we will examine the medical staff of Memorial Hospital (the name has been changed to protect the hospital's confidentiality). We must first ask whether the medical staff is likely to grow over the next few years. Table 8–8 shows the number of physicians on the medical staff with active or courtesy privileges. Table 8–9 shows that almost 20 percent of the active medical staff is over 60, and that almost 40 percent is over 50. This indicates that the hospital may have to find physicians to replace a substantial proportion of its active medical staff over the next few years. Table 8–10 shows the number of staff additions and deletions over the last 5 years. The hospital has shown an ability to attract physicians and a willingness to grant new physicians admitting privileges.

Exhibit 8–1 Information on the Medical Staff That Is Useful in Risk Analysis

1. **Assumption:** The size of the medical staff will grow at the projected rate, or remain the same.
   Information:
   - number of active and associate staff members and the specialties represented[a]
   - net additions to or deletions from the staff over the last three years
   - age distribution of the current staff
   - teaching programs and the percentage of residents remaining on the medical staff
   - resources devoted to staff recruitment, and types of programs undertaken

2. **Assumption:** The medical staff will have the expertise needed to attract the volume and type of patients projected.
   Information:
   - age, specialty, and board certification of the current medical staff, and of staff added or deleted over the last three years

3. **Assumption:** The hospital's share of the patients admitted by its medical staff will grow or remain the same.
   Information:
   - index of physician investment
   - number of physicians' offices adjacent to or close to the hospital
   - current percentage of patients each physician admits to the hospital
   - medical staff affiliations with other hospitals

4. **Assumption:** The rate at which the medical staff admits patients will increase or remain the same.
   Information:
   - number of physicians participating in HMOs, primary care networks, and other organizations intended to reduce hospitalization
   - number of physicians in large group practices

5. **Assumption:** The subgroup of physicians who provide most of the hospital's patients will continue to do so.
   Information:
   - list of the top ten admitting physicians, by age, specialty, and percentage of total hospital admissions[a]
   - list of physicians (by age and specialty) who provide more than one percent of the hospital's patient days

[a]From "Standard & Poor's Approach to Rating Hospital Revenue Bonds," in *Debt Financing and Capital Formation in Health Care Institutions*, ed. Geoffrey B. Shields (Rockville, Md.: Aspen Systems Corp., 1983), pp. 42–53.

Table 8–8 Memorial Hospital Medical Staff by Specialty and Privileges

	Privileges		
Specialty	*Active*	*Courtesy*	*Total*
Primary care:			
General/Family practice	27	4	31
Internal medicine	11	4	15
Obstetrics/Gynecology	5	2	7
Pediatrics	5	2	7
Subtotal	48	12	60
Other:			
Anesthesiology	2	–	2
Audiology	–	1	1
Emergency	2	–	2
Gastroenterology	2	1	3
General Surgery	9	5	14
Nephrology	1	–	1
Neurology	3	–	3
Neurosurgery	2	–	2
Ophthalmology	4	–	4
Orthopedic surgery	1	2	3
Otolaryngology	2	1	3
Pathology	3	1	4
Plastic surgery	2	–	2
Psychiatry	1	7	8
Radiology	3	2	5
Urology	6	–	6
Subtotal	43	20	63
Total	91	32	123

Source: Reprinted with permission of Block, McGibony + Associates, Inc., Silver Spring, Md.

Memorial Hospital is involved in a joint family practice residency program that started in 1975 with two other hospitals. Of the 11 residents who graduated in the first 5 years, 5 have stayed in the area. However, the amount of training that is done at Memorial has decreased due to the lack of interest on the part of the medical staff. There has never been a full- or part-time director of medical education employed by Memorial to supervise the residency program. A survey of the medical staff revealed that only 52 percent of the medical staff believe that Memorial should make a stronger commitment to the residency program. Finally, the hospital does not have a physician recruitment program, nor does it offer inducements, such as office space, to attract new staff members.

Table 8–9 Memorial Hospital Active Medical Staff, by Specialty and Age Group

Specialty	*Age Groupings* 31–40	41–50	51–59	60+	*Total*
Primary care:					
General/Family practice	8	5	7	7	27
Internal medicine	–	9	–	2	11
Obstetrics	2	1	–	2	5
Pediatrics	2	1	2	–	5
Subtotal	12	16	9	11	48
Other:					
General surgery	1	3	3	2	9
E.R. physicians	1	1	–	–	2
Anesthesiology	1	–	1	–	2
Gastroenterology	1	1	–	–	2
Nephrology	1	–	–	–	1
Neurology	2	1	–	–	3
Neurosurgery	1	1	–	–	2
Ophthalmology	–	–	4	–	4
Otolaryngology	1	–	–	1	2
Orthopedics	–	–	1	–	1
Pathology	1	1	–	1	3
Plastic surgery	1	–	–	1	2
Psychiatry	1	–	–	–	1
Radiology	1	1	–	1	3
Urology	3	2	–	1	6
Subtotal	16	11	9	7	43
Totals	28	27	18	18	91
Percentage of total	30.7%	29.7%	19.8%	19.8%	100%

Source: Reprinted by permission of Block, McGibony + Associates, Inc., Silver Spring, Md.

While the number of new physicians suggests that the hospital is able to replace those who retire or resign due to age, Memorial Hospital currently takes little positive action to ensure that that ability will continue in the future. Unless the reasons for physicians to join the medical staff are better understood, and appropriate actions taken, a substantial risk exists that, in the future, a sufficient number of physicians will not be found.

The assumption that the medical staff will have the expertise it needs to attract a sufficient number of patients then has to be examined. As Table 8–8 shows,

Table 8–10 Memorial Hospital Additions/Deletions to Medical Staff from 1975 through 1979 (June)

Year	*Additions*	*Resigned*	*Deletions*[a]	*Appointment Discontinued*
1975	15	–		–
1976	13	2		–
1977	24	3		–
1978	18	3		4
1979	12	2		5
Totals	82[b]	10		9

[a]Does not include three physicians who are deceased
[b]Of those physicians admitted to staff during and since 1975, 41 now have active or associate privileges and 25 now have consulting privileges.

Source: Reprinted with permission of Block, McGibony + Associates, Inc., Silver Spring, Md.

more than half of the active staff are in primary care specialties. No information on board certification or eligibility is reported in the hospital's long-range plan.

The adequacy of the medical staff's expertise could be assessed in a number of ways. The need for physicians in the hospital's service area could be determined by using certain quantitative techniques.[23] Memorial's medical staff could be compared with those in similar hospitals, defined in terms of bed size, urban/rural location, and other factors. Finally, the medical staff could be surveyed to determine what specialties are underrepresented on the medical staff.

Table 8–11 shows the need for physicians in Memorial Hospital's service area in 1975 and 1985. Need was determined by multiplying the national physician-to-population ratio for each specialty by the appropriate population projection. The additional physicians needed to meet the national norm is indicated. The table shows a need for more primary care physicians, as well as physicians in other medical care specialties, in particular, general surgeons, psychiatrists, and anesthesiologists.

This method of determining physician need has an number of shortcomings. It assumes that the distribution of specialists in the United States is ideal (e.g., the calculation results in a decrease in the need for general family physicians and an increase in internists), and it does not take into account the possible substitution of nurse practitioners and other health workers for physicians. It has the advantage, however, that the data required to estimate the number of physicians needed in the service area are readily available.

The medical staff of Memorial Hospital were surveyed to determine their opinion on the need for additional physicians. They were asked whether the

Table 8–11 Physician Requirements in Memorial Hospital's Area

		1975		*1985*	
Specialty	*Physicians*	*Phys. Needed*[a]	*Additional Required*	*Phys. Needed*[a]	*Additional Required*
Primary care:					
General/Family practice	107.0	68	(39.0)	71	(36.0)
Internal medicine	23.5	62	38.5	64	40.5
OB/GYN	11.0	26	15.0	27	16.0
Pediatrics	9.5	25	15.5	26	16.5
Subtotal	151.0	181	30.0	188	37.0
Medical specialties:					
Cardiology	7.0	7	0.0	7	0.0
Dermatology	4.0	6	2.0	6	2.0
Gastroenterology	1.0	2	1.0	2	1.0
Pulmonary disease	0.5	2	1.5	2	1.5
Subtotal	12.5	17	4.5	17	4.5
Surgical specialties:					
General surgery	13.5	38	24.5	39	25.5
Neurosurgery	3.0	4	1.0	4	1.0
Ophthalmology	11.0	14	3.0	14	3.0
Orthopedics	6.5	14	7.5	14	7.5
Otolaryngology	7.0	7	0.0	7	0.0
Plastic surgery	3.0	3	0.0	3	0.0
Thoracic surgery	5.0	2	(3.0)	2	(3.0)
Urology	8.0	8	0.0	8	0.0
Subtotal	57.0	90	33.0	91	34.0
Other specialties:					
Anesthesiology	6.0	15	9.0	16	10.0
Neurology	2.0	4	2.0	4	2.0
Pathology	7.5	12	4.5	12	4.5
Psychiatry	12.0	25	13.0	26	14.0
Radiology	13.5	17	3.5	18	4.5
Other	6.0	5	(1.0)	6	0.0
Subtotal	47.0	78	31.0	82	35.0
Grand totals	267.5	366	98.5	378	110.5

[a]Physicians needed to meet national norms.

Source: Reprinted with permission of Block, McGibony + Associates, Inc., Silver Spring, Md.

medical staff currently needed more physicians. As Table 8–12 shows, 56 percent said more were needed. The need for orthopedists was most frequently cited.

No information is available on the specialties of physicians who joined the medical staff of Memorial Hospital over the last few years. This information would help in evaluating the ability of the hospital to attract various types of physicians.

Memorial is a community hospital of just under 300 beds located in an area that has a supply of primary care physicians proportionately below that in the nation as a whole. The fact that the majority of its active medical staff consists of primary care specialists is not inconsistent with what we know about the hospital and its role. However, the hospital needs to consider the opportunities to expand the medical staff in areas such as psychiatry and orthopedics. On the other hand, our risk analysis does not suggest that the hospital faces a significant risk of lower-than-expected utilization due to a lack of expertise in its medical staff.

Table 8–12 Memorial Hospital Medical Staff Questionnaire Responses: Need for Physicians on the Medical Staff

Question 18: Do you believe that the Medical Staff needs more physicians?

	Number	*%*
Yes	37	56.1
No	29	43.9
Totals	66	100.0%

If yes, what type?

	No. of Responses		*No. of Responses*
Orthopedics	16	Primary care	1
Neurology	5	Allergy	1
Psychiatry	5	Emergency med.	1
General practice	4	Physiatrist	1
OB/GYN	4	Internal medicine	1
Subspecialists	3	Pathologists	1
Family practice	3	Internists	1
ENT	2	Hematologist	1
Pediatrics	2	Dermatology	1
Anesthesiology	2	Gastroenterology	1
Nephrology	2		
Neonatology	2		

Source: Reprinted with permission of Block, McGibony + Associates, Inc., Silver Spring, Md.

Admissions and Referrals

Another assumption that could be questioned is whether Memorial's share of the patients admitted by its medical staff will grow or remain the same. Sufficient information was not available to calculate the index of physician investment (see Table 8–2). However, the number of physicians with offices in or adjacent or close to the hospital can indicate an ongoing commitment to admit patients to the hospital.

Table 8–13 and Figure 8–3 show the location of physicians' offices. Of the 91 active physicians, 53 have offices located in the city in which Memorial is located, 12 have offices in the hospital (specialists in anesthesiology, emergency medicine, pathology, and radiology), and another 12 have offices in an adjacent medical arts building. The medical arts building operates at full capacity. A survey of the medical staff showed that 11 of the 61 physicians who do not rent

Table 8–13 Memorial Hospital: Location of Active Medical Staff Offices, April, 1979

Location	*Medical Staff*		
	Primary	*Other*	*Total*
Zip code area 01	2	3	5
Zip code area 02	11	12	23
Zip code area 03	1	–	1
Medical Arts Bldg.	7	5	12
Hospital	2	10	12
Subtotal	23	30	53
Zip code area 04	6	14	20
Zip code area 05	2	–	2
Zip code area 06	2	–	2
Zip code area 07	2	1	3
Zip code area 34	3	1	4
Zip code area 40	1	1	2
Zip code area 43	2	–	2
Zip code area 51	2	–	2
Zip code area 12	1	–	1
Subtotal	21	17	38
Totals	44	47	91

Source: Reprinted with permission of Block, McGibony + Associates, Inc., Silver Spring, Md.

Figure 8–3 Memorial Hospital: Percentage of Active Medical Staff Members in Cities and Towns of Hawthorne County

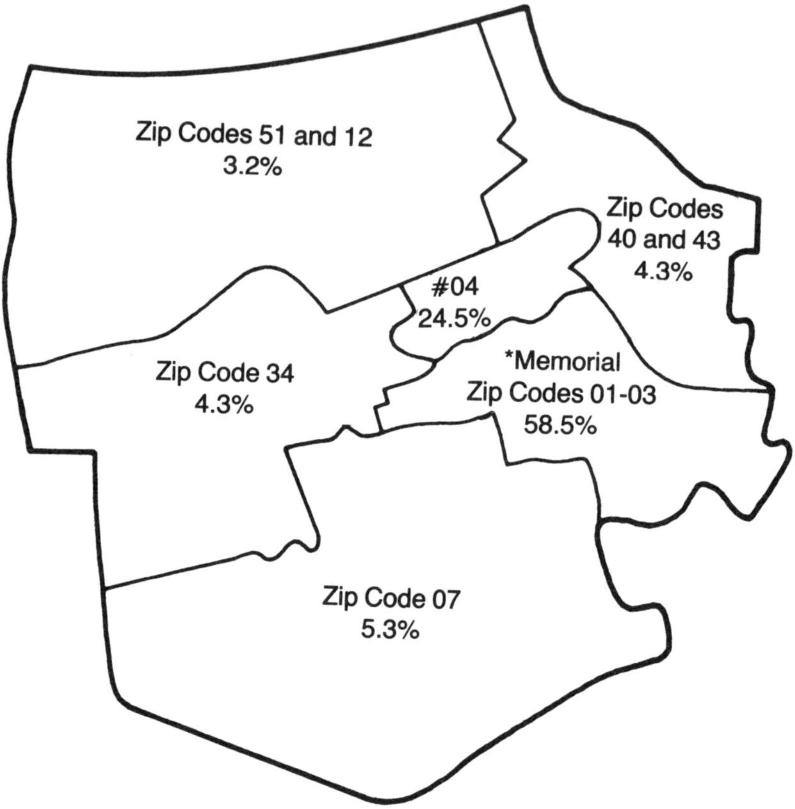

Source: Reprinted with permission of Block, McGibony + Associates, Inc., Silver Spring, Md.

space near the hospital would be interested in moving closer. Of the physicians not working in the city, most have offices in an adjacent town.

Information was not available on the number of affiliations of the medical staff with other hospitals or the percentage of their patients that physicians admit to Memorial. A review of hospital records did show, however, that only 1 of the 15 physicians who joined the medical staff in the last 3 years admits a significant number of patients to Memorial.

The survey questionnaire (to which 88, or 59 percent of the medical staff responded) did yield useful information on the attitudes of physicians who admit less than 30 percent of their patients to Memorial. Table 8–14 shows that, for

Table 8–14 Memorial Hospital Medical Staff Questionnaire Responses: Reasons for Lower Admissions to the Hospital

Question 9: If you admit less than 30 percent of your patients to Memorial Hospital, please indicate your reasons for this. Please rank your answers using number one (1) as the most serious; number ten (10) as the least serious.

Most serious reason:	*Number*	*Percent*
As a specialist, most of my referrals come from physicians on the staffs of other hospitals.	22	57.9
Lack of patient referrals from Memorial staff physicians	20	52.6
Physician's convenience	16	42.1
Other[a]	16	42.1
Patient's preference	13	34.2
Lack of specialized services	10	26.3
Location	7	18.4
Deficiencies in Anesthesia	6	15.8
Deficiencies in Nursing	5	13.2
Deficiencies in Laboratory	5	13.2
Deficiencies in X-ray	5	13.2
Lack of available beds when needed	5	13.2
Inadequate house staff	3	7.9

[a]Only 38 respondents; does not apply to top admitters.

Source: Reprinted with permission of Block, McGibony + Associates, Inc., Silver Spring, Md.

20 physicians, the lack of referrals from physicians on Memorial's staff was the most serious reason. Deficiencies in Memorial's services and facilities were less frequently cited. Table 8–15 shows that 31 physicians would increase their admissions to Memorial if they could get more referrals from Memorial's medical staff.

The available information suggests that Memorial Hospital's share of the admissions of its staff could decrease. If new physicians are not admitting a significant number of patients, the hospital could soon be left with a medical staff with little commitment to the hospital. Another group of physicians is unable to increase its commitment to the hospital because of the lack of referrals. Unless this situation changes, Memorial faces the risk of lower utilization as members of the current medical staff retire.

The risk to the hospital if physicians alter the rate at which they hospitalize patients also needs to be assessed. Medical practice in Memorial's service area is predominantly solo practice; the service area is in a part of the United States that has historically had few HMOs.

Table 8–15 Memorial Hospital Medical Staff Questionnaire Responses: Reasons for Increasing Admissions to the Hospital

Question 10: What single factor would cause you to increase your number of admissions to Memorial Hospital?

	Number	*Percent*
More referrals from Memorial's medical staff	31	41.9
Other	22	29.7
Availability of beds	8	10.8
More adequate equipment or facilities	5	6.8
Better availability of nursing staff	3	4.1
Office space at or near Memorial	3	4.1
Better availability of other ancillary staff	2	2.7
Totals	74	100.0%[a]

Comments:
- Sterilization
- CAT Scanner
- A high quality Psychiatric Staff
- E.R. call schedule for oral and maxillo facial surgeons.

[a]May not add to 100 percent due to rounding.

Source: Reprinted with permission of Block, McGibony + Associates, Inc., Silver Spring, Md.

A majority of the studies that have been undertaken on this subject show that members of group practice HMOs (i.e., prepaid group practices) are admitted less often to the hospital and have shorter lengths of stay. The evidence that this also is true for members of individual practice associations (a form of HMO in which physicians continue to practice in their existing offices) is less convincing.[24] Group practices can also become large enough to sponsor outpatient surgery centers and to offer other services that hospitals now provide on an inpatient basis. No information is available on the number of physicians in group practices, or on the possible start-up of an HMO, in Memorial Hospital's service area.

Another assumption that could also be questioned is that the group of physicians that provides most of Memorial Hospital's patients will continue to do so. Table 8–16 provides a list of physicians ranked according to the number of patient days they contributed to Memorial in 1978. The top ten physicians were responsible for approximately 41.89 percent of the patient days. Eight of the ten were in primary care specialties and the remaining two were general surgeons, which confirms the hospital's dependence on primary care specialists. Two of the ten, responsible for 6.23 percent of the hospital's total patient days, were

Table 8–16 Memorial Hospital Physicians Ranked by Number of Patient Days Contributed, July 1 to December 31, 1978

Physician No.	*(Age)*	*Type of Practice*	*Privileges*	*No. of Pt. Days*	*% of Total Pt. Days*	*Cumulative*
1.	50	Gen. Practice	Active	2,876	7.35	7.35
2.	49	Gen. Practice	Active	2,625	6.71	14.06
3.	44	Int. Medicine	Active	1,698	4.33	18.38
4.	44	Int. Medicine	Active	1,605	4.10	22.48
5.	59	Gen. Surg.	Active	1,313	3.35	25.84
6.	65	Gen. Practice	Active	1,293	3.30	29.17
7.	38	Pediatrics	Active	1,286	3.29	32.46
8.	65	Gen. Practice	Active	1,136	2.90	35.36
9.	53	Family Practice	Active	1,089	2.78	38.14
10.	42	Gen. Surgery	Active	1,077	2.75	40.89
11.	44	I.M./Cardiology	Active	1,072	2.74	43.63
12.	61	Gen. Practice	Active	982	2.50	46.13
13.	53	Orthopedics	Active	856	2.19	48.32
14.	—	Gen. Practice	Active	837	2.14	50.46
15.	40	Gen. Surgery	Active	808	2.06	52.52
16.	50	Gen. Practice	Active	735	1.88	54.40
17.	64	Gen. Practice	Active	723	1.85	56.25
18.	55	Gen. Practice	Active	710	1.81	58.06
19.	63	Urology	Active	690	1.76	59.82
20.	45	Psychiatry	Consulting	685	1.75	61.57
21.	37	Gen. Practice	Active	660	1.69	63.26
22.	65	Family Practice	Active	604	1.54	64.80
23.	60	OB/Gynecology	Active	595	1.52	66.32
24.	65	Gen. Surgery	Active	583	1.49	67.81

Table 8–16 continued

Physician No.	(Age)	Type of Practice	Privileges	No. of Pt. Days	% of Total Pt. Days	Cumulative
25.	58	Gen. Practice	Active	569	1.45	69.26
26.	43	I.M./Hematology	Active	565	1.44	70.70
27.	45	I.M./Cardiology	Active	561	1.43	72.13
28.	66	OB/Gynecology	Active	511	1.31	73.44
29.	57	Gen. Practice	Active	470	1.20	74.64
30.	56	Gen. Surgery	Active	453	1.16	75.80
31.	54	Pediatrics	Active	445	1.14	76.94
32.	42	Pediatrics	Active	437	1.12	78.06
33.	41	Plastic Surg.	Active	408	1.04	79.10
34.	51	Gen. Sur./Thorac.	Active	390	1.00	80.10
35.	42	Psychiatric	Consulting	389	.99	81.09
36.	68	Gen. Practice	Active	385	.98	82.07
37.	45	Int. Medicine	Active	383	.98	83.05
38.	73	Gen. Practice	Active	246	.63	83.68
39.	55	Ophthalmology	Active	243	.62	84.30
40.	44	I.M./Pulmonary	Active	241	.62	84.91
41.	52	Gen. Practice	Active	229	.59	85.50
42.	61	Plastic Surg.	Active	225	.57	86.07
43.	71	Gen. Practice	Honorary	212	.54	86.61
44.	54	Gen. Practice	Active	207	.53	87.14
45.	42	Gen. Surgery	Active	205	.52	87.66
46.	36	I.M./Cardiology	Active	197	.50	88.16
47.	39	Otolaryngology	Active	179	.46	88.62
48.	51	Urology	Active	162	.41	89.03
49.	37	Int. Medicine	Consulting	155	.40	89.43
50.	65	Int. Medicine	Active	154	.39	89.82

Table 8–16 continued

Physician No.	*(Age)*	*Type of Practice*	*Privileges*	*No. of Pt. Days*	*% of Total Pt. Days*	*Cumulative*
51.	61	Pediatrics	Active	143	.37	90.19
52.	58	Ophthalmology	Active	138	.35	90.54
53.	39	Urology	Active	138	.35	90.89
54.	38	Neurosurgery	Active	130	.33	91.22
55.	—	Ophthalmology	Honorary	126	.32	91.54
56.	32	OB/Gynecology	Active	122	.31	91.85
57.	32	I.M./Cardiology	Active	107	.27	92.12
58.	—	Pediatrics	*	107	.27	92.39
59.	—	Gen. Practice	*	106	.27	92.66
60.	—	Gen. Practice	*	103	.26	92.92
61.	—	Pediatrics	*	101	.26	93.18
62.	—	Gen. Practice	*	91	.23	93.41
63.	33	Gastroent.	Active	75	.19	93.60
64.	32	Orthopedics	*	66	.17	93.77
65.	—	Pediatrics	*	57	.15	93.92
66.	50	Pathology	Consulting	56	.14	94.06
Sub-Total				36,825	94.09	94.06
67. Maternal Health				1,051	2.69	96.75
68. Unassigned and Other				1,262	3.22	100.0
Totals:				39,138	100.0%	100.0%

*Do not have staff privileges, but admit a small number of patients.

Source: Reprinted with permission of Block, McGibony + Associates, Inc., Silver Spring, Md.

over 65. Of the 66 physicians who provided 94.06 percent of the hospital's patient days, 15 were 60 years or older and accounted for 21.70 percent of total patient days.

An analysis of the distribution of admissions by physician in each medical specialty reveals another possible risk. In OB/GYN, two physicians, age 60 and 65, accounted for over 90 percent of admissions. The retirement of either or both could drastically reduce the capabilities of the hospital in this specialty.

As noted earlier, Memorial Hospital appears to have little difficulty attracting new staff, but none of those who have received staff privileges over the last 3 years admit a significant number of patients. Other physicians are having difficulty obtaining referrals. The risk to the hospital is that older physicians who are responsible for a substantial proportion of the hospital's utilization will not be replaced with physicians who have a similar level of commitment. This risk appears significant.

Physician Characteristics and Environment

Block, McGibony + Associates emphasize the importance of the professional environment in determining whether physicians—especially potential medical staff—utilize the hospital. While the location of physician offices in relationship to the hospital and the array of services available are critical for some physicians, for others the professional environment is just as important.

The professional environment includes:

1. The attitudes and values of the medical staff with respect to medicine and medical practice, including the organization of medical practice.
2. The rules and practices of the medical staff with regard to:
   (a) the granting and use of clinical privileges
   (b) professional responsibility
   (c) quality assurance and continuing education programs
3. Medical staff organization and the involvement of the staff in the planning and decision making processes.
4. The treatment accorded new staff members, e.g., privileges, referrals.[25]

An understanding of this environment requires a combination of data analysis, interviews, and observation of the hospital's day-to-day workings. As the data presented above suggest, the ability of Memorial Hospital to increase or maintain its current level of utilization depends on whether new physicians are attracted to the medical staff and whether physicians with a similar level of commitment to the hospital replace those who are approaching retirement.

Of particular concern is the absence of any formal process for dealing with the problem of physician recruitment and physician investment in the hospital. The establishment of a committee or task force composed of members of the board, administration, and medical staff and the development of specific goals (e.g., to have two new OB/GYN physicians on the staff within six months) would lower the risks of falling levels of physician recruitment and investment.

If Memorial is successful in recruiting new, younger physicians, it will have to begin to estimate what the effect will be on the need for beds and services. Figure 8–4 and Table 8–17 show the age distribution of physicians in St. Joseph's Hospital's Department of Medicine and the percentage of discharges, patient days, and surgical cases attributed to each age group. It shows that physicians 60 and over are responsible for a much smaller share of hospital utilization than other age groups.

The relationship between surgery and age is also highlighted. Physicians under 40 represent about 20 percent of the staff and less than 5 percent of patient days, but they perform about 18 percent of the surgery. Physicians over 60 represent about 15 percent of the medical staff and 12 percent of the patient days, but they do only about 4 percent of the surgery. Other data reveal that the average length of stay for patients of physicians under 40 is four days shorter than for physicians over 60, seven days shorter than for physicians 40–49 and five days shorter than for physicians 50–59.

It is impossible to say from these data from St. Joseph's if the difference among physicians in these age groups is due to the type of patient they are seeing (e.g., differences in diagnosis or severity), their medical education, or their clinical subspecialty. However, if Memorial Hospital follows the same pattern, it could have serious consequences for the hospital. While younger physicians may use the hospital's ancillary services as intensely as older physicians, they may not fill as many beds. Projections of hospital use could be highly inaccurate unless this situation is examined and taken into account.

It would, of course, be useful to have more information than we have provided here. Still, the examples of data we have presented from hospital plans illustrate what planners, bankers, and bond rating agencies look at as they question the assumptions underlying projections of utilization. This questioning is an iterative process, that is, each piece of information is capable of suggesting new information that should be looked at. There is no formula that defines where the questioning stops. The desire of decision makers to see additional information will depend on personal factors (e.g., the management style referred to in Chapter 1), the cost of acquiring the additional information, and the financial and other risks involved.

MEDICAL STAFF ANALYSIS IN THE STRATEGIC PLANNING PROCESS

Medical staff analysis is only one part of the strategic planning process, but it provides useful information for all of the planning tasks discussed in Chapter 2. Table 8–18 shows the types of analysis required for each task in the strategic

Figure 8–4 St. Joseph's Hospital Department of Medicine: Age Distribution and Utilization Patterns, 1980

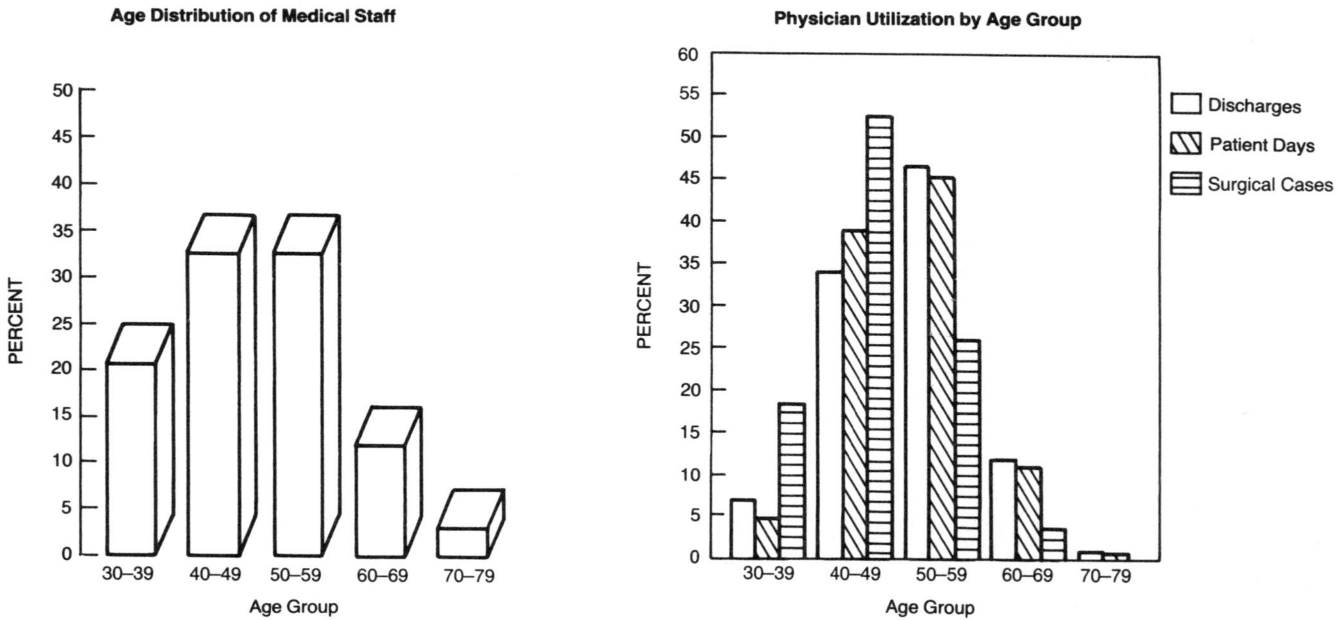

Source: Confidential communication with the hospital.

Table 8–17 St. Joseph's Hospital Department of Medicine: Utilization of Acute Care Facilities by Age Group

Physician Number	1980 Discharges #	1980 Discharges %	1980 Patient Days #	1980 Patient Days %	Average Length of Stay	Surgical Cases #	Surgical Cases %
Age Group: 30–39							
372	79	3.1	833	2.1	10.5	3	1.2
Other (6)	95	3.7	988	2.5	10.4	45	17.3
Summary: Age 30–39	174	6.9	1,821	4.6	10.5	48	18.5
Age Group: 40–49							
342	217	8.6	3,908	9.8	18.0	3	1.2
850	157	6.2	1,968	4.9	12.5	12	4.6
365	130	5.1	1,375	3.5	10.6	3	1.2
361	107	4.2	2,428	6.1	22.7	99	38.1
364	71	2.8	3,089	7.8	43.5	17	6.5
481	59	2.3	582	1.5	9.9	—	—
362	56	2.2	767	1.9	13.7	—	—
Other (4)	63	2.5	1,332	3.3	19.7	2	0.8
Summary: Age 40–49	860	33.9	15,449	38.8	17.9	136	52.3
Age Group: 50–59							
307	284	11.2	4,814	12.1	17.0	4	1.5
327	205	8.1	2,247	5.7	11.0	46	17.7
300	153	6.0	1,513	3.8	9.9	5	1.9
355	126	5.0	1,523	3.8	12.1	1	0.4
301	111	4.4	3,013	7.6	27.1	2	0.8
359	102	4.0	1,414	3.6	13.9	6	2.3
356	98	3.9	2,067	5.2	21.1	—	—
303	87	3.4	1,164	2.9	13.4	1	0.4
Other (3)	14	0.6	169	0.4	11.4	2	0.8
Summary: Age 50–59	1,180	46.5	17,924	45.1	15.2	67	25.8
Age Group: 60–69							
310	136	5.4	2,530	6.4	18.6	6	2.3
318	101	4.0	1,227	3.1	12.1	2	0.8
367	63	2.5	549	1.4	8.7	1	0.4
Other (1)	1	—	1	—	1.0	—	—
Summary: Age 60–69	301	11.9	4,307	10.8	14.3	9	3.5
Age Group: 70–79							
Other (1)	22	0.9	272	0.7	12.4	—	—
Summary: Age 70–79	22	0.9	272	0.7	12.4	—	—
Total Staff (34)	2,537	100.0	39,773	100.0	15.7	260	100.0

Source: Confidential communication with the hospital.

Table 8–18 Medical Staff Analysis Required in the Strategic Planning Process

Planning Tasks	Analysis Required
1. Internal analysis	Identify physician groups served, needs met, and technologies used. Examine the professional environment and management style of physicians.
2. External analysis	Identify total potential physician market, served and unserved. Identify competitors for physician loyalty.
3. Assessment of present position	Determine change over time in the portion of potential market served and the impact of that change on the hospital.
4. Development and evaluation of alternative scenarios	Forecast utilization and financial conditions, assuming no change in physician markets served, and then assuming decreases or increases in physicians served due to competition and other factors.
5. Revision of mission statement and development of goals	Compare current and future markets with those in initial mission statement. Assess impact of market goals.
6. Development and evaluation of alternative strategies	Assess impact of alternative changes in physician groups served, functions performed, and technology used. Estimate use, financial impact, and competitor response.
7. Determination of strategies and objectives	Describe physician groups, functions, and technologies over the time frame of the plan.
8. Development of contingency plans	Determine what changes in physician markets would have the most serious negative consequences. Assess the impact of alternative strategies for limiting their impact. Set "trigger points" for signaling a need to act.
9. Development and implementation of program and operational plans	Specify characteristics of physician markets to be served.
10. Development of an evaluation, monitoring, and control system	Monitor changes in the use of services by the physician markets selected. Compare changes with goals in plan. Explain and determine impact of variances.
11. Revision and implementation of contingency plans	Reexamine assumptions about physician groups, their needs, and the technologies to be used.

planning process. These analyses parallel those involved in gaining market and service area information, as described in Table 6–8.

Though all of the analyses listed in Table 8–18 are not described in this chapter, the analyses related to service area and market definition, market-attractiveness/business-position, and risk will supply much of the information

Exhibit 8–2 Information on Physicians To Support Selected Strategic Planning Decisions

1. **Task: Internal Analysis**
   - *Decision/question:*Is there a need and/or demand for other services and technologies in the physician groups we now serve?
   - *Information:*
     a. use of other hospitals (or alternative facilities) by hospital physicians
     b. differences in the services and technologies offered by alternative facilities
     c. net additions or deletions to the medical staff over the last three years; age distribution of the medical staff
2. **Task: External Analysis**
   - *Decision/question:*What physician market is not being served by the hospital?
   - *Information:*
     a. age, specialty, and office location of physicians who admit less than a majority of their patients to the hospital
     b. differences in the age and specialty of the hospital's medical staff and the staffs of its principal competitors
     c. age, specialty, and office location of physicians engaged in alternative forms of practice (e.g., HMOs, free-standing ambulatory surgery centers)
3. **Task: Assessment of Present Position**
   - *Decision/question:* Has the hospital demonstrated the ability to gain or retain the loyalty of the physicians it needs?
   - *Information:*
     a. change in the hospital medical staff's age and specialty distribution, in relation both to past years and to the hospital's competitors
     b. admissions per physician by department and age group; rate of admissions among older and younger physicians
     c. percentage of medical staff who are board certified and board eligible
4. **Task: Development and Evaluation of Alternative Scenarios**
   - *Decision/question:* What would be the impact on utilization of continuing current trends in the physician groups served?
   - *Information:*
     a. forecast of patient days based on the rate of admissions and length of stay for the current medical staff 40–55 years of age (thereby excluding younger and older physicians whose practices are changing)
     b. forecast of the number of physicians in each department in 5 years, based on current rate of additions and deletions
5. **Task: Revision of the Mission Statement and Development of Goals**
   - *Decision/question:*Can the hospital provide in 5 years the services listed in its initial mission statement with its forecasted supply of physicians?
   - *Information:*
     a. forecast of admissions and procedures by department and specific services, based on forecasts of the number of physicians and the current use rate
     b. comparison of licensure and certification requirements for specific services; forecasted availability of physicians

Exhibit 8–2 continued

6. **Task: Development and Evaluation of Alternative Strategies**
   - *Decision/question:* Should the hospital attempt to attract established physicians or new physicians arriving in the community?
   - *Information:*
     a. extent to which physicians invest heavily in individual hospitals by concentrating their admissions
     b. hospital's location in relationship to the offices of physicians not on the medical staff
     c. hospital's location in relationship to areas of population growth
     d. ability of the hospital to match or exceed others in making equipment and other services available to physicians
7. **Task: Setting of Strategies and Objectives**
   - *Decision/question:* Which physician groups will the hospital serve? With what services? Using what technologies?
   - *Information:*
     a. annual estimates of additions to the medical staff by specialty
     b. a prioritized list of capital expenditures needed to attract and retain physicians in specific specialties
     c. estimates of the annual volume of admissions and procedures by type
8. **Task: Development of Contingency Plans**
   - *Decision/question:* What changes in the medical staff would have the most serious impact on the number of admissions?
   - *Information:*
     a. names, ages, and specialties of the top ten admitters to the hospital over the next 5 years, percentage of total admissions and patient days they represent, level of their investment in the hospital
     b. expected average waiting time to recruit a physician in each specialty

that is needed. For example, the market definition and risk analysis will provide information needed for internal and external analyses and the assessment of the hospital's current position.

SUPPORT FOR SPECIFIC PLANNING DECISIONS

Each of the planning tasks listed in Table 8–18 requires many decisions and answers to numerous questions. Some of these questions and decisions are listed in Exhibit 8–2. These decisions and questions and related information parallel those required for service area and market analyses, as listed in Exhibit 6–6. Hospitals that have recently undertaken financial feasibility studies will have some of the necessary information (see Exhibit 8–1). However, it may be necessary for some hospitals to develop the capability to capture the necessary data and to develop systems for analyzing them. This can be done through a special study, or computers can be used routinely to implement the necessary data collection and analysis (see Chapter 11).

REFERENCES

1. R. Kropf and S.B. Goldsmith, "Innovation in Hospital Plans," *Health Care Management Review,* (Spring 1983), pp. 7–16.

2. This research is summarized in G.W. Shannon and G.E.A. Dever, *Health Care Delivery—Spatial Perspectives* (New York: McGraw-Hill, 1974), pp. 121–128.

3. O.L. Peterson et al., "The Doctor and the Medical Community," *Journal of Medical Education* 31 (December 1956):95.

4. T.F. Williams et al., "Patient Referrals to a University Clinic: Patterns in a Rural State," *American Journal of Public Health* 50, no. 10 (1960):1503.

5. M.S.T. Hobbs and E.D. Acheson, "Perinatal Mortality and the Organization of Obstetric Services in the Oxford Area in 1962," *British Medical Journal* (February 26, 1966), p. 502.

6. Williams et al., "Patient Referrals," p. 1503.

7. This term was suggested by S.B. Goldsmith, Sc.D., Professor of Health Administration, University of Massachusetts at Amherst.

8. *American Medical Directory* (Chicago: American Medical Association, 1982).

9. *Directory of Medical Specialists* (Chicago: Marquis Who's Who, Inc., 1981).

10. One such company is MMS, Inc., Chicago, which is authorized by the AMA and the American Osteopathic Association to publish and distribute lists of physicians and osteopaths.

11. A useful discussion of physician inventories is contained in A. Oreglia et al., *A Guide to the Development of Health Resource Inventories,* DHEW Publication no. (HRA) 76-14504 (Rockville, Md.: U.S. Department of Health, Education, and Welfare, 1976), pp. 99–129.

12. H. Luft, "How Do Health Maintenance Organizations Achieve Their 'Savings'?: Rhetoric and Evidence," *New England Journal of Medicine* 298, no. 24 (June 15, 1978):1338–1342.

13. E. Friedson, "The Organization of Medical Practice" in H.E. Freeman, S. Levin, and L.G. Reader, *Handbook of Medical Sociology*. Englewood Cliffs, N.J.: Prentice-Hall, 1963, p. 348.

14. W. McClure, *Reducing Excess Hospital Capacity* (Excelsior, Minn.: InterStudy, 1976), p. 24.

15. D.F. Abell and J.S. Hammond, *Strategic Market Planning* (Englewood Cliffs, N.J.: Prentice-Hall, 1979), p. 212.

16. P. Kotler, *Marketing Management: Analysis, Planning and Control* (Englewood Cliffs, N.J.: Prentice-Hall, 1980), p. 78.

17. Abell and Hammond, *Strategic Market Planning,* p. 216–220.

18. Kotler, *Marketing Management,* p. 79.

19. R.A. Milch, "Product-Market Differentiation: A Strategic Planning Model for Community Hospitals," in *Strategic Planning In Health Care Management,* ed. W.A. Flexner, E.N. Berkowitz, and M. Brown (Rockville, Md.: Aspen Systems Corp., 1981), p. 40.

20. A. Spiegel and H. Hyman, *Basic Health Planning Methods* (Germantown, Md.: Aspen Systems Corp., 1978), pp. 179–238.

21. Abell and Hammond, *Strategic Market Planning,* p. 219.

22. J.M. Ziff and J.W. Hlywak, "Financial Feasibility Studies," *Handbook of Health Care Accounting and Finance,* ed. W.O. Cleverley (Rockville, Md.: Aspen Systems Corp., 1982), pp. 1097–1109.

23. Abt Associates, *Methods For Determining Physician Requirements* (Washington, D.C.: Public Health Service DHEW, 1979). DHEW Publication No. HRA79-12, p. 15.

24. Luft, "How Do Health Maintenance Organizations," p. 1338.

25. Excerpt from a confidential plan prepared by Block, McGibony, + Associates, Inc., Silver Spring, Md.

Chapter 9

Case Studies of Market and Medical Staff Analysis

INTRODUCTION

This chapter describes the use of the generic techniques presented in Chapters 6 and 8 for strategic planning analysis and decision making. Two illustrative examples are presented, each representing issues of potential importance to hospital strategic planning in the current cost-containment environment: (1) the merging of the pediatric departments in two hospitals and (2) the establishment of an ambulatory surgery center. The two case studies are not intended to illustrate the full range of strategic analytic techniques required to address comprehensively all the relevant issues. They do show, however, how market analysis and medical staff analysis can be integrated in strategic planning.

In terms of the major steps in the strategic planning process described in Exhibit 2–1, the two case studies involve the evaluation of alternative scenarios. The first case study evaluates alternative methods of merging the pediatric departments of two hospitals. It demonstrates the use of data from a survey of the two hospitals' admitting pediatricians to define the physician market for the proposed merged pediatric inpatient unit. It also illustrates the use of the two merging hospitals' pediatric patient discharge abstracts in a patient origin study in order to define the merged unit's primary and secondary service areas. The information yielded by the survey and the patient origin study is then used to estimate the market penetration in the merged unit's service area. This information is then used to estimate the utilization level of the unit. The case study discusses some potentially erroneous assumptions in its analysis and suggests ways in which it could have been improved. It concludes with a discussion of specific strategies for ensuring that the proposed merged unit will attract enough patients to achieve an appropriately high average occupancy rate.

The second case study evaluates the impact in a hospital of the creation of an ambulatory surgery (AS) center. It involves the use of case-mix techniques to estimate the utilization of the new center. It also examines the effect of the proposed center on the future utilization of the hospital's existing medicine-surgery (med-surg) inpatient unit. The techniques that are employed include (1) a survey of the hospital's admitting surgeons and (2) a projection of the future utilization of the med-surg unit and the AS center, using a case-mix projection model. The case study uses several of the techniques presented in Chapter 8 to explore the risk that future changes in the hospital's admitting surgery staff or staff treatment practices could affect the accuracy of the projections of future utilization of the med-surg unit and AS center. The risk analysis uses hospital administrative and discharge abstract data to estimate the chances that the projected utilization will be lower than expected because the hospital's surgery staff (1) has low levels of investment in the hospital, (2) contains a high proportion of surgeons close to retirement age, (3) contains a high proportion of surgeons who are just beginning their careers, or (4) will lower its surgery rate in future years. Finally, the case study attempts to identify deficiencies in its analysis and ways to improve this analysis accordingly.

MERGING OF TWO HOSPITALS' DEPARTMENTS

Empirical information and rational analysis are both important in deciding how to integrate departments in two merging hospitals. On the basis of these combined resources, planners can decide how best to (1) satisfy the needs of the medical staffs in the merging departments, (2) maximize revenue and market share, and (3) meet the needs of the communities in the merged service area. Unfortunately, available evidence suggests that empirical information and rational analysis are often less important in the merging process than such factors as interdepartmental rivalry and community political forces.[1–5] Nevertheless, the case study presented here illustrates the use of empirical information and rational analysis in the consolidation of the pediatric departments in two merging hospitals. However, it does not address a number of important aspects of hospital mergers, for example, the financial and architectural aspects. Also, it does not include sensitivity or demand-projection analyses. Finally, it does not deal with the type of risk analysis described in Chapter 8.

The case study involves two hospitals, Memorial and Recovery, that have agreed to merge and are presently in the process of combining their operations, organizations, and plants. The pediatric service at Memorial has 30 beds and six admitting pediatricians. The pediatric service at Recovery has 20 beds and six admitting pediatricians, two of whom also have admitting privileges at Memorial. In the past year, Memorial's pediatric service had 1,095 admissions, an average length of stay of 5.5 days, and an occupancy rate of 55.0 percent. The equivalent utilization statistics for Recovery were 472 admissions, 6.4 days, and 41.4 percent. The facility at Memorial was renovated and modernized 5 years ago, while that at Recovery is 17 years old and in need of upgrading. In addition, the Memorial facility has a wider range of modern pediatric diagnostic and therapeutic equipment than does Recovery. Tabulations of the past year's discharge diagnoses from the two facilities, using computerized chart abstract data, revealed a very similar pediatric diagnostic mix in the two facilities.

These data suggested that it might be sensible to merge the two pediatric departments by closing the service at Recovery and expanding that at Memorial. This seemed even more logical in light of the fact that the merger of the two hospitals was expected to yield about 25 extra beds at Memorial, which beds could be used to expand Memorial's pediatric inpatient facility to 55 beds, if necessary.

However, the possibility of locating the merged pediatrics department at Memorial Hospital raised a number of important questions. For example:

- Would Memorial's and Recovery's admitting pediatricians be in favor of the move? Would they continue to admit their patients at the merged facility?
- Would Recovery's pediatric patients have to travel so much farther to reach Memorial Hospital that they would seek hospitalization elsewhere?

To answer these questions, a survey of the admitting pediatricians was conducted at the two hospitals. Its purpose was to define the potential physician market for the proposed merged pediatric unit (see Chapter 8). In addition, a pediatric inpatient origin study was performed, using computerized chart abstracts from the two hospitals, to define the primary and secondary service areas of the proposed merged facility (see Chapter 6). Figure 9–1 presents a map showing the location of the merging hospitals in their combined primary pediatric inpatient catchment area. The primary catchment area includes those towns whose patients constitute 90 percent of the two hospitals' admissions and for which the value of the index of relevance to either of the two merging hospitals is equal to or greater than 5 percent. The index of relevance for a particular town to a particular hospital is the ratio of the number of discharges from that hospital who reside in that town to the total number of discharges who reside in that town. Figure 9–1 also indicates the geographic location of the private-practice offices of the pediatricians who admit patients at Memorial and/or Recovery Hospitals.

The survey questionnaire asked the admitting pediatricians to provide the total number of patients each pediatrician admitted to all hospitals in the past year and estimates of the number of patients each pediatrician would admit to the upgraded merged facility. Table 9–1 shows the type of information that could be obtained from such a survey. The data in columns 1 and 5–10 were derived from the physician survey. The data in columns 2, 3, and 4 could be obtained from pediatric patient discharge abstracts or from hospital administrative records. Table 9–2 presents the patient-origin tabulations. These tabulations could be

Figure 9–1 Map of Combined Primary Catchment Area of Pediatric Departments in Merging Hospitals

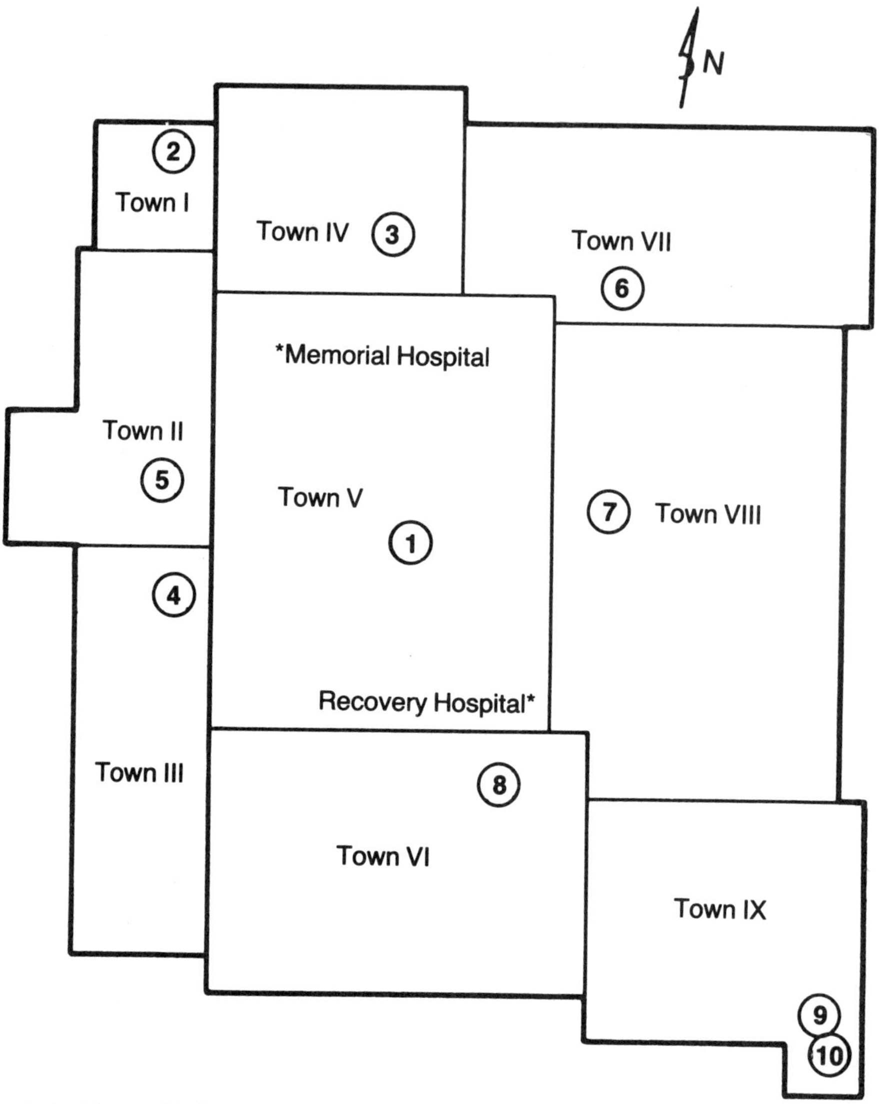

Scale: 1 inch = 10 miles

Notes: 1) Numbers in circles represent offices of pediatricians who admit patients at Memorial and/or Recovery hospitals

2) Hospitals other than the merging hospitals are not depicted on this map for the sake of clarity

Table 9–1 Profile of Admitting Pediatricians at Memorial and Recovery Hospitals

	Column Number									
	1	*2*	*3*	*4*	*5*	*6*	*7*	*8*	*9*	*10*
			1982 Adm. to Memorial and/or Recovery Hospital				*Estimate of Total 1983 Adm. to Merged Facility*		*Estimate of Maximum Future (1993) Adm. to Merged Facility*	
Hospital	*Adm.-Ped. No.*	*Total No. of 1982 Adm. to All Hospitals*	*No.*	*%*	*Willing to Use Merged Facility*	*Estimate of Extra 1983 Adm. to Merged Facility*	*No.*	*%*	*No.*	*%*
Memorial	1[a]	396	270	17.2	Yes	—	270	15.1	270	13.6
"	2	325	151	9.6	Yes	75	226	12.7	266	13.4
"	3	276	258	16.5	Yes	—	258	14.5	344	17.3
"	4[a]	191	157	10.0	Yes	—	157	8.8	174	8.8
"	5	178	165	10.5	Yes	—	165	9.3	174	8.8
"	6	123	94	6.0	Yes	—	94	5.3	111	5.6
Recovery	1[a]	(396)[b]	126	8.0	Yes	—	126	7.1	126	6.4
"	7	384	102	6.5	Yes	100	202	11.3	202	10.2
"	8	361	173	11.0	Yes	80	253	14.2	281	14.2
"	9	318	22	1.4	No	−22	—	—	—	—
"	4[a]	(191)[b]	32	2.0	Yes	—	32	1.8	36	1.8
"	10	165	17	1.1	No	−17	—	—	—	—
Total		2,717	1,567	100.0		216	1,783	100.0	1,984	100.0

[a]These pediatricians currently admit to both Memorial and Recovery Hospitals.
[b]Parentheses indicate that the enclosed numbers of admissions are already included in the column list and therefore are not included in the total.

most efficiently and conveniently derived using computerized chart abstract data from the two merging hospitals.

Tables 9–1 and 9–2 provide important information for determining the manner in which the two pediatric facilities are merged. For example, column 5 in Table 9–1 indicates that eight of the ten admitting pediatricians would be willing to use only the inpatient facility at Memorial Hospital if it were upgraded. It also appears that the closing of the Recovery pediatric facility would result in only a very small loss of patients. The two pediatricians who would not be willing to use Memorial Hospital (9 and 10) are responsible for only 2.5 percent of current admissions to the merging departments (column 4 in Table 9–1). They have a joint private practice in the far southeastern corner of the merging departments' primary catchment area (see Figure 9–1), and over 70 percent of their

Table 9–2 Annual Pediatric Admissions to Memorial and Recovery Hospitals, by Town of Patients' Residence and Admitting Pediatrician, 1982

	Admitting Pediatrician											
Town	*1*	*2*	*3*	*4*	*5*	*6*	*7*	*8*	*9*	*10*	*Total*	*% of Total*
I		111	14	17	9	2	20	18			191	12.2
II				1	153						154	9.8
III	9			171	3						183	11.7
IV		31	231								262	16.7
V	383										383	24.4
VI								155			155	9.9
VII						92	82		1		175	11.2
VIII	4		13								17	1.1
IX									5	5	10	0.6
Other[a]		9							16	12	37	2.4
Total	396	151	258	189	165	94	102	173	22	17	1,567	100.0
% of Total	25.2	9.6	16.5	12.1	10.5	6.0	6.5	11.0	1.4	1.1	100.0	

[a]Towns in the "other" category are those outside the primary catchment area of the merging hospitals, that is, they are in the secondary catchment area.

admissions to the merging hospitals reside outside the primary catchment area (see Table 9–2). In addition, it is unlikely that these two pediatricians would be seriously inconvenienced by the closure of Recovery's facility, because less than 10 percent of their combined current admissions (39 out of 483, as indicated in columns 2 and 3 in Table 9–1) are to the merging hospitals.

The admitting pediatricians estimated that they would admit 216 more patients annually to the expanded, upgraded facility at Memorial than they were currently admitting to the separate departments (column 6 in Table 9–1). This represents a potential 13.8 percent increase over the current 1,567 annual admissions (column 3 in Table 9–1). It would give the expanded upgraded facility an estimated 1,783 admissions in its first year of operation (column 7 in Table 9–1).

It is also apparent from the last column in Table 9–2 that only 2.4 percent of the current admissions to the merging departments resided outside the primary catchment area. Assuming that the longest travel time from Memorial to any residential community in the primary pediatric catchment area is three-quarters of an hour, it would seem reasonable to conclude that closure of Recovery's inpatient pediatric unit would not inconvenience a significant number of patients who currently use that facility.

Table 9–3 contains data and projections of importance in planning future operations and plant size in the expanded, upgraded Memorial facility. The data

Table 9–3 Estimated Market Penetration—Upgraded Pediatric Service at Memorial Hospital

	Column Number				
	1	2	3	4	5
		1982 Pediatric Admissions to Merging Hospitals		Estimated 1983 Pediatric Admissions to Upgraded Memorial Hospital	
Town	*1982 Pediatric Admissions To All Hospitals*	*No.*	*Market Penetration (%)*	*No.*	*Market Penetration (%)*
I	496	191	38.5	280	56.5
II	198	154	77.8	154	77.8
III	185	183	98.9	183	98.9
IV	451	262	58.1	272	60.3
V	383	383	100.0	383	100.0
VI	384	155	40.4	226	58.9
VII	524	175	33.4	254	48.5
VIII	18	17	94.4	17	94.4
IX	136	10	7.4	0	00.0
Other[a]	439	37	8.4	14	3.2
Total	3,214	1,567	48.8	1,783	55.5

[a]Towns in the "other" category are those outside the primary catchment area of the merging hospitals, that is, in the secondary catchment area.

in column 1 could be produced from a patient origin study using computerized pediatric patient chart abstracts (see Chapter 6 for a description of patient origin study techniques). Only those chart abstracts from hospitals with pediatric admissions of patients who reside in the merging hospitals' combined catchment area would be employed in the study. In addition, only the chart abstracts of patients admitted by a pediatrician who admits patients at Memorial or Recovery Hospital would be reflected in columns 2 and 4 of the table. The data in column 2 are also derivable from a patient origin study of the merging hospitals' pediatric inpatients. Incidentally, these data are the same as those in the second last column in Table 9–2.

The data in column 4 of Table 9–3 show total admissions (including the physicians' estimates of additions to the 1982 caseload) to the merged facility. They are based on the admitting pediatricians' estimates of the number of their inpatients who were not currently being admitted to one of the merging hospitals but who would be admitted to the merged facility. In determining the geographic distribution of the residences of each admitting pediatrician's extra patients who would be admitted to the new expanded, upgraded facility at Memorial, it was assumed that those residences would be distributed in the same manner as those of the admitting pediatricians' inpatients who are now treated at Memorial or Recovery. The numbers of the admitting pediatricians' new patients in each town in the primary catchment area were then summed for all admitting pediatricians and added to the data in column 2 to yield the data in column 4 in Table 9–3. A similar calculation was performed for those patients living in the secondary catchment area, to yield the number for "other" (14) in column 4 of the table.

However, there are two assumptions underlying the data in Table 9–3 that could be incorrect. The first assumption is that each admitting pediatrician's caseload will not change between 1982 and 1983. The second assumption is that the geographic distribution of each admitting pediatrician's caseload will not change during this period. These assumptions could be incorrect for a number of reasons. First, each admitting pediatrician might not continue to attract the same proportion of the population in each neighboring town as patients. Second, the admitting pediatrician might not continue to admit the same proportion of patients residing in each neighboring town. Third, the population might grow at different rates in different neighboring towns.

These factors could be investigated, and their effect, if any, on the data in column 4 in Table 9–3 could be estimated and incorporated in the data. The first two factors would probably be investigated by interviewing each admitting pediatrician. Investigation of the third factor would require an examination of census data and trends for each town in the primary and secondary catchment areas.

It should also be remembered that patients have their own tastes and preferences with respect to hospitals. We could, therefore, be incorrect in our implicit assumption that Recovery's patients would agree to use Memorial. It may be that some of them, for instance, would not be willing to travel the extra distance to reach Memorial. Other patients might not wish to use Memorial because they believe that the quality of the hospital's food is poor or that the neighborhood surrounding the hospital is dangerous. These factors, although not addressed in this case, could be important in a merger.

Column 4 in Table 9–3 indicates that the new Memorial pediatric facility would have an estimated 1,783 admissions in its first year of operation. If one assumes that the merged facility would have a first-year average length of stay (ALOS) equal to the weighted average of ALOSs in the existing merging facilities, the ALOS of the merged facility would be 5.77 days. With an ALOS of 5.77 days, 1,783 admissions would represent a 51.3 percent occupancy rate in the new 55-bed facility at Memorial.

Column 9 in Table 9–1 indicates that the admitting pediatricians believed that, by expanding their practices to maximum capacity, they could increase their admissions at the upgraded, merged facility to 1,984 per annum. This represents an increase of 201 patients, or 11.3 percent, over the estimated 1,783 admissions during the first year of operation. At the same expected first-year ALOS of 5.77 days, this would yield an average occupancy rate of 57.0 percent.

This would be an unacceptably low admission rate, for two reasons. First, the ideal occupancy rate in a 55-bed pediatric inpatient unit is generally agreed to be 70 percent. Second, the anticipated extra 201 annual admissions would probably not be fully realized for about 10 years. This estimate is based on forecasts (not shown here) indicating that there would be no change in pediatric inpatient admission rates, no change in the birth rate, and a seven-percent population growth rate in the primary catchment area over the next 10 years.

Thus, additional admissions would be needed for the proposed merged facility. An extra 652 admissions would yield a total annual admission rate of 2,435, corresponding to the ideal occupancy rate of 70 percent.

There are a number of possible strategies for generating these extra 366 admissions. The information in Figure 9–1 and Table 9–3 could be used in defining and evaluating the various strategies. The anticipated market penetration rates of the upgraded merged facility are shown in column 5 of Table 9–3. These indicate the geographic areas within which it might be fruitful to attempt to find more patients, that is, they indicate the areas in which the merged facility's initial market penetration would be expected to be low (with low market penetration arbitrarily defined as being below 60 percent), in Towns I, VI, VII, and IX and in the secondary catchment area ("other"). In fact, a comparison of columns 1 and 4 in Table 9–3 reveals that there are 216 pediatric admissions in Town I, 156 in Town VI, 270 in Town VII, 136 in Town IX, and 425 in the secondary catchment area who would not be expected to use the merged facility when it begins operating. This is a total of 1,203 patients who could become users of the upgraded, merged facility.

Several tactics for transferring some of these patients into users of the merged facility could be investigated. First, the hospitals' strategic planner could identify those pediatricians who are responsible for a large portion of these admissions and examine the possibility of inducing them to admit their patients to the merged facility. One approach might be to survey them to ascertain what, if any, types of improvements, special services, or equipment would cause them to use the merged facility, and then provide the indicated improvements, services, or equipment. Another approach might be to investigate the possibility of the merged facility assisting one or more of its admitting pediatricians to purchase practices in low market penetration areas. This would not only immediately bring extra admissions to the merged facility, it would also create for the merged facility the potential for increased admission rates as the acquired practices expanded.

Second, the planner could analyze inpatient admission rates in the pediatric-aged population in the merged facility's primary and secondary catchment area. This would involve tabulations using the data in column 1 of Table 9–3 and population data from the U.S. census. The purpose of this analysis would be the identification of geographical areas, if any, in which admission rates are low. Such areas could offer potential for generating additional third-party-covered pediatric inpatients. If any such areas were identified, the merged facility could attempt to realize some of the additional patients as extra admissions either by acquiring or creating pediatric office practices to tap into the low admission rate areas or by encouraging or assisting one or more of the merging facilities' admitting pediatricians to expand their practices into such areas.

An analysis of these factors might indicate that they would not yield the estimated 652 extra admissions that would lead to an initial average occupancy rate of 70 percent. In that event, consideration should be given to reducing initially the number of beds below the planned level of 55 in the merged facility, particularly if none, or only a small portion of the 652 extra admissions could be realized. This is because an average occupancy rate much lower than 70 percent would imply unnecessarily high operating expenses and low profitability.

There are a number of ways in which this analysis could be improved. For example, the planner could:

- examine the risk that the actual utilization of the merged department would be lower than projected in Table 9–1, due to the fact that (1) a large proportion of the merging hospitals' admitting pediatricians with large inpatient case loads are close to retirement age, or (2) a large proportion of the merging hospitals' admitting pediatricians are likely to leave the staff for other reasons.
- survey the pediatricians who practice in the merged service area, and who do not currently admit patients to either of the merging hospitals, to find out if they would be willing to use the merged facility if it were upgraded.
- survey the past and current patients of the merging departments to determine their willingness to use the proposed merged, upgraded facility.

ESTABLISHING AN AMBULATORY SURGERY CENTER

Background

Although surgery has been performed outside the hospital for many years, it is only in the past two decades that ambulatory surgery (AS) centers (also known as same-day, come-and-go, in-and-out, or outpatient surgery centers) have begun to be established in the United States.[6] One of the earliest reports of successful, large-scale, outpatient surgery was that of J.H. Nichol of the Royal Glasgow Hospital for children in 1909.[7] A total of 7,320 surgical procedures, performed on an outpatient basis, yielded results as successful as those for children who were treated on an inpatient basis.[8]

There are several reasons for the recent popularity of ambulatory surgery. The most important is that it has the potential for being far less expensive than inpatient surgery because it eliminates several days of hospitalization.[9–15] While this is an extremely significant consideration in the current cost-reduction environment, there are grounds for believing that the potential cost savings of ambulatory surgery are not always realized.[16–19] These include the fact that, from a hospital, community, or third party payer perspective, the creation of an AS unit does not generally lead to a reduction of expenses associated with inpatient capital or fixed costs. Instead, it usually leads only to additional capital and fixed-cost expenses—those of the AS unit. It is possible that the investment in AS capital and the fixed costs in a particular hospital or community would lead to an even greater reduction in inpatient capital and fixed costs in the long run. However, this has not yet been demonstrated to be true.[20–22]

Three clinical developments have facilitated the growth of ambulatory surgery. The first is improved anesthetics, such as Pentathol and Nitrous Oxide, that act and wear off faster than their predecessors.[23,24] The second is improved techniques for controlling bleeding.[25] The third is the relatively recent demonstration of the advantages of early postsurgery ambulation.[26]

Other reasons for favoring ambulatory surgery include the added convenience for both patient and surgeon, the reduced congestion in inpatient surgery units, less lost-work time for patient and employer, less preoperative and postoperative medication and diagnostic tests for the patient, and less risk of contracting in-hospital nosocomial infections.[27]

Not all of these advantages of ambulatory surgery have been conclusively demonstrated, nor is there reason to believe that they apply to all patients and surgeons. Nevertheless, a growing body of opinion is calling for the establishment of more AS units.[28] Authorities estimate that between 20 and 40 percent of all surgical procedures can now be safely and effectively performed on an ambulatory basis.[29]

In this context, the following case study illustrates a strategic issue that is likely to be addressed by planners in the next few years. It involves a 560-bed community hospital, Suburban, whose board of directors decided to investigate the possibility of establishing an AS center that would be integrated with the hospital's other surgery services. The impetus for the decision was the fact that the hospital's 350-bed inpatient med-surg unit reached 97-percent occupancy in the current year and the rate of admissions to the unit had been growing steadily at an annual average 2-percent rate for the past decade. Consequently, many elective surgery patients were experiencing a wait of several weeks and were sometimes "bumped" just prior to surgery by more critical patients. Complaints were made by both the hospital's admitting surgeons and their patients. The creation of an AS unit was seen as a means to expand Suburban Hospital's surgery capacity with a minimum of capital outlay. This was an important consideration, given the currently constrained capital environment in the U.S. hospital system—an environment created by reduced philanthropy, high interest rates leading to high borrowing costs, and termination of federal construction grants and loan guarantees.

Preliminary Analysis

An initial, cursory business-position/market-attractiveness analysis suggested that the creation of the center would be a desirable investment. Suburban's business position was strong for a number of reasons. First, the hospital currently provided about one-half of the surgery in its service area. The hospital's med-surg unit had about 40 percent of market share in its service area, and this share had grown slowly but surely over the past 5 years.

The two-percent annual growth rate in Suburban's med-surg admissions was due to two factors: (1) a fairly steady 1.5-percent service area population growth rate, and (2) a 0.5-percent increase in the size of the med-surg admitting staff. The hospital seemed to be in a good position, therefore, to feed the proposed center with patients—a consideration that would be particularly important in the early months of the center's existence. In addition, there was only one other AS unit in Suburban's service area. This unit was small (about 750 patients per year) and in a distant corner of the service area. Also, none of the three other inpatient med-surg units in Suburban's service area had increased its size or range of services, nor had any of them experienced significant utilization levels in the past five years. There was therefore not likely to be serious competition to Suburban's proposed center. Finally, it appeared that the third party payers in Suburban's service area, both private and governmental, were enthusiastic about reimbursing Suburban for ambulatory surgery.

The attractiveness of the market for the proposed center appeared to be high. This was due to a number of factors, including the encouragement of the local certificate-of-need and health care evaluation agencies. In addition, several of Suburban's senior admitting surgeons had informally expressed enthusiasm for the center. Finally, there was the fact that there had been a steady growth in admissions of med-surg patients at Suburban over the past 10 years.

Thus, there appeared to be every reason to believe that, with respect to the proposed AS center, Suburban Hospital had a strong position in an attractive market and the center would be successful. If this expectation were fulfilled, the center would provide an important impetus to the achievement of Suburban's primary objective—reducing the occupancy rate in the med-surg unit and thus its overcrowded state resulting from its strong position in an attractive market.

However, further analysis was necessary to confirm the expected benefits of the proposed AS center. In addition, planning was needed to describe, comprehensively and specifically, the size and type of center and the precise future effect it would have on the utilization of Suburban's inpatient units. Some of the relevant issues were:

- the anticipated number and type of procedures to be performed in the center during the first 5 years of its existence
- the resulting change in the occupancy rate in the inpatient med-surg service during the first 5 years of the center's existence
- the risk that the above estimates would be inaccurate due to Suburban's admitting surgery staff shrinking or changing its treatment practices.

Expected Utilization of the Proposed AS Center

Estimation of the level of utilization of the proposed AS center involved four steps:

1. creation of a list of procedures eligible for ambulatory surgery
2. determination of the number of each of the AS eligible procedures currently being performed by each of Suburban's admitting surgeons
3. determination of the number of each AS eligible procedure each of Suburban's admitting surgeons would be willing to treat in the proposed AS center
4. estimation of the rate of growth of the proposed AS center's case load

The list of AS eligible procedures was developed by an ad hoc committee of ten members—two from each of the following departments at Suburban: Medicine, Surgery, Pediatrics, Obstetrics/Gynecology, and Anesthesiology. The committee reviewed the literature on ambulatory surgery, sent delegates to visit AS units at Presbyterian Hospital in Dallas, Texas,[30] and at Virginia Mason Hospital in Seattle, Washington.[31] In the light of their literature review, the site visits to Dallas and Seattle, and their own clinical experience, the committee members drew up a list of 18 procedures (see Table 9–4). The 18 procedures were abstracted from a list of 280 procedures that the literature review had suggested as suitable for ambulatory treatment.[32] The committee recommended that these 18 procedures be eligible for treatment in the proposed AS center during its first 5 years. It was also recommended that the 18 procedures be evaluated for possible modification every few years. Modification might be necessitated by the experiences of the staff of the proposed center or by developments in AS therapy or technology. The list of 18 AS eligible procedures and other aspects of the proposed AS center were then discussed in medical-staff committee meetings in the departments of medicine, surgery, pediatrics, obstetrics/gynecology, and anesthesiology.

The number of AS eligible procedures currently being performed by each of Suburban's admitting surgeons was determined from the hospital's computerized

Table 9–4 Estimated Utilization of Proposed Ambulatory Surgery Center in Suburban Hospital, 1982

			Estimate of Procedures Surgeons Would Have Treated in AS Center					
			From Suburban Admissions					
Procedure	*Inpt Services*[a]	*1982 Suburban Admissions*	*Gyn*	*M/S*	*Ped.*	*Total*	*From Non-Suburban Admissions*	*Total*
Dilation and curettage	O	1,087	780	—	—	780	201	981
Tonsillectomy or T & A	P,M	1,032	—	14	631	645	143	788
Cystoscopy & Pyelogram	P,M	943	—	751	9	760	293	1,053
Inguinal herniorrhaphy	P,M	786	—	455	199	654	131	785
Myringotomy	P,M	485	—	280	—	280	52	332
Laparoscopy	P,M	417	—	—	—	—	22	22
Tubal ligation	O	278	145	—	—	145	33	178
Excision masses	P,M	243	—	159	6	165	21	186
Excision lesions	P,M	239	—	137	3	140	47	187
Adenoidectomy	P,M	206	—	116	145	261	34	295
Breast biopsy	M	159	—	95	—	95	21	116
Laryngoscopy	P,M	74	—	37	8	45	11	56
Scar revisions	P,M	72	—	42	13	55	17	72
Septoplasty	P,M	63	—	21	4	25	15	40
Blepharoplasty	P,M	57	—	30	10	40	15	55
Cast changes	P,M	56	—	24	11	35	9	44
Vasectomy	M	31	—	25	—	25	1	26
Muscle recissions or resections	P,M	27	—	12	3	15	7	22
Total		6,255	925	2,198	1,042	4,165	1,073	5,238

[a]O = obstetrics/gynecology, P = pediatrics, M = medicine/surgery.

chart abstracts. Both surgical procedure and physician number are coded on Suburban's chart abstracts (see Exhibit 3–1). Hence it was a relatively simple matter for the hospital's computer center to tabulate the number of each of the 18 AS eligible procedures performed by each admitting surgeon in the current year. These data were entered on questionnaires sent to each of Suburban's admitting surgeons (see Exhibit 9–1). The questionnaires were used primarily

Exhibit 9–1 Surgeon's Questionnaire Regarding Suburban Hospital's Proposed AS Center

Dear Dr. Doe:

Suburban hospital is considering the establishment of an ambulatory surgery center. We are therefore surveying our admitting surgeons to obtain estimates of their likely future use of the proposed center and the hospital's inpatient surgery service. Please consider the following six questions carefully because we will use your answers to make decisions on important issues, such as whether to establish the proposed center and how large it should be.

Below is a list of procedures considered by our Ad Hoc Committee on Ambulatory Surgery to be eligible for ambulatory treatment. The data on the number of these procedures you performed at Suburban during 1982 were derived from the hospital's computerized chart abstracts.

Questions:

1. Are the data on the number of these procedures you performed at Suburban in 1982 accurate? If not, please correct.
2. How many of these procedures that you performed at Suburban in 1982 would you have performed in the proposed center if it had existed in 1982?
3. If the current four-week average wait for elective surgery admissions were reduced to one week, how many more such patients would you admit to Suburban's med-surg unit? ____________ patients.
4. How many of these procedures did you perform at hospitals other than Suburban in 1982?
5. How many of these procedures that you performed at hospitals other than Suburban would you have performed at the proposed center if it had existed in 1982?
6. What is the total number of patients you hospitalized at all hospitals (including Suburban) in 1982? ____________ patients.

	Memorial Utilization		*Non-Memorial Utilization*	
Procedure	*No. You Performed in 1982 (Please Correct)*	*No. You Would Have Performed in Proposed AS Center*	*No. You Performed in 1982 (Your Estimate)*	*No. You Would Have Performed in Proposed AS Center*
Dilation and Curettage	—	—	—	—
Tonsillectomy or T & A	53	—	—	—
Cystoscopy & Pyelogram	—	—	—	—
Inguinal Herniorrhaphy	14	—	—	—

Exhibit 9–1 *continued*

	Memorial Utilization		*Non-Memorial Utilization*	
Procedure	*No. You Performed in 1982 (Please Correct)*	*No. You Would Have Performed in Proposed AS Center*	*No. You Performed in 1982 (Your Estimate)*	*No. You Would Have Performed in Proposed AS Center*
Myringotomy	1	—	—	—
Laparoscopy	—	—	—	—
Tubal ligation	—	—	—	—
Excision masses	—	—	—	—
Excision lesions	—	—	—	—
Adenoidectomy	3	—	—	—
Breast biopsy	—	—	—	—
Laryngoscopy	—	—	—	—
Scar revisions	—	—	—	—
Septoplasty	—	—	—	—
Blepharoplasty	—	—	—	—
Cast changes	—	—	—	—
Vasectomy	—	—	—	—
Muscle recissions or resections	—	—	—	—

to determine the number of AS eligible procedures each of Suburban's surgeons was willing to perform in the proposed AS center. However, they were also used as a rough check on the level of disagreement between the surgeons' memories and the tabulations derived from the chart abstract data (see Question 1 in Exhibit 9–1).

The results of the questionnaire are presented in Tables 9–4 and 9–5. Table 9–5 summarizes the results for each surgeon separately, and Table 9–4 focuses on all the surgeons' estimates of their use of the proposed center. The "total" row in Table 9–4 shows that Suburban's admitting surgeons were willing to perform 4,165 (third from last column) of the hospital's 6,255 1982 AS eligible procedures in the proposed center. The majority, 2,198 (52.8 percent), of those 4,165 procedures had been admitted to the med-surg unit; 1,042 (25.0 percent) had been admitted to the pediatric unit; and 925 (22.2 percent) had been admitted to the obstetrics/gynecology unit. Suburban's admitting surgeons were also willing to perform in the proposed center another 1,073 procedures currently being performed at hospitals other than Suburban. This would have yielded a total estimated 1982 case load for the proposed center of 5,238 procedures.

The growth rate of the proposed center's case load was estimated to be two percent per year. This estimate was based on two assumptions. The first assumption was that the number of AS center admissions from Suburban's AS-

Table 9–5 Results of Suburban Hospital Physician Survey

Physician: Doe, P — Service: Surgery — Specialty: Pediatric Surgery

Index of investment: 0.86 — 1982 Admissions to Suburban: 146 — 1982 Surgery admissions to Suburban: 105

1982 Admissions to all hospitals: 170 — Extra elective surgery admissions if med-surg wait period was reduced: 0

AS Eligible Procedure	*Current Suburban Admis-sions*	*Estimated Suburban Admissions to be Treated in AS Center*	*Estimated Non-Suburban Admissions*	*Estimated Non-Suburban Admissions to be Treated in AS Center*
Tonsillectomy or T & A	53	30	4	2
Inguinal herniorrhaphy	14	9	2	2
Myringotomy	1	—	—	—
Adonoidectomy	3	2	—	—
Cast changes	—	—	4	1
Total	71	41	10	5

eligible case load would grow at a two percent annual rate. This was based on the observation that the annual number of admissions to Suburban's obstetrics/gynecology, pediatrics and med-surg units (see third column in Table 9–6, for example) grew at a steady annual rate of about two percent over the past ten years. The second assumption was that the number of AS center admissions from the non-Suburban case loads of Suburban surgeons willing to use the center would also grow at two percent per annum. This was based on the fact that the overall number of hospital admissions from persons residing in Suburban's service area had been growing at a steady annual rate of two percent per annum for the past decade. And there were no indications that this rate would change in the near future.

Expected Utilization of the Medical-Surgical Unit

The main, though not the only, reason for considering the creation of an AS center at Suburban was that it would be desirable to reduce the excessively high occupancy rate and resulting excessive waiting periods for elective surgery ad-

Table 9–6 Utilization of Suburban Hospital Inpatient Med-Surg Unit without an Ambulatory Surgery Center: Trends

Year	*Admissions*	*Actual Annual Growth Rate (%)*	*Average Length of Stay (Days)*	*Patient Days*	*Occupancy Rate (%)*	*Patient Days in Excess of 90% Occupancy*
1972	17,835	—	5.80	103,443	81.0	—
1974	18,607	2.2	5.79	107,734	84.3	—
1976	19,300	1.9	5.75	110,975	86.9	—
1978	20,121	2.1	5.74	115,495	90.4	—
1980	20,861	1.8	5.72	119,325	93.4	4,350
1982	21,741	2.0	5.70	123,923	97.0	8,948
1983	22,176		5.69	126,182	98.8	11,207
1984	22,618		5.68	128,484	100.6	13,509
1985	23,070		5.67	130,809	102.4	15,834
1986	23,533		5.66	133,214	104.3	18,239
1987	24,004		5.65	135,621	106.1	20,646
1988	24,483		5.64	138,118	108.1	23,143
1989	24,973		5.63	140,596	110.1	25,621
1990	25,473		5.62	143,203	112.1	28,228
1991	25,983		5.61	145,765	114.1	30,790
1992	26,502		5.60	148,476	116.2	33,501

Note: Data for the period 1972 to 1982 are based on actual experience. Data for the period 1983 to 1992 are projections based on actual experience in the period 1972–1982.

missions in the med-surg unit. It was necessary, therefore, to determine the extent to which the creation of the AS center would in fact reduce occupancy in the med-surg unit. This involved three separate steps:

1. determination of the level of utilization of the med-surg unit without the proposed AS center
2. estimation of the amount of med-surg utilization that would be transferred to the proposed AS center
3. calculation of the resulting reduced levels of utilization in the med-surg unit

Table 9–6 shows the past, current, and projected future levels of utilization in the med-surg unit. Data on past and current (1972–1982) utilization levels were obtained from the hospital's administrative records. Estimates of future utilization were based on two assumptions: (1) that the average annual rate of growth of med-surg admissions during the past 10 years (2 percent) would continue during the next decade; (2) that the average annual rate of reduction in the average length of stay in the med-surg unit (0.17 percent) would continue until 1992 if the AS center were not created and utilized.

Suburban's med-surg committee decided that a med-surg occupancy level of 90 percent would be ideal. Experience indicated that this level would provide sufficient utilization for efficient operation, yet would be low enough to allow flexibility in scheduling admissions, with a reasonable waiting period of one to two weeks for elective procedures. The last column in Table 9–6 shows the patient days in excess of the 90-percent occupancy level. The proposed AS center would need to absorb at least this number of med-surg patients in order to keep the occupancy rate in the med-surg unit at its desired level of 90 percent.

The next question, therefore, was how many of Suburban's med-surg patients the proposed AS center would absorb. A simple case-mix model, shown in Table 9–7, was developed to address this question. On the left in this table is a list of AS eligible procedures traditionally treated on the med-surg service. Column 1 shows the average length of stay for patients with these procedures on the med-surg unit in 1982. These data were developed from the hospital's computerized chart abstracts. These abstracts contain both admission and discharge date (see Exhibit 3–1). They also contain the treatment service code, which was used to derive the number of 1982 med-surg admissions and patient days (columns 2 and 3 in Table 9–7) for each procedure.

The expected reduction in med-surg admissions due to use of the proposed AS center is shown in column 4 in Table 9–7. These data were derived from the results of the survey of admitting surgeons (see Table 9–4 and Exhibit 9–1). They are aggregations of the number of the AS eligible procedures that the admitting surgeons who used the med-surg unit were willing to perform in the proposed AS center. In other words, the data in column 4 represent the admitting surgeons' estimates of the amount by which their med-surg admissions would drop if they used the AS center.

Column 5 of Table 9–7 shows the anticipated reduction in med-surg patient days. These data were derived by multiplying the estimated reduction in admissions for each AS eligible procedure (column 4) by the corresponding average length of stay (column 1). The assumption here was that the patients whom the med-surg admitting surgeons would be willing to treat in the proposed AS center would require the same length of hospitalization as those whom the surgeons would not be willing to treat in the proposed center. The effects of errors in this assumption (which are not examined here) could easily be explored by means of a sensitivity analysis based on different hypothesized levels of error in the assumption. A more elaborate analysis could include a review of the ambulatory surgery literature and a survey of the med-surg admitting surgeons willing to use the proposed AS center to determine if, and to what extent, the assumption might be in error. The assumption could then be modified accordingly and used

Table 9–7 Effect of Suburban Hospital's Ambulatory Surgery Center on the Utilization of the Med-Surg Inpatient Unit, by Procedure, 1982

	Column Number						
	1	*2*	*3*	*4*	*5*	*6*	*7*
	Avg Length of Stay	*1982 Med-Surg Utilization*		*Expected Reduction in Med-Surg Utilization*		*Expected Remaining Med-Surg Utilization*	
Procedure	*(Days)*	*Admissions*	*Pt. Days*	*Admissions*	*Pt. Days*	*Admissions*	*Pt. Days*
Cystoscopy & Pyelogram	1.7	823	1,399	751	1,276	72	123
Inguinal herniorrhaphy	2.9	786	2,279	455	1,320	231	959
Myringotomy	1.6	485	776	280	448	205	328
Excision masses	1.5	237	354	159	240	78	114
Excision lesions	3.4	234	796	137	466	97	330
Adenoidectomy	2.7	191	516	116	313	175	203
Breast biopsy	2.2	159	350	95	209	64	141
Laryngoscopy	3.0	61	183	37	111	24	72
Scar revisions	1.2	55	66	42	50	13	16
Septoplasty	1.1	54	59	21	24	33	35
Blepharoplasty	1.6	43	69	30	48	13	21
Cast changes	1.1	39	43	24	27	15	16
Vasectomy	2.3	31	71	25	58	6	13
Tonsillectomy or T & A	1.2	23	28	14	17	9	11
Muscle Recissions or Resections	1.4	22	31	12	17	10	14
Admissions eligible for Amb. surg.		3,243	7,020	2,198	4,624	1,045	2,396
Admissions not eligible for Amb. surg.		18,498	116,898			18,498	116,898
Total	5.70	21,741	123,918			19,543	119,294

as a basis for determining the estimated reduction in med-surg patient days (column 5) from the estimated reduction in med-surg admissions (column 4) and the corresponding average lengths of stay (column 1).

The expected level of utilization of the med-surg unit if the proposed AS center were operational (columns 6 and 7) was determined by subtracting the expected reduction in utilization due to the AS center (columns 4 and 5) from the current utilization of the med-surg unit (columns 2 and 3).

The figures at the bottom of Table 9–7 show the overall effect of the AS center on med-surg utilization. The utilization of the med-surg unit by patients not eligible for AS treatment (18,498 admissions and 116,898 patient days) would not be affected by the creation of the AS center. However, it could be expected that the 3,243 admissions and the 7,020 patient days due to admissions with procedures eligible for AS treatment would be reduced to 1,045 admissions and 2,396 patient days due to the proposed AS center. This would reduce the overall utilization of the med-surg unit from 21,741 admissions and 123,918 patient days to 19,543 admissions and 119,294 patient days. It would also increase the average length of med-surg stay from 5.70 days (Table 9–7) to 6.10 days (see Table 9–8). This is due to the fact that patients eligible for treatment in an AS center generally stay in the med-surg unit for shorter periods than patients not eligible for AS treatment. Hence, removal of patients eligible for AS treatment would increase the average length of stay of the remaining patients.[33]

The case-mix model in Table 9–7 was used to estimate utilization of the med-surg unit for each year between 1982 and 1992 (Table 9–8). Four assumptions were made in applying the model to the years beyond 1982: (1) the average lengths of stay for all med-surg patients would drop 0.17 percent per year—equal to the average annual percentage drop in the med-surg average length of

Table 9–8 Projected Utilization of Suburban Hospital Inpatient Med-Surg Unit with Ambulatory Surgery Center

			Med-Surg Utilization with AS Center			
Year	*Med-Surg Admissions without AS Center*	*Expected Admissions to AS Center*	*Admis-sions*	*Average Length of Stay (Days)*	*Patient Days*	*Occupancy Rate (%)*
1982	21,741	2,198	19,543	6.10	119,294	93.4
1983	22,176	2,242	19,934	6.09	121,398	95.0
1984	22,618	2,287	20,331	6.08	123,612	96.8
1985	23,071	2,333	20,738	6.07	125,880	98.5
1986	23,533	2,379	21,154	6.06	128,193	100.4
1987	24,003	2,427	21,576	6.05	130,535	102.2
1988	24,483	2,457	22,026	6.04	133,037	104.1
1989	24,973	2,525	22,448	6.03	135,361	106.0
1990	25,473	2,575	22,898	6.02	137,846	107.9
1991	25,981	2,627	23,354	6.01	140,358	109.9
1992	26,502	2,679	23,823	6.00	142,938	111.9

stay during the period 1972 to 1982; (2) the number of admissions would increase at an annual average rate of 2 percent for all types of med-surg patients—equal to the annual average rate of increase in overall med-surg admissions between 1972 and 1982; (3) the proportion of med-surg patients with each type of AS eligible procedure treated in the AS center would remain constant; and (4) the increases in the med-surg occupancy level shown in Table 9–8 would not affect the demand for med-surg beds. The effect of errors in these assumptions on the projections in Table 9–8 could be investigated by means of sensitivity or other types of analyses (not undertaken here).

The most important conclusion to be drawn from Table 9–8 is that creation of the AS center would not reduce the crowding in the med-surg unit to acceptable levels. Without the AS center, the med-surg occupancy rate was estimated to be 98.8 percent in 1983 and to increase at a steady rate of about 2 percent per year thereafter (Table 9–6). With the AS center, the med-surg occupancy rate was projected to be 95 percent in 1983 and to increase at about 2 percent per year thereafter (Table 9–8). Hence, creation of the AS center would not reduce the crowding in the med-surg unit to acceptable levels—an occupancy rate of 90 percent—as desired by Suburban's med-surg committee.

This does not suggest that the AS center should not be built. It does suggest that the hospital would have to adopt another strategy to alleviate the crowding in the med-surg unit. This could involve an expansion of the med-surg unit or restrictions on the numbers and/or types of admissions to the unit. Use of the AS center alone would not absorb enough med-surg cases to reduce med-surg occupancy rates to acceptable levels.

Risk Analysis

This section explores the risk that future changes in Suburban's admitting surgery staff and/or their treatment practices could affect the accuracy of the projected utilization of the proposed AS center and med-surg unit.

The AS Center

One of the major unquantifiable risks concerning the AS center is that the 54 surgeons who expressed a willingness to use the center might not do so for a number of reasons: fear of malpractice suits; inconvenience in terms of scheduling in, or location of, the AS center; discomfort with new procedures and an unknown, unproven regimen; or simply a change of heart. However, two other factors, also unquantifiable, might alleviate these possible negative consequences. The first is that some of Suburban's 69 surgeons who did not express a willingness to use the AS center in the survey (see Exhibit 9–1 and Table 9–5) might actually use the center. The second is that some of the approximately

100 surgeons who have not previously used Suburban but who have practices in Suburban's service area might be willing and able to use the proposed AS center. This latter factor might be especially significant since, as noted earlier, there was currently only one small AS facility in a far corner of Suburban's service area.

Tables 9–9 and 9–10 contain data on the 54 Suburban admitting surgeons who were willing to use the proposed AS center. These data would be relevant to the analysis of the risk that these surgeons might not use the proposed center for any of the following reasons: (1) the surgeons might have low values of the index of investment, suggesting a high likelihood that they might discontinue their use of Suburban altogether; (2) a high proportion of these surgeons might be close to retirement age and might therefore cause a significant drop in use of the center when they retire; (3) a high proportion of these surgeons might be in the early stages of their careers and thus would be more likely to leave Suburban and relocate to advance their careers; or (4) the young surgeons who would be willing to use the AS center might have lower surgery rates and less desire to use the center than their older colleagues who would be willing to use the center, suggesting that as the older physicians retire, the use of the center would drop.

The last row in Table 9–10 shows that the average value of the index of investment of the 54 surgeons was 0.76, suggesting a high dependence on Suburban Hospital and little likelihood that they would stop using it. In similar vein, the value of the index of investment for subgroups of these surgeons in the age ranges of ≤30, 31–40, 41–50, 51–60 and 61+ was between 0.62 and 0.79. This suggests that it is unlikely that Suburban would lose any of these subgroups of surgeons in the near future. There were two surgeons with indexes of investment below 0.5. Physician No. 14 in the 41–50 category accounted for 4.0 percent of the total expected admissions (column 9); physician No. 49 in the 61+ group accounted for 4.2 percent of the total (column 9). Therefore, their combined expected total level of utilization of the center constituted only 8.2 percent of the total. Also, their lowest value of the index of investment, for physician No. 49 was 0.42, which represents a relatively high level of dependence on Suburban. Hence, on the basis of their relatively high values of the index of investment, it appeared unlikely that any of the surgeons willing to use the AS center would discontinue their use of Suburban in the near future, since that would have a large and possibly disruptive effect on their current hospitalization patterns.

Table 9–10 also shows that 43.0 percent of the expected admissions to the AS center would be from surgeons in the 41–50 year age group and that 28.3 percent would be from surgeons in the 51–60 year age group (column 9). This was reassuring in that it meant that a total of 71.3 percent of the expected admissions would be from surgeons between the ages of 41 and 60—the mid-to-late career years—in which their practice locations and treatment styles would

Table 9–9 Characteristics of Physicians Willing To Utilize Ambulatory Surgery Center at Suburban Hospital: Current Utilization

	Column Number							
	1	*2*	*3*	*4*	*5*	*6*	*7*	*8*
				Current Annual Utilization of Suburban Hospital Services				
Age (Yrs)	*M.D. No.*[a]	*Specialty*[b]	*Index of Investment*	*Total Admissions*	*Surgical Admissions*	*Rate of Surgery (%)*	*AS Eligible Procedures*	*% of Total*
≤30	1	O	0.64	199	182	91.5	126	2.6
	2 Others		0.72	36	31	86.1	23	0.5
Subtotal	3 (5.6%)[c]		0.65	235	213	90.6	149	3.1
31–40	4	P	0.75	367	363	98.9	255	5.3
	5	GS	0.72	268	256	95.5	178	3.7
	3 Others		0.77	113	92	81.4	63	1.3
Subtotal	5 (9.3%)		0.73	748	711	95.1	496	10.4
41–50	9	O	1.00	554	489	88.3	353	7.4
	10	U	0.73	543	450	82.9	344	7.2
	11	PS	0.55	485	480	99.0	321	6.7
	12	P	0.81	469	462	98.5	321	6.7
	13	O	0.68	402	343	85.3	240	5.0
	14	O	0.44	311	221	71.1	153	3.2
	14 Others		0.72	453	413	91.2	287	6.0
Subtotal	20 (37.0%)		0.73	3,217	2,858	88.9	2,019	42.3
51–60	29	I	0.88	566	470	83.0	359	7.5
	30	P	0.84	504	495	98.2	343	7.2
	31	GS	0.85	452	440	97.4	305	6.4
	32	U	0.64	304	275	90.5	149	3.1
	33	I	0.51	143	109	76.2	76	1.6
	13 Others		0.73	476	449	94.3	301	6.3
Subtotal	18 (33.3%)		0.79	2,445	2,238	91.5	1,533	32.1
61+	47	O	0.64	326	312	95.7	206	4.3
	48	P	0.58	295	255	86.4	177	3.7
	49	FP	0.42	199	196	98.5	126	2.6
	5 Others		0.75	108	99	91.7	67	1.4
Subtotal	8 (14.8%)		0.62	928	862	92.8	576	12.1

Table 9–9 continued

	Column Number							
	1	*2*	*3*	*4*	*5*	*6*	*7*	*8*
				Current Annual Utilization of Suburban Hospital Services				
Age (Yrs)	*M.D. No.*[a]	*Spe-cialty*[b]	*Index of Invest-ment*	*Total Admis-sions*	*Surg-ical Admis-sions*	*Rate of Sur-gery (%)*	*AS Eli-gible Proce-dures*	*% of Total*
All 54 M.D.s	54 (100%)		0.76	7,573	6,882	90.9	4,773	100.0

[a]This column lists only surgeons who were willing to admit more than 50 patients per year to the proposed AS center. Surgeons willing to admit less than 50 are included in the "others" category.

[b]O = obstetrics/gynecology, P = pediatric surgery, I = internal medicine, U = urology, PS = plastic surgery, GS = general surgery, FP = family practice.

[c]Percentages in parentheses are the percentages of the 54 M.D.s in each age group.

be unlikely to change significantly. Specifically, they would be unlikely to leave Suburban, stop performing surgery, or make other changes that would lead to their not using the AS center.

In similar vein, only a relatively small proportion, 28.7 percent of the expected admissions to the center, would be from surgeons not in the mid-to-late career years. Of these, 3.3 percent would be from surgeons 30 years of age or younger. These surgeons were in their very early careers and thus more likely than their older colleagues to relocate their practices and hence possibly leave Suburban. Of the total expected admissions, 10.3 percent would be from surgeons between 31 and 40 years of age. These surgeons were in their early careers and also likely (although less so than their younger colleagues) to move, and to therefore stop using Suburban. Surgeons over the age of 61 years accounted for 15.1 percent of expected admissions. These surgeons were in their late careers and could leave Suburban as a result of retirement. Overall however, the vast majority, over 70 percent of the expected admissions to the center, would be from surgeons in their stable mid-to-late careers (41–60 years of age), and who would consequently be unlikely to leave Suburban. This conclusion was supported by the fact that only 5.6 percent of the surgeons willing to use the center were 30 years or younger, only 14.8 percent of them were 61 years or older, and 70.3 percent of them were between 41 and 60 years of age (column 1 in Table 9–10).

Column 6 in Table 9–9 shows that the overall rate of surgery (percent of admissions involving surgery) in the group of 54 surgeons willing to use the AS

Table 9–10 Characteristics of Physicians Willing To Utilize Ambulatory Surgery Center at Suburban Hospital: Expected Utilization

	1	2	3	4	5	6	7	8	9
				Expected Annual Utilization of Ambulatory Surgery Center					
Age (Yrs)	M.D. No.[a]	Specialty[b]	Index of Investment (%)	Admissions from Suburban Case Load	% of Total	Admissions from non Suburban Case Load	% of Total	Total Admissions	% of Total
≤30	1	O	0.64	120	2.9	30	2.8	150	2.9
	2 Others		0.72	20	0.5	5	0.5	25	0.5
Subtotal	3 (5.6%)[c]		0.65	140	3.4	35	3.3	175	3.3
31–40	5	P	0.75	240	5.8	35	3.3	275	5.3
	6	GS	0.72	172	4.1	28	2.6	200	3.8
	3 Others		0.77	58	1.4	7	0.7	65	1.2
Subtotal	5 (9.3%)		0.73	470	11.3	70	6.5	540	10.3
41–50	9	O	1.00	330	7.9	0	0.0	330	6.3
	10	U	0.73	325	7.8	60	5.6	385	7.4
	11	PS	0.55	315	7.6	35	3.3	350	6.7
	12	P	0.81	310	7.4	100	9.3	410	7.8
	13	O	0.68	210	5.0	5	0.5	215	4.1
	14	O	0.44	140	3.4	70	6.5	210	4.0
	14 Others		0.72	250	6.0	100	9.3	350	6.7
Subtotal	20 (37.0%)		0.73	1,880	45.1	370	34.5	2,250	43.0
51–60	29	I	0.88	325	7.8	35	3.3	360	6.9
	30	P	0.84	310	7.4	30	2.8	340	6.5
	31	GS	0.85	230	5.5	30	2.8	260	5.0
	32	U	0.64	100	2.4	110	10.3	210	4.0
	33	I	0.51	50	1.2	0	0.0	50	1.0
	13 Others		0.73	230	5.5	33	3.1	263	5.0
Subtotal	18 (33.3%)		0.79	1,245	29.9	238	22.2	1,483	28.3
61+	47	O	0.64	145	3.5	100	9.3	245	4.7
	48	P	0.58	135	3.2	115	10.7	250	4.8
	49	FP	0.42	90	2.2	130	12.1	220	4.2
	5 Others		0.75	60	1.4	15	1.4	75	1.4
Subtotal	8 (14.8%)		0.62	430	10.3	360	33.6	790	15.1
All 54 M.D.s	54 (100%)		0.76	4,165	100	1,073	100	5,238	100

[a]This column lists only surgeons who were willing to admit more than 50 patients per year to the proposed AS center. Surgeons willing to admit less than 50 are included in the "others" category.

[b]O denotes obstetrics/gynecology, P denotes pediatric surgery, I denotes internal medicine, U denotes urology, PS denotes plastic surgery, GS denotes general surgery, FP denotes family practice.

[c]Percentages in parentheses are the percentages of the 54 M.D.s in each age group.

center was 90.9 percent. There was some variation in this rate between age groups, with the 41- to 50-year olds having the lowest rate (88.9 percent) and the 31- to 40-year olds the highest (95.1 percent). However, there was no indication of a trend that could threaten to reduce the utilization of the AS center. For instance, the rate of surgery did not decrease with age. If it had, it would suggest that use of the AS center could drop in the future as Suburban's older surgeons died or retired, leaving an overall lower rate of surgery in future years.

There is a suggestion in Tables 9–9 and 9–10 that Suburban's surgeons would increase over time the proportion of their admissions they treat in the AS center. Comparison of column 8 in Table 9–9 and column 5 in Table 9–10 suggests that the younger surgeons would be willing to perform a higher proportion of their AS eligible procedures in the AS center than their older colleagues. For example, AS eligible procedures for the 30-years-and-under age group constituted 3.1 percent of the total for all physicians (column 8 in Table 9–9). On the other hand, the number of AS admissions they expected to make from their Suburban case loads was 3.4 percent of the total for all physicians (column 5 in Table 9–10). In other words, relative to all physicians willing to use the AS center, the under-30-year-old group indicated a greater willingness to use the center. For the 61-years-and-over group, the equivalent statistics were 12.1 percent and 10.3 percent. Relative to all physicians, therefore, the over-61-year-old group indicated less willingness to use the center. Hence, the over-61-year-old group appeared to be less willing to admit their AS eligible patients to the center than the under-30-year-old group. The same conclusions were reached when the 31- to 40-year-old group was compared with the 51- to 60-year-old group.

It was not possible to rely on actual past experiences in analyzing the risk of errors in expected AS utilization patterns in the future because Suburban had no past experience with ambulatory surgery. However, an attempt was made to examine the past admitting and surgery patterns of the surgeons who were willing to use the AS center (see Table 9–11). The examination focused on the 41 surgeons who had been admitting patients to Suburban for at least 5 years. These 41 surgeons represented about 85 percent of the anticipated 5,238 AS center patients, so that conclusions drawn from their past behavior could be expected to be reliably generalized to the expected use of the center. Table 9–11 shows that, for the 41 surgeons, the annual growth rates of total number of admissions, surgical admissions, and AS eligible admissions had all been about 2 percent per annum between 1977 and 1982. The data on AS eligible admissions were tabulated from Suburban's computerized chart abstracts, using procedure code, physician code, and discharge date.

Table 9–11 also shows that the surgery rate for the 41 surgeons was relatively constant, at about 90 percent between 1977 and 1982. While there were year-to-year variations in the admission and surgery rates, there was no evidence to suggest overall upward or downward trends. These stable past patterns of the

Table 9–11 Ambulatory-Surgery Eligible Admissions of 41 Surgeons Willing To Use Proposed AS Center at Suburban Hospital, 1977–1982

Year	*Total Admis-sions*	*Annual Growth Rate (%)*	*Surgical Admis-sions*	*Annual Growth Rate (%)*	*Surgery Rate (%)*	*AS Eligible Admis-sions*	*Annual Growth Rate (%)*
1977	5,876		5,254		89.4	3,215	
1978	5,932	1.0	5,403	2.8	91.1	3,296	2.5
1979	6,101	2.9	5,483	1.5	90.0	3,372	2.3
1980	6,175	1.2	5,618	2.5	91.0	3,385	0.4
1981	6,327	2.5	5,701	1.5	90.1	3,456	2.1
1982	6,437	1.7	5,849	2.7	90.9	3,540	2.4
	Avg. Annual Growth Rate 1977–1982:	1.9		2.2			2.0

Note: This table includes only those surgeons who had been admitting patients to Suburban for at least 5 years (representing 85 percent of proposed AS center admissions from current Suburban inpatient case load).

41 surgeons suggested that there was little reason to expect their future admitting and surgery habits to change. Hence, there appeared to be good reason to expect future admissions to the center from Suburban's AS eligible case load to increase at a stable 2 percent per annum.

The risk that, in the future, expected AS center admissions from the non-Suburban case loads of Suburban surgeons would grow at a rate other than the assumed 2 percent per annum is not addressed here. Analysis of this risk would involve examination of surgery rates and population growth rates in Suburban's service area. It would also explore the recent rate of growth of the non-Suburban AS eligible case loads of Suburban's surgeons who were willing to use the proposed AS center.

The Medical-Surgery Unit

The risk analysis of the med-surg unit focused on the likelihood that changes in the unit's admitting staff or in the staff's admitting or treatment patterns might lead to errors in projections of future utilization of the unit (see Table 9–6). This is important because, if Suburban decided to address the problem of excessive med-surg occupancy by expanding the med-surg unit, the size of the expansion would depend on the size of the projected future utilization of the unit.

The data in Table 9–12, which apply to the current med-surg admitting staff, were assembled to analyze the risk of an unexpected drop in med-surg utilization due to the following possibilities:

- A large proportion of the med-surg staff were in the very early stages of their careers and might, therefore, relocate and leave Suburban; alternatively, a large proportion of the med-surg staff were in the very late stages of their careers and might, therefore, retire and leave Suburban.
- A large proportion of the staff had low values of the index of investment, which would represent a high risk that this portion of the staff might stop using Suburban.
- The average length of stay in the unit was lower for younger than for older med-surg admitting physicians, creating the possibility that as time passed the older physicians would die or retire, and thus reduce the overall average length of stay in the unit.

Table 9–12 shows that only 3.4 percent of the med-surg unit's admitting physicians were 30 years of age or younger. These young physicians were responsible for only 0.8 percent of the unit's admissions and only 0.9 percent of its patient days. Hence, there was only a small risk that a significant unexpected future drop in med-surg utilization would result from a large proportion of these young physicians relocating in the very early stages of their careers and hence leaving Suburban, since they accounted for only a very small (less than 1 percent) proportion of the unit's current utilization.

Similarly, the elderly physicians also accounted for too small a part of the unit's utilization for their possible retirements to cause unexpected significant drops in future utilization. Physicians 61 years and older constituted 9.5 percent of the med-surg staff and were responsible for only 4.5 percent of the unit's admissions and 3.4 percent of its patient days. In contrast, the med-surg physicians in their more stable, mid-to-late career years, 41 to 60 years of age, represented 66.3 percent of all med-surg physicians and were responsible for most of the unit's admissions (78.8 percent) and patient days (79.3 percent). It seemed unlikely, therefore, that there would be significant future reductions in med-surg staff utilization due to young physicians relocating and/or older physicians retiring.

The overall value of the index of investment of the med-surg staff was 0.71, suggesting little risk of future reductions in utilization due to physicians discontinuing their use of Suburban. A high value of the index of investment at Suburban meant that the majority (71 percent) of the physicians' inpatients were treated at Suburban. Hence, it was unlikely that they would elect to stop admitting their patients at Suburban and concentrate their hospital activities at other local hospitals. Closer examination revealed that only 16 of the 116 med-surg admitting

Table 9–12 Characteristics of Physicians Responsible for Admissions to the Medical-Surgery Unit at Suburban Hospital, 1982

				Current Utilization of Med/Surg Unit				
Age (Yrs)	*M.D. Number*[a]	*Specialty*[b]	*Index of Investment*	*Admissions*	*% of Total*	*Avg. Length of Stay (Days)*	*Patient Days*	*% of Total*
≤30	1	Ob	.64	114	0.5	6.7	761	0.6
	3 Others		.73	57	0.3	5.3	299	0.2
Subtotal	4 (3.4%)[c]		.68	171	0.8	6.2	1,060	0.9
31–40	5	I	.91	452	2.1	6.3	2,867	2.3
	6	I	.76	376	1.7	5.4	2,018	1.6
	7	P	.87	353	1.6	5.3	1,893	1.5
	8	G	.94	299	1.4	6.2	1,864	1.5
	9	IC	.91	284	1.3	5.9	1,676	1.4
	10	G	.66	272	1.3	7.0	1,905	1.5
	11	IH	.82	253	1.2	6.3	1,594	1.3
	12	G	.89	237	1.1	6.3	1,498	1.2
	13	P	.85	226	1.0	4.1	933	0.8
	14	PS	.66	196	0.9	5.9	1,156	0.9
	15	IP	.54	149	0.7	5.2	779	0.6
	16	Ob	.13	139	0.6	6.6	920	0.7
	17	Ob	.23	44	0.2	8.2	359	0.3
	11 Others		.74	176	0.8	5.3	938	0.8
Subtotal	24 (20.7%)		.83	3,456	15.9	5.9	20,390	16.5
41–50	29	GP	.99	722	3.3	5.5	3,917	3.2
	30	GP	1.00	686	3.2	4.6	3,756	3.0
	31	GP	.93	666	3.1	6.1	4,040	3.3
	32	FP	.97	657	3.0	5.8	3,788	3.1
	33	P	.84	585	2.7	6.1	3,573	2.9
	34	GP	1.00	583	2.7	6.1	3,561	2.9
	35	GP	.92	499	2.3	4.4	2,177	1.8
	36	GP	.56	471	2.2	6.2	2,916	2.4
	37	U	.73	448	2.1	6.4	2,883	2.3
	38	O	.64	438	2.0	7.4	3,226	2.6
	39	G	1.00	410	1.9	4.6	1,864	1.5
	40	GP	.51	338	1.6	5.5	1,849	1.5
	41	IC	.57	326	1.5	5.5	1,780	1.4
	42	P	.62	318	1.5	6.4	2,034	1.6
	43	P	.70	306	1.4	6.1	1,864	1.5
	44	I	.61	298	1.4	4.8	1,418	1.1
	45	G	.56	286	1.3	5.8	1,649	1.3
	46	PS	.73	279	1.3	5.4	1,509	1.2

Table 9–12 continued

Age (Yrs)	M.D. Number[a]	Specialty[b]	Index of Investment	Admissions	% of Total	Avg. Length of Stay (Days)	Patient Days	% of Total
				Current Utilization of Med/Surg Unit				
	47	IC	.90	245	1.1	5.4	1,313	1.1
	48	P	.48	235	1.1	6.6	1,555	1.3
	49	I	.45	220	1.0	6.7	1,469	1.2
	50	Op	.31	171	0.8	5.2	886	0.7
	51	Ob	.20	146	0.7	4.4	642	0.5
	52	Ob	.15	64	0.3	7.3	469	0.4
	17 Others		.72	241	1.1	5.8	1,390	1.1
Subtotal	41 (35.3%)		.79	9,638	44.3	5.8	55,528	44.8
51–60	70	G	1.00	751	3.5	6.5	4,881	3.9
	71	GP	1.00	724	3.3	6.5	4,727	3.8
	72	GP	.96	591	2.7	4.4	2,969	2.1
	73	GP	.84	577	2.7	5.0	2,889	2.3
	74	U	1.00	543	2.5	6.8	3,695	3.0
	75	FP	1.00	515	2.4	4.3	2,235	1.8
	76	G	.91	473	2.2	4.4	2,096	1.7
	77	Op	.72	441	2.0	7.1	3,114	2.5
	78	Ob	1.00	372	1.7	5.7	2,120	1.7
	79	Ob	.92	321	1.5	6.0	1,930	1.6
	80	PS	.41	257	1.2	6.1	1,565	1.3
	81	I	.71	210	1.0	4.8	997	0.8
	82	P	.32	176	0.8	4.6	803	0.7
	83	Op	.68	169	0.8	4.5	763	0.6
	84	G	.71	163	0.8	8.2	1,329	1.1
	85	Ob	.85	153	0.7	5.7	872	0.7
	86	P	.37	146	0.7	5.0	732	0.6
	87	P	.46	144	0.7	6.4	921	0.7
	88	I	.61	138	0.6	6.4	887	0.7
	89	FP	.27	133	0.6	3.4	458	0.4
	90	Ob	.32	117	0.5	7.4	867	0.7
	91	GP	.31	84	0.4	6.9	579	0.5
	92	P	.17	63	0.3	7.3	459	0.4
	13 Others		.69	234	1.1	5.3	1,234	1.0
Subtotal	36 (31.0%)		.77	7,495	34.5	5.7	42,722	34.5
61+	106	FP	.73	497	2.3	3.9	1,937	1.6
	107	G	.87	215	1.0	4.8	1,024	0.8
	108	GP	1.00	92	0.4	6.5	596	0.5
	109	GP	.32	59	0.3	2.6	154	0.1
	110	I	1.00	27	0.1	6.2	166	0.1

Table 9–12 continued

Age (Yrs)	M.D. Number[a]	Specialty[b]	Index of Investment	Current Utilization of Med/Surg Unit: Admissions	% of Total	Avg. Length of Stay (Days)	Patient Days	% of Total
	6 Others		.72	91	0.4	3.8	341	0.3
Subtotal	11 (9.5%)		.83	981	4.5	4.3	4,218	3.4
All 116 M.D.s	116 (100%)		.71	21,741	100.0	5.7	123,918	100.0

[a]This column lists only those physicians who currently provided more than 0.1 percent of the admissions to the medical-surgery unit. Those who admitted less than 0.1 percent are included in "others."

[b]I = internal medicine, IC = cardiology, IH = hematology, IP = pulmonary, FP = family practice, GP = general practice, G = general surgery, O = orthopedic surgery, Ob = obstetrics/gynecology, Op = ophthalmology, P = pediatrics, PS = plastic surgery, U = urology.

[c]Percentages in parentheses are the percentages of the 116 M.D.s in each age group.

physicians, or 14 percent, had values of the index of investment below 0.50. These physicians treated fewer than half of their inpatients at Suburban. They were more likely than their colleagues with higher values of the index of investment to discontinue use of Suburban and to transfer their inpatient activities to other local hospitals at which they had higher values of the index of investment. However, they accounted for only 10.1 percent of admissions and 10.4 percent of patient days. Hence, there appeared to be little risk of significant drops in future med-surg utilization due to low values of the index of investment for the med-surg staff.

The current average length of stay in the med-surg unit was 5.7 days. It was 6.2 days for the physicians 30 years of age and younger, 5.9 days for those between 31 and 40 years of age, 5.8 days for those between 41 and 50 years of age, 5.7 days for those between 51 and 60 years of age, and 4.3 days for those over 61 years of age. In other words, the average length of stay decreased with increasing physician age. This may or may not be true in other hospitals, and it is difficult to explain without more information on Suburban's med-surg physicians' current treatment practices and the case-mix severity of their patients. However, it does suggest that as the older members of the staff died or retired, they would be replaced by physicians who had higher average length of stay patterns. This should lead to an increase in med-surg patient days.

The last issue to be addressed in this risk analysis is whether past changes in the size of the med-surg staff indicated a risk of unexpected future reductions—which could lead to unexpected future reductions in med-surg utilization. The data in Table 9–13 show that the med-surg staff increased an average of 0.5 percent per annum, from 113 to 116, between 1977 and 1982. During this same period, med-surg admissions grew at an average of 2.1 percent per annum, from 19,641 to 21,741. Hence, the unit's staff grew more slowly than its admissions. This suggests that the average number of admissions per physician increased during the period. At the same time, the med-surg staff's average value of the index of investment grew from 0.68 to 0.71. This suggests that, on average, the unit's staff were slowly concentrating their inpatient activities at Suburban. This agrees with the informal, "from-the-grapevine" opinion that Suburban's med-surg unit was regarded as desirable. The fact that the med-surg staff grew more slowly than the unit's admissions between 1977 and 1982 was probably due to a combination of three factors: (1) an increase in the average size of the med-surg physicians' practices; (2) the med-surg staff's concentration of their inpatient activities at Suburban; and (3) the fact that the med-surg unit, after expanding steadily after 1972, began approaching its maximum capacity in about 1980 (see Table 9–6).

Overall, Table 9–13 indicates that the med-surg staff at Suburban Hospital had been extremely stable over the previous five years. In addition, the hospital appeared to have had little or no problem replacing vacancies that occurred during this period (Table 9–13). Hence, there appeared to be very little risk of a sudden drop in med-surg utilization due to a sudden drop in staff size.

Table 9–13 Medical-Surgical Admitting Staff at Suburban Hospital, 1977–1982

						Changes in Admitting Staff					
						Additions	*Deletions*				
	Total Admissions	*Annual Growth Rate (%)*	*Admitting Staff*	*Annual Growth Rate (%)*	*Avg. Index of Investment*	*Total*	*Discontinuations*	*Resignations*	*Retirements*	*Deaths*	*Total*
1977	19,641	—	113		0.68	15	4	1	5	4	14
1978	20,121	2.4	114	0.8	0.69	6	1	—	3	2	6
1979	20,490	1.8	114	—	0.70	12	3	2	3	3	11
1980	20,861	1.8	115	0.9	0.73	16	6	5	3	1	15
1981	21,201	1.6	116	0.9	0.73	9	5	3	—	1	9
1982	21,741	2.6	116	—	0.71						
Avg Annual Growth Rate 1977–1982 (%)		2.1		0.5							

Finally, there was the risk that med-surg utilization would drop if med-surg admitting physicians discontinued their use of Suburban due to dissatisfaction with the services at the hospital. While this issue was not addressed in this case study, it could be examined by means of a survey of the med-surg admitting physicians that would probe their satisfaction or dissatisfaction with the hospital's services. This survey could also solicit recommendations for improvements in those services.

REFERENCES

1. D.B. Starkweather, *Hospital Mergers in the Making* (Ann Arbor, Mich.: Health Administration Press, 1981), pp. 77–123.

2. M.B. Hadley, *A Study of the Administrative Problems Experienced in Hospital Mergers in the United States,* unpublished DBA Thesis (Washington, D.C.: George Washington University, 1977).

3. H. Williams, *Hospital Closures and Mergers, New York City, 1960–1975* (New York, N.Y.: Health and Hospital Planning Council of Southern New York, Inc., 1976).

4. R.J. Taylor, "Human Dynamics in Hospital Mergers," Research fellowship papers prepared for the American College of Hospital Administrators, Washington, D.C., 1978.

5. D.B. Starkweather and D.C. Walden, eds., *Conference on Analysis of Hospital Mergers: Transcript of Proceedings* (Rockville, Md.: National Center for Health Services Research, 1970).

6. T.R. O'Donovan, *Ambulatory Surgical Centers: Development and Management* (Germantown, Md.: Aspen Systems Corp., 1976), pp. 5–6.

7. J.H. Nichol, "Paper presented to the British Medical Society," *British Medical Journal* 2 (1909):753.

8. Ibid., p. 753.

9. A. Weltmann, "Cost Determinations and Constants in Ambulatory Surgery," *Ambulatory Surgical Centers: Development and Management,* ed. T.R. O'Donovan (Germantown, Md.: Aspen Systems Corp., 1976), pp. 157–162.

10. R. Raatjes, "Financial Aspects of Ambulatory Surgery," *Ambulatory Surgical Centers: Development and Management,* ed. T.R. O'Donovan (Germantown, Md.: Aspen Systems Corp., 1976), pp. 95–98.

11. J.C. McCabe, "Major Issues in the Total Escalation of Health Care Costs," *Ambulatory Surgical Centers: Development and Management,* ed. T.R. O'Donovan (Germantown, Md.: Aspen Systems Corp., 1976), pp. 163–170.

12. T.R. O'Donovan, "The Pros and Cons of Ambulatory Surgery," *Ambulatory Surgical Centers: Development and Management,* ed. T.R. O'Donovan (Germantown, Md.: Aspen Systems Corp., 1976), pp. 11–18.

13. R.M. Grossman, "Is Ambulatory Surgery Less Expensive," *Hospitals, JAHA* 53 (May 16, 1979):112–116.

14. L.A. Burns and M.S. Ferber, "Ambulatory Surgery in the United States: Development and Prospects," *Journal of Ambulatory Care Management* 4, no. 3 (August 1981):1.

15. G.J. Hill, "Outpatient Surgery—What Are the Indications for It?" *Surgery* 77, no. 3 (March 1975):333–335.

16. Weltman, "Cost Determinations," pp. 157–162.

17. Raatjes, "Financial Aspects," pp. 95–98.

18. O'Donovan, "Pros and Cons," pp. 11–18.

19. Grossman, "Is Ambulatory Surgery Less Expensive," pp. 112–116.

20. Weltman, "Cost Determinations," pp. 157–162.

21. Raatjes, "Financial Aspects," pp. 95–98.

22. Grossman, "Is Ambulatory Surgery Less Expensive," pp. 112–116.

23. T.R. O'Donovan, "Major Concepts and Definitions," *Ambulatory Surgical Centers: Development and Management,* ed. T.R. O'Donovan (Germantown, Md.: Aspen Systems Corp., 1976), pp. 3–10.

24. L.D. Brindenbaugh, "A Hospital-Based Ambulatory Surgery Unit," *Ambulatory Surgical Centers: Development and Management,* ed. T.R. O'Donovan (Germantown, Md.: Aspen Systems Corp., 1976), pp. 105–112.

25. O'Donovan, "Ambulatory Surgical Centers," p. 3.

26. O'Donovan, "Major Concepts," pp. 3–10.

27. O'Donovan, "Pros and Cons," pp. 11–18.

28. Grossman, "Is Ambulatory Surgery Less Expensive," pp. 112–116.

29. T.R. O'Donovan, "Major Conclusions Ambulatory Surgery," *Ambulatory Surgical Centers: Development and Management,* ed. T.R. O'Donovan (Germantown, Md.: Aspen Systems Corp., 1976), pp. 19–26.

30. D.D. Hawthorne, "Hospital-Based Unit Improves Utilization," *Ambulatory Surgical Centers: Development and Management,* ed. T.R. O'Donovan (Germantown, Md.: Aspen Systems Corp., 1976), pp. 77–84.

31. Brindenbaugh, "Hospital-Based Ambulatory Surgery Unit," pp. 105–112.

32. T.R. O'Donovan, ed., *Ambulatory Surgical Centers: Development and Management* (Germantown, Md.: Aspen Systems Corp., 1976), pp. 203–207.

33. J.B. Johnson, "Ambulatory Surgery: A New Look at an Old Concept," *Ambulatory Surgical Centers: Development and Management,* ed. T.R. O'Donovan (Germantown, Md.: Aspen Systems Corp., 1976), pp. 85–94.

Chapter 10

Financial Planning

INTRODUCTION

Financial planning is more than a single component of the strategic planning process. Though it is an integral part of strategic planning, it requires the carrying out of a series of tasks that parallel those of the larger strategic planning process (see Table 10–1). Financial planning's major roles in strategic planning are to define some of the important constraints under which the hospital must operate (including financial resources, goals, and objectives), and to define the financial implications of alternative strategies. Financial planning therefore serves both to limit the kinds of decisions that can be made and to test the financial feasibility of each choice as it is considered in the planning process.

The importance of financial planning and control has led to the development of specialized staff and computer resources in hospitals. Financial planning can also share data and other resources with important and well-developed administrative functions, such as patient and third party billing. This could lead hospitals to view financial planning as independent from strategic planning. In fact, the two must be closely integrated. Many of the assumptions about the markets to be served and the volume and types of services to be provided that must be made in financial planning should be the result of a strategic planning process.

The major objective of this chapter is not to provide the reader with the knowledge and skills necessary to carry out the financial planning tasks listed in Table 10–1. That would require far more space than is available here; in any event, a number of other volumes are already available on those detailed aspects. Rather, because financial planning is so frequently discussed as a separate activity with its own base of knowledge and skills, our objective in this chapter is to attempt to demonstrate how financial and strategic planning can be integrated. To this end, we examine here the first six steps listed in Table 10–1, following the process from the preparation of the initial mission statement through the development and evaluation of alternative strategies.

Table 10–1 Financial Planning in the Strategic Planning Process

Strategic Planning Tasks	*Financial Planning Tasks and Analyses*
1. Preparation of initial mission statement	Develop initial financial goals
2. Internal analysis	Evaluate financial position against initial goals • rate of return on equity and/or growth in assets • internal sources and uses of capital
3. External analysis	Evaluate external financial environment • financial position and objectives of competing and complementary organizations • growth and availability of sources of revenue • growth and availability of external sources of capital
4. Assessment of present position	Assess current financial position • comparative financial performance • share of available revenue received • access to and use of available capital
5. Revision of mission statement and development of goals	Revise financial goals
6. Development and evaluation of alternative strategies	Determine financial impact of alternative strategies • on financial goals • on the use of capital To do this, • estimate capital and operating budgets • estimate impact on utilization, revenues, and expenses
7. Setting of strategies and objectives	Set financial objectives • determine what movement toward achieving the financial goals should occur each year • set targets for the acquisition and use of working and long-term capital
8. Development of contingency plans	Develop a financial contingency plan • set financial "trigger points" • determine financial consequences of alternative strategies • investigate alternative sources of working and long-term capital
9. Development and implementation of program and operational plans	Develop program and operational budgets • develop a capital budget • evaluate working capital needs • prepare departmental and program budgets • develop a financing plan • set rates and estimate reimbursement

Table 10–1 continued

Strategic Planning Tasks	*Financial Planning Tasks and Analyses*
10. Development of evaluation, monitoring, and control system	Establish a financial control system • implement management by objectives • determine and evaluate program and department budget variances • monitor achievement of financial objectives • monitor capital budgets
11. Revision and implementation of contingency plans	Revise financial plan and implement contingency plan • reassess assumptions about the external financial environment • evaluate achievement of financial objectives

For this purpose, we use the example of City Hospital that was introduced in Chapters 6 and 8 to demonstrate one way in which financial and strategic planning can be integrated. In preparing this case study, we have relied extensively on the assistance of Mark Toso, CPA, Vice-President of Amherst Associates, and the library of computer models developed by Amherst Associates.

CASE STUDY: CITY HOSPITAL

City Hospital's major mission is to provide acute inpatient services to residents of Adams, Schuyler, Morris, and Jefferson counties. The hospital's market share for acute inpatients is 85 percent in Adams and Schuyler counties. Physicians and patients from Morris and Jefferson counties come to the hospital primarily for cancer treatment, since City has the only medical oncology department in the four-county area.

The hospital's cancer patients from Morris and Jefferson counties are almost entirely Medicare patients. Younger cancer patients tend to use University Hospital, about 30 miles away. Morris and Jefferson county physicians under 40 use University Hospital for cancer referrals. Patients from Morris and Jefferson counties who require radiation therapy are treated at University Hospital and at hospitals in an adjacent metropolitan area.

Using the three-dimensional market definition introduced in Chapter 6, City Hospital's market in Morris and Jefferson counties can be described as follows: City Hospital now focuses primarily on one payer group, Medicare; it meets the need for a range of hospital diagnostic and therapeutic services (the major exception being radiation therapy), the technologies it uses cover a wide range, and include chemotherapy and surgery.

If the hospital wishes to increase the number of patients from Morris and Jefferson counties, it has numerous options in developing a market strategy. Possibilities include some combination of changes in patient groups served, needs met, and technologies used. Or, instead of changing the scope of its market it could improve its position by differentiation (i.e., by treating one or more segments of its market differently or by differentiating itself from competitors). For example, it could offer ambulance transfer services to patients at a reduced rate or develop a hospice. It could also offer radiation therapy, which would both expand its scope of services and technologies and differentiate the hospital from those of its competitors that don't offer radiation therapy.

Looking at its physician market, City might also attempt to change the scope of the physician group it now serves (e.g., by attracting younger physicians). It might differentiate between segments of its physician market (e.g., by offering continuing education programs on cancer treatment to physicians in Morris and Jefferson counties). City could also attempt to differentiate itself from other hospitals (especially University) in ways that would make it attractive to physicians (e.g., through selected equipment purchases). A combination of changes in physician groups, needs served, and technologies used could result in an increase in the volume of patients treated.

The above information on City Hospital is only a small portion of the information that would be contained in the strategic plan for the entire hospital. We will assume, however, that expanding the number of cancer patients it treats from Morris and Jefferson counties is critical to the fulfillment of what the hospital's leadership feels is City's mission. Thus, increased service to people in these counties and the development of the hospital's capabilities for cancer treatment are high priority goals. Capabilities for cancer treatment and the market for services in these two counties are of course not the only subjects of City Hospital's strategic plan; however, we will focus on these two subjects in order to illustrate the integration of strategic and financial planning.

The Financial Environment for Strategy Development

The definition of the hospital's financial environment encompasses the first five tasks listed in Table 10–1. At the end of this stage of its financial planning (and strategic planning) process, through a careful review of its internal and external environment, City Hospital will have determined what its mission and goals are. The assessment of its current position could lead the hospital to reassess the mission and goals it had at the beginning of the planning process.

Developing Initial Financial Goals

A hospital's initial mission statement has significant implications for the development of its financial goals. A statement of responsibilities toward the communities it serves will likely suggest the need to maintain or expand existing sources of revenue and capital. For both for-profit and nonprofit hospitals, the internal and external generation of capital is necessary to replace existing plant and equipment and to provide new services.[1,2] In addition, for-profit hospitals have the responsibility to investors to provide a return on equity and to pay dividends consistent with the hospital's need for capital for other purposes (and with the expectations of shareholders).[3]

As a nonprofit hospital that wishes to provide additional services to new population groups, City Hospital needs to combine internally generated capital (operating and nonoperating income) with externally generated capital (debt and contributions). It has therefore set the following initial financial goal: to generate sufficient capital to maintain its current services, provide for future replacement of plant and equipment, and provide some additional services consistent with the hospital's mission. It has also set four initial financial objectives:

1. an operating margin of at least 3 percent
2. a return on fund balance of at least 15 percent
3. a current ratio of from 1.5 to 2.0
4. a debt-to-asset ratio of no greater than 60 percent.

Rather than set objectives in terms of the dollars of working and long-term capital that need to be raised, City has chosen—through the attainment of the above objectives—to ensure access to a steady stream of capital from both external and internal sources. We assume that banks and other sources of debt continue to view hospitals with these financial characteristics as good candidates, although other factors, discussed in Chapter 8, are also considered.

Evaluating Financial Position against Initial Goals

The two major topics of an internal analysis in both strategic and financial planning are (1) how resources are currently being used and (2) the capabilities of the hospital (see Chapter 2).

The hospital's financial reports, prepared internally and by its auditors, describe how working and long-term capital have been allocated to meet the needs of staff, patients, and physicians. There are a number of ways in which these data can be evaluated, for example, using financial ratios,[4] productivity indicators,[5] or patterns of practice data.[6] The hospital will also be concerned about whether its financial capabilities match or surpass the capabilities of staff and other hospital resources. While the money for a new service might be found, for example, the hospital may not be able to recruit necessary staff. An assessment of the new service in light of the hospital's initial financial goals is also critically important.

In addition to the information cited above, City Hospital's internal analysis (not presented in its entirety here) revealed that:

- The hospital's decision several years ago to specialize in a limited number of tertiary services resulted in growth in these areas and a drop in routine admissions, especially in maternity and pediatrics. The average annual increase in admissions between 1978 and 1982 was only 1.7 percent. Admissions actually fell by 1.5 percent in 1982 (see Table 10–2).
- The hospital's medical staff is primarily composed of older physicians (average age 55). The hospital has fewer primary care physicians and more specialists than comparable hospitals in its state.

In order to evaluate its financial position against its initial objectives, City Hospital used the Amherst Multiyear Model, a financial forecasting model developed by Amherst Associates. The hospital first had to make some assumptions about future (post-1982) demand for inpatient and outpatient services. Because of the aging of its medical staff and competition from University Hospital, it adopted the conservative assumption that admissions would drop by one percent per year between 1983 and 1988. It assumed that its length of stay would remain constant at 9.2 days, with a continuing drop in ALOS for routine admissions being counterbalanced by an increase in ALOS for more acutely ill patients as the hospital's tertiary care activities expanded. The net result would be an annual one percent decrease in patient days between 1983 and 1988. The effect on patient days is shown in Table 10–2. All of this decrease was expected to be in routine care units; admissions to the hospital's critical care, coronary care, and burn units were expected to continue to grow due to the hospital's emphasis on tertiary care.

Table 10–2 City Hospital Multiyear Profile, 1978–1988

	Patient Days	*Admissions*	*ALOS*	*ADC*	*Visits*	*Beds*
1978	113,384	13,000	8.72	311	64,508	396
1979	118,642	13,175	9.01	325	68,566	396
1980	125,869	13,645	9.22	344	75,454	396
1981	125,710	14,104	8.91	345	79,512	396
1982	127,797	13,892	9.20	350	83,709	402
1983	126,519	13,753	9.20	347	84,546	402
1984	125,253	13,615	9.20	343	85,392	402
1985	124,001	13,479	9.20	340	86,245	402
1986	122,761	13,345	9.20	336	87,108	402
1987	121,534	13,211	9.20	333	87,979	402
1988	120,318	13,079	9.20	330	88,859	402

Source: Amherst Multiyear Model. Reprinted with permission of Amherst Associates, Inc., Chicago, Ill.

The emphasis on tertiary care resulted in an increase in outpatient visits, which rose at an average annual rate of 7.4 percent between 1978 and 1982. However, the rate of increase slowed to an average of 5.5 percent per year between 1980 and 1982, so the hospital used the conservative assumption that outpatient visits would rise only one percent per year during the forecast period (see Table 10–2).

In order to prepare a forecast of revenues and expenses, the hospital made the following assumptions:

- Administrative expenses are primarily determined by inpatient services and would therefore decline by one percent per year in accordance with the one percent annual decrease in inpatient days.
- The number of full-time equivalent personnel (FTEs) could be forecast on the basis of the current ratio of FTEs to units of service. The FTEs needed for inpatient and outpatient services could be calculated separately and then combined.
- Salaries could be forecast on the basis of the current salary per FTE. Salaries would increase by 7.5 percent per year and benefits would remain at 14 percent of salaries.
- Nonsalary expenses would increase by 9 percent per year; 50 percent of these expenses would be fixed, while 50 percent would vary with the volume of services provided.
- Rates for all payers would increase a total of 9 percent per year. The proportion of revenue from Medicare would increase, that from Medicaid would remain the same, and that from Blue Cross would decrease.
- Capital expenditures of $5 million per year would be needed to maintain the hospital's current services and level of quality. After 1983, this sum would be increased 10 percent per year to account for the effects of inflation and new technology.

We will not take the time here to explain the reasoning behind each of these assumptions. Any of them could be changed, and the resulting adjusted financial statements could be produced in a short period of time. Table 10–3 shows the forecast of revenue and expense that was produced based on the above assumptions. Operating income was expected to decline during the forecast period. A decline in nonoperating income was also expected, as a result of a decline in interest income. The negative interest income shown in Table 10–3 was the result of the depletion of the hospital's investments and subsequent borrowing for the hospital's capital expenditures program.

As Table 10–4 shows, in order to meet the need for capital, the Amherst model depletes investments rather than add to long-term debt. When capital needs exceed investments, negative investments are shown and an interest charge

Table 10–3 City Hospital Forecast of Revenue and Expense, 1982–1988

FORECAST STATEMENT OF REVENUE AND EXPENSE
(000s omitted)

	For the year ending June 30						
	Actual 1982	*1983*	*1984*	*1985*	*1986*	*1987*	*1988*
Revenue:							
Routine patient revenue	$31,543	$33,770	$37,618	$41,208	$44,739	$48,362	$52,209
Ancillary inpatient revenue	29,318	33,564	37,860	41,786	44,824	49,713	55,183
Outpatient revenue	6,419	7,381	8,457	9,506	10,976	12,465	14,203
Total patient service revenue	67,280	74,715	83,935	92,500	100,539	110,540	121,595
Deductions from patient revenue:							
Contractual allowances	12,902	16,197	19,307	21,955	24,021	27,148	30,733
Free care and bad debts	1,009	1,252	1,459	1,588	1,733	1,890	2,073
Total deductions	13,911	17,449	20,766	23,543	25,754	29,038	32,806
Net patient service revenue	53,369	57,266	63,169	68,957	74,785	81,502	88,789
Other operating revenue	806	869	939	1,012	1,093	1,179	1,273
Net operating revenue	54,175	58,135	64,108	69,969	75,878	82,681	90,062
Operating expense:							
Salaries, wages, and benefits	27,185	29,424	32,408	35,137	37,841	40,853	44,123
Nonsalary expense	21,754	24,110	26,777	29,361	31,836	34,968	38,440
Patient service expense	48,939	53,534	59,185	64,498	69,677	75,821	82,563
Operating income prior to depreciation and interest	5,236	4,601	4,923	5,471	6,201	6,860	7,499
Depreciation	1,929	2,466	2,982	3,582	4,232	4,932	5,602
Interest expense	625	653	510	442	437	432	427
Total operating expense	51,493	56,653	62,677	68,522	74,346	81,185	88,592
Operating income	2,682	1,482	1,431	1,447	1,532	1,496	1,470
Nonoperating revenue:							
Interest income	688	494	292	87	(21)	(123)	(223)
Other income	30	30	30	30	30	30	30
Total nonoperating revenue	718	524	322	117	9	(93)	(193)
Net income	$3,400	$2,006	$1,753	$1,564	$1,541	$1,403	$1,277

This statement was prepared on the basis of the accompanying assumptions and rationale.

Source: Amherst Multiyear Model. Reprinted with permission of Amherst Associates Inc., Chicago, Ill.

(underestimated by using the rate of return on investments) is shown on the income statement (Table 10–3). The model requires that the user specify whether the shortfall will be met by adding long-term debt (and the interest rate expected) or whether other assumptions should be made (e.g., an increase in contributions).

As can be seen in Table 10–4, by 1984, City Hospital would have liquidated its investments and would still need additional capital, amounting to $5.3 million in 1988. Reducing the hospital's capital expenditures might at first seem a logical way to reduce the need for borrowing. However, the routine capital expenditures in Table 10–4 would not be enough to ensure that the value of the hospital's assets in 1988 would be equal to what they were in 1982. If inflation were assumed to remain at 9 percent during the forecast period, the future value of the hospital's 1982 net fixed assets would be $50.2 million (this calculation is done by the user, not the model). Table 10–5 shows that City Hospital's net fixed assets were forecast to be $43.7 million in 1988. Using the data in this table, the user could calculate that net fixed assets were forecast to increase at an annual rate of only 6.5 percent.

The erosion of the hospital's fund balance or equity is shown in Table 10–6. Fund balances were expected to increase by only 4.5 percent during the forecast period (a calculation by the user), far less than what recent history suggests may be the rate of inflation.

A decline in real net fixed assets and fund balance does not necessarily mean that the hospital would be unable to meet its goal of maintaining current services and replacing existing plant and equipment. Improvements in technology and hospital management might make it possible to provide current services with less resources. However, the hospital would have to consider the source and magnitude of such economies before it scaled down its capital expenditure program.

Table 10–7 shows that the hospital was not expected to meet its initial financial objectives of an operating margin of 3 percent or a return on fund balance of 15 percent. It also shows that the hospital would have no problem meeting its objectives for current and debt-to-asset ratios.

The leverage and coverage ratios in Table 10–7 show that the hospital was expected to have considerable unused capacity to acquire new long-term debt. Additional debt would not necessarily solve the problem of declining inpatient utilization. However, long-term debt could be used to provide the hospital with the resources it needed to increase utilization. Market strategies that required a level of capital expenditure of $5 million per year (or more) were therefore not out of the question for City Hospital. Any evaluation of alternative strategies would, however, have to include an estimate of the extent to which such strategies would solve the problem of declining utilization.

The use of the Amherst financial model shows that, given the assumptions listed earlier, City Hospital was facing a period of declining utilization, declining

Table 10–4 City Hospital Forecast of Cash Flow, 1982–1988

FORECAST STATEMENT OF CASH FLOW
(000s omitted)

	For the year ending June 30						
	Actual 1982	*1983*	*1984*	*1985*	*1986*	*1987*	*1988*
Cash investments, and other long term assets at beginning of year	$5,497	$6,492	$5,987	$2,766	$1,596	$523	($500)
Sources of funds:							
From operations:							
Net income	$3,400	$2,006	$1,753	$1,564	$1,541	$1,403	$1,277
Add items not affecting cash							
Depreciation	1,929	2,466	2,982	3,582	4,232	4,932	5,602
Total from operations	5,329	4,472	4,735	5,146	5,773	6,335	6,879
New long term debt	—	—	—	—	—	—	—
Change in other long term liabilities	—	—	—	—	—	—	—
Restricted contributions	679	600	350	350	350	350	350
Total sources of funds	6,008	5,072	5,085	5,496	6,123	6,685	7,229
Uses of funds:							
Project expenditures	—	—	—	—	—	—	—
Routine capital expenditures	5,690	5,000	5,500	6,000	6,500	7,000	7,500
Repayment of debt net of change in current portion	362	2,516	370	375	380	390	400
Change in current portion of long term debt	(24)	(2,154)	2,146	(5)	(5)	(10)	(10)
Change in working capital items:							
Net receivables	689	591	841	825	830	957	1,038
Inventories	320	47)	147	142	136	172	191
Other current assets	246	75)	113	106	104	122	135
Trade payables	(1,492)	(356)	(576)	(558)	(534)	(677)	(749)
Accrued salary	(646)	(100)	(134)	(123)	(122)	(135)	(148)
Other current liabilities	(132)	(42)	(101)	(96)	(93)	(111)	(121)
Total for working capital items		215	290	296	321	328	346
Total uses of funds	5,013	5,577	8,306	6,666	7,196	7,708	8,236
Cash, investments, and other long term assets at end of year	$6,492	$5,987	$2,766	$1,596	$523	($500)	($1,507)
Consisting of:							
Cash	$784	$803	$888	$967	$1,045	$1,138	$1,239
Investments	3,210	2,636	(670)	(1,919)	(3,070)	(4,186)	(5,294)
Other long term assets	2,498	2,548	2,548	2,548	2,548	2,548	2,548)
	$6,492	$5,987	$2,766	$1,596	$523	($500)	($1,507)

This statement was prepared on the basis of the accompanying assumptions and rationale.

Source: Amherst Multiyear Model. Reprinted with permission of Amherst Associates, Inc., Chicago, Ill.

Table 10–5 City Hospital Forecast Balance Sheet, 1982–1988

FORECAST BALANCE SHEET
(000s omitted)

	For the year ended June 30						
	Actual 1982	*1983*	*1984*	*1985*	*1986*	*1987*	*1988*
Assets							
Current assets:							
Cash	$784	$803	$888	$967	$1,045	$1,138	$1,239
Net receivables	7,567	8,158	8,999	9,824	10,654	11,611	12,649
Inventory	1,279	1,326	1,473	1,615	1,751	1,923	2,114
Other current assets	996	1,071	1,184	1,290	1,394	1,516	1,651
Total current assets	10,626	11,358	12,544	13,696	14,844	16,188	17,653
Gross fixed assets	40,148	45,148	50,648	56,648	63,148	70,148	77,648
Less accumulated depreciation	10,190	12,656	15,638	19,220	23,452	28,384	33,986
Net fixed assets	29,958	32,492	35,010	37,428	39,696	41,764	43,662
Investments	3,210	2,636	(670)	(1,919)	(3,070)	(4,186)	(5,294)
Other long term assets	2,108	2,548	2,548	2,548	2,548	2,548	2,548
Total assets	$46,292	$49,034	$49,432	$51,753	$54,018	$56,314	$58,569
Liabilities and fund balance							
Current liabilities:							
Trade payables	$4,851	$5,207	$5,783	$6,341	$6,875	$7,552	$8,301
Accrued salary	1,224	1,324	1,458	1,581	1,703	1,838	1,986
Other current liabilities	922	964	1,065	1,161	1,254	1,365	1,486
Current portion long term debt	362	2,516	370	375	380	390	400
Total current liabilities	7,359	10,011	8,676	9,458	10,212	11,145	12,173
Long term debt net of current portion:							
Unsecured debt	2,151	—	—	—	—	—	—
Secured debt	9,812	9,447	9,077	8,702	8,322	7,932	7,532
Total long term debt	11,963	9,447	9,077	8,702	8,322	7,932	7,532
Other long term liabilities	—	—	—	—	—	—	—
Total liabilities	19,322	19,458	17,753	18,160	18,534	19,077	19,705
Fund balance	26,970	29,576	31,679	33,593	35,484	37,237	38,864
Liabilities and fund balance	$46,292	$49,034	$49,432	$51,753	$54,018	$56,314	$58,569

This statement was prepared on the basis of the accompanying assumptions and rationale.

Source: Amherst Multiyear Model. Reprinted with permission of Amherst Associates, Inc., Chicago, Ill.

Table 10–6 City Hospital Forecast of Changes in Fund Balance, 1982–1988

FORECAST STATEMENT OF CHANGES IN FUND BALANCE
(000s omitted)

	For the year ending June 30						
	Actual 1982	*1983*	*1984*	*1985*	*1986*	*1987*	*1988*
Balance at beginning of year	$22,891	$26,970	$29,576	$31,679	$33,593	$35,484	$37,237
Net income	$3,400	$2,006	$1,753	$1,564	$1,541	$1,403	$1,277
Restricted contributions	679	600	350	350	350	350	350
Adjustment to fixed assets	—	—	—	—	—	—	—
Assumption and cancellation of long term debt	—	—	—	—	—	—	—
Balance at end of year	$26,970	$29,576	$31,679	$33,593	$35,484	$37,237	$38,864

This statement was prepared on the basis of the accompanying assumptions and rationale.

Source: Amherst Multiyear Model. Reprinted with permission of Amherst Associates, Inc., Chicago, Ill.

real assets, and declining profitability. It had, however, considerable capacity to acquire new long-term debt and to make investments that might reduce its financial problems, increase utilization, and allow it to maintain services and replace its plant and equipment.

Evaluating the External Financial Environment

An external analysis in strategic planning focuses on defining the hospital's total market (served and unserved) and the identity and intentions of competing and complementary organizations. The policies and future intentions of government, other third party payers, and other groups that could affect the hospital's future must also be examined. This information is used in financial planning to estimate the growth and availability of sources of revenue and capital.

The flow of revenue into the hospital can be either augmented or threatened by the availability or nonavailability of unserved markets, the actions of organizations competing for the same markets, and the actions of organizations who complement those of the hospital in such a way as to alter the demand for services (e.g., prevention programs and home care for the elderly). The actions of third party payers also have an impact, and government has additional ways of affecting the flow of revenue (e.g., through the certificate-of-need process). The resulting changes in revenue can affect the ability of the hospital to generate capital internally (i.e., through profits).

Table 10–7 City Hospital Forecast of Financial Ratios, 1982–1988

FORECAST FINANCIAL RATIOS
(000s omitted)

	For the year ending June 30						
	Actual 1982	*1983*	*1984*	*1985*	*1986*	*1987*	*1988*
Liquidity ratios							
Current ratio	1.44	1.13	1.45	1.45	1.45	1.45	1.45
Acid	1.13	0.90	1.14	1.14	1.15	1.14	1.14
Absolute	0.11	0.08	0.10	0.10	0.10	0.10	0.10
Leverage ratios							
Debt/Assets	41.7%	39.7%	35.9%	35.1%	34.3%	33.9%	33.6
Current liabilities/Assets	15.9%	20.4%	17.6%	18.3%	18.9%	19.8%	20.8%
Long term debt/Assets	25.8%	19.3%	18.4%	16.8%	15.4%	14.1%	12.9%
Secured debt/Net fixed assets	32.8%	29.1%	25.9%	23.3%	21.0%	19.0%	17.3%
Assets/Fund balance	1.72	1.66	1.56	1.54	1.52	1.51	1.51
Composition ratios							
Current assets/Assets	23.0%	23.2%	25.4%	26.5%	27.5%	28.7%	30.1
Net fixed assets/Assets	64.7%	66.3%	70.8%	72.3%	73.5%	74.2%	74.5
Investments/Assets	12.3%	10.6%	3.8%	1.2%	(1.0)%	(2.9)%	(4.7)%
Activity ratios							
Assets	1.17	1.19	1.30	1.35	1.40	1.47	1.54
Current assets	5.10	5.12	5.11	5.11	5.11	5.11	5.10
Fixed assets	1.81	1.79	1.83	1.87	1.91	1.98	2.06
Profitability ratios							
Operating income/Fund balance	9.9%	5.0%	4.5%	4.3%	4.3%	4.0%	3.8%
Net income/Fund balance	12.6%	6.8%	5.5%	4.7%	4.3%	3.8%	3.3%
Return on assets	7.3%	4.0%	3.5%	3.0%	2.8%	2.4%	2.1%
Operating return	5.8%	3.0%	2.9%	2.8%	2.8%	2.7%	2.5%
Operating margin	5.0%	2.5%	2.2%	2.1%	2.0%	1.8%	1.6%
Profit margin	6.1%	3.4%	2.7%	2.2%	2.0%	1.7%	1.4%
Coverage ratios							
Interest	9.52	7.84	10.28	12.64	14.21	15.66	17.11
Debt service	6.18	5.05	1.73	6.88	7.65	8.33	8.94

This statement was prepared on the basis of the accompanying assumptions and rationale.

Source: Amherst Multiyear Model. Reprinted with permission of Amherst Associates, Inc., Chicago, Ill.

The flow of long-term capital can also be affected by these same factors. The failure to generate a steady flow of revenue can threaten the hospital's ability to raise long-term capital through borrowing or the issuance of stock and securities. Through their reimbursement policies (e.g., by limiting the reimbursement of interest payments on long-term debt), government and third party payers can affect the hospital's ability to acquire long-term capital.

The external analysis undertaken for City Hospital (not presented in its entirety here) showed that a substantial unserved market for tertiary services existed in its four-county region. It also showed that University Hospital had set as its major goal the attainment of a dominant role in the provision of those services.

The state government had not made any moves to grant monopolies through the certificate-of-need process by selecting only one provider for each tertiary service in the region. The state had also indicated its intention to hold increases in the Medicaid budget to a level of 4 percent over the next 5 years. At the same time, Blue Cross and other insurers (and businesses) were pressing for some relief from what they saw as imminent cost shifting.

Thus, if City Hospital wished to offer additional services to cancer patients, it had to determine whether it had the resources, in terms of both staff and money, to compete effectively with University Hospital and meet the requirements of third party payers.

Assessing the Current Financial Position

The assessment of a hospital's current position in the strategic planning process results in a statement of the hospital's current strengths, weaknesses, opportunities, and threats. It identifies imminent threats to the hospital's survival and the rate of change in its situation. The assessment of a hospital's current financial position covers the same topics. The hospital's financial position can be either the cause or the outcome of the hospital's internal and external environment, as identified in strategic planning.

To review a few of the pertinent facts, City Hospital's strengths were its large market share in two of the counties in its primary service area and a qualified medical staff in a mature stage of their careers. Its primary weaknesses were its low market share and limited market served in two counties of its region and its inability to attract referrals from younger physicians in these counties. It was also threatened by the intentions of a university-based hospital. Its objective was to define and gain a larger share of a market in two counties while pursuing its goal of providing community service and expanding its role in cancer treatment.

Revising Financial Goals

Based on an assessment of its current position, a hospital should consider whether to revise its mission statement and goals. What decision makers in the hospital and the community it serves want must be compared to what can actually be accomplished. The desires of other affected groups (e.g., government and competing hospitals) can suggest the need to change course. Financial planning can suggest the financial necessity to make such a change. It can also produce estimates of the financial impact of changes in mission and goals that are made for nonfinancial reasons.

The assessment of City's position resulted in a decision to modify the hospital's mission statement. Rather than seek to develop a full array of tertiary services, City decided to develop those related to cancer treatment. Because of demographic trends in its service area and the age of the population it now serves, City also decided to devote its resources to the treatment of cancers found in adults. It would not seek to develop pediatric oncology services.

After this assessment, City Hospital decided not to revise its initial financial goal and objectives, because it felt they were reasonable, given the standards being applied by lenders. The question was how to increase the hospital's profitability sufficiently to achieve its first two financial objectives—an operating margin of at least 3 percent and a return on fund balance of at least 15 percent. At this point, various alternatives for improving profitability had to be evaluated.

The Financial Impact of Alternative Market Strategies

In the strategic planning process, the hospital develops and evaluates alternative strategies for achieving its mission and goals. The selection of strategies has implications for, and is constrained by, the financial condition and goals of the hospital. As described in Chapter 2, two major types of strategies are (1) those that concern a change in the hospital's markets and (2) those that imply a change in the hospital's organizational structure. The primary emphasis in the present context is on strategies that concern a change in a hospital's markets. For each such alternative strategy, the following three tasks must be carried out in the financial planning process:

1. Capital and operating budgets must be estimated.
2. The impact of the strategy on hospital utilization, revenues, and expenses must be determined.
3. The impact of the strategy on the attainment of the hospital's financial goals and objectives must be assessed.

City Hospital was considering possible changes in its market. One of the strategies that it wanted to evaluate carefully in the financial planning process was the development of a radiation therapy service, the development of which would change the needs being met and the technologies being used by the hospital. Other strategies would then be considered. Here we confine our examination to a comparison of City's strategy of developing a radiation therapy service with one other strategy, that of making no changes and proceeding on the hospital's current course.

Development of a Radiation Therapy Department

The development of a radiation therapy department would allow City Hospital to expand the scope of the patient and physician needs that it met and the technologies that it used to meet those needs. The leadership of City Hospital was interested in doing both, but it was also concerned about the impact that such a new service would have on the hospital's financial condition and whether it would help or hinder the hospital's ability to meet its financial goal and objectives. Again, a financial model would be used to support decision making. Before the model could be used, however, an operating and capital budget had to be prepared. Also, estimates had to be made of the future utilization not only of the new service but of other ancillary and routine services in the hospital as well.

Demand Forecast. Assumptions about future demand must be made based on a hospital's past experience, its understanding of the population it wishes to serve, and its position in relation to competitors.

In an attempt to estimate the current total demand for radiation therapy in its HSA region, City Hospital gathered data from government records (i.e., the volume of services provided, which is submitted to the rate-setting authority) and requested a tabulation from the statewide data consortium of the number of patients in its HSA region who left the region for radiation therapy. The tumor registry operating in the area provided the number of new cancer patients by both place of residence and place of hospitalization. Total demand in 1982 for radiation therapy was estimated to be 44,820 treatments (see Table 10–8).

Using the data it obtained, City Hospital determined that most of the patients going to hospitals in the adjacent metro area were utilizing high energy linear accelerators not now available in their own regions. City Hospital estimated that

Table 10–8 Hospital Market Share for Radiation Therapy in City Hospital's HSA Region, 1982

	Treatments	*Market Share*
University Hospital	10,500	23.4%
Memorial Hospital	7,450	16.6
Suburban Hospital	4,650	10.4
Subtotal	22,600	50.4
Patients on waiting lists at local hospitals	12,500	27.9
Area residents treated outside the region	7,200	16.1
Residents of adjacent region who cross region and seek care in an adjacent metro area	2,520	5.6
Total	44,820	100.0

it could attract 50 percent of patients currently leaving its region for treatment if it obtained a 20-million electron volt (mev) linear accelerator. It estimated that it could also attract 20 percent of patients crossing from an adjacent region to reach the metro area. The accuracy of these assumptions could be tested by the use of physician interviews, but the hospital management decided against such a survey at that time, concluding that such an expense was not necessary until the hospital had examined the potential impact of developing a radiation therapy department, given the above assumptions about market share.

The acquisition of a midrange 6 million volt (MV) linear accelerator, in addition to the 20-mev accelerator, would enable City to attract an additional substantial number of the patients who now had to wait for treatment in area hospitals. City estimated that 50 percent of the patients who were on waiting lists would use its new radiation therapy service. Based on these assumptions, Table 10–9 shows City Hospital's estimates of the patients it could have served in 1982 with a radiation therapy service that included the two linear accelerators.

City Hospital felt that these were conservative estimates, since it had not assumed that the hospital would attract patients now being seen by other hospitals in its region. Also, it had not included in the estimated numbers any of its own patients who were currently being referred to other hospitals.

An examination of trends in the incidence of cancer in the surrounding regions and projections of the age of the population had led state planners to forecast an annual 1.06 percent increase in the incidence of cancer. City Hospital felt that the demand for radiation therapy would grow much faster, since the number of cancers for which treatments were being prescribed had increased rapidly as new equipment made radiation therapy safer and more effective. The availability of the new equipment and of board-certified radiation therapists (a new specialty that was part of radiology until 1976) would also increase demand from those physicians who had not been referring patients—even when radiation therapy would have been appropriate—because of a lack of knowledge of or access to the service.

However, City Hospital made the conservative assumption that treatments would grow at an annual rate of only 1.06 percent per year. This led to the forecast of total demand shown in Table 10–10.

As the table indicates, City forecast that its share of the market would grow, especially after the first year of operations. This would be primarily the result of higher utilization of the 20-mev linear accelerator, which was expected to be the only such machine outside the adjacent metro area. Use of the 20-mev machine was forecast to increase by 3,500 treatments by the end of 1985 and by another 1,500 treatments by the end of 1986. Use of the equipment would reach 9,000 treatments per year in 1986 and remain at that level in the following years. City Hospital's share of the market was expected to decrease after 1986 unless additional equipment were added.

Table 10–9 City Hospital Estimates of Patient Use of Radiation Therapy Service, 1982

	Patients	*Treatments*[a]
6-MV linear accelerator	347	6,250
20-mev linear accelerator	228	4,104
Total	575	10,354

[a]Assumes 18 treatments per patient.

Capital Expenditures. Table 10–11 shows City Hospital's capital budget for the new radiation therapy department. It was assumed that $400,000 for renovations and construction would have to be paid in 1983 in preparation for the new department but that payment for the remaining items could be delayed until 1984. The amount for renovations and construction was less than would have been needed if the Hospital had not designed part of a new addition to the Hospital (completed 2 years ago) to house radiation therapy equipment. The rooms designed to house the equipment had been built with sufficient shielding for such use. The proposed funds were thus needed primarily to prepare the therapy rooms for installation of the equipment and to finish approximately 7,000 net square feet of space (put in plaster walls, etc.).

The $2.6 million in capital expenditures was therefore added to the amounts already included in the model for 1983 and 1984. A 10-year weighted average depreciation was assumed for the entire capital expenditure.

Table 10–10 City Hospital Forecast of Total Demand for Radiation Therapy Service

	Total	*City Hospital*	
Year	*Treatments*	*Treatments*	*Market Share*
1982	44,820	10,354	23.1%
1983	45,295	10,464	23.1
Service begins operation			
1984	45,775	10,528	22.9
1985	46,260	16,000	34.6
1986	46,750	18,500	39.6
1987	47,246	18,500	39.2
1988	47,747	18,500	38.7

Table 10–11 Capital Expenditures for a Radiation Therapy Department at City Hospital

1. Major therapy-related equipment	
6-MV linear accelerator	$465,000
20-mev linear accelerator	920,000
Fluoroscopic simulator	00,000
Treatment planning computer	200,000
Brachytherapy "kit"	45,000
Subtotal	$2,030,000
2. Support equipment and furnishings	
Polystyrene phantom	$6,000
Automated water phantom	15,000
Film dosimetry system	6,000
Thermoluminescent dosimetry system	15,000
Video camera system	16,000
Intercom system	5,000
Crash cart	8,000
Other	121,022
Subtotal	$192,022
3. Renovations and construction	$400,000
Total	$2,622,022

Operating Budget. After considering the expected volume of treatments and the types of equipment being purchased, City Hospital staff prepared an operating budget for the new department. Table 10–12 summarizes the budget forecast. The hospital chose not to include salaries for physicians in the budget, assuming that the new medical director and other physicians would be compensated through patient fees and research funds they would be able to acquire.

Tables 10–13 and 10–14 show forecasts of activity for the new department as prepared by the Amherst Multiyear Model after staff had entered the data

Table 10–12 Operating Cost Projections for the Radiation Therapy Service at City Hospital

			Direct Expenses		
Year	*Treatments*	*Paid FTEs*	*Salaries*	*Nonsalary*	*Salary per FTE*
1983	0	1.5	$50,517	$46,101	$33,678
1984	10,528	20.0	405,800	198,250	20,290
1985	16,000	22.0	478,230	296,776	21,738
1986	18,500	24.0	537,063	399,934	22,378
1987	18,500	25.0	642,051	439,527	25,682
1988	18,500	25.0	707,254	483,479	28,290

Table 10–13 Activity Data for the New Radiation Therapy Service at City Hospital: Treatments

Dept. 48 Therapeutic radiology (ancillary)
Unit of activity: Treatments

	Units	*FTEs*	*Salaries*	*Nonsalary*	*Revenue*
1978	0	0.0	0	0	0
1979	0	0.0	0	0	0
1980	0	0.0	0	0	0
1981	0	0.0	0	0	0
1982	0	0.0	0	0	0
1983	0	1.5	50,517	46,101	0
1984	10,528	20.0	405,800	198,250	1,231,776
1985	16,000	22.0	478,230	296,776	2,040,480
1986	18,500	24.0	537,063	399,934	2,571,685
1987	18,500	25.0	642,051	439,527	2,803,120
1988	18,500	25.0	707,254	483,479	3,055,460

Source: Amherst Multiyear Model. Reprinted with permission of Amherst Associates, Inc., Chicago, Ill.

from Table 10–12. Total revenue was also entered, with the forecasts based on the number of treatments and an estimated charge of $117 per treatment (increasing by an average of 9 percent per year).

Since the model being used was capable of preparing separate forecasts for inpatient and outpatient activity for each ancillary department, City Hospital staff estimated that 90 percent of the treatments would be given to outpatients and 10 percent to inpatients. The model then used these proportions to allocate the other cost and staffing data (Table 10–14).

Additional Expenses and Revenues. The addition of the radiation therapy service as a new department would result in additional revenues and expenses and revenues that were not included in Tables 10–13 and 10–14. Administrative and other indirect costs were assigned to the department as expenses. Moreover, radiation therapy patients would use other services in the hospital, and hence generate additional expenses and revenues, and this additional utilization had to be estimated if the impact of the new department were to be determined.

There are several methods that could be used to forecast the use of other hospital services by radiation therapy patients. Physicians and other professionals could be asked what services should be used; this would provide a normative definition of the services needed. The hospital could conduct empirical research to determine the services that patients with diagnoses and problems similar to

Table 10–14 Activity Data for the New Radiation Therapy Service at City Hospital

Dept. 48 Therapeutic radiology (ancillary)
Unit of activity: Treatments

Inpatient:	*Units*	*FTEs*	*Salaries*	*Nonsalary*	*Revenue*
1978	0	0.0	0	0	0
1979	0	0.0	0	0	0
1980	0	0.0	0	0	0
1981	0	0.0	0	0	0
1982	0	0.0	0	0	0
1983	0	0.2	5,052	4,610	0
1984	1,053	2.0	40,580	19,825	123,178
1985	1,600	2.2	47,823	29,678	204,048
1986	1,850	2.4	53,706	39,993	257,169
1987	1,850	2.5	64,205	43,953	280,312
1988	1,850	2.5	70,725	48,348	305,546
Outpatient:	*Units*	*FTEs*	*Salaries*	*Nonsalary*	*Revenue*
1978	0	0.0	0	0	0
1979	0	0.0	0	0	0
1980	0	0.0	0	0	0
1981	0	0.0	0	0	0
1982	0	0.0	0	0	0
1983	0	1.4	45,465	41,491	0
1984	9,475	18.0	365,220	178,425	1,108,598
1985	14,400	19.8	430,407	267,098	1,836,432
1986	16,650	21.6	483,357	359,941	2,314,517
1987	16,650	22.5	577,846	395,574	2,522,808
1988	16,650	22.5	636,529	435,131	2,749,914

Source: Amherst Multiyear Model. Reprinted with permission of Amherst Associates, Inc., Chicago, Ill.

those expected actually use at other hospitals. The hospital could also look at average service use by its current patients. City Hospital chose to use the latter two methods, since its physicians lacked experience with the new service, and the Hospital's administration was concerned that the use of normative criteria would overstate the volume of services that would actually be used.

A hospital of a similar size and patient case mix provided City Hospital with a summary of the ancillary services used by its 711 radiation therapy patients in 1982 (see Table 10–15). City Hospital maintained separate cost centers for

Table 10–15 Ancillary Services Used by Radiation Therapy Patients at Mercy Hospital

Department and Test/Procedure	*Mercy Hospital (No. for 711 Pts.)*	*Number per Patient*
Radiology (diagnostic and treatment planning):		
CT:		
Diagnostic	199	.28
Treatment planning	256	.36
Chest x-ray	768	1.08
Ultrasound scans	557	.78
Other x-ray and scans	711	1.00
Laboratory:		
CBC	2,133	3.00
Hem/Heg'l	1,849	2.60
Other blood	171	.24
SMA-12	1,308	1.84
Other chem.	28	.04
Urinalysis	85	.12
Misc. lab.	114	.16
Pathology:		
Path reviews	370	.52
Biopsies	171	.24

CT and ultrasound scanning. The number of scans per patient in Table 10–15 was multiplied by the number of expected inpatients and outpatients, and the number of additional scans was then added to the totals for each service for each of the forecast years (see Table 10–16).

Laboratory and pathology posed more difficult problems. City Hospital did not use a relative value scale to aggregate the total number of standard units of these services that were provided. While a forecast for each specific test could be prepared, hospital staff felt that this would be excessively detailed for a 5-year forecast and provide more detail than the hospital's board and administration would want to see. Thus, while recommending that the hospital implement the use of a relative value scale, the staff chose for immediate use as a basis for forecasting the average service utilization of hospital inpatients. They added the number of additional inpatient days that radiation therapy inpatients would use to the current total used for forecasting, and the model added the additional laboratory and pathology revenues and expenses that would be produced. This understated the actual use, since most radiation therapy patients are outpatients, and their laboratory and pathology use is not included in the forecast.

Since they lacked data on the length of stay of radiation therapy patients, the hospital staff used the average length of stay of all inpatients (ten days) to estimate

Table 10–16 Inpatient and Outpatient Use of Ultrasound Scans by Radiation Therapy Patients at City Hospital

	Outpatients		*Inpatients*	
Year	*Patients*[a]	*Scans*[b]	*Patients*[a]	*Scans*[b]
1984	526	410	59	46
1985	800	624	89	69
1986	925	721	103	80
1987	925	721	103	80
1988	925	721	103	80

[a]The number of treatments (see Table 10–14) is divided by 18, the average number of treatments per patient, to give the number of patients treated.

[b]The number of patients is multiplied by .78, the average number of ultrasound scans per patient (see Table 10–15), to determine the number of scans.

the number of patient days that would result from opening the new department. Revenues and expenses for a number of departments were forecast on the basis of patient days. This included laboratory and pathology, as well as central medical supply and pharmacy. Expenses in nonrevenue-producing areas such as administration were also forecast on the basis of patient days, so that the financial impact of increased inpatient admissions could be estimated.

This method for forecasting the impact of radiation therapy patients on the hospital is far from perfect. It does not include an estimation of the impact of radiation therapy outpatients on ancillary services other than CT and ultrasound scanning. It assumes that radiation therapy inpatients consume ancillary and routine hospital services (other than CT and ultrasound scanning) at the same rate as the average hospital patient. Finally, the method does not include an estimate of the additional volume for a number of ancillary services, including surgery.

Thus, in general, the impact on City Hospital of adding a radiation therapy department was underestimated. It is important to remember that the speed and flexibility of computer modeling enable us to repeat an analysis quickly, when and if new information becomes available. City Hospital chose to minimize the amount of new empirical research to support decision making. It utilized data that were readily available to hospital staff. It adopted a conservative methodology for predicting the financial impact of the new department. The financial model was capable of accommodating that level of analysis. However, it could have accepted much more detailed data if City Hospital decision makers had been willing to spend the money necessary to fill the gaps outlined above.

Financial Impact

The financial model could now be used to assess the impact on City Hospital of developing a radiation therapy department. Tables 10–17 to 10–21 were produced and then compared to the financial statements prepared earlier. Table 10–22 presents forecasts for 1988 with and without the development of a radiation therapy department.

While it is important to examine year-to-year changes, looking at 1988 enabled City Hospital to see the cumulative effect of 5 years of operation under the assumptions that were made. As shown in Table 10–22, the forecast for 1988 showed that total patient service revenue would be $3,834,000 higher if the radiation therapy department were opened. However, because of higher deductions from revenue and operating expenses, operating income would be only $363,000 higher. The increase in net income of $293,000 would be even smaller because of higher interest charges (shown as negative interest income) resulting from additional debt. Interest charges in 1988 ($293,000) were understated, since the cost of capital was calculated as equal to the interest rate on investments. This debt (shown as negative "investments" in Table 10–22), the result of the hospital's need for additional capital, would rise to $5.8 million in 1988 for the radiation therapy alternative. The ratios in Table 10–22 show that City Hospital would come somewhat closer in meeting its objectives for profitability if it developed the radiation therapy department, but would not meet them.

Our analysis also suggests that the development of the radiation therapy department would not impede City Hospital in meeting its financial objectives, despite the need for capital expenditures beyond what was initially assumed. The financial ratios in Table 10–22 did not change significantly. City Hospital would be able to increase its net income by developing the service and also would be able to meet some of the additional capital requirements. The total increase in needed capital (shown as negative "investments") would amount to about $500,000 in 1988, while over $2.6 million in capital expenditures would be used to develop the service. Added depreciation income would also assist in meeting the need for capital.

Once again, we need to note that City Hospital had considerable unused capacity to acquire and service long-term debt. The debt service coverage ratio for City under our initial assumptions was forecast to be 8.94 in 1988; and its debt-to-asset ratio was forecast to be 33.6 percent. City could clearly afford to make an investment which would not hurt its profitability.

It is also important that the broader strategic issues be considered. City Hospital was facing competition from University Hospital, had an aging medical staff, and was failing to win referrals from younger physicians. An emphasis on tertiary services might not be the most desirable solution; but, if the hospital wished to stick with its mission statement, secure a position in the region as a tertiary

Table 10–17 City Hospital Forecast of Revenue and Expense, 1982–1988, with the Proposed Radiation Therapy Service

FORECAST STATEMENT OF REVENUE AND EXPENSE
(000s omitted)

	For the year ending June 30						
	Actual 1982	*1983*	*1984*	*1985*	*1986*	*1987*	*1988*
Revenue:							
Routine patient revenue	$31,543	$33,770	$37,753	$41,429	$45,019	$48,666	$52,542
Ancillary inpatient revenue	29,318	33,564	38,086	42,160	45,294	50,226	55,741
Outpatient revenue	6,419	7,381	9,644	11,471	13,453	15,164	17,146
Total patient service revenue	67,280	74,715	85,483	95,060	103,766	114,056	125,429
Deductions from patient revenue:							
Contractual allowances	12,902	16,065	19,505	22,618	25,027	28,267	32,015
Free care and bad debts	1,009	1,252	1,566	1,765	1,956	2,132	2,337
Total deductions	13,911	17,317	21,071	24,383	26,983	30,399	34,352
Net patient service revenue	53,369	57,398	64,412	70,677	76,783	83,657	91,077
Other operating revenue	806	869	939	1,012	1,093	1,179	1,273
Net operating revenue	54,175	58,267	65,351	71,689	77,876	84,836	92,350
Operating expense:							
Salaries, wages, and benefits	27,185	29,479	32,922	35,787	38,591	41,724	45,076
Nonsalary expense	21,754	24,156	27,066	29,809	32,426	35,615	39,150
Patient service expense	48,939	53,635	59,988	65,596	71,017	77,339	84,226
Operating income prior to depreciation and interest	5,236	4,632	5,363	6,093	6,859	7,497	8,124
Depreciation	1,929	2,506	3,245	3,845	4,495	5,195	5,864
Interest expense	625	653	510	441	437	431	427
Total operating expense	51,493	56,794	63,743	69,882	75,949	82,965	90,517
Operating income	2,682	1,473	1,608	1,807	1,927	1,871	1,833
Nonoperating revenue:							
Interest income	688	474	165	(113)	(183)	(240)	(293)
Other income	30	30	30	30	30	30	30
Total nonoperating revenue	718	504	195	(83)	(153)	(210)	(263)
Net income	$3,400	$1,977	$1,803	$1,724	$1,774	$1,661	$1,570

This statement was prepared on the basis of the accompanying assumptions and rationale.

Source: Amherst Multiyear Model. Reprinted with permission of Amherst Associates, Inc., Chicago, Ill.

Table 10–18 City Hospital Forecast of Cash Flow, 1982–1988, with the Proposed Radiation Therapy Service

FORECAST STATEMENT OF CASH FLOW
(000s omitted)

	For the year ending June 30,						
	Actual 1982	*1983*	*1984*	*1985*	*1986*	*1987*	*1988*
Cash, investments, and other long term assets at beginning of year	$5,497	$6,492	$5,588	$358	($425)	($1,013)	($1,526)
Sources of funds:							
From operations:							
Net income	$3,400	$1,977	$1,803	$1,724	$1,774	$1,661	$1,570
Add items not affecting cash							
Depreciation	1,929	2,506	3,245	3,845	4,495	5,195	5,864
Total from operations	5,329	4,483	5,048	5,569	6,269	6,856	7,434
New long term debt	—	—	—	—	—	—	—
Change in other long term liabilities	—	—	—	—	—	—	—
Restricted contributions	679	600	350	350	350	350	350
Total sources of funds	6,008	5,083	5,398	5,919	6,619	7,206	7,784
Uses of funds:							
Project expenditures	—	—	—	—	—	—	—
Routine capital expenditures	5,690	5,400	7,722	6,000	6,500	7,000	7,500
Repayment of debt net of change in current portion	362	2,516	370	375	380	390	400
Change in current portion of long term debt	(24)	(2,154)	2,146	(5)	(5)	(10)	(10)
Change in working capital items:							
Net receivables	689	610	1,000	892	870	979	1,057
Inventories	320	50	160	150	144	176	194
Other current assets	246	77	127	112	108	127	138
Trade payables	(1,492)	(366)	(628)	(592)	(566)	(688)	(764)
Accrued salary	(646)	(103)	(154)	(129)	(127)	(141)	(150)
Other current liabilities	(132)	(43)	(115)	(101)	(97)	(114)	(124)
Total for working capital items	(1,015)	225	390	332	332	339	351
Total uses of funds	5,013	5,987	10,628	6,702	7,207	7,719	8,241
Cash, investments, and other long term assets at end of year	$6,492	$5,588	$358	($425)	($1,013)	($1,526)	($1,983)
Consisting of:							
Cash	$784	$804	$899	$984	$1,066	$1,160	$1,264
Investments	3,210	2,236	(3,089)	(3,957)	(4,627)	(5,234)	(5,795)
Other long term assets	2,498	2,548	2,548	2,548	2,548	2,548	2,548
	$6,492	$5,588	$358	($425)	($1,013)	($1,526)	($1,983)

This statement was prepared on the basis of the accompanying assumptions and rationale.

Source: Amherst Multiyear Model. Reprinted with permission of Amherst Associates, Inc., Chicago, Ill.

Table 10–19 City Hospital Forecast Balance Sheet, 1982–1988, with the Proposed Radiation Therapy Service

FORECAST BALANCE SHEET
(000s omitted)

	For the year ending June 30,						
	Actual 1982	*1983*	*1984*	*1985*	*1986*	*1987*	*1988*
Assets							
Current assets:							
Cash	$784	$804	$899	$984	$1,066	$1,160	$1,264
Net receivables	7,567	8,177	9,177	10,069	10,939	11,918	12,975
Inventory	1,279	1,329	1,489	1,639	1,783	1,959	2,153
Other current assets	996	1,073	1,200	1,312	1,420	1,547	1,685
Total current assets	10,626	11,383	12,765	14,004	15,208	16,584	18,077
Gross fixed assets	40,148	45,548	53,270	59,270	65,770	72,770	80,270
Less accumulated depreciation	10,190	12,696	15,941	19,786	24,281	29,476	35,340
Net fixed assets	29,958	32,852	37,329	39,484	41,489	43,294	44,930
Investments	3,210	2,236	(3,089)	(3,957)	(4,627)	(5,234)	(5,795)
Other long term assets	2,498	2,548	2,548	2,548	2,548	2,548	2,548
Total assets	$46,292	$49,019	$49,553	$52,079	$54,618	$57,192	$59,760
Liabilities and fund balance							
Current liabilities:							
Trade payables	$4,851	$5,217	$5,845	$6,437	$7,003	$7,691	$ 8,455
Accrued salary	1,224	1,327	1,481	1,610	1,737	1,878	2,028
Other current liabilities	922	965	1,080	1,181	1,278	1,392	1,516
Current portion long term debt	362	2,516	370	375	380	390	400
Total current liabilities	7,359	10,025	8,776	9,603	10,398	11,351	12,399
Long term debt net of current portion:							
Unsecured debt	2,151	—	—	—	—	—	—
Secured debt	9,812	9,447	9,077	8,702	8,322	7,932	7,532
Total long term debt	11,963	9,447	9,077	8,702	8,322	7,932	7,532
Other long term liabilities	—	—	—	—	—	—	—
Total liabilities	19,322	19,472	17,853	18,305	18,720	19,283	19,931
Fund balance	26,970	29,547	31,700	33,774	35,898	37,909	39,829
Liabilities and fund balance	$46,292	$49,019	$49,553	$52,079	$54,618	$57,192	$59,760

This statement was prepared on the basis of the accompanying assumptions and rationale.

Source: Amherst Multiyear Model. Reprinted with permission of Amherst Associates, Inc., Chicago, Ill.

Table 10–20 City Hospital Forecast of Changes in Fund Balance, 1982–1988, with the Proposed Radiation Therapy Service

FORECAST STATEMENT OF CHANGE IN FUND BALANCE
(000s omitted)

	For the year ending June 30						
	Actual 1982	*1983*	*1984*	*1985*	*1986*	*1987*	*1988*
Balance at beginning of year	$22,891	$26,970	$29,547	$31,700	$33,774	$35,898	$37,909
Net income	$3,400	$1,977	$1,803	$1,724	$1,774	$1,661	$1,570
Restricted contributions	679	600	350	350	350	350	350
Adjustment to fixed assets	—	—	—	—	—	—	—
Assumption and cancellation of long term debt	—	—	—	—	—	—	—
Balance at end of year	$26,970	$29,547	$31,700	$33,774	$35,898	$37,909	$39,829

This statement was prepared on the basis of the accompanying assumptions and rationale.

Source: Amherst Multiyear Model. Reprinted with permission of Amherst Associates, Inc., Chicago, Ill.

hospital, and attract new physicians, it might be essential to meet a growing need for a technology not found elsewhere in its four-county area.

This type of analysis should provide the decision makers in City Hospital with a better understanding of whether creating a radiation therapy service would move the hospital toward or away from achieving its financial goal and objectives.

Structural Options for Radiation Therapy

The analysis undertaken could have included other options that were not considered here. For example, and as noted earlier, we have focused here on the strategic alternatives for changing a hospital's markets rather than on alternative changes in a hospital's corporate structure. However, radiation therapy is a good example of why both types of alternatives need to be considered.

Free-standing radiation therapy services are being developed, and the implementation of limits on a hospital's cost per case under Medicare is likely to make the establishment of such services attractive to some hospitals (or make them more willing to see such services provided by others in the community). At the same time, an arrangement in which the hospital bills for the service and pays physicians a percentage of total charges will become increasingly unattractive to those hospitals whose expenses are equal to or exceed their allowable costs per case under Medicare.

Table 10–21 City Hospital Forecast of Financial Ratios, 1982–1988, with the Proposed Radiation Therapy Service

FORECAST FINANCIAL RATIOS
(000s omitted)

	For the year ending June 30						
	Actual 1982	*1983*	*1984*	*1985*	*1986*	*1987*	*1988*
Liquidity ratios							
Current ratio	1.44	1.14	1.45	1.46	1.46	1.46	1.46
Acid	1.13	0.90	1.15	1.15	1.15	1.15	1.15
Absolute	0.11	0.08	0.10	0.10	0.10	0.10	0.10
Leverage ratios							
Debt/Assets	41.7%	39.7%	36.0%	35.1%	34.3%	33.7%	33.4%
Current liabilities/Assets	15.9%	20.5%	17.7%	18.4%	19.0%	19.8%	20.7%
Long term debt/Assets	25.8%	19.3%	18.3%	16.7%	15.2%	13.9%	12.6%
Secured debt/Net fixed assets	32.8%	28.8%	24.3%	22.0%	20.1%	18.3%	16.8%
Assets/Fund balance	1.72	1.66	1.56	1.54	1.52	1.51	1.50
Composition ratios							
Current assets/Assets	23.0%	23.2%	25.8%	26.9%	27.8%	29.0%	30.2%
Net fixed assets/Assets	64.7%	67.0%	75.3%	75.8%	76.0%	75.7%	75.2%
Investments/Assets	12.3%	9.8%	(1.1%)	(2.7%)	(3.8%)	(4.7%)	(5.4%)
Activity ratios							
Assets	1.17	1.19	1.32	1.38	1.43	1.48	1.55
Current assets	5.10	5.12	5.12	5.12	5.12	5.12	5.11
Fixed assets	1.81	1.77	1.75	1.82	1.88	1.96	2.06
Profitability ratios							
Operating income/Fund balance	9.9%	5.0%	5.1%	5.4%	5.4%	4.9%	4.6%
Net income/Fund balance	12.6%	6.7%	5.7%	5.1%	4.9%	4.4%	3.9%
Return on assets	7.3%	4.0%	3.6%	3.3%	3.2%	2.9%	2.6%
Operating return	5.8%	3.0%	3.2%	3.5%	3.5%	3.3%	3.1%
Operating margin	5.0%	2.5%	2.5%	2.5%	2.5%	2.2%	2.0%
Profit margin	6.1%	3.3%	2.7%	2.4%	2.2%	1.9%	1.7%
Coverage ratios							
Interest	9.52	7.86	10.90	13.61	15.35	16.89	18.41
Debt service	6.18	5.06	1.84	7.41	8.26	8.98	9.62

This statement was prepared on the basis of the accompanying assumptions and rationale.

Source: Amherst Multiyear Model. Reprinted with permission of Amherst Associates, Inc., Chicago, Ill.

Table 10–22 Comparison of Selected Financial Information from Two 1988 Forecasts for City Hospital

	1988 Forecasts ($000s omitted)	
	Initial	*With XRT*
From Forecast of Revenue and Expense		
Total patient service revenue	$121,595	$125,429
Total deductions	32,806	34,352
Net patient service revenue	88,789	91,077
Net operating revenue	90,062	92,350
Total operating expense	88,592	90,517
Operating income	1,470	1,833
Nonoperating revenue:		
Interest income	(223)	(293)
Other income	30	30
Total nonoperating revenue	(193)	(263)
Net income	1,277	1,570
From Forecast of Cash Flow		
Cash, investments and long-term assets at beginning of year	(500)	(1,526)
Total sources of funds	7,229	7,784
Total uses of funds	8,236	8,241
Cash, investments, and long-term assets at end of year	(1,507)	(1,983)
Investments	(5,294)	(5,795)
From Forecast Financial Ratios		
Profitability ratios:		
Net income fund balance	3.3%	3.9%
Operating margin	1.6%	2.0%
Current ratio	1.45%	1.46%
Debt/Asset ratio	33.6%	33.4%

Source: Based on data from Tables 10–17 through 10–21.

There are four components of a radiation therapy service that generate income: (1) the ownership of the physical space, (2) the ownership of the equipment, (3) the use of the equipment for providing treatment, and (4) the professional knowledge of which treatment to provide. Hospitals have traditionally assumed that they must own the space and provide the technicians to use the equipment. However, they have been willing to leave the other two components—ownership of the equipment and professional knowledge—to others (e.g., through equipment leasing and separate billing arrangements with physicians). Hospitals will now need to consider whether control of all four components should pass to a separate corporate entity, thereby giving them more of the rewards of ownership and control and fewer negative financial consequences.[7]

REFERENCES

1. W.H. Nelson and S.D. Nadauld, "An Approach to Capital Expenditure Planning," *Financial Planning, Topics In Health Care Financing* 7, no. 4 (Summer 1981):17.

2. H.W. Long, "Valuation as a Criterion in Not-for-Profit Decision-making," *Health Care Management Review* 1, no. 3 (Summer 1976):34–46.

3. Hospital Corporation of America, *1981 Annual Report* (Nashville, TN: Hospital Corporation of America, 1981), pp. 26–27.

4. W.O. Cleverley, "Financial Ratio Analysis," *Handbook of Health Care Accounting and Finance*, ed. W.O. Cleverley (Rockville, Md.: Aspen Systems Corp., 1982), pp. 497–524.

5. An example of productivity indicators are the data produced by the American Hospital Association's MONITREND program (see Chapter 5).

6. An example of patterns-of-practice data are those produced by the Commission on Professional and Hospital Activities (see Chapter 5).

7. The ideas presented here about ownership of the components of a radiation therapy service are derived, with some modification in the terms used, from presentations by Clayton D. Pruett and Lynn D. Colquitt of CDP Associates at the Annual Meeting of the American Society of Therapeutic Radiologists in Orlando, Florida, in 1982.

Chapter 11

Developing a Decision Support System

INTRODUCTION

Numerous organizations are now offering hospitals information services and products that range from printed reports to computer hardware and software that can be used to generate management reports internally. In this chapter, we examine a few of those services and products. We do not provide a survey or evaluation of their quality; such an attempt would be quickly outdated. Instead, we focus on the ability of the services and products to contribute to the strategic planning process. Particular attention is paid to their usefulness in carrying out the tasks described in Chapters 6, 8, and 10.

Rather than use a series of separate, independent products and services, hospital managers may wish to integrate them to develop a more comprehensive "decision support system." In the following pages we describe such a system and discuss its objectives and components. Finally, we discuss the current status of decision support systems for hospital strategic planning.

HOSPITAL INFORMATION PRODUCTS AND SERVICES

Service Area and Market Analysis

We suggested in Chapter 6 that a hospital might benefit from segmenting consumer groups and using a three-dimensional definition of its consumer markets. To do this, it needs both a data base and the software that can retrieve and analyze the data. The sources of such data were described in Part II. In this section, several examples of software for data analysis are described.

Two important characteristics of the software now on the market that affect their usefulness in strategic planning are (1) the extent to which the manager needs to learn a computer language that does not resemble spoken or written English, and (2) the extent to which the software can customize reports.

The ASK interactive data inquiry program offered by the Missouri Health Data Corporation (one of the shared data systems discussed in Chapter 5) provides the user with considerable flexibility in producing customized reports, but it requires that the user learn a computer language that is considerably different from spoken English. ASK allows the user to select portions of a data base, to retrieve data, and to have it displayed in a user-defined sequence. For example, data can be displayed by name (e.g., patient, physician, payer), by number (e.g., patient account, social security), or by amount (e.g., total charges, room charges).[1]

If, for example, the user wanted to know how many male Medicare patients under age 60 were admitted to the hospital in October, the following statement would be entered:[2]

> COUNT WHERE SEX = MALE, PAYER = MEDICARE, DOB (date of birth) => (equal to or greater than) 100121. ADMIT DATE => 100181 AND <= (equal to or less than) 103181

The explanations in parentheses would not be typed in.

While the words in this statement are familiar, the symbols and syntax are not part of ordinary speech. A translation into ordinary spoken English would be:

> "Look at each record in the file and count the number of records that show that the patient was male, eligible for Medicare, born on or before October 1, 1921, and was admitted between October 1, 1981, and October 31, 1981."

Learning the language used by ASK saves time in the long run, but initially it takes time that some busy managers will not have or want to devote. Other software programs used to retrieve data and generate reports allow managers to respond to questions, rather than having themselves to develop a complete set of statements that instructs the computer to produce a report. Exhibit 11–1 shows the system and user responses needed to produce a patient origin analysis by physician using Shared Medical System's COMMAND AD HOC REPORT WRITER. Table 11–1 shows the report that is produced. Managers must still learn some new terms (e.g., "down axis") and syntax (e.g., that titles must be put in quotation marks). The system, however, assists in developing a complete request by asking questions. Managers are also not required to know the order in which information is to be provided to the computer.

Both ASK and COMMAND leave it to the manager to define the information that would be relevant, and how it will be presented. Some software programs provide a list of standardized reports considered relevant to the problem or topic, thus restricting the flexibility of the manager. However, such programs also reduce considerably the amount of work to be done by the manager in producing reports. Reports might be selected from lists (called "menus") and/or by re-

Exhibit 11–1 Request for a Patient Origin Analysis by Physician Using Shared Medical Systems' COMMAND AD HOC REPORT WRITER

System and User Responses[a]	Explanation
REQUEST TITLE *'PATIENT ORIGIN ANALYSIS BY PHYSICIAN'*	User specifies title
CONTINUE TITLE ? (Y,N) *N*	User indicates title is complete
FOOTING ? (Y,N) *Y*	User requests note at bottom of table
FOOTING *'ROUTE TO ADMINISTRATION'*	User indicates content of footing
CONTINUE FOOTING (Y,N) *N*	User indicates footing is complete
ITEMS FUNCTIONS: *CNT* COMPONENT: *''PT NO WOSCD''*	User indicates that the data used in the table will be counts of patient numbers (defined as numbers ''Without self-check digit'' or ''WOSCD'' in this system)
PERCENTS? (Y,N) *Y*	User indicates that percents should also appear
PCT OR CUM PCT? (P,C) *P*	User indicates that row or column percentages should not be cumulative
ROW, COL OR GRAND TOT? (R,C,G) *R*	User indicates that row percentages should appear
ROW, COL OR GRAND TOT? (R,C,G) *C*	User indicates that column percentages should appear
AS A PCT OF COLUMN TOTAL ANOTHER FUNCTION? (Y,N) *N*	System confirms choice and asks if another is desired. User says no.
DOWN AXIS? (Y,N) *Y*	User indicates that there will be a row variable
DOWN COMPONENT: *''ATN DR NO''*	User indicates that the attending physician's identification number will be on the rows
EXPLICIT VALUES? (Y,N) *N*	User indicates that all values of variable are to be used
TOTALS ? (Y,N) *Y*	User requests row totals
WITH TOTALS	System confirms choice
ACROSS AXIS? (Y,N) *Y*	User indicates there will be a column variable

Exhibit 11–1 continued

System and User Responses[a]	Explanation
ACROSS COMPONENT: *"PT ZIP CD"*	User selects patient zip code as the column variable
EXPLICIT VALUES ? (Y,N) *Y*	User indicates that only certain values are to be used
ACROSS EXPLICIT VALUES: *IN ('09001', '09002', '09003', '09004', '09005', '09006')*	User selects zip codes to be included
TOTALS ? (Y,N) *Y*	User requests column totals
WITH TOTALS	System confirms choice
WHERE SEGMENT/COMPONENT: *"DSCH DATE"*	User indicates that discharge date is to be used to segment patients
EXPLICIT VALUES ? (Y,N) *Y*	User indicates that only patients with specific discharge dates are to be included
EXPLICIT VALUES: *(01/01/83 THRU 10/31/83)*	User selects patients discharged between January 1st and October 31st of 1983.

Note: Not all system and user responses have been shown. Additional systems and user statements would be required to produce Table 11–1.

[a]User entries are in italics.

Source: Produced by SMS's COMMAND AD HOC REPORT WRITER. Reprinted with permission of Shared Medical Systems © 1983.

sponding to a series of questions that define the user's needs. The more complex and unique the request made by the user, however, the less likely it is that it can be met through the use of a menu or by responding to computer-generated questions. COMMAND allows the user to either produce customized reports, as illustrated above, or to select from a list of reports previously defined.

The Case Mix System developed by Arthur Andersen & Co. is an example of a software that allows hospital managers to select from a useful set of standardized reports for segmenting and defining consumer markets.[3] Figure 11–1 shows the hierarchy of Case Mix reports available on the cost of care. Exhibit 11–2 presents the hierarchy of reports outlined in boldface type in Figure 11–1. The reports present base period, year-to-date and projected data on volumes and charges (cost based on cost-to-charge ratios and actual cost per unit can also be used).

Table 11–1 Patient Origin Analysis by Physician

CNT "PT NO WOSCD"
CNT "PT NO WOSCD" AS A PCT OF ROW TOTAL
CNT "PT NO WOSCD" AS A PCT OF COLUMN TOTAL

"ATN DRN O"	*"PT ZIP CD"* 09001	09002	09003	09004	09005	09006	TOTALS
019990	496	10	53	64	3	1	627
	79.1%	1.6%	8.5%	10.2%	0.5%	0.2%	100.0%
	15.8%	5.7%	12.0%	10.3%	2.1%	0.8%	13.5%
100020	12	4	5	15	4	1	41
	29.3%	9.8%	12.2%	36.6%	9.8%	2.4%	100.0%
	0.4%	2.3%	1.1%	2.4%	2.9%	0.8%	0.9%
100030	2	0	1	5	1	1	10
	20.0%	0.0%	10.0%	50.0%	10.0%	10.0%	100.0%
	0.1%	0.0%	0.2%	0.8%	0.7%	0.8%	0.2%
100050	8	0	0	3	0	2	13
	61.5%	0.0%	0.0%	23.1%	0.0%	15.4%	100.0%
	0.3%	0.0%	0.0%	0.5%	0.0%	1.7%	0.3%
100100	5	0	2	1	0	0	8
	62.5%	0.0%	25.0%	12.5%	0.0%	0.0%	100.0%
	0.2%	0.0%	0.5%	0.2%	0.0%	0.0%	0.2%
100130	140	5	23	36	0	9	213
	65.7%	2.3%	10.8%	16.9%	0.0%	4.2%	100.0%
	4.5%	2.8%	5.2%	5.8%	0.0%	7.6%	4.6%
100190	0	1	1	0	0	1	3
	0.0%	33.3%	33.3%	0.0%	0.0%	33.3%	100.0%
	0.0%	0.6%	0.2%	0.0%	0.0%	0.8%	0.1%
100200	0	0	1	0	0	0	1
	0.0%	0.0%	100.0%	0.0%	0.0%	0.0%	100.0%
	0.0%	0.0%	0.2%	0.0%	0.0%	0.0%	0.0%
TOTALS	3143	176	441	624	140	118	4642
	67.7%	3.8%	9.5%	13.4%	3.0%	2.5%	100.0%
	100.0%	100.0%	100.0%	100.0%	100.0%	100.0%	100.0%

Source: Reprinted with permission of Shared Medical Systems © 1983. Produced by SMS's COMMAND AD HOC REPORT WRITER.

A hospital manager can use the reports in Exhibit 11–2 to define some of the hospital's markets. The first report (counting from the top) segments the hospital's patients by type. The second report segments inpatients by hospital service. The third segments medical patients by DRG (one way of defining patient need). The fourth segments the cost centers (e.g., Lab-Chemistry) that provide services to patients in each DRG. The fifth report segments the specific services used within each cost center.

Figure 11–1 Cost of Care Report Hierarchy: Case Mix System™

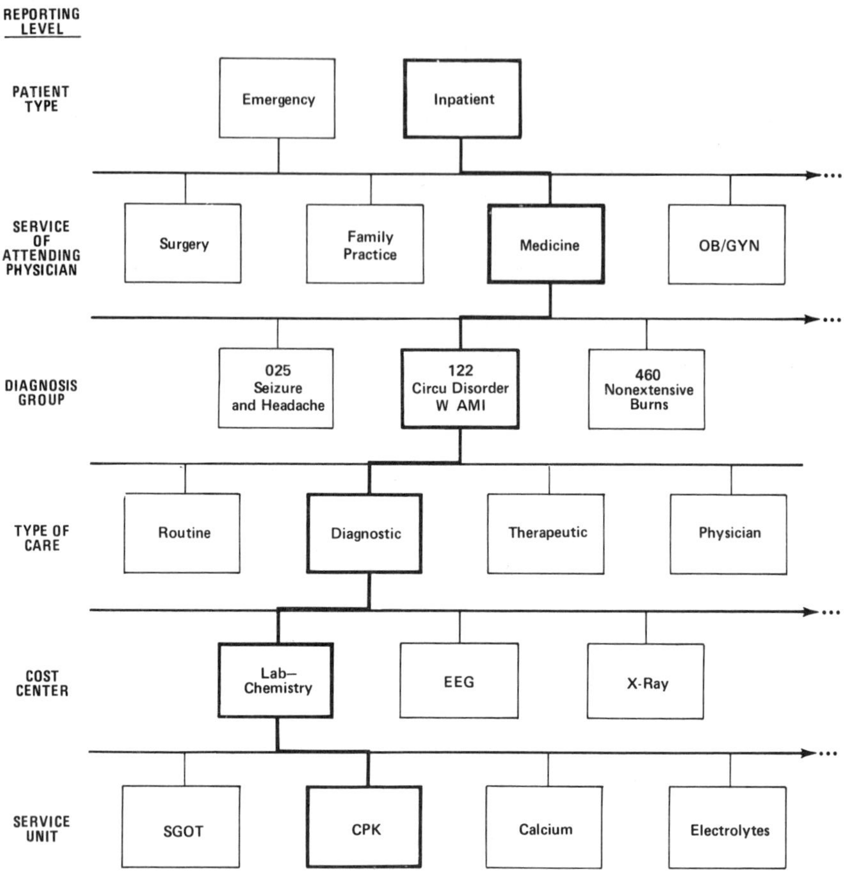

Note: Reporting of DRGs within treating cost centers is also provided.

Source: Reprinted from *Case Mix System*™ with permission of Arthur Andersen & Co., © 1983.

With this type of software, the manager gains a reduction in the number of specific instructions that must be given to the computer to produce a report, and also the benefit of the knowledge and experience of the individuals who initially developed and subsequently refined the software. However, the manager is not able to look at markets in ways other than those presented by the hierarchy. For example, cost centers cannot be segmented according to type of service. Thus, the extent to which physical therapy charges or costs are incurred by outpatients

Exhibit 11–2 Cost of Care Reports Sample: Case Mix System™

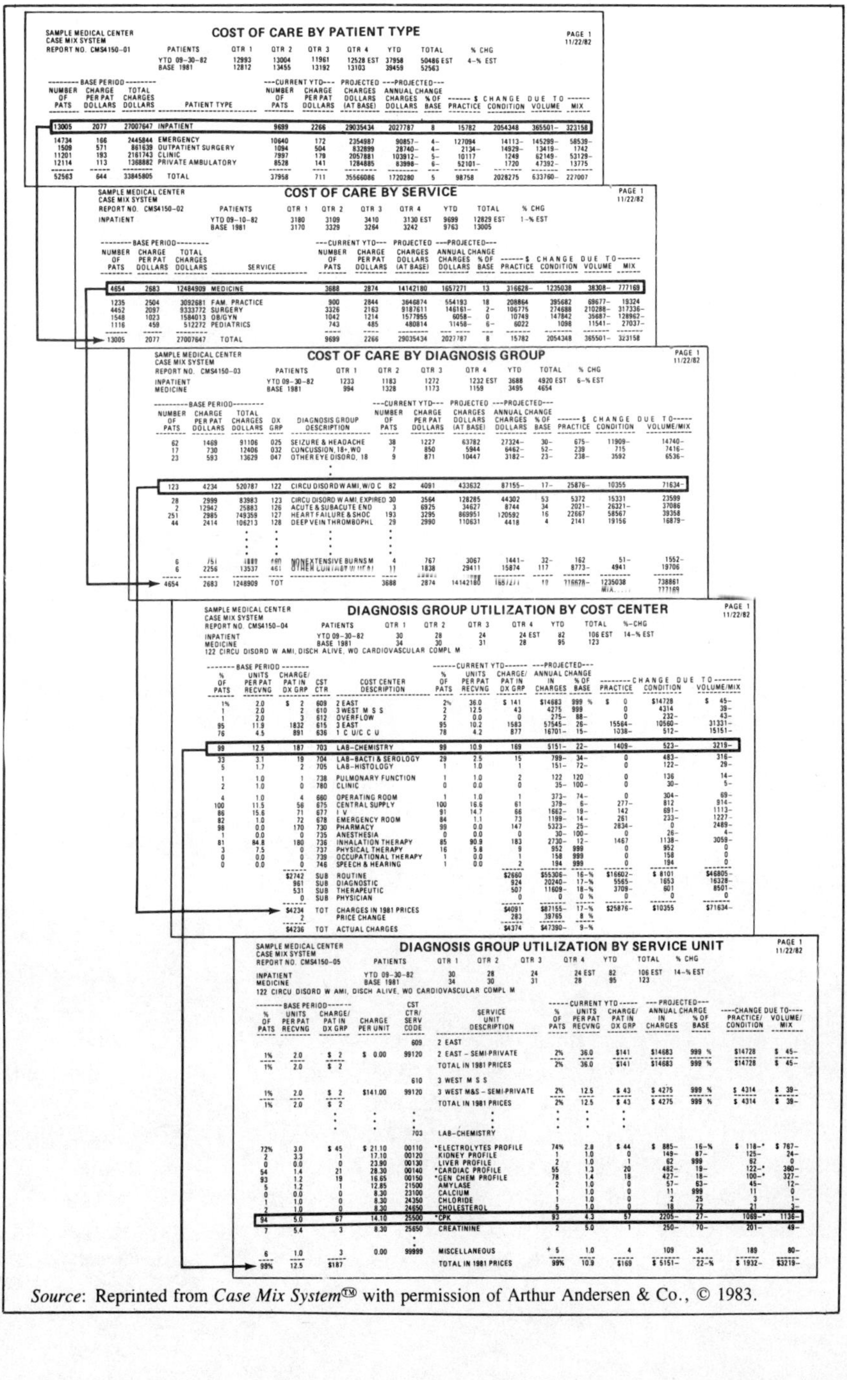

Source: Reprinted from *Case Mix System*™ with permission of Arthur Andersen & Co., © 1983.

cannot easily be determined. The Case Mix System could, however, be interfaced with a report writer (e.g., similar to ASK) that could produce such a table.

As noted in Chapter 6, there are numerous ways in which the hospital can define the consumer markets it serves. Software acquired for market analysis thus needs to be flexible. At the same time, it must not be so complex and time-consuming as to discourage its use by managers and planners. Each hospital must evaluate the available products on the basis of its own needs.

Medical Staff Analysis

The resources available to some hospitals to examine the characteristics of their medical staffs and probe the resulting implications for the future have grown in recent years. The storage of medical record information in computers now allows some hospitals to ask what impact physicians have on utilization. If cost and billing information is also stored, the hospital can ask what impact physicians have on costs and revenues. At some hospitals, the data base on physicians has accordingly grown from a list of names and staff privileges to include important data on the impact that physicians have on the hospital.

However, storing the data is not enough; software is needed to retrieve and analyze the data. ASK, Shared Medical Systems' COMMAND AD HOC REPORT WRITER,[4] and other flexible report generators are capable of retrieving data and preparing tables from any appropriately structured data bases, including those that contain data on physicians.

Amherst Associates offers software, called MEDSTAFF, that is specifically written to prepare reports on physicians.[5] MEDSTAFF offers advantages similar to those of Arthur Andersen's Case Mix System, that is, less time and effort in preparing reports. To use MEDSTAFF, the hospital must provide Amherst Associates with data captured by the hospital's clinical and financial information systems (e.g., number of patient days or discharges aggregated from discharge abstracts or bills) and also aggregated data from other files (e.g., on board certification, staff affiliations with other hospitals). Exhibit 11–3 presents a list of the files and data items used in, and the reports produced by, MEDSTAFF. Procedures can be established for routine updating of data to permit analyses to be prepared when needed.

The MEDSTAFF physician data file can also be used for several applications in integrated systems and can serve as a master file of information on physicians for billing, maintaining medical records, and other purposes.

Exhibit 11–4 presents a computer request for a MEDSTAFF table showing physicians by age and specialty in 1980—data that appear in Table 11–2. Different column and row variables and the periods of time can be selected. The requested data can also be limited to physicians with certain staff status, board certification, or membership in certain physician groups. The age cat-

Exhibit 11–3 MEDSTAFF Files, Data Items, and Tables

1. Files:

Data Description	File Name
Physician data	PHYINF.XXX
Specialty names	PHYSPC.XXX
Location names	PHYLOC.XXX
Patient day data	PHYDAY.XXX
Admissions data	PHYADM.XXX
Affiliation names	PHYAFN.XXX
Affiliation data	PHYAFD.XXX

2. Data items in the physician data file:
   - Physician code number
   - Physician name
   - Specialty name code
   - Staff status code
   - Board status code
   - Year joined staff
   - Year left staff
   - Year of birth
   - Group code
   - Location code
3. Tables that can be produced by MEDSTAFF:
   - Specialties by:
     a. staff status
     b. specialty board status
     c. physician group
     d. age
   - Admissions by:
     a. age
     b. age and specialty
     c. specialty
     d. office location
   - Patient days by:
     a. age
     b. age and specialty
     c. year and specialty
     d. specialty
     e. office location
   - Average length of stay by:
     a. age
     b. age and specialty
     c. specialty
   - Ranks of individual physicians:
     a. for each available data year by admissions, patient days, or average length of stay
     b. for admissions, patient days, or average length of stay for specified year
     c. by specialty and by admissions, patient days, or average length of stay for specified year

Exhibit 11–3 continued

- Affiliations with other hospitals:
  a. hospitals with affiliated physicians
  b. affiliations by individual physicians

Source: Amherst Associates, Inc., Chicago, Ill.

egories to be used in the table can also be changed. Finally, the system permits ranking to be done either numerically or by alphabetical order.

The production of this type of table does not require a knowledge of mnemonics or acronyms specific to the system or the computer. The analyst is continually reminded that, by typing "?", assistance in the form of a list of options can be produced on the screen. The analyst is not required to produce a line in computer language to specify which data are to be included in the table and where those data are located. Instead, the MEDSTAFF system asks questions in a language close to conversational English. It reminds the analyst what the choices are and what default values will be used if no choice is made. The MEDSTAFF program thus illustrates the type of "user-friendly" computer languages being developed to facilitate the acquisition of useful information by decision makers.

Financial Planning

Financial planning can utilize the data base of a hospital financial information system that is designed to perform other tasks (see fiscal services and patient accounting categories in Figure 3–1). Alternatively, the data collected and stored by financial information systems can be transferred to a separate financial planning data base, which is then updated periodically. In this section we illustrate both methods for acquiring the data needed for financial planning. We also provide examples of software for data retrieval, data analysis, and financial forecasting.

Amherst Associates' Hospital Systems Library is used for financial planning by hospitals. It is an example of a system that uses a specific financial planning data base. Hospitals maintain, in Amherst's computers, separate financial planning data bases that contain activity and staffing statistics, data on assets and liabilities, fund balance information, and revenue and expense data. These data are stored by cost center, by account, and by month. Each data base contains up to 12 months or 13 periods of data. Separate data bases are maintained (1) for as many years of historical data as the hospital wishes to maintain, (2) for the current fiscal year actual, and (3) for the current fiscal year budget. The hospital may maintain as many data bases as it desires for forecasting purposes.[6]

The extent to which data from other applications of the hospital's information system can be accessed is of critical importance in the integration of financial

Exhibit 11–4 Computer Request for a MEDSTAFF Table Showing Physicians by Age and Specialty in 1980

System and User Responses[a]		Explanation
RUN AA: *MEDSTAFF*		MEDSTAFF is requested.
MEDSTAFF, VERSON 1.0 30-Mar-83 09:13 MEDICAL STAFF ANALYSIS PROGRAM		System responds that MEDSTAFF is available.
THREE (MAX) LETTER FILE CODE? *RHR*		System asks for name of file wanted and user responds.
MEDSTAFF OPTION (?=INSTRUCTION) ? *?*		System asks for option desired and user requests instructions.
AT "MEDSTAFF OPTION" RESPOND:		System displays options.
<CR>	TO TERMINATE THE PROGRAM	
INS OR ?	TO OBTAIN THESE INSTRUCTIONS	
STATUS	TO OBTAIN A REPORT ON FILE CHARACTERISTICS AND CODE SETTING	
MODIFY	TO MODIFY THE STATUS REPORT	
SORT	TO LIST AND SORT YOUR DATA FILES	
TABLE	TO ACCESS "TABLE OPTION"	
PERIODS	TO INITIALIZE AND MODIFY THE DATA/ANALYSIS PERIODS	
MEDSTAFF OPTION (?=INSTRUCTIONS)? *TAB*		User requests the table option.
TABLE OPTION (?=INSTRUCTIONS)? *?*		User asks for instructions.
AT "TABLE OPTIONS" RESPOND:		System displays options.
<CR>	TO RETURN TO "MEDSTAFF OPTIONS"	
SELECT	SELECTION OF TABLES	
GROUP	TABLE GROUP NO. 1	
GR2	TABLE GROUP NO. 2	
RANK	RANKING OF TABLES[b]	
AFFILIATION	AFFILIATION TABLES	
INS OR ?	INSTRUCTIONS	
TABLE OPTION (?=INSTRUCTIONS)? *SEL*		User chooses option of selecting tables.

Exhibit 11–4 continued

System and User Responses[a]	Explanation
STAFF STATUSES TO INCLUDE (<CR> = ALL; ? = INSTRUCTIONS)? *<CR>*	By pressing carriage return, user chooses to have all physicians included on the tables.
BOARD STATUSES TO INCLUDE (<CR> = ALL; ? = INSTRUCTIONS)? *<CR>*	By pressing carriage return, user chooses to have all physicians included.
GROUPS TO INCLUDE (<CR> = ALL; ? = INSTRUCTIONS)? *<CR>*	User presses carriage return to include all groups.
WANT TO SEE AVERAGE DAILY CENSUS INSTEAD OF PATIENT DAYS (Y OR N = <CR>)? *<CR>*	User presses carriage return to request patient days.
TABLE NO. (? = INSTRUCTIONS)? *6*	User selects Table 6, Physicians By Age And Specialty. A list of all tables available would be printed if desired. The user can select specific tables or predefined groups of tables.
ENTER ANALYSIS PERIODS (<CR> = ALL; ? = INSTRUCTIONS)? *4*	Each year is a separate analysis period. The number 4 is a code for the year 1980. Typing "?" would provide a list of options.
ENTER THE UPPER LIMITS OF THE AGE GROUPS (? = INSTRUCTIONS)? *<CR>*	By pressing carriage return, the user chooses not to set an upper limit.
PLEASE ADVANCE TO NEXT PERFORATION AND <CR>	User adjusts the paper so that the table will appear on a single page. The table is then printed.

[a]User responses are in italics. <CR> means: press carriage return.

[b]Ranking here refers to the rank order in which physicians will be listed on the tables. Unless otherwise requested, for example, physician specialties would be shown in alphabetical order, as in Table 11–1.

Note: The MEDSTAFF program contains other options not shown in this example.

Source: Amherst Associates, Inc., Chicago, Ill.

and strategic planning. For example, data from patient discharge abstracts are needed to define what patient needs the hospital serves, while financial data can be used to determine the cost of hospital services. Both types of data are required to assess the impact of starting a new service. In addition, data are needed from sources outside the hospital on the external environment (e.g., census and regional patient origin data).

Software for linking data bases and retrieving and analyzing data is therefore essential for strategic planning. A data base management system (DBMS) con-

Table 11–2 MEDSTAFF Program Output: Physicians by Age and Specialty in 1980

TABLE NO. 6
PHYSICIANS BY AGE AND SPECIALTY 1980

SPECIALTY	*1-35*	*36-39*	*40-49*	*50-59*	*60-UP*	*TOTAL*	*AV. AGE*
ALLERGY	0	0	1	0	0	1	46.0
ANESTHESIOLOGY	1	0	1	1	0	3	43.0
CARDIOVASCULAR DISEASES	2	2	2	4	0	10	45.1
DERMATOLOGY	1	1	1	1	0	4	43.0
DENTISTRY	1	3	2	1	1	8	43.9
EMERGENCY MEDICINE	1	3	5	0	0	9	41.7
ENDOCRINOLOGY	0	1	0	1	0	2	45.0
FAMILY PRACTICE	4	1	5	7	9	26	53.0
GASTROENTEROLOGY	0	0	3	0	0	3	42.3
HEMATOLOGY	0	0	1	0	0	1	43.0
INTERNAL MEDICINE	2	12	10	3	1	28	41.8
NEPHROLOGY	0	0	1	0	0	1	40.0
NEUROLOGY	2	0	2	0	0	4	38.3
NUCLEAR MEDICINE	0	0	1	0	0	1	47.0
OB/GYN	2	0	4	11	1	18	51.6
OCCUPATIONAL MEDICINE	0	0	1	0	1	2	51.5
OPHTHALMOLOGY	0	2	2	2	1	7	49.7
OTORHINOLARYNGOLOGY	1	1	3	2	0	7	45.1
PATHOLOGY	0	1	2	1	0	4	44.5
PEDIATRICS	2	2	5	6	2	17	47.0
PSYCHIATRY	0	0	3	1	0	4	47.8
PULMONARY DISEASE	1	1	2	0	0	4	37.3
RADIOLOGY	0	3	3	0	0	6	42.5
SURGERY-GENERAL	2	2	9	1	3	17	46.2
SURGERY-NEUROLOGICAL	0	0	4	1	0	5	46.4
SURGERY-ORAL	4	6	5	0	1	16	40.0
SURGERY-ORTHOPEDIC	0	5	2	2	0	9	42.9
SURGERY-PEDIATRIC	1	0	3	0	0	4	42.0
SURGERY-PLASTIC	0	1	3	0	1	5	47.2
SURGERY-THORACIC	0	1	4	1	2	8	49.3
UROLOGY	0	1	2	1	1	5	48.6
ONCOLOGY	0	2	0	0	0	2	38.0
TOTAL	27	51	92	47	24	241	45.6

AGE CALCULATED RELATIVE TO THE INITIAL YEAR OF THE ANALYSIS PERIOD.
NO. OF PHYSICIANS INCLUDED: 241
NO. NOT ON STAFF FOR ANALYSIS PERIOD REQUESTED: 31

Source: Amherst Associates' MEDSTAFF Medical Staff Analysis Program. Reprinted with permission of Amherst Associates, Inc., Chicago, Ill.

sists of software capable of retrieving data items from separate files without requiring that the files be merged. For instance, a DBMS could retrieve the name and specialty of a physician from a physician file (such as one maintained by MEDSTAFF) and data on the DRGs in which the physician's patients are found from a file containing discharge abstracts (which might contain only the physician's identification code). These retrieved data, saved in a new file, can then be analyzed and a report can be prepared, using a report writer such as ASK or a general purpose statistical program such as the Statistical Package for the Social Sciences (SPSS).[7]

Shared Medical Systems' (SMS) COMMAND Patient Information Reporting System allows both the linkage of financial and utilization data and the development of reports.[8] It combines a DBMS with a report writer capable of performing numerical calculations and selecting subsets of the data (e.g., by using the "less than," "equal to," and "greater than" operators in the ASK example presented earlier).

COMMAND could, for example, group Medicare patients by DRG and by physician, and then present a report showing the difference between total charges and allowable billing rates. This is information that a hospital would want to examine as it considers the attractiveness of the markets it now serves (and the performance of physician groups in the hospital) in light of the prospective reimbursement system established by the Social Security Amendments of 1983. Of course, a system like COMMAND would also be useful in a service area and market analysis for consumers and in a medical staff analysis, since retrieving and analyzing data from a number of files are important tasks for these types of analyses (see Chapters 6 to 9).

Since some of the information needs of managers are predictable, COMMAND contains the software for preparing a number of standard reports that can be easily requested. The system will produce each standard report at a specified interval. Hospital management may also request that the SMS staff provide the software to produce additional reports in a format suited to a hospital's specific needs. As we illustrated earlier, COMMAND's AD HOC REPORT WRITER allows managers to produce customized reports of themselves at any time.

Reimbursement on the basis of patient diagnosis or the severity of the patient's medical condition (using DRGs or some other system) is likely to accelerate the development of methods for linking financial and utilization data. Competition among hospitals and other providers may stimulate the development of the type of shared data bases discussed in Chapter 5, especially if government and other payers require the collection and submission of the relevant data.

In our discussion of products and services up to this point we have focused on the retrieval and analysis of historical information. Managers are also interested in preparing forecasts that are based on alternative assumptions. Software available from Mediflex Systems Corporation, Amherst Associates and other firms allows managers to test the effect of alternative assumptions and forecasting techniques on forecasts of utilization, manpower, revenues, and expenses.

Exhibit 11–5 shows a request for a forecast of a statistic using Mediflex. Table 11–3 shows the resulting report. The statistic has been forecast for 12 periods into the future. The forecasting technique has also been applied to the 12 periods of the current year (marked 1–12) and the 12 periods of the previous year (marked −1 to −12) to show what the forecasting technique would have predicted for these periods. These predicted values are shown in the column labeled "MODEL". The variance between actual (or budgeted) and predicted values (i.e., between BASE and MODEL) is shown in absolute numbers and as a percent.

These tests can be repeated using different forecasting techniques. In this example, a straight line extrapolation has been used. Mediflex also allows the use of a simple percentage increase, a weighted moving average and exponential smoothing for trend forecasting. Forecasts can also be based on the relation between known variables and Mediflex, which contains ten types of formulas for such "relational" forecasting.

Forecasts can also be prepared using a model, which is a set of mathematical equations (some using just simple arithmetic) that express the relationships among a set of variables. The critical test of a model is whether it closely replicates what occurs in the real world. If it does, hospital managers can use the model for forecasting. Such a model can of course be tested to see if it would have predicted what occurred in the past, but its accuracy in predicting the future is always unknown. Still, managers need such forecasts to support decisions on changes in services and markets, among other things. A number of firms—including Mediflex Systems, Ernst & Whinney, and Amherst Associates—offer financial models for this purpose to hospitals.

The Health Central System, a multihospital corporation in Minneapolis, has developed demand and financial forecasting models in a joint effort with Planmetrics, Inc., of Chicago. In a review of existing models, Health Central System discovered that most had excellent capabilities for forecasting financial operating results, some had the capability of projecting cash flow statements, balance sheets, and key financial ratios, but none had the capability to forecast demand for specific health care services. This is an important technique for many strategic analyses, and Health Central's model offers it.[9]

The data inputs, calculations, and outputs of the Health Central System demand forecasting model are summarized in Figure 11–2. Figure 11–3 shows how the output of the demand forecasting model is used in the financial forecasting model. The number of patient days and ancillary procedures (i.e., measures of demand) for each specialty group in the hospital are used to create operating budgets, which in turn are combined with a forecast of the revenue that would be produced by a particular level of demand to prepare operating statements for each specialty group and for the hospital as a whole. Health Central can then evaluate the

Exhibit 11–5 Request for a Forecast Using Mediflex

System and User Responses[a]	Explanation
REPORT, FORECAST, EDIT, OR END? *F*	User requests forecast
RELATIONAL OR TREND FORECAST [R T]: *T*	User requests trend forecast
STATISTICS OR ACCOUNTS? *S*	User requests forecast of one or more statistics
STATISTICS TO FORECAST [ALL OR NUMBERS]? *611*	User requests a forecast of statistic number 611
STARTING PERIOD NUMBER OF BASE DATA – *12*	User requests that the 12 periods of last year be included in calculations
NUMBER OF PERIODS TO CONSIDER IN BASE DATA? *24*	User asks that the 12 periods of data from last year and 12 from the current year (a total of 24) be included
WHICH FILE FOR PERIODS 7 TO 12 BUDGET OR FORECAST [B F] *B*	User requests that budget data be used for the periods of the current year not yet completed
ENDING PERIOD OF FORECAST? *24*	User requests a one-year forecast (24 periods from beginning of current year)
TEST OR FORECAST [T F] *T*	User requests that forecast not be added to existing data base, but kept in a temporary test file
DEFINE NEW TECHNIQUE OR PARAMETERS? *Y*	User chooses to define new technique or parameters for forecast
STATISTIC NUMBER TO ADD? *611*	User selects statistic
TECHNIQUE FOR STATISTIC 611? *1*	User selects straight line extrapolation
DEFINE ANY MORE? *N*	User desires no further technique or parameter changes
STATS SUCCESSFULLY FORECAST	System reports that forecast is completed
PRINT REPORT? *Y*	User requests printed report
ALIGN PAPER	System asks user to align paper on printer/terminal

[a]User responses appear in italics.

Source: Reprinted with permission of Mediflex Systems Corp.

Table 11–3 Forecast of a Statistic Prepared Using Mediflex

MEDIFLEX MEMORIAL HOSPITAL
TRIAL FORECAST REPORT

STATISTICS: 611

BASE DATA COMPARISON					*FORECAST*	
PER	*BASE*	*MODEL*	*VARIANCE*	*PER-CENT*	*PER*	*FORECAST*
–12	623	628	(5)	(0.80)	13	603
–11	631	627	4	0.63	14	602
–10	635	626	9	1.42	15	601
–9	620	625	(5)	(0.80)	16	600
–8	649	624	25	3.85	17	599
–7	628	623	5	0.80	18	598
–6	649	622	27	4.16	19	597
–5	643	621	22	3.42	20	596
–4	635	620	15	2.36	21	595
–3	637	619	18	2.83	22	594
–2	627	618	9	1.44	23	593
–1	650	617	33	5.08	24	592
1	616	616		0.00		
2	584	615	(31)	(5.31)		
3	501	614	(113)	(22.55)		
4	362	613	(251)	(69.34)		
5	662	612	50	7.55		
6	592	611	(19)	(3.21)		
7	729	610	119	16.32		
8	591	609	(18)	(3.05)		
9	641	608	33	5.15		
10	642	607	35	5.45		
11	600	606	(6)	(1.00)		
12	649	605	44	6.78		
TOT	14,796	14,796				7,170
AVG	616	616				597

TECHNIQUE USED: STRAIGHT LINE
PARAMETERS USED:

Source: Reprinted with permission of Mediflex Systems Corp.

forecasted financial performance of each hospital and of the physician specialty groups in each hospital. This allows them to consider the impact of physician behavior on financial performance and alternative investment strategies.

Table 11–4 shows a Health Central summary of operations for general medicine for the period 1981–1990. By altering the assumptions made in the model, Health

Figure 11–2 The Health Central System and Planmetrics: Summary of Demand Forecasting Method

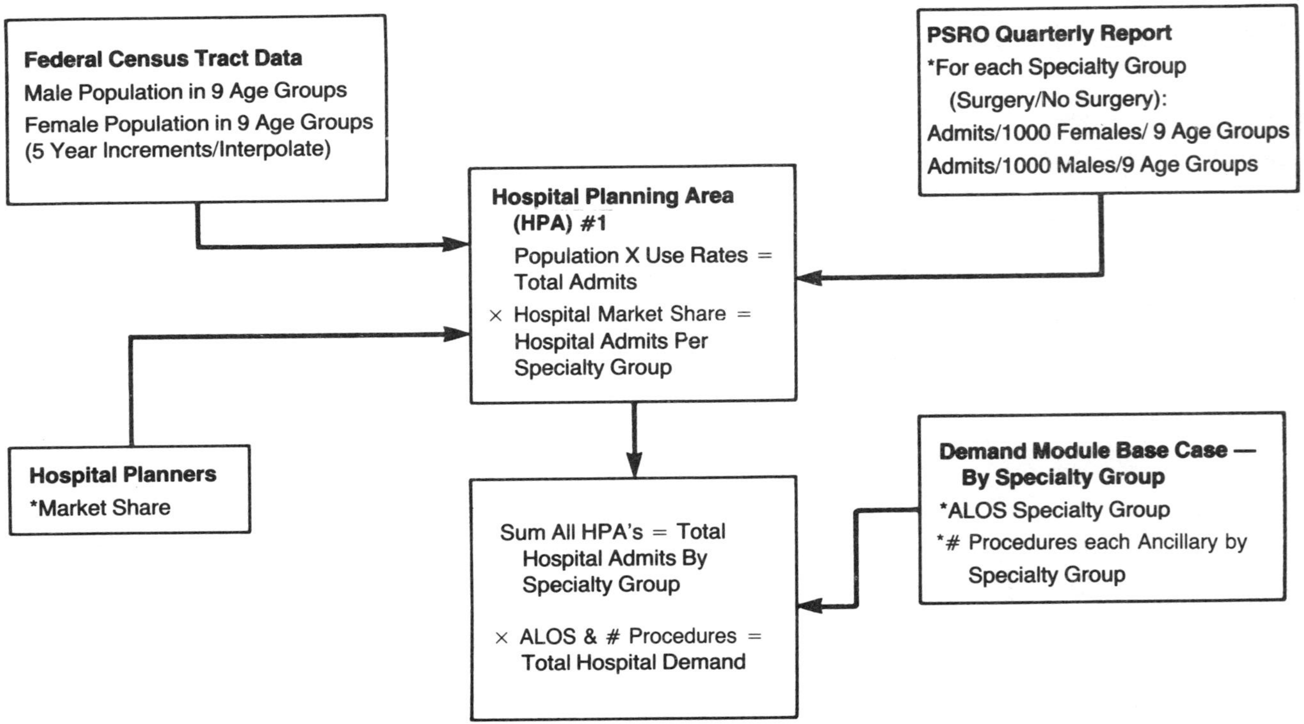

Source: Reprinted from *Computerized Forecasting Models Developed by a Multi-Hospital System* by Charles Ego with permission of the Health Central System, Minneapolis, Minn.

Figure 11–3 Health Central System and Planmetrics: Summary of Financial Forecasting Method

Interface from Demand Module

By Specialty Group:
No. Admits
ALOS
No. Days
No. Procedures for Ancillary Service

Manual Input for Forecasting

Inflation Percent(s)
Third Party Discount Percent
Bad Debt Percent
Capital Expenditures in Current Dollars (movable equipment auto option)
Interest Rates: Borrow/Invest
New Debt (auto option)
Pricing Option
Changes in Cost Allocation Statistics
Changes in Fixed Cost Levels

Computer Forecasting Logic

1. Calculate Depreciation and Changes in Fixed Assets
2. Borrow Funds
3. Calculate Debt Service (principal and interest)
4. Calculate Department Fixed and Variable Cost
5. Develop Department Cost Statements
6. Allocate All Costs to Specialty Groups
7. Calculate Specialty Group & Total Hospital Revenue: Prior Rates × New Volume
8. Calculate Revenue Increase Due to Price Change, Bad Debts, and Third Party Discounts for Total Hospital
9. Calculate Revenue Increase Due to Price Change, Bad Debts, Third Party Discounts to Specialty Groups
10. Develop Total Hospital Operating Statement, Balance Sheet, Cash Flow, Ratios
11. Develop Operating Statement for Each Specialty Group
12. Develop Operating Statements for Combination of Selected Specialty Groups

Source: Reprinted from *Computerized Forecasting Models Developed by a Multi-Hospital System* by Charles Ego with permission of the Health Central System, Minneapolis, Minn.

Table 11–4 Health Central System Summary of Operations by Specialty

	1981	*1982*	*1983*	*1984*	*1985*	*1986*	*1987*	*1988*	*1989*	*1990*
GENERAL MEDICINE										
REVENUE DATA										
REVS BEFORE INCR	5429.53	5485.59	5607.78	6011.99	6475.58	9167.16	10127.41	10852.18	11746.36	12644.48
REV AFTER INCR										
BOARD AND CARE	2247.96	2315.76	2501.62	2715.05	3850.47	4253.59	4558.19	4893.63	5267.30	5679.53
ANCILLARY	3181.57	3234.51	3448.33	3693.37	5168.93	5710.25	6118.86	6569.08	7071.76	7626.37
TOTAL	5429.53	5550.27	5949.95	6408.42	9019.40	9963.84	10677.05	11462.71	12339.06	13305.90
LESS:										
3RD PARTY DISCOUNT	698.02	434.65	475.36	520.43	714.23	770.93	830.31	895.69	968.64	1049.04
BAD DEBT FREECARE	43.96	44.94	48.18	51.89	73.03	80.68	86.45	92.82	99.91	107.74
NET PATIENT REVENUES	4687.55	5070.68	5426.41	5836.10	8232.14	9112.23	9760.29	10474.20	11270.51	12149.12
ADD:										
INTEREST INCOME	22.33	0.00	130.35	255.90	274.07	274.11	274.14	274.18	274.23	274.28
MISCELLAN INCOME	123.27	0.00	0.00	0.00	306.07	0.00	0.00	0.00	0.00	0.00
TOTAL REVENUES	4833.15	5070.67	5556.76	6092.00	8812.28	9386.34	10034.43	10748.38	11544.74	12423.40
TOTAL EXPENSES	4398.60	4817.66	5279.07	5787.13	8395.69	8938.53	9551.69	10227.18	10980.63	11812.00
NET REV FROM OPER	434.55	253.01	277.69	304.87	416.59	447.81	482.74	521.20	564.11	611.40
DEPR FUND INCOME	0.00	52.32	39.91	30.75	57.86	104.52	172.72	247.28	328.71	417.49
EXCS OF REV OVER EXP	434.55	305.33	317.60	335.62	474.45	552.33	655.46	768.48	892.82	1028.89
PCT OF TOTL REVENUES	8.99%	6.02%	5.72%	5.51%	5.38%	5.88%	6.53%	7.15%	7.73%	8.28%

Table 11–4 continued

	1981	*1982*	*1983*	*1984*	*1985*	*1986*	*1987*	*1988*	*1989*	*1990*
PCT PRICE INCREASE	0.00%	1.18%	6.10%	6.59%	39.28%	8.69%	5.43%	5.63%	5.05%	5.23%
REV PER ADM/VISIT	1908.45	1919.38	1952.57	2083.15	2232.96	3110.67	3381.44	3563.93	3764.86	3953.87
REVENUE PER DAY	341.03	338.41	339.78	357.77	378.47	527.15	572.95	604.04	638.08	670.33
COST PER ADM/VISIT	1546.08	1685.67	1838.12	2005.24	2895.06	3033.09	3189.21	3358.68	3519.43	3693.56
COST PER DAY	276.28	297.20	319.87	344.39	490.69	514.00	540.38	569.25	596.48	626.20

Source: Reprinted from *Computerized Forecasting Models Developed by a Multi-Hospital System* by Charles Ego with permission of the Health Central System, Minneapolis, Minn.

Central can examine the sensitivity of its forecast to changes in the rate of admissions, market share, third party discounts, interest rates, and other input variables.

The importance of basing financial planning on reasonable assumptions about utilization has led to the development of Health Central's model and other demand forecasting models.[10,11] Payment based on patient case-mix, diagnosis or severity will accelerate this trend, since hospitals will probably have to consider how their present and future patient population will affect their financial condition, and then make decisions on which markets to serve. Usually, such case-mix reimbursement systems will also require the creation and maintenance of detailed data bases that allow hospitals to make detailed analyses of the factors affecting their present and future financial condition.

Computer models, like the software we have examined, can be easy or difficult to use, provide the user with few or many options, and produce standard or custom reports and analyses. Before selecting a model, hospital managers should ask for a demonstration of the model's capabilities and features. This includes looking at an actual process of generating a report.

Exhibit 11–6 shows the instructions needed by Ernst & Whinney's Executive Decision Model to generate an estimated statement of revenue and expense that reflects a 15 percent shift in payer mix. Table 11–5 shows a statement of revenue and expense produced by the Executive Decision Model that reflects the change in payer mix. Since it is in a standard report format, the user has not been asked to indicate what information should appear on the rows and columns, where the data are located, and what calculations need to be performed. The model also allows for the generation of custom reports.[12]

With the Executive Decision Model, a hospital manager is not required to learn FORTRAN, BASIC, COBOL or any of the other computer languages offered with computers. Nor is the manager required to remember a large set of acronyms or to learn the proper sequence of commands to produce the table. It is necessary, however, that the user refer to (or remember parts of) a user's manual that lists the available options for analysis and the codes for revenue class and cost centers. The typed statements are far simpler than those in the ASK example presented earlier. The offsetting sacrifice, however, is a loss of flexibility.

Nevertheless, most, if not all, of a hospital manager's requirements for financial forecasts may be met by such systems as Ernst & Whinney's Executive Decision Model, Mediflex, and Amherst Associates' Hospital Systems Library. Competition in the financial modeling field is producing further refinements in the capabilities of such models, in response to requests from hospital managers. In this context, managers must ensure that the development of financial planning programs by the hospital itself does not duplicate the efforts of other hospitals

Exhibit 11–6 Ernst and Whinney's Executive Decision Model: Example of the Use of Report Generation (RG) and Management Analysis (MA) Components

System and User Responses[a]	Explanation
SYSTEM: *EDM* Ernst & Whinney Executive Decision Model	User requests Executive Decision Model. System confirms choice.
DATABASE NAME: */HOSPITAL*	User requests data base.
EDM > *MA*	User selects Management Analysis function.
MA > *CHANGE*	User selects a change in the value of a variable as the procedure.
AREA: *PAYER MIX*	User selects payer mix as the variable to be changed.
ENTER DESCRIPTION OF THIS ALTERATION: *SHIFT MEDICARE UTILIZATION WITH BLUE CROSS*	User enters description of desired change.
REVENUE CLASS: *100*	User selects Medicare.
DEPARTMENT/COST CENTER: *ALL*	User indicates desired change is for entire hospital.
TYPE OF CHANGE: *PERCENT*	User requests percentage change.
CHANGE: *–15*	User stipulates that the percentage of Medicare patients should decrease by 15 percent.
REVENUE CLASS: *102*	User selects Blue Cross.
DEPARTMENT/COST CENTER: *ALL*	User indicates desired change is for entire hospital.
TYPE OF CHANGE: *PERCENT*	User requests percentage change.
CHANGE: *15*	User stipulates that the percentage of Blue Cross patients should increase by 15 percent.
REVENUE CLASS: *<CR>*	System asks if another change is to be made. User indicates none.
MA > *REPORT*	System asks for the next task. User requests a report.
RG > *FS*	User requests a financial statement.
FINANCIAL STATEMENT: *INCOME*	The system asks which one is desired. User specifies income statement.

Exhibit 11–6 continued

System and User Responses[a]	Explanation
DESIRED LEVEL OF DETAIL: *HOSPITAL*	User specifies report by hospital. The alternative is report by cost center.
REPORT TO BE PREPARED WHERE: /*INCOME2*	User asks that report be printed in a particular file.
SELECT PROCESSING PRIORITY (I,D,O): *O*	User specifies overnight priority. Significant cost savings may be achieved by use of deferred or overnight priority.
RECEIPT #1155	
RG > SYSTEM	The user leaves the EDM system.
SYSTEM: COPY /INCOME2 TO TERMINAL	When the processing is complete, the report is copied from the file /INCOME2 to the terminal.

[a]User responses are in italics. <CR> means: press carriage return.

Source: Reprinted with permission of Ernst & Whinney.

and consulting firms. They can do this by examining the products already on the market after a careful assessment of their information needs.

DECISION SUPPORT SYSTEMS

There are a number of problems that have kept hospital managers from benefiting from the use of computer-based management information systems. In many instances, computer languages can inhibit rather than facilitate the manager's use of the computer. The learning of FORTRAN or BASIC, for instance, is a poor use of a manager's time, yet programers who are capable of translating the needs of the manager into computer instructions are expensive and/or scarce. Moreover, because strategic decisions are not routine, the effort to learn a computer language often seems unjustified. While the languages used by such products as COMMAND and the Executive Decision Model are simpler to learn than FORTRAN or BASIC, the manager must still learn a separate set of instructions for each product. The use of only one language or set of instructions for all the software used by hospital managers would clearly encourage the use of data and analytical techniques for strategic planning.

In some cases, of course, the data needed for planning may be inaccessible. Or, while the files may contain the necessary data, they may be too costly to

Table 11–5 Executive Decision Model Statement of Revenue and Expense

TOTAL HOSPITAL
MAY 23, 1983 11:37 AM

REVENUES			
INPATIENT SERVICES	18,170,240		
ANCILLARY INPATIENT	20,475,024		
ANCILLARY OUTPATIENT	5,749,003		
TOTAL PATIENT SERVICE REVENUES		44,394,267	
DEDUCTIONS FROM REVENUE:			
CONTRACTUAL ALLOWANCES	(3,225,446)		
BAD DEBTS	(879,905)		
CHARITY CARE	(203,176)		
TOTAL DEDUCTIONS FROM REVENUE		(4,308,527)	
OTHER OPERATING REVENUES		20,000	
TOTAL OPERATING REVENUES			40,105,740
EXPENSES			
SALARIES AND WAGES	18,560,285		
EMPLOYEE BENEFITS	4,813,024		
PROFESSIONAL FEES	1,534,961		
SUPPLIES AND OTHER	8,334,261		
SUBTOTAL		33,242,531	
INTEREST EXPENSE	1,187,286		
DEPRECIATION	2,649,774	3,837,060	
TOTAL OPERATING EXPENSES			37,079,591
REVENUE FROM OPERATIONS			40,105,740
NON-OPERATING REVENUE			0
EXCESS OF REVENUES OVER EXPENSES			3,026,149

Source: Reprinted with permission of Ernst & Whinney.

retrieve. Finally, new files may have to be created for a decision that might be made only once. Database management systems can alleviate these problems by allowing data to be retrieved easily from existing files, but only if the needed files have been appropriately constructed.

In other cases, procedures for analysis may not be linked to each other. Files prepared for use by one computer program may not be accepted by another, or the output of one analytical procedure may not be accepted by another. Instead of quickly performing an analysis, the manager might be left waiting for a programer to change a file, or be forced to use a pocket calculator to finish an analysis that another program could perform. Competition among the firms that sell computer services to hospitals may alleviate these problems to some extent. For example, if all of the computer firm's programs accept data in the same format and from each other, the client is less likely to want to pay the cost of file conversion to use other programs offered by a competing firm.

Existing software usually requires that the manager know the appropriate data and analytical procedures for the problem or decision at hand. Currently, a hospital manager cannot ask computers for data on low occupancy and then be presented with choices as to how the manager might proceed to examine the problem. The manager does not have in storage certain paths to follow (i.e., problem algorithms) that have been developed with the advice of other managers who had had similar problems and had made decisions on how to deal with them. Rather than be relayed through conversation, books, or journals, the problem-solving advice could be given through the computer. The computer could also be programed to ask questions designed to ensure that the advice was appropriate and to explain the advantages and disadvantages of each of the analytical techniques available.

The ideal solution to these problems would be a single system composed of hardware, software, and data that would meet all, or most, of the manager's information needs. However, when those needs are broad, complex, and difficult to define—as in strategic planning—this poses a formidable challenge. Currently, there is no system that is adequate for hospital strategic planning. Hospital managers need what has been called a decision support system (DSS). In this section, we define such a system, describe its objectives and components, discuss its importance in hospital strategic planning, and examine the current status of efforts to provide a decision support system for hospital managers.

Definition and Objectives of a Decision Support System

There is no widely accepted definition of a decision support system. The term *decision support system* will be used in this book to describe a combination of computer hardware, software, and data that is designed to support a decision-making process.[13,14] The adjective *support* is used because the operations researchers, computer scientists, and experts on decision making who work on such systems believe that many decisions—particularly those in strategic planning—require the knowledge and experience of a human being. The rationale for this belief is that strategic decisions are unstructured or semistructured.[15]

Structured decisions are those in which the nature of the problem, the available alternatives, and the rules that govern the selection of alternatives are all known. The ongoing control of inventory in the hospital's pharmacy is an example. The decision to be made concerns how many of what items to order, and when to order them. Past experience and a knowledge of current utilization levels in the hospital usually provide an adequate basis for making such a decision.

In unstructured decisions, the nature of the problem, the available alternatives, and the rules for selecting alternatives, are all unknown. For semistructured decisions, some information on these factors is available. We might, for example, know that a hospital's utilization is dropping because its physicians are retiring, and we may have selected a number of alternatives for attracting new physicians but not be sure which alternative to select because of a lack of previous experience with some of the proposed alternatives (e.g., a physicians' office building).

A system composed of computer hardware, software, and data cannot provide optimal solutions to unstructured and semistructured problems, but such a system can still support the decision maker. As the above example suggests, many of the decisions in the strategic planning process are semistructured. The decision maker needs information to make a choice, but it is doubtful that a single model, no matter how well-constructed, could select a solution without the benefit of the knowledge, experience, and creativity of one or more human beings.

The developers of decision support systems attempt to facilitate interaction between people, computers, and data in order to improve the decision-making process. They envision the use of a DSS in strategic planning in a number of iterative cycles. The development of initial information is followed by consideration of the information's implications, which is then followed by the framing of new questions, and the development of further information. This process is repeated until the decision maker elects to terminate it and make one or more decisions.

As Keen and Morton have pointed out, various levels of support can be provided by a DSS:[16]

- access to facts, or information retrieval
- pattern recognition ability and filters
- computations, comparisons, projections
- useful models

Exhibit 11–7 shows the levels of support and the analytical methods and procedures available in a few of the decision support systems for hospital financial planning now on the market.

Exhibit 11–7 Levels of Support Provided by Existing Decision Support Systems for Hospital Financial Planning: Selected Examples of Procedures and Techniques

1. Pattern recognition ability and filters:
   Graphics (e.g., histograms, scatterplots)
   Regression analysis (simple and multiple)
   Variance analysis (comparison of actual performance against initial or revised targets, as in flexible budgeting)
   Exception reporting (only information that is above or below specific values is reported)
2. Computations, comparisons, projections:
   Automatic recalculation (if desired, all values in a table are recalculated if one or more are changed)
   Projections (using techniques such as simple and multiple regression, exponential smoothing, moving averages)
   Spreading (total amounts are distributed according to instructions defined by the user)
   Cost allocation (using single apportionment, double apportionment, or simultaneous solution)
   Calculation of rates and ratios
3. Useful models:
   Revenues and expenses (information on demand, rates of payment, costs, and productivity are combined and projections are made for one or more years)
   Rate-setting (the rate of payment from third party payers is calculated)
   Budgeting (fixed or flexible budgets are calculated)
   Cash flow (projects monthly cash receipts and disbursements)

Imagine the situation of a hospital manager, who, because of low occupancies, has been asked to look into the hospital's utilization. The manager might first ask to see weekly statistics on occupancy by hospital service. This would require retrieval of the relevant data. Then, a graph showing occupancy and patient days would be prepared, and a time series analysis would be carried out so that patterns could be detected. The manager would then ask for a projection that showed what the patient days and occupancy levels would be under several different assumptions, including the continuation of past trends. Finally, the manager and the staff would use a model that showed the effect of a number of important variables, such as the age of the population and the hospital's market share, on utilization. Assumptions concerning market share would then be changed in order to judge the sensitivity of the hospital's occupancy rate to changes in market share.

All of these levels of support are neither necessary nor possible for every strategic planning decision. Models and projections, for example, cannot be produced for many decisions; and, in some cases, we have too little information or understanding of the situation to perform numerical calculations and prepare projections. Decision support systems must therefore, above all, be flexible. Emphasis must be placed on giving the administrator control over what the system does in order to facilitate the administrator's use of the system.

In addition, the designers of a DSS must confront the realities of the human personality, that is, the managerial ''style'' referred to in Chapter 2. While individual styles may differ, there are certain common characteristics that must be taken into account.[17]

- In the selection of alternative strategies—particularly when a degree of complexity prevails, the greater the ''cognitive strain'' (i.e., stress associated with learning or knowing) imposed by problem constraints (such as time, information availability, and recall capability), the simpler the rules of search. Individuals usually try to minimize cognitive strain in part by their choice among problem-solving strategies.
- Problem-solving behavior is adaptive. Individuals start with a tentative solution, search for information, modify the initial solution, and then continue until there is some balance between expected and realized results.
- Even in the most restricted problem-solving situation, a person's personality and aversion to or preference for risk enter into that person's choice of strategies, use of information, and ultimate solution.

Components of a Decision Support System

What we are looking for is a means of providing the various levels of support discussed earlier that takes into account the characteristics of the individuals involved in each decision-making situation. There are a number of ways to describe the components of a decision support system. Bonczek and his colleagues have come up with a useful way of doing this. For them, a decision support system consists of three components: a language system, a knowledge system, and a problem-processing system.[18]

A language system consists of the words and symbols used to direct the retrieval and analysis of data. The general trend in computer-based systems is toward the use of languages that are similar to those used in human communications and that do not require the user to understand the structure or processes of the computer and its data bases.[19]

Thus, the manager who, in our earlier example, has been asked to look into the hospital's utilization might ask for occupancy rates without being required to stipulate where such information is located and the procedures for retrieving it. Similarly, the manager could ask for a time-series analysis without specifying how such an analysis should be performed.

The knowledge system contains the data files and data bases considered relevant for the decisions to be made. The trend here has been toward the development of data bases and software (database management systems) that allow the user to relate data from various files without being concerned with their physical organization on tapes or disks.[20] For example, a manager might ask what the relationship is between patient diagnosis and occupancy rates, even though the data on the former resided in patient chart abstract files and those on the latter in administrative files.

Finally, the problem-processing system relates the language and knowledge systems to each other in order to produce information that supports the decision-making process. When a language system is used to request a report or state a problem, the problem-processing system seeks out and manipulates data to yield useful information. The trend here is toward problem-processing systems that can accept a number of different computer languages and utilize many knowledge systems.[21]

Problem processing systems may also contain procedures and models that can be used to solve various problems. In our example, the manager might state that the problem was low occupancy. The problem-processing system would then respond by linking procedures and models with the appropriate data files to produce graphs and statistical analyses. Such problem-processing systems have yet to be developed for hospitals and other health care organizations. Until such systems are available, the manager has access to libraries of computer programs and models from which those that appear to be useful can be selected.

In summary, a decision support system could have a potentially positive impact on the willingness and ability of hospital managers to use data and analytical procedures to support decision making in strategic planning if such a system had the following features:

- A computer language system that closely approximated conversational English.
- A knowledge system that contained relevant data files in formats that allowed a data base management system to retrieve, combine, and analyze data from any or all of the files.
- A problem-processing system that was appropriate to the types of decisions for which the DSS was designed.

The DSS should permit the output from one analytical technique to be used as the input to another. Finally, it should have a single computer language that allowed the manager to use all of the available analytical techniques.

Current Status of Decision Support Systems for Hospital Management

Much of the progress in the development of decision support systems for hospital strategic planning has occurred in the area of financial analysis and planning. This is not an unexpected development, considering the critical financial environment that hospitals are moving into (see Chapter 1). Hospitals can now purchase or lease the software and hardware to develop integrated information systems in which financial and clinical information can be linked by a database management system. Libraries of computer programs for financial planning and analysis are being offered to hospitals. These libraries either use data available in the hospital or require that data be periodically transferred to a central computer. Many of the programs in these libraries use the same format for data files and accept the output from other programs.

In other words, the language and knowledge systems for hospital financial planning have already been developed. The hospital may still have to purchase separate products and services from several firms and need staff and/or consultants to link them. For example, a hospital may acquire financial and clinical information systems oriented toward day-to-day transactions and link them with a database management system that allows the retrieval of data from any of the systems' files. Financial modeling and other analytical capabilities might then be acquired from another firm whose software accepts data in the format produced by the hospital's information systems. The question then is whether the systems the hospital has acquired or developed will provide the data and analytical techniques that are needed for strategic planning.

However, though important components of a DSS for financial planning are now available to hospitals, less progress has been made in developing a DSS that will carry out the type of consumer and physician market analyses described in Chapters 6 and 8. While the data files for such analyses may be available, and a database management system may be available to link them, in many cases the hospital must still rely on computer programs written by staff, on manual tabulations, on reports developed for other purposes (e.g., utilization review), or on flexible report generators to conduct an analysis. Moreover, only a few demand forecasting models are available for use in hospital financial planning.

In any event, problem-processing systems for financial and strategic planning have yet to emerge. This may be because they require more developmental effort and expense than the potential market justifies. Meanwhile, management consultants provide services to fill the problem-processing need.

Finally, it is important to note that computer technology and the products and services being offered to hospitals are changing so rapidly that many of our observations may not apply soon after this book appears. Indeed, we would hope that a DSS for strategic planning will have already appeared as this is read. If one has not, our words will serve as an argument for its development.

REFERENCES

1. Missouri Health Data Corporation, *ASK* (Jefferson City, Mo.: MHDC, 1981), p. 1.
2. Ibid., p. 2.
3. Arthur Andersen & Co., *Case Mix System Business Description* (Detroit, Mich.: Arthur Andersen & Co., n.d.).

4. Shared Medical Systems, *Take COMMAND* (King of Prussia, Pa.: Shared Medical Systems, n.d.).

5. Amherst Associates, *Amherst Computer Models* (Chicago: Amherst Associates, Inc., n.d.).

6. Amherst Associates, *Hospital Systems Library* (Chicago: Amherst Associates, n.d.), p. II–1.

7. N.H. Nie et al., *Statistical Package For The Social Sciences,* 2nd ed. (New York: McGraw-Hill, 1975).

8. Shared Medical Systems, *Take COMMAND*.

9. C. Ego, *Computerized Forecasting Models Developed by a Multi-Hospital System* (Minneapolis: Minn.: Health Central System, n.d.).

10. M. Warner, J. Steinberg, and M. Brown, "A Strategic Planning Model for Multihospital Systems," *Inquiry* 18, no. 3 (Fall 1981):214–223.

11. L. Friedman et al., "A Computer Simulation Model of Hospital Mergers," *Health Care Management Review* (Summer 1980):53–65.

12. Ernst & Whinney, *Executive Decision Model: The Challenge of Financial Planning* (Cleveland, Ohio: Ernst & Whinney, n.d.).

13. P.G.W. Keen and M.S. Scott Morton, *Decision Support Systems: An Organizational Perspective* (Reading, Mass.: Addison-Wesley, 1978).

14. R.H. Bonczek, C.W. Holsapple, and A.W. Winston, *Foundations of Decision Support Systems* (New York: Academic Press, 1981), p. 12.

15. Keen and Morton, *Decision Support Systems,* p. 11.

16. Ibid., p. 97.

17. M. Alexis and C.Z. Wilson, eds., *Organizational Decision Making* (Englewood Cliffs, N.J.: Prentice-Hall, 1967), pp. 73–74.

18. Bonczek, Holsapple, and Winston, *Foundations,* p. 69.

19. Ibid., p. 58.

20. Ibid., p. 125.

21. Ibid., p. 73.

Index

M

N

About the Authors

Roger Kropf is an Assistant Professor in the Health Administration Program in the Division of Public Health at the University of Massachusetts at Amherst. He teaches graduate courses in institutional and regional planning and in health care management information systems.

Before joining the faculty of the University of Massachusetts, Dr. Kropf was responsible for consulting and training in the areas of data analysis and information systems development at the Alpha Center for Health Planning. He has served as a consultant to the National Center for Health Statistics and the New York State Office of Health Systems Management in the areas of information systems evaluation and development.

Dr. Kropf holds a Masters in Regional Planning and a Ph.D. from the Maxwell School of Public Affairs at Syracuse University, where his doctoral research focused on management information systems in health maintenance organizations. He is a member of the editorial board of the Journal of Ambulatory Care Management and a contributor to the *Handbook of Health Care Accounting and Finance,* published by Aspen Systems Corporation.

James Greenberg is an Associate Professor on the Health Science faculty at Brooklyn College. He has a Ph.D. from the University of California, Berkeley, and has had planning and administrative positions and consultantships in several health-care institutions, including the New York Health Services Administration, the Montefiore Hospital and Medical Center, and the Alpha Center for Health Planning.

Dr. Greenberg's current interests are hospital planning and reimbursement. He has conducted research, with federal funding, on the use of case-mix measures in hospital planning, and has had several articles on this topic published.